尾田栄一郎

Vending machines have these labels that say
"war~m" on them during the winter. I feel so relaxed
when I read it as "deadlines coming clo~se." In
the first chapter, if Luffy had said "I'll become the
Pirate Ki~ng!" it would have seemed really weird.
Time to star~t volume 52!

-Eiichiro Oda, 2008

Eiichiro Oda began his manga career at the age of
17, when his one-shot cowboy manga **Wanted!**
won second place in the coveted Tezuka manga
awards. Oda went on to work as an assistant to
some of the biggest manga artists in the industry,
including Nobuhiro Watsuki, before winning the
Hop Step Award for new artists. His pirate
adventure **One Piece**, which debuted in
Weekly Shonen Jump in 1997, quickly became
one of the most popular manga in Japan.

ONE PIECE VOL. 52
SABAODY PART 3

SHONEN JUMP Manga Edition

STORY AND ART BY EIICHIRO ODA

English Adaptation/Megan Bates
Translation/Taylor Eagle, HC Language Solutions
Touch-up Art & Lettering/HudsonYards
Design/Sean Lee
Supervising Editor/Alexis Kirsch
Editor/Megan Bates

Printed in the U.S.A.

Published by VIZ Media, LLC
P.O. Box 77010
San Francisco, CA 94107

10 9 8 7
First printing, June 2010
Seventh printing, December 2016

www.viz.com

RATED T FOR TEEN

PARENTAL ADVISORY
ONE PIECE is rated T for Teen and is recommended for ages 13 and up. This volume contains fantasy violence and tobacco usage.

ratings.viz.com

THE WORLD'S MOST POPULAR MANGA
SHONEN JUMP
www.shonenjump.com

SHONEN JUMP MANGA

ONE PIECE

Vol. 52
ROGER AND RAYLEIGH

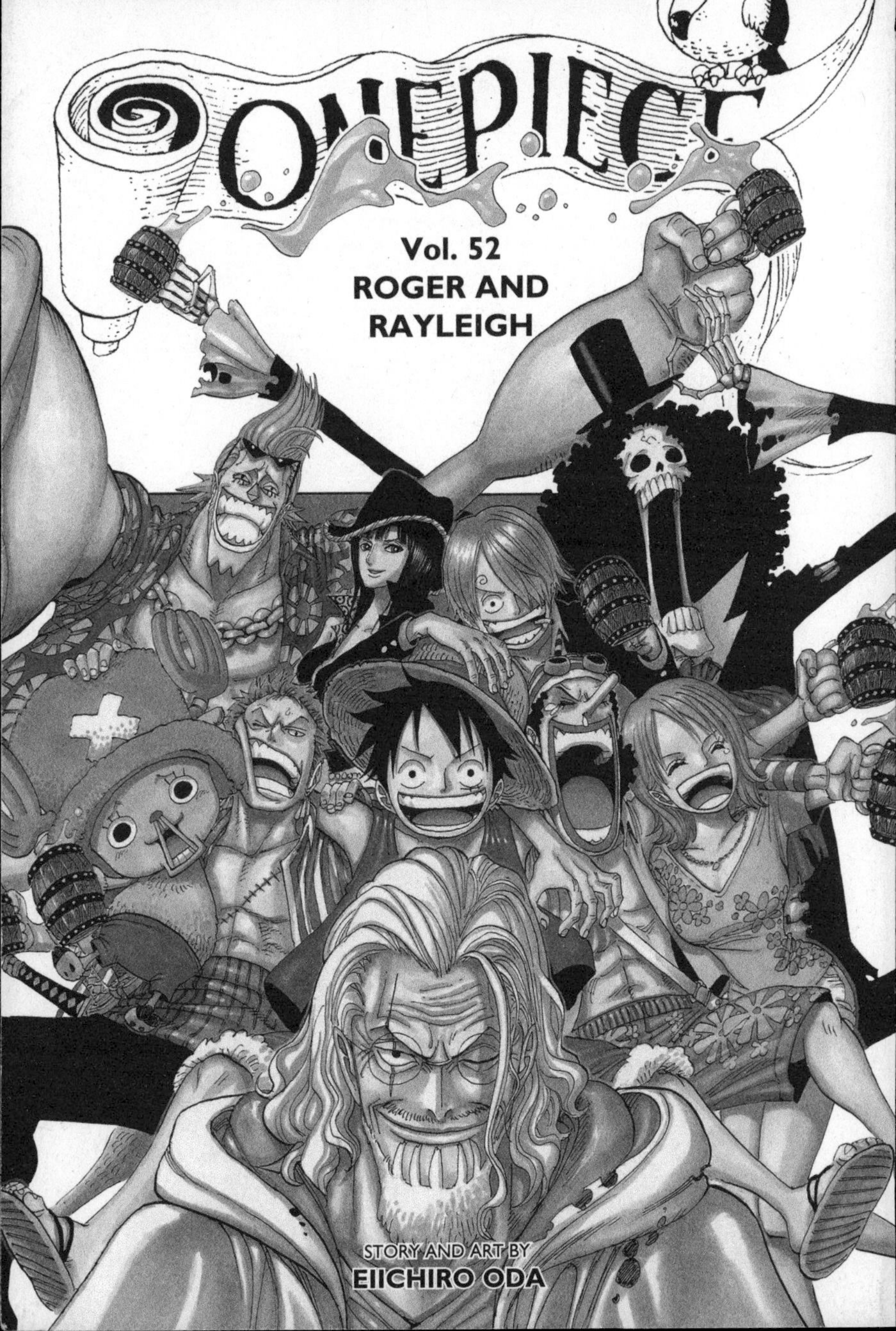

STORY AND ART BY
EIICHIRO ODA

100 Million+ Bounty Rookies

South Blue
Captain, Kid Pirates
Bounty: 315 million berries
Eustass "Captain" Kid

South Blue
Fighter, Kid Pirates
Bounty: 162 million berries
"Murder Machine" Killer

North Blue
Captain, Hawkins Pirates
Bounty: 249 million berries
"Magician" Basil Hawkins

North Blue
Captain, Drake Pirates
Bounty: 220 million berries
"Red Flag" X. Drake

North Blue
Captain, Heart Pirates
Bounty: 200 million berries
"Surgeon of Death" Trafalgar Law

Grand Line
(Long-Arm Race)
Captain, On-Air Pirates
Bounty: 198 million berries
"Roar of the Seas" Scratchmen Apoo

South Blue
Captain, Bonney Pirates
Bounty: 140 million berries
"Glutton" Jewelry Bonney

West Blue
Captain, Fire Tank Pirates
Bounty: 138 million berries
Capone "Gang" Bege

Sky Island
Captain, Fallen Monk Pirates
Bounty: 180 million berries
"Mad Monk" Urouge

The Straw Hats

Total bounty: 700,000,050 berries

Boundlessly optimistic and able to stretch like rubber, he is determined to become King of the Pirates.
Bounty: 300 million berries
Monkey D. Luffy

A former bounty hunter and master of the "three-sword" style. He aspires to be the world's greatest swordsman.
Bounty: 120 million berries
Roronoa Zolo

A thief who specializes in robbing pirates. Nami hates pirates, but Luffy convinced her to be his navigator.
Bounty: 16 million berries
Nami

A village boy with a talent for telling tall tales. His father, Yasopp, is a member of Shanks's crew.
Bounty: 30 million berries (Sniper King)
Usopp

The bighearted cook (and ladies' man) whose dream is to find the legendary sea, the "All Blue."
Bounty: 77 million berries
Sanji

A blue-nosed man-reindeer and the ship's doctor.
Bounty: 50 berries
Tony Tony Chopper

A mysterious woman in search of the Ponegliff on which true history is recorded.
Bounty: 80 million berries
Nico Robin

A softhearted cyborg and talented shipwright.
Bounty: 44 million berries
Franky

A skeleton warrior with an afro. He dreams of being reunited with Laboon, the tame whale he parted with fifty years ago.
Bounty: 33 million berries
Brook

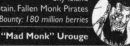

THE STORY OF ONE PIECE

Volume 52

Monkey D. Luffy started out as just a kid with a dream—to become the greatest pirate in history! Stirred by the tales of pirate "Red-Haired" Shanks, Luffy vowed to become a pirate himself. That was before the enchanted Devil Fruit gave Luffy the power to stretch like rubber, at the cost of being unable to swim—a serious handicap for an aspiring sea dog. Undeterred, Luffy set out to sea and recruited some crewmates—master swordsman Zolo; treasure-hunting thief Nami; lying sharpshooter Usopp; the high-kicking chef Sanji; Chopper, the walkin' talkin' reindeer doctor; mysterious archaeologist Robin; cyborg shipwright Franky; and Brooks, a musical skeleton!

Now in the Grand Line, Luffy and the crew are headed for Fish-Man Island aboard their new vessel, *Thousand Sunny*. After defeating one of the Seven Warlords of the Sea, Gecko Moria, on the enormous ghost ship *Thriller Bark*, they meet up with a mermaid named Camie and the Fish-Man Hatchan. In order to reach the underwater Fish-Man Island and pass over the Red Line, *Thousand Sunny* will require a special coating, so the Straw Hats make their way to the renowned coating craftsman at Sabaody Archipelago, a gathering ground for high-bounty rookie pirates and Celestial Dragons! Camie is kidnapped while the crew isn't looking and then purchased by a Celestial Dragon, while Hatchan is persecuted for being a Fish-Man. Enraged, Luffy reneges on his promise to leave the Celestial Dragons alone and strikes back…and now there are Navy battleships hot on the Straw Hats' trail!!

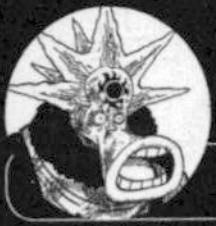

Octopus fritter store owner and former Arlong Pirate Octopus Fish-Man

Hatchan (Hachi)

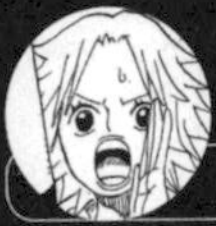

Designer in training and Octopus fritter store clerk Kissing Gourami Mermaid

Camie

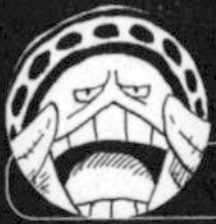

Starfish and Designer of Criminal brand

Pappagu

Flying Fish Riders

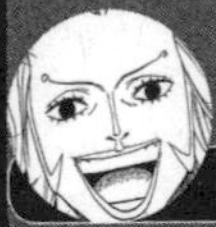

Leader

Iron Mask Duval

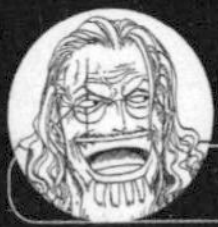

Former first mate with the Roger Pirates and the Pirate King's right-hand man

Silvers Rayleigh

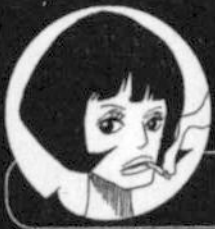

Bar owner and former pirate

Shakuyaku (Shakky)

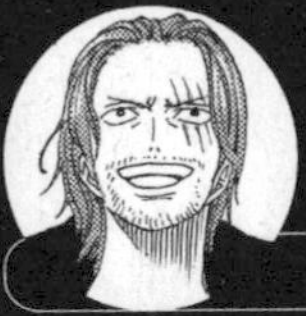

A pirate that Luffy idolizes. Shanks gave Luffy his trademark straw hat.

"Red-Haired" Shanks

Vol. 52
Roger and Rayleigh

CONTENTS

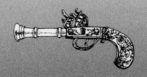

ONE PIECE

Hereafter, 52 volumes will start.

Chapter 503: AGGRAVATED ISLAND

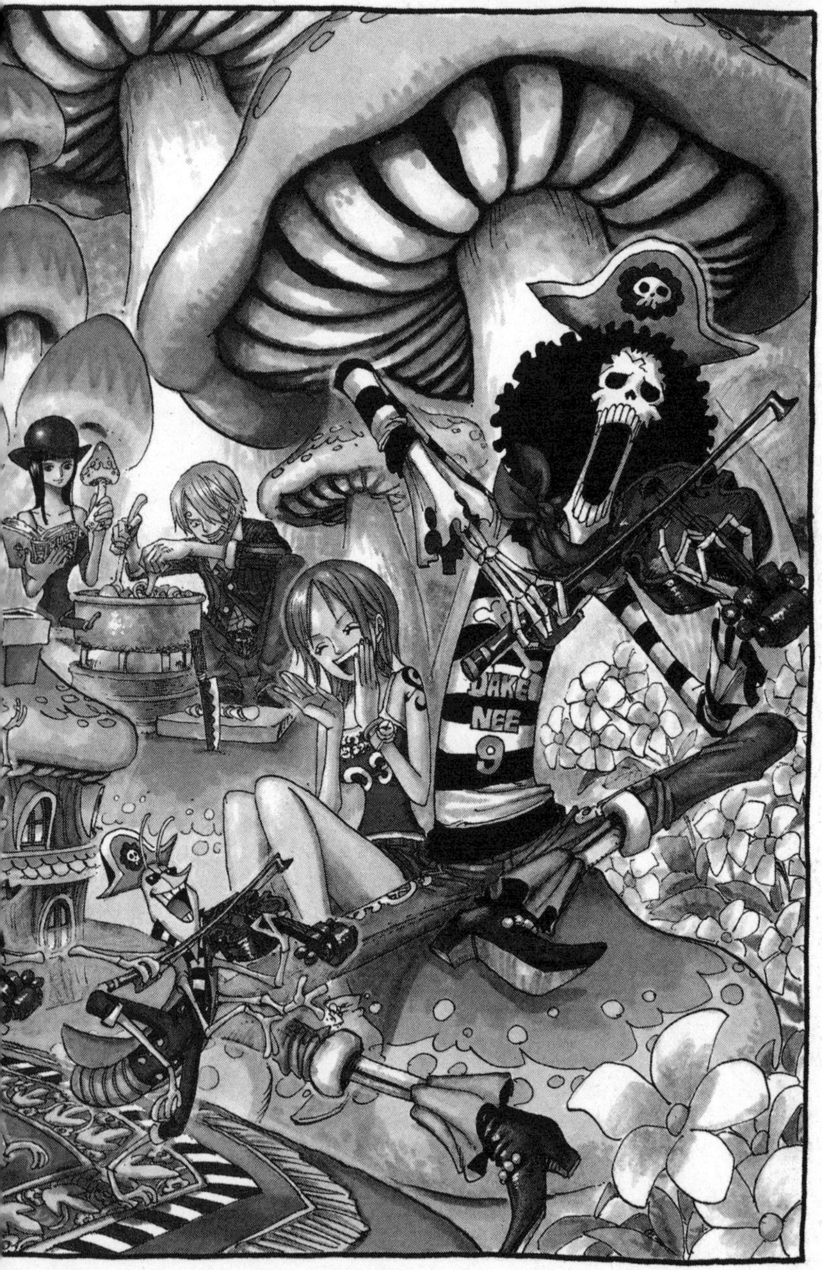

DAKE
NEE
9

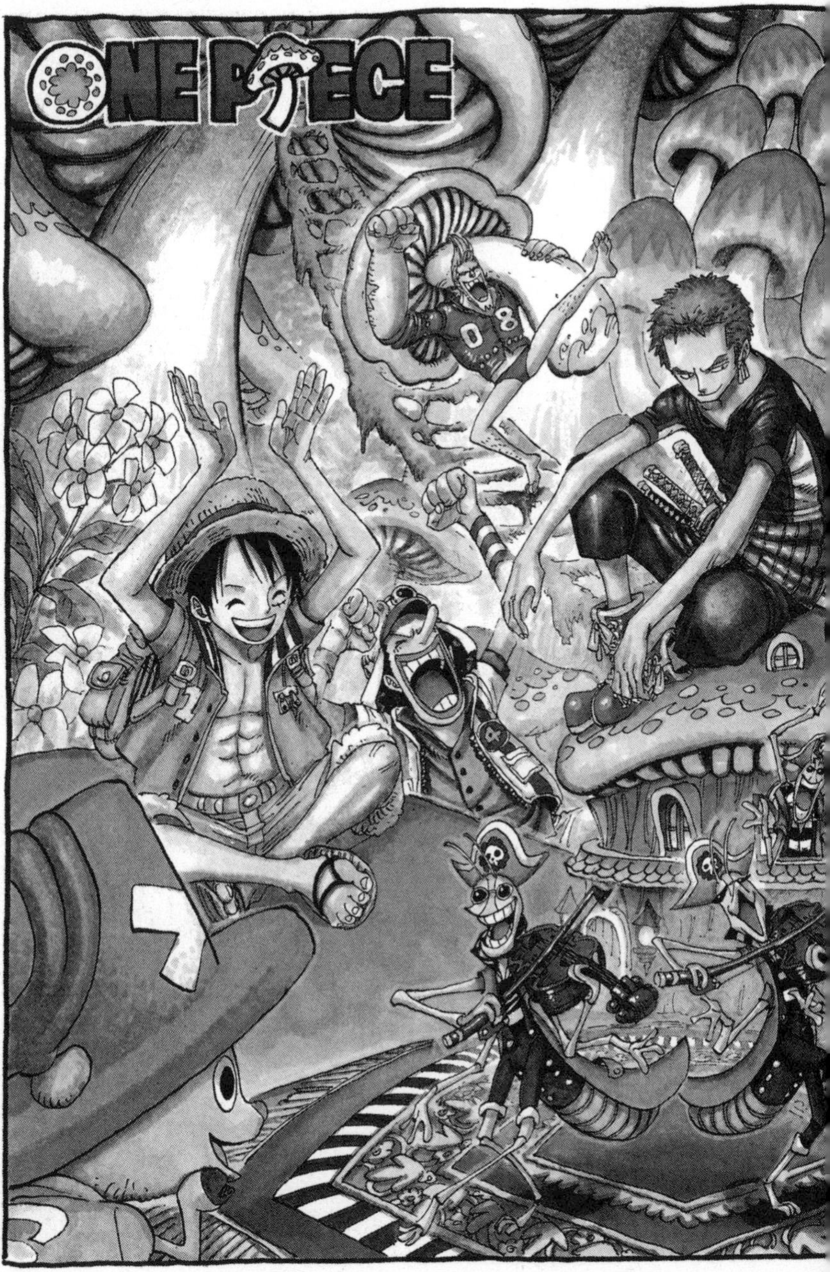
ONE PIECE

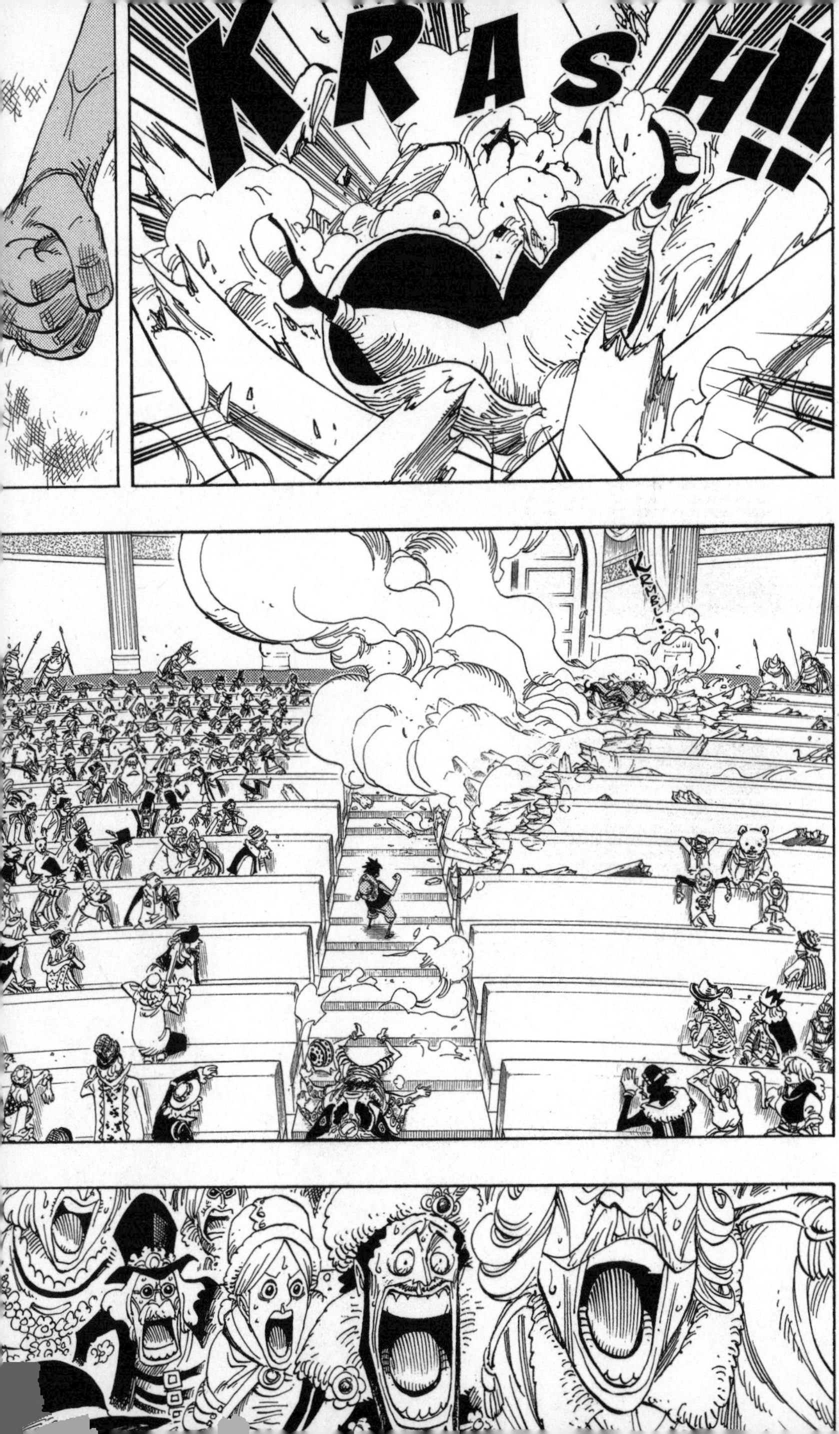
KRASH!!
KRMBL...

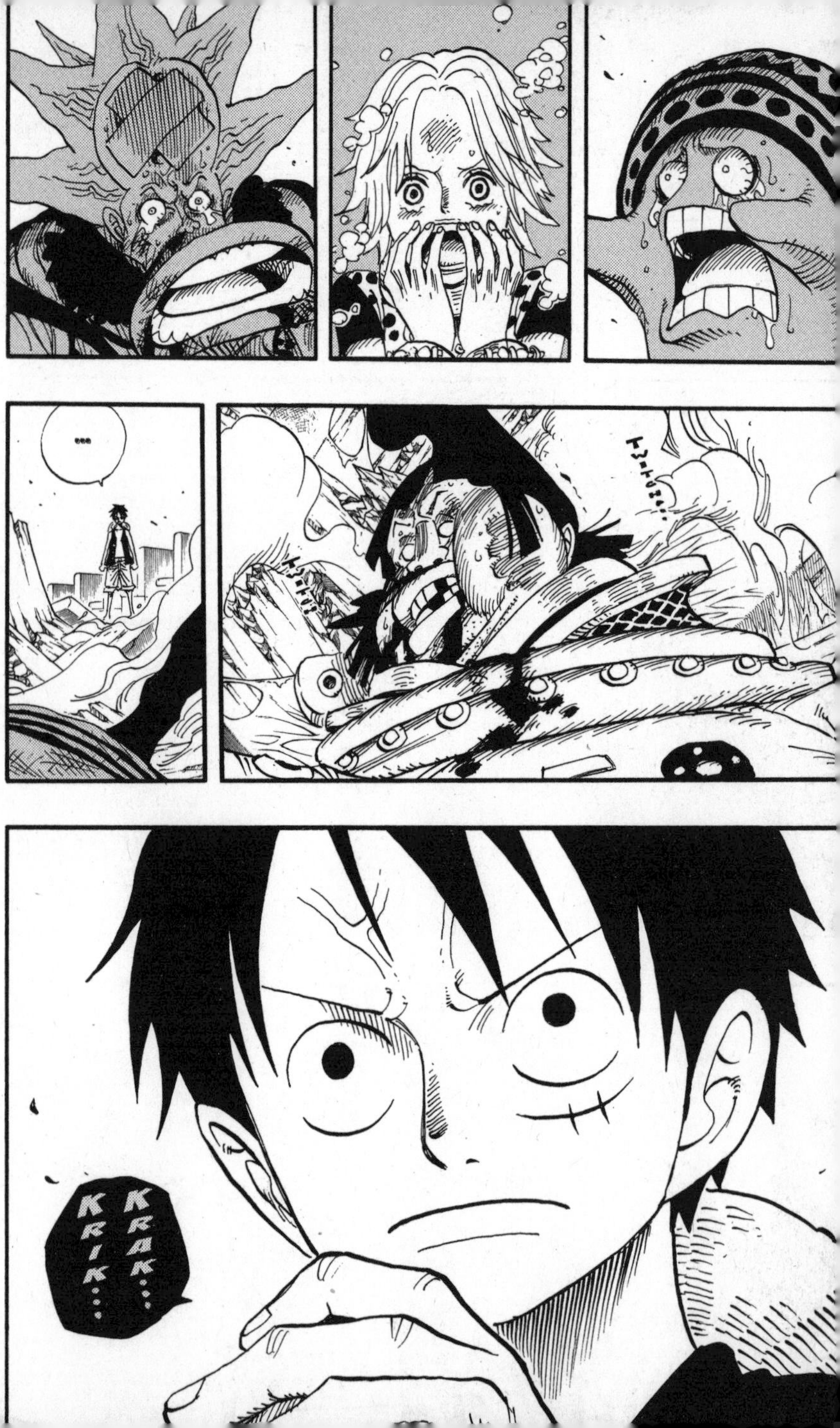
TWITCH...
TWITCH!!
...
KRIK... KRAK...

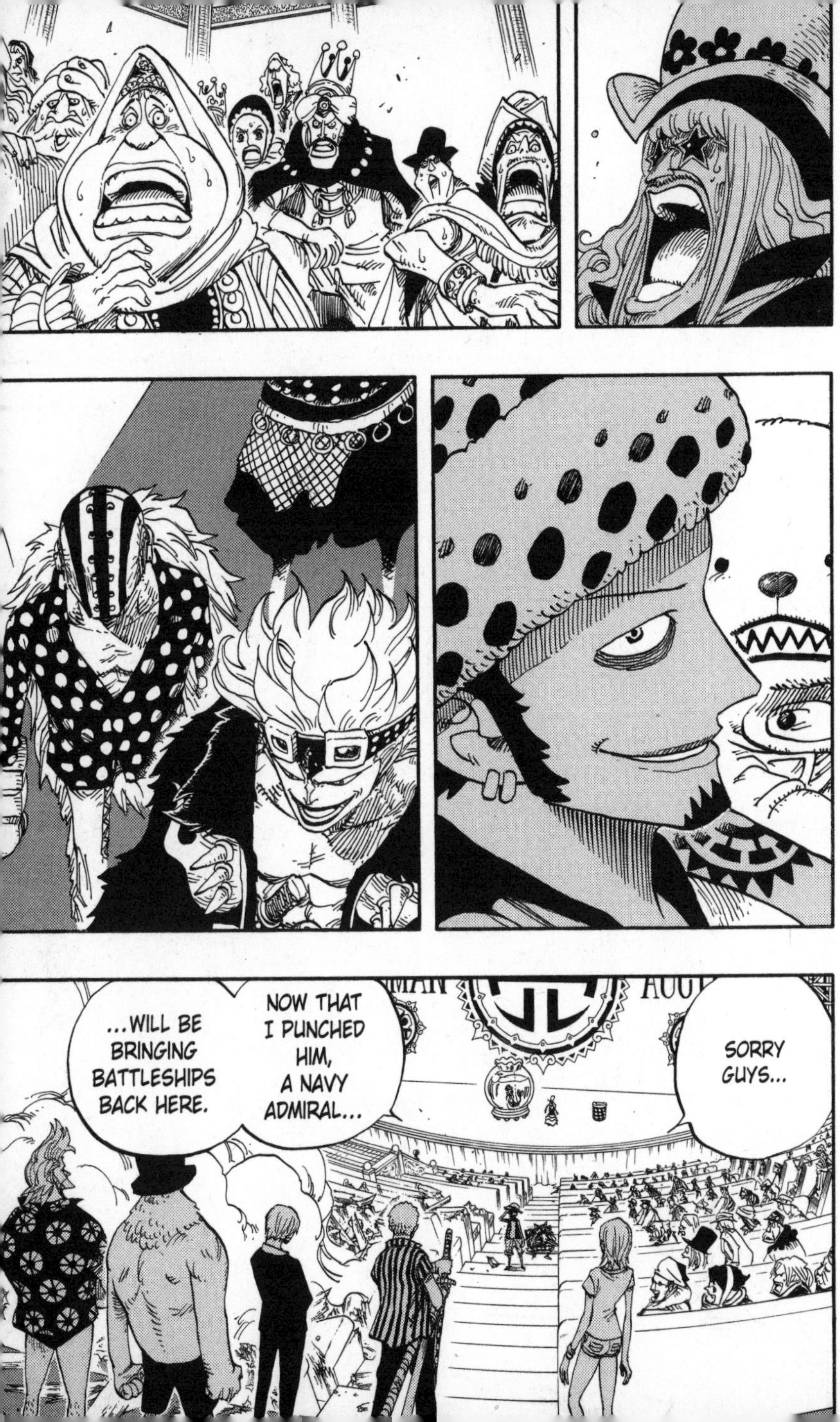
SORRY GUYS...
NOW THAT I PUNCHED HIM, A NAVY ADMIRAL...
...WILL BE BRINGING BATTLESHIPS BACK HERE.

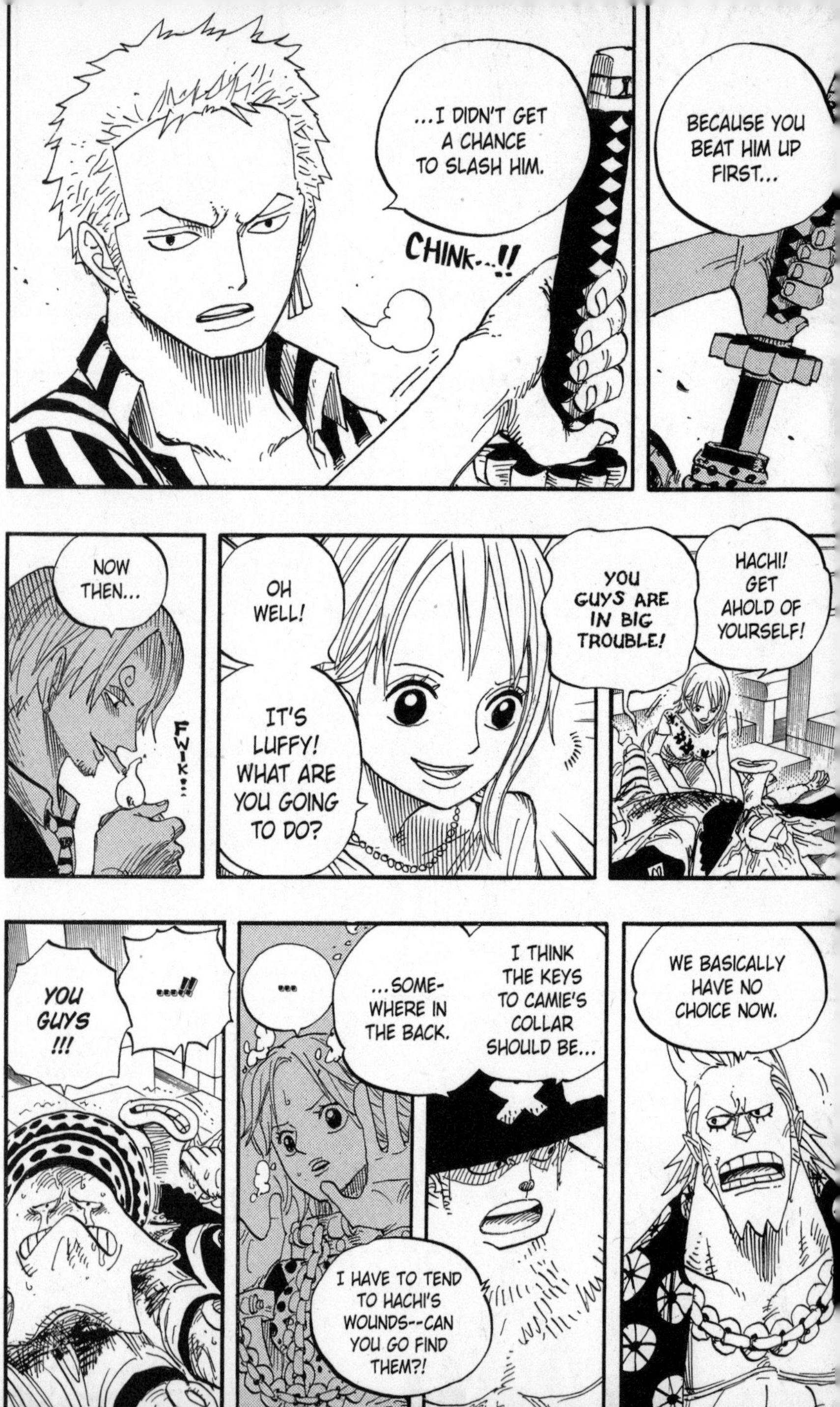
BECAUSE YOU BEAT HIM UP FIRST...
...I DIDN'T GET A CHANCE TO SLASH HIM.
CHINK...!!
HACHI! GET AHOLD OF YOURSELF!
YOU GUYS ARE IN BIG TROUBLE!
OH WELL!
IT'S LUFFY! WHAT ARE YOU GOING TO DO?
NOW THEN...
FWIK...
WE BASICALLY HAVE NO CHOICE NOW.
I THINK THE KEYS TO CAMIE'S COLLAR SHOULD BE...
...SOME-WHERE IN THE BACK.
...
I HAVE TO TEND TO HACHI'S WOUNDS--CAN YOU GO FIND THEM?!
...!!
YOU GUYS!!!

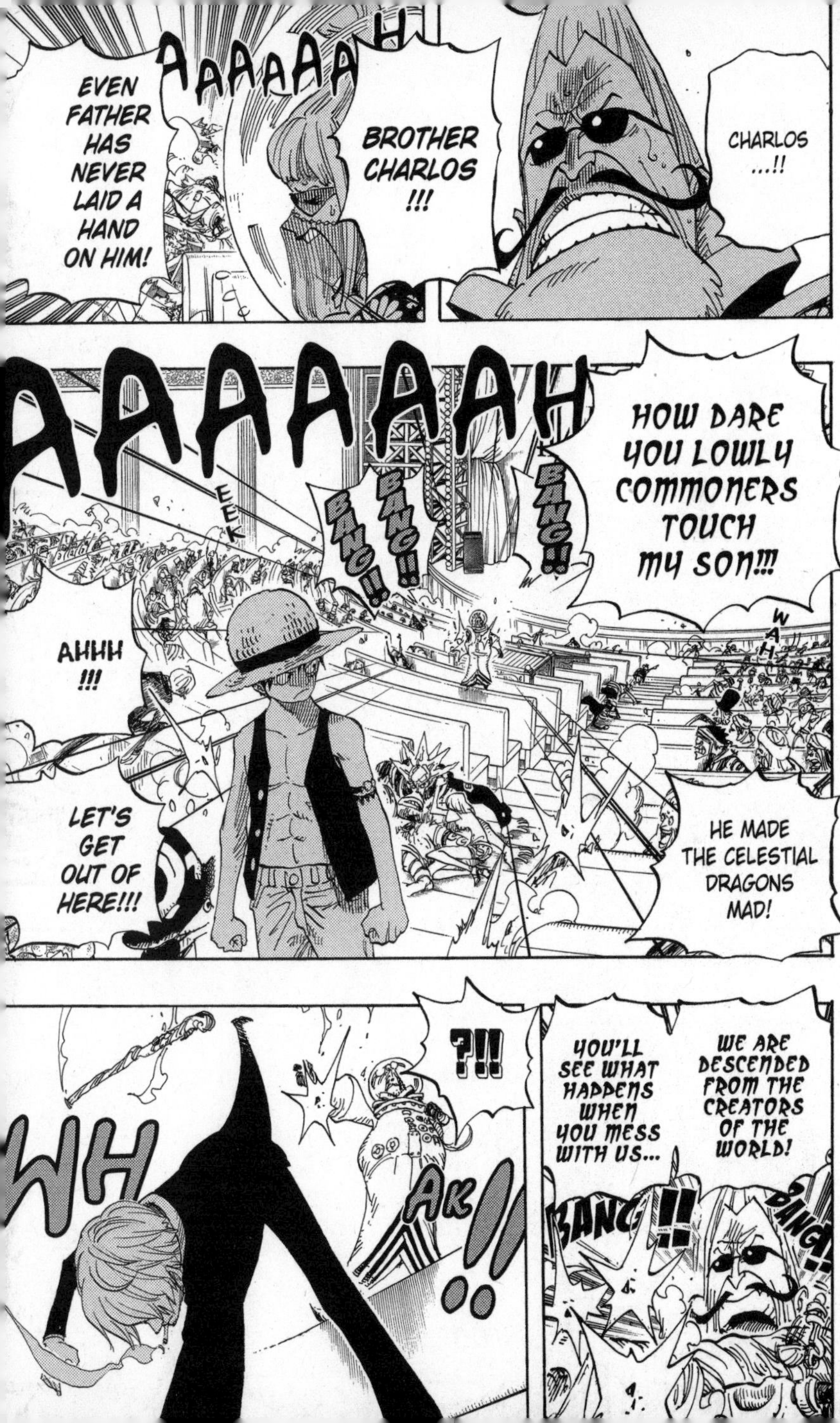
CHARLOS ...!!
AAAAAAH
BROTHER CHARLOS !!!
EVEN FATHER HAS NEVER LAID A HAND ON HIM!
HOW DARE YOU LOWLY COMMONERS TOUCH MY SON!!!
BANG!!
BANG!!
BANG!!
AAAAAAAAH
WAH
EEK
HE MADE THE CELESTIAL DRAGONS MAD!
AHHH !!!
LET'S GET OUT OF HERE!!!
WE ARE DESCENDED FROM THE CREATORS OF THE WORLD!
YOU'LL SEE WHAT HAPPENS WHEN YOU MESS WITH US...
BANG!!
BANG!!
?!!
WHAK!!

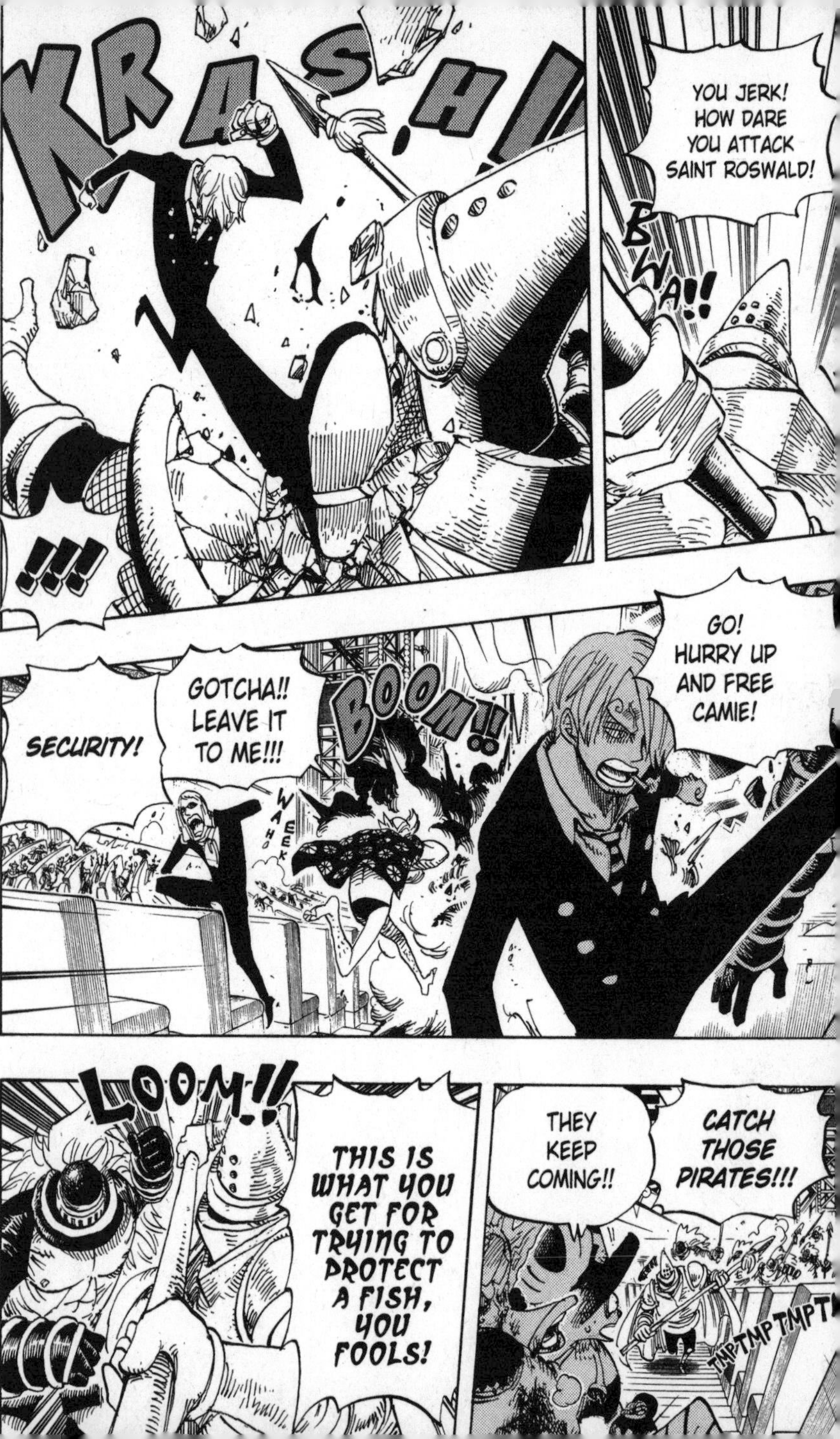
YOU JERK! HOW DARE YOU ATTACK SAINT ROSWALD!
BWA!!
KRASH!
!!!
GO! HURRY UP AND FREE CAMIE!
BOOM!!
WAH EEK
GOTCHA!! LEAVE IT TO ME!!!
SECURITY!
CATCH THOSE PIRATES!!!
THEY KEEP COMING!!
TMP TMP TMPT
THIS IS WHAT YOU GET FOR TRYING TO PROTECT A FISH, YOU FOOLS!
LOOM!!

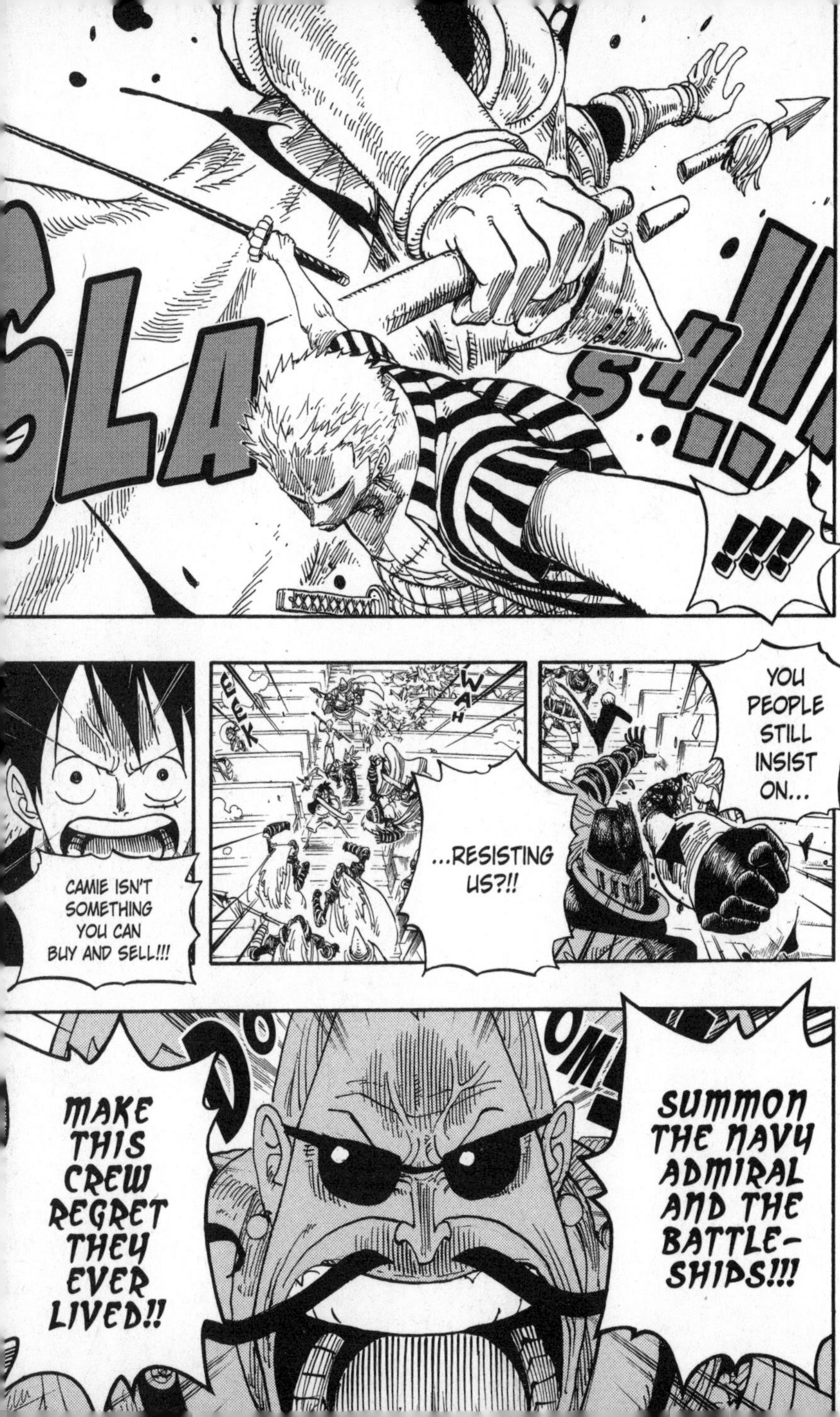
SLASH!!
!!!
YOU PEOPLE STILL INSIST ON...
...RESISTING US?!!
WAH
CAMIE ISN'T SOMETHING YOU CAN BUY AND SELL!!!
SUMMON THE NAVY ADMIRAL AND THE BATTLE-SHIPS!!!
MAKE THIS CREW REGRET THEY EVER LIVED!!

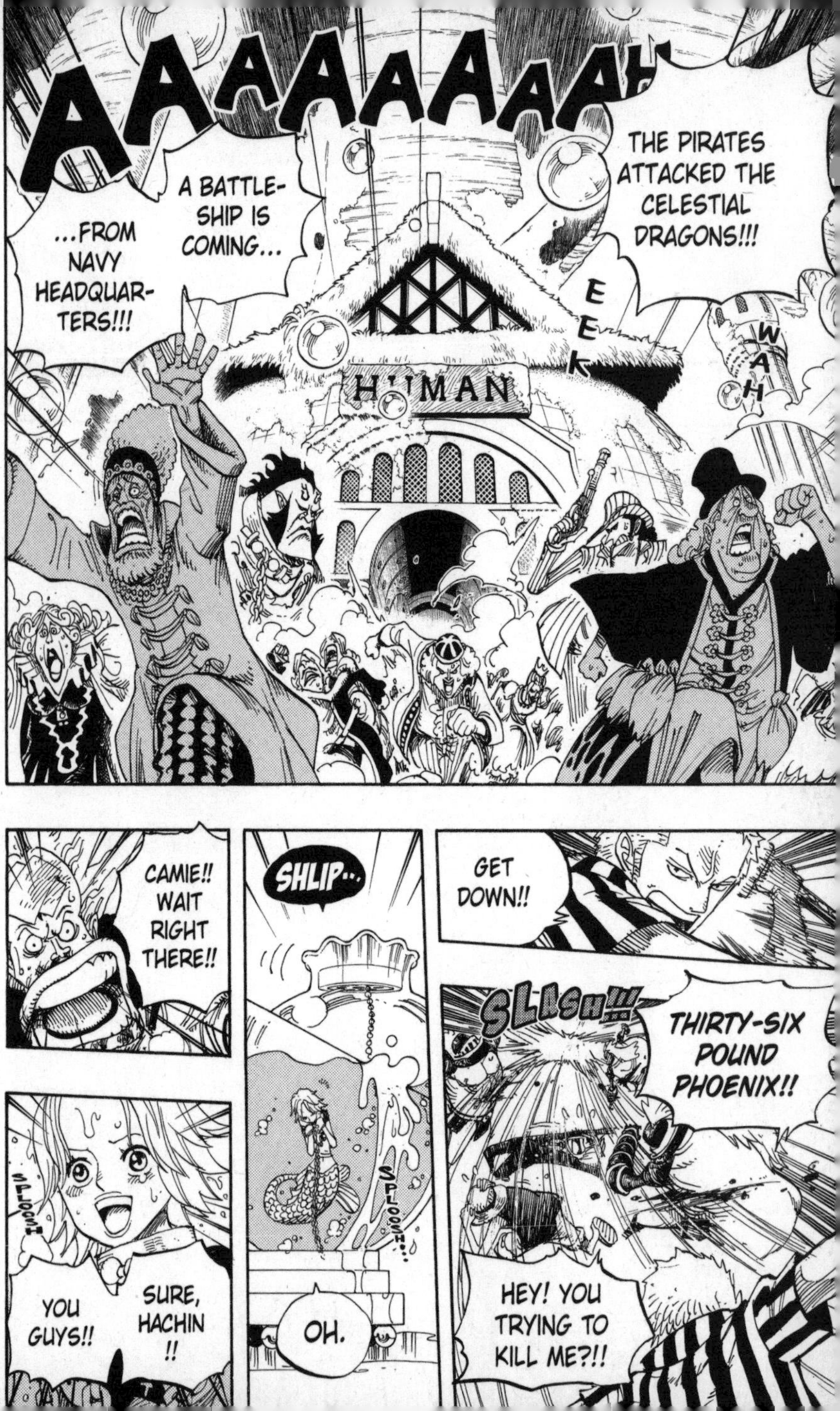
AAAAAAAH
THE PIRATES ATTACKED THE CELESTIAL DRAGONS!!!
WAH
EEK
A BATTLE-SHIP IS COMING...
...FROM NAVY HEADQUAR-TERS!!!
HUMAN
GET DOWN!!
SLASH!!!
THIRTY-SIX POUND PHOENIX!!
HEY! YOU TRYING TO KILL ME?!!
SHLIP...
SPLOOSH...
OH.
CAMIE!! WAIT RIGHT THERE!!
SPLOOSH
SURE, HACHIN!!
YOU GUYS!!

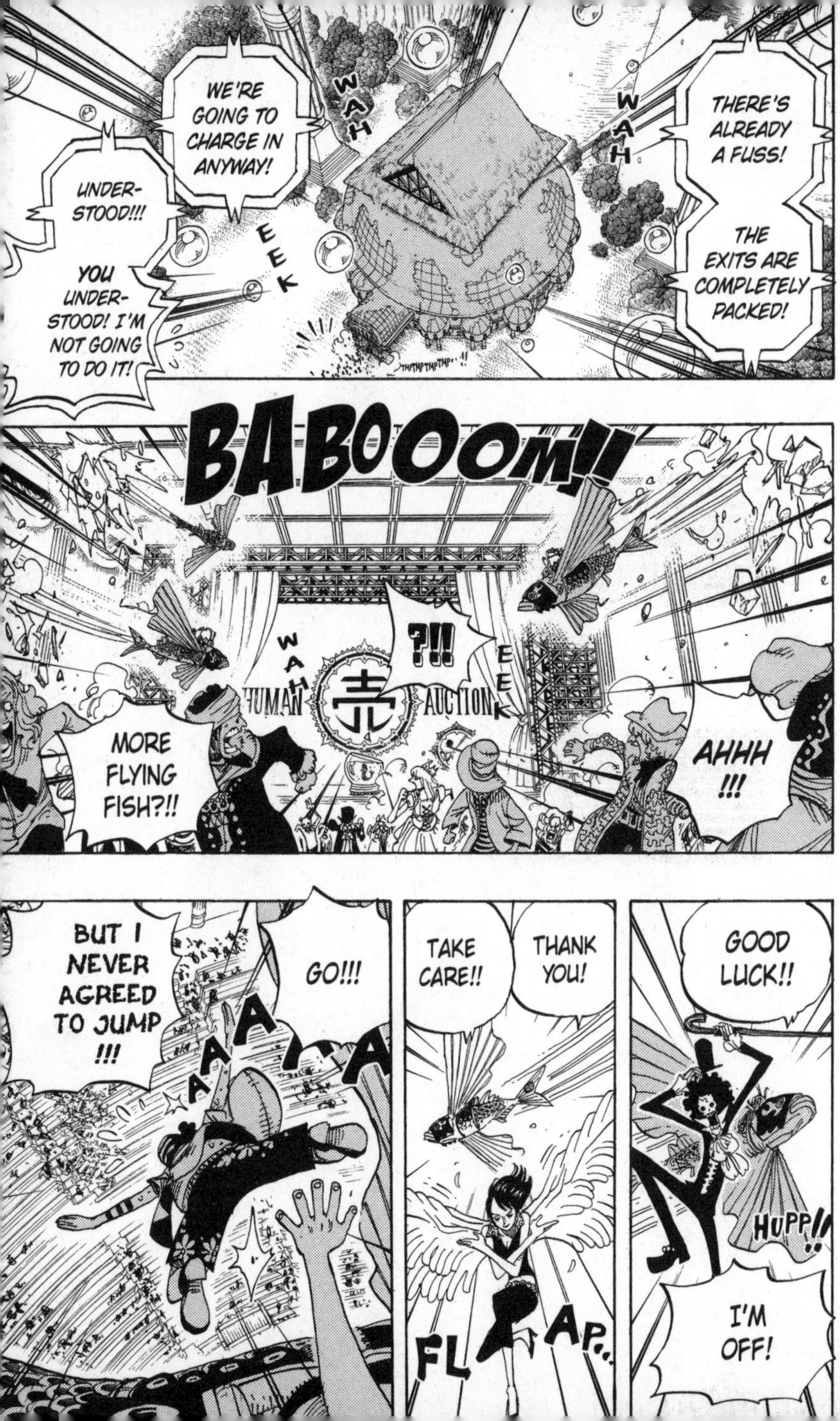
THERE'S ALREADY A FUSS!
THE EXITS ARE COMPLETELY PACKED!
WAH
WAH
WE'RE GOING TO CHARGE IN ANYWAY!
EEK
UNDER-STOOD!!!
YOU UNDER-STOOD! I'M NOT GOING TO DO IT!
TMPTMPTMPTMP
BABOOOM!!
AHHH!!!
EEEK
?!!
WAH
HUMAN AUCTION
MORE FLYING FISH?!!
GOOD LUCK!!
HUPP!!
I'M OFF!
THANK YOU!
TAKE CARE!!
FLAP...
GO!!!
BUT I NEVER AGREED TO JUMP!!!
AAAA

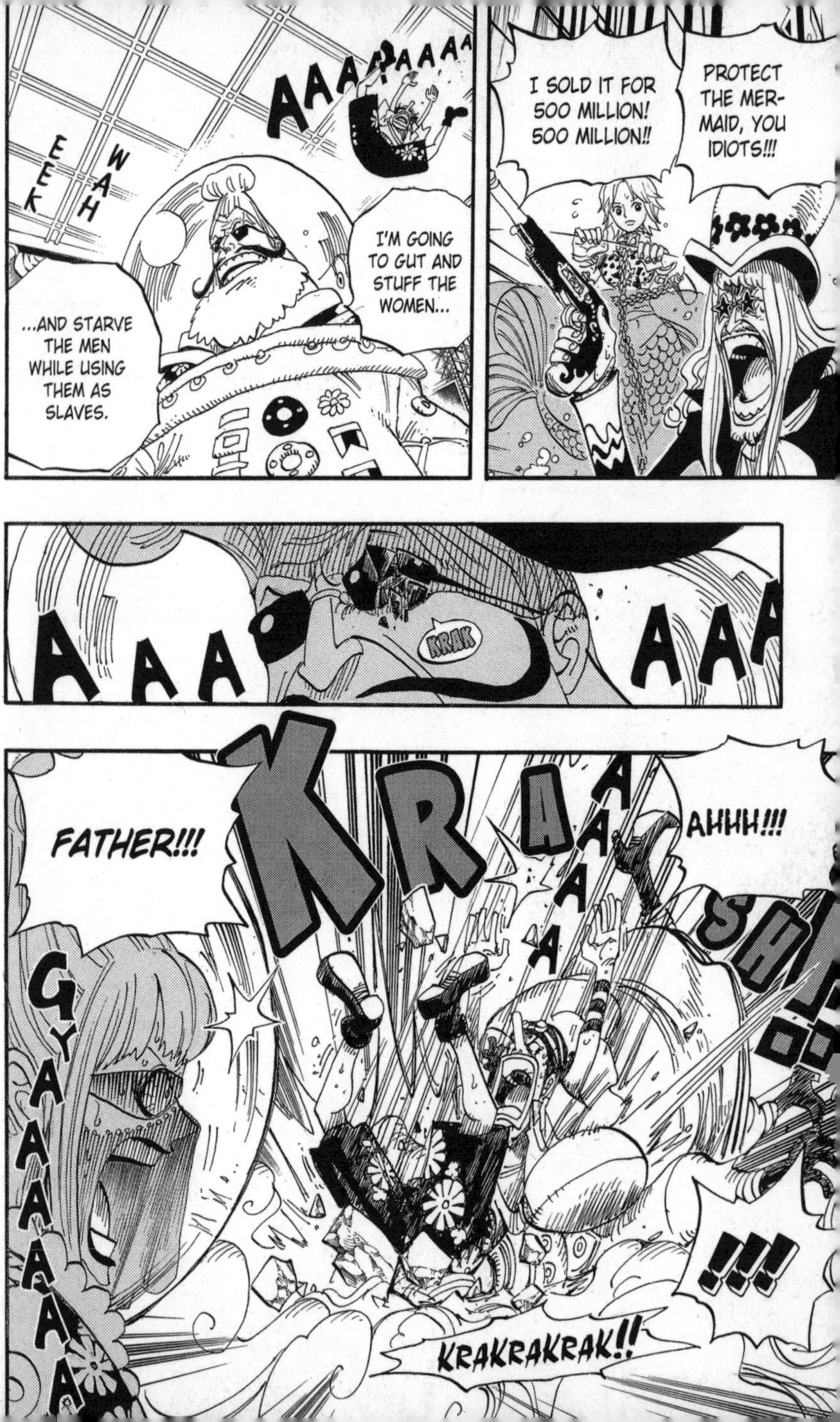

PROTECT THE MER-MAID, YOU IDIOTS!!!
I SOLD IT FOR 500 MILLION! 500 MILLION!!
AAAAAAAA
I'M GOING TO GUT AND STUFF THE WOMEN...
...AND STARVE THE MEN WHILE USING THEM AS SLAVES.
WAH
EEEK
AAA
KRAK
AAA
AHHH!!!
SH!!
!!!
KRAAAAAA
FATHER!!!
GYAAAAAAAA
KRAKRAKRAK!!

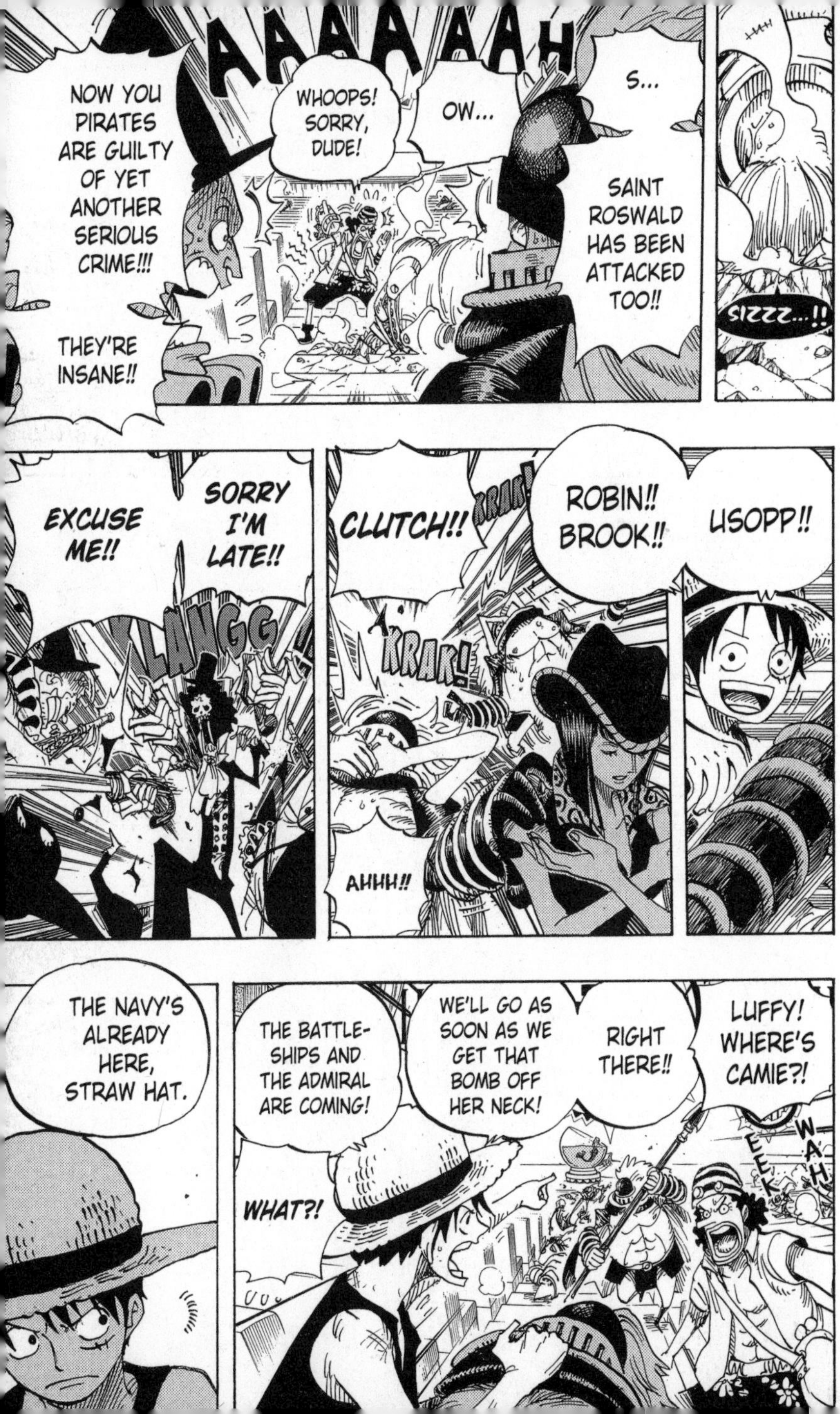
SIZZZ...!!
AAAAAAH
S...
SAINT ROSWALD HAS BEEN ATTACKED TOO!!
OW...
WHOOPS! SORRY, DUDE!
NOW YOU PIRATES ARE GUILTY OF YET ANOTHER SERIOUS CRIME!!!
THEY'RE INSANE!!
USOPP!!
ROBIN!! BROOK!!
KRAK!
CLUTCH!!
KRAK!
AHHH!!
SORRY I'M LATE!!
EXCUSE ME!!
KLANGG
LUFFY! WHERE'S CAMIE?!
RIGHT THERE!!
WE'LL GO AS SOON AS WE GET THAT BOMB OFF HER NECK!
THE BATTLE-SHIPS AND THE ADMIRAL ARE COMING!
WAH
EEEK
WHAT?!
THE NAVY'S ALREADY HERE, STRAW HAT.

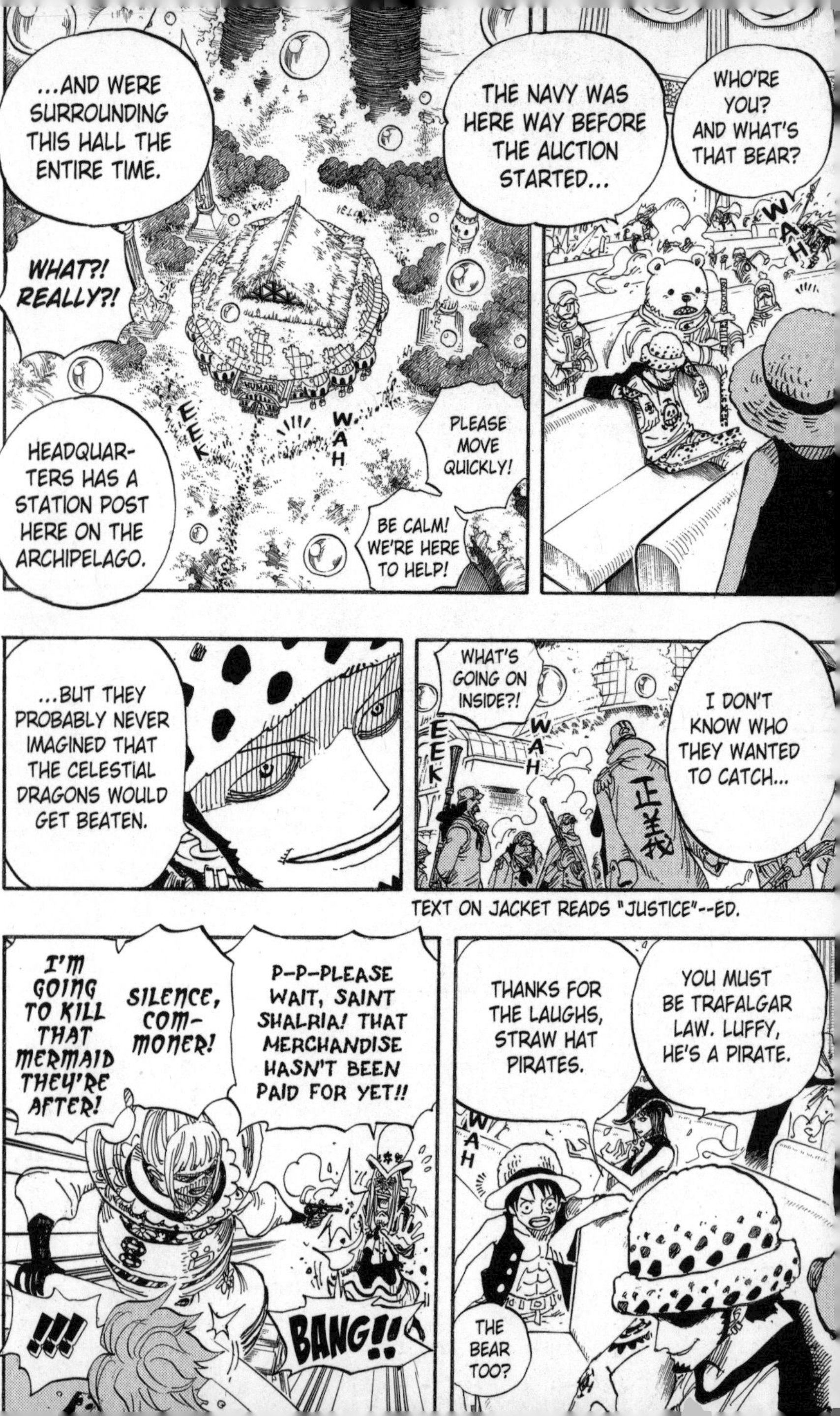
WHO'RE YOU? AND WHAT'S THAT BEAR?
WAH
THE NAVY WAS HERE WAY BEFORE THE AUCTION STARTED...
...AND WERE SURROUNDING THIS HALL THE ENTIRE TIME.
WHAT?! REALLY?!
PLEASE MOVE QUICKLY!
WAH
EEK
BE CALM! WE'RE HERE TO HELP!
HEADQUARTERS HAS A STATION POST HERE ON THE ARCHIPELAGO.
I DON'T KNOW WHO THEY WANTED TO CATCH...
WHAT'S GOING ON INSIDE?!
WAH
EEK
...BUT THEY PROBABLY NEVER IMAGINED THAT THE CELESTIAL DRAGONS WOULD GET BEATEN.
YOU MUST BE TRAFALGAR LAW. LUFFY, HE'S A PIRATE.
THANKS FOR THE LAUGHS, STRAW HAT PIRATES.
WAH
THE BEAR TOO?
P-P-PLEASE WAIT, SAINT SHALRIA! THAT MERCHANDISE HASN'T BEEN PAID FOR YET!!
SILENCE, COMMONER!
I'M GOING TO KILL THAT MERMAID THEY'RE AFTER!
BANG!!
!!!
TEXT ON JACKET READS "JUSTICE"--ED.

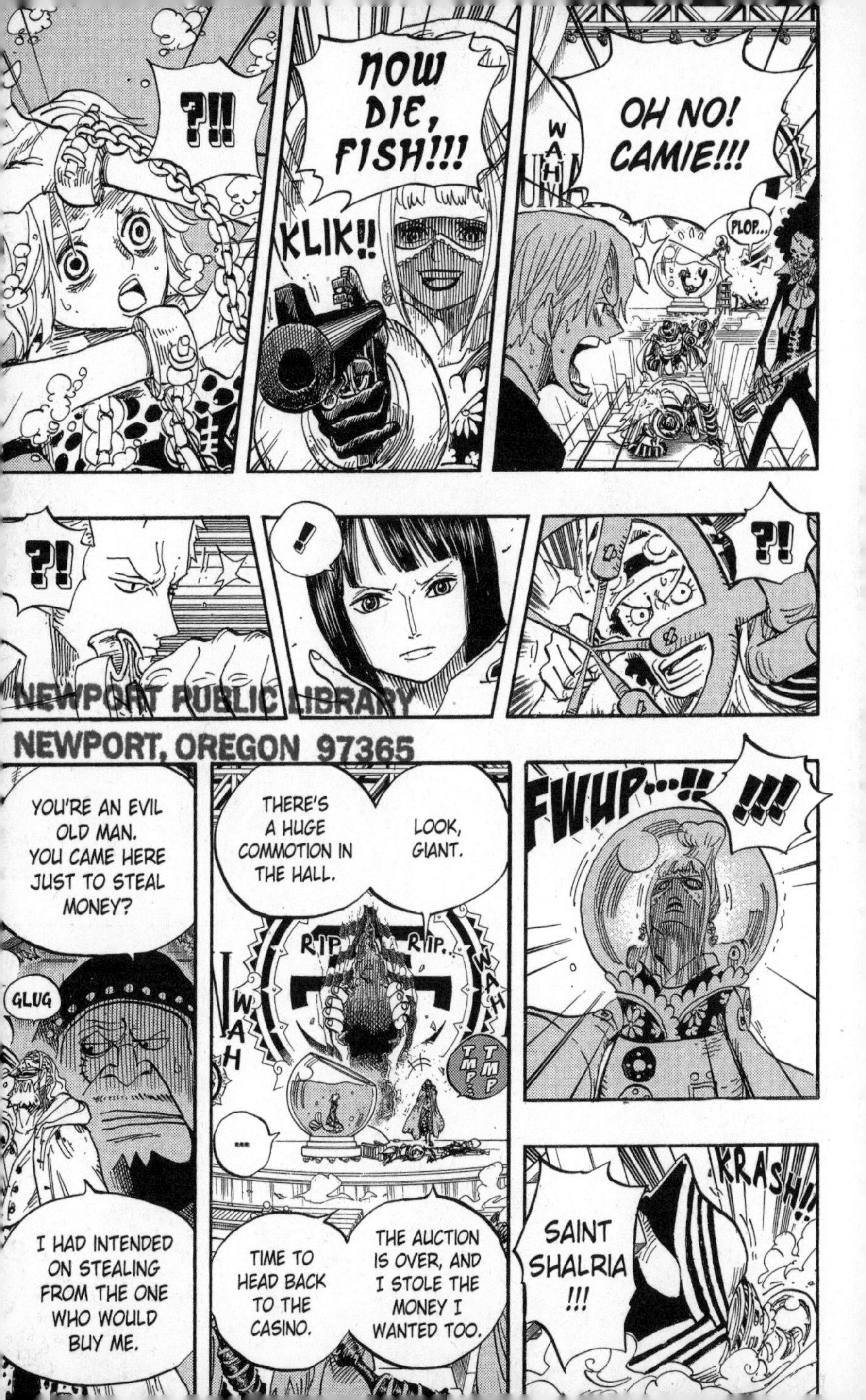
WAH
OH NO! CAMIE!!!
PLOP...
NOW DIE, FISH!!!
KLIK!!
?!!
?!
!
?!
FWUP...!!
!!!
KRASH!!
SAINT SHALRIA !!!
LOOK, GIANT.
THERE'S A HUGE COMMOTION IN THE HALL.
RIP
RIP..
WAH
WAH
TMP TMP
...
THE AUCTION IS OVER, AND I STOLE THE MONEY I WANTED TOO.
TIME TO HEAD BACK TO THE CASINO.
YOU'RE AN EVIL OLD MAN. YOU CAME HERE JUST TO STEAL MONEY?
GLUG
I HAD INTENDED ON STEALING FROM THE ONE WHO WOULD BUY ME.

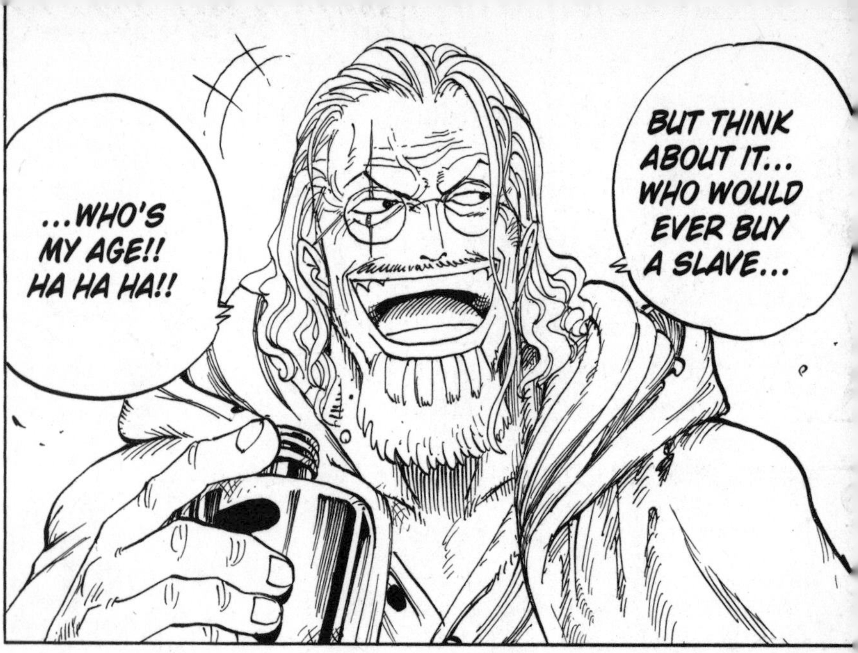
BUT THINK ABOUT IT... WHO WOULD EVER BUY A SLAVE...
...WHO'S MY AGE!! HA HA HA!!

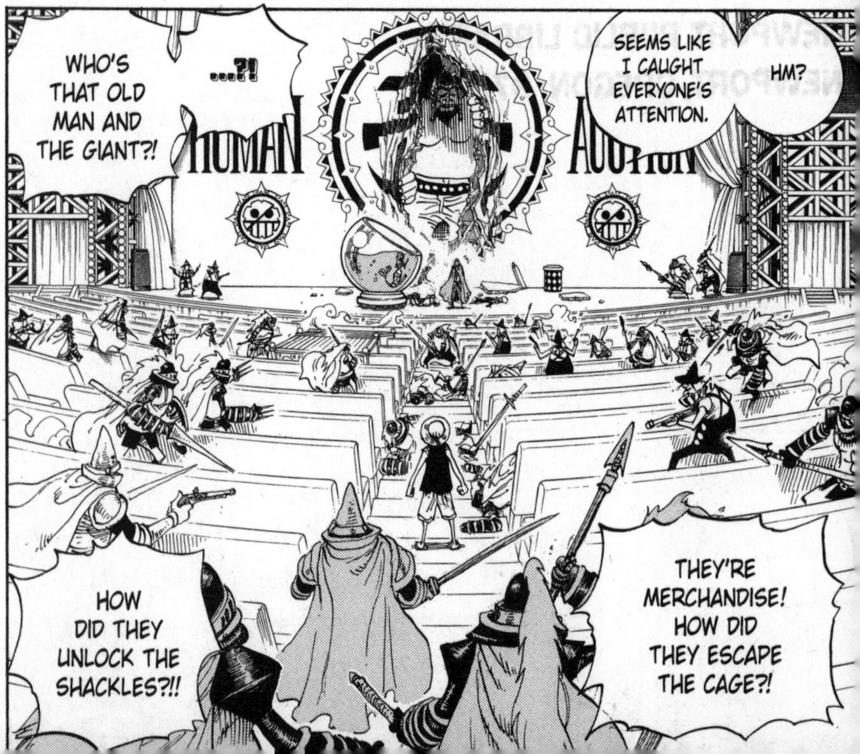
HM?
SEEMS LIKE I CAUGHT EVERYONE'S ATTENTION.
...?!
WHO'S THAT OLD MAN AND THE GIANT?!
HUMAN
THEY'RE MERCHANDISE! HOW DID THEY ESCAPE THE CAGE?!
HOW DID THEY UNLOCK THE SHACKLES?!!

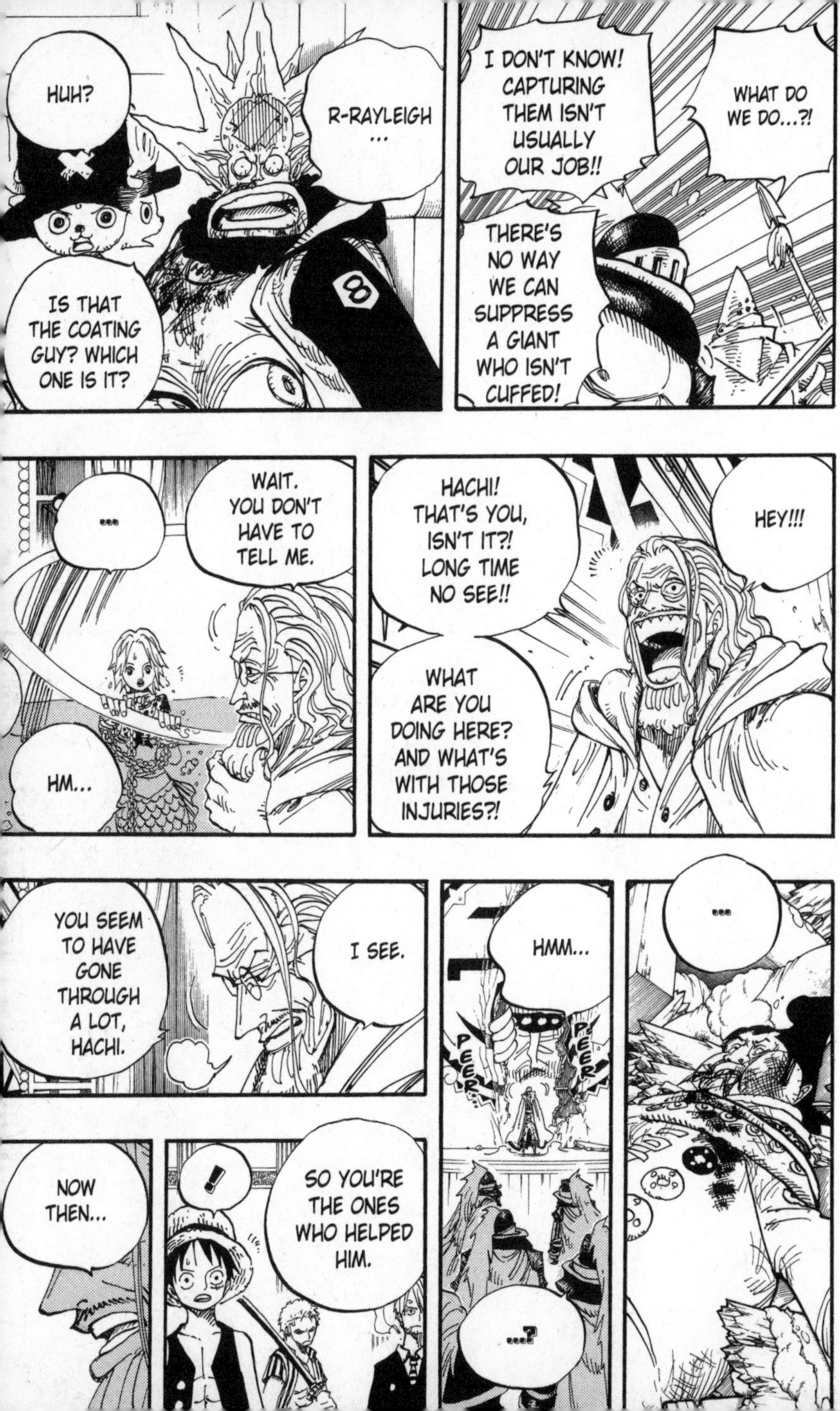
WHAT DO WE DO...?!
I DON'T KNOW! CAPTURING THEM ISN'T USUALLY OUR JOB!!
THERE'S NO WAY WE CAN SUPPRESS A GIANT WHO ISN'T CUFFED!
R-RAYLEIGH ...
HUH?
IS THAT THE COATING GUY? WHICH ONE IS IT?
HEY!!!
HACHI! THAT'S YOU, ISN'T IT?! LONG TIME NO SEE!!
WHAT ARE YOU DOING HERE? AND WHAT'S WITH THOSE INJURIES?!
WAIT. YOU DON'T HAVE TO TELL ME.
...
HM...
...
HMM...
PEER
PEER
...?
I SEE.
YOU SEEM TO HAVE GONE THROUGH A LOT, HACHI.
SO YOU'RE THE ONES WHO HELPED HIM.
!
NOW THEN...

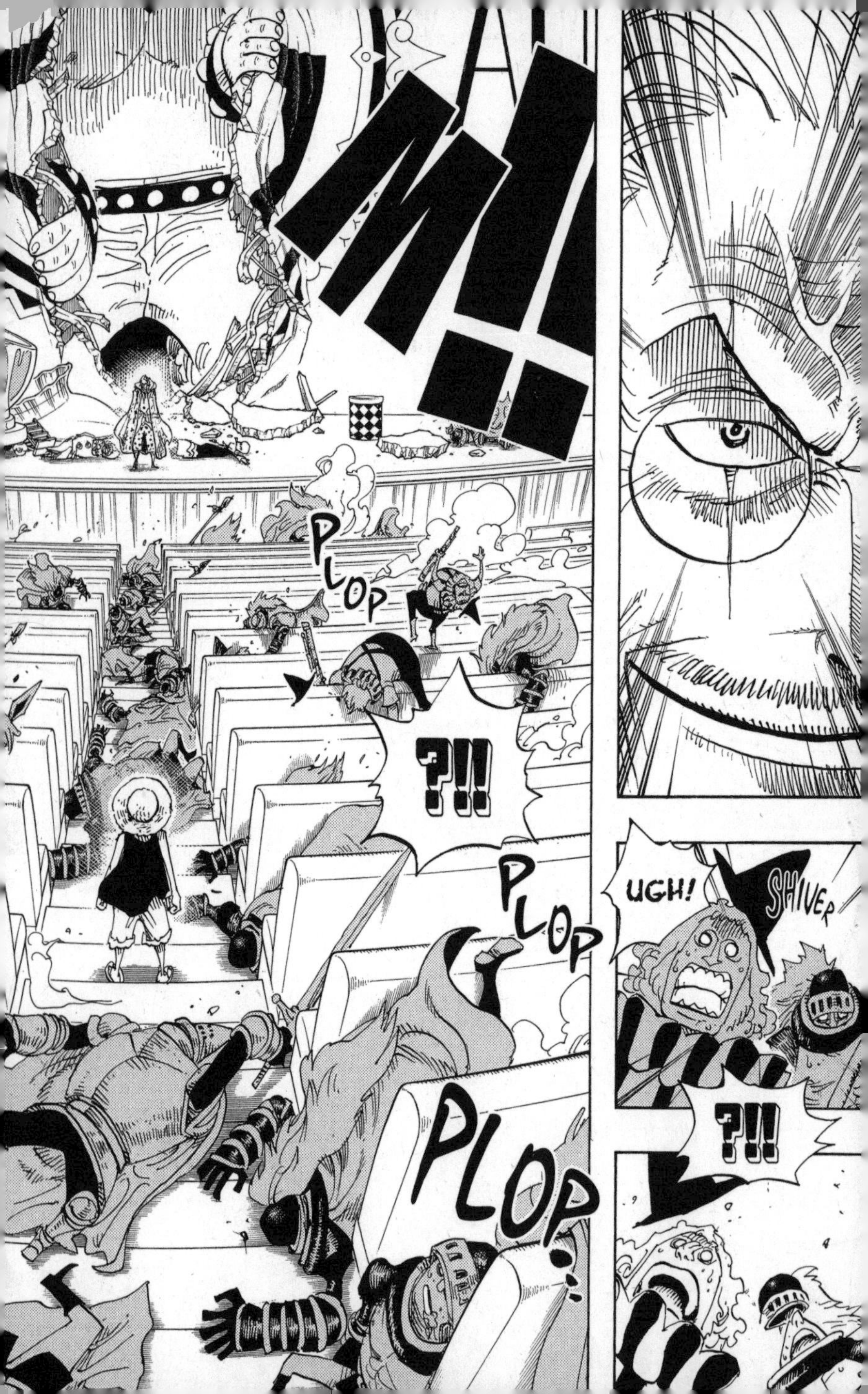
UGH!
SHIVER
?!!
PLOP
?!!
PLOP
PLOP

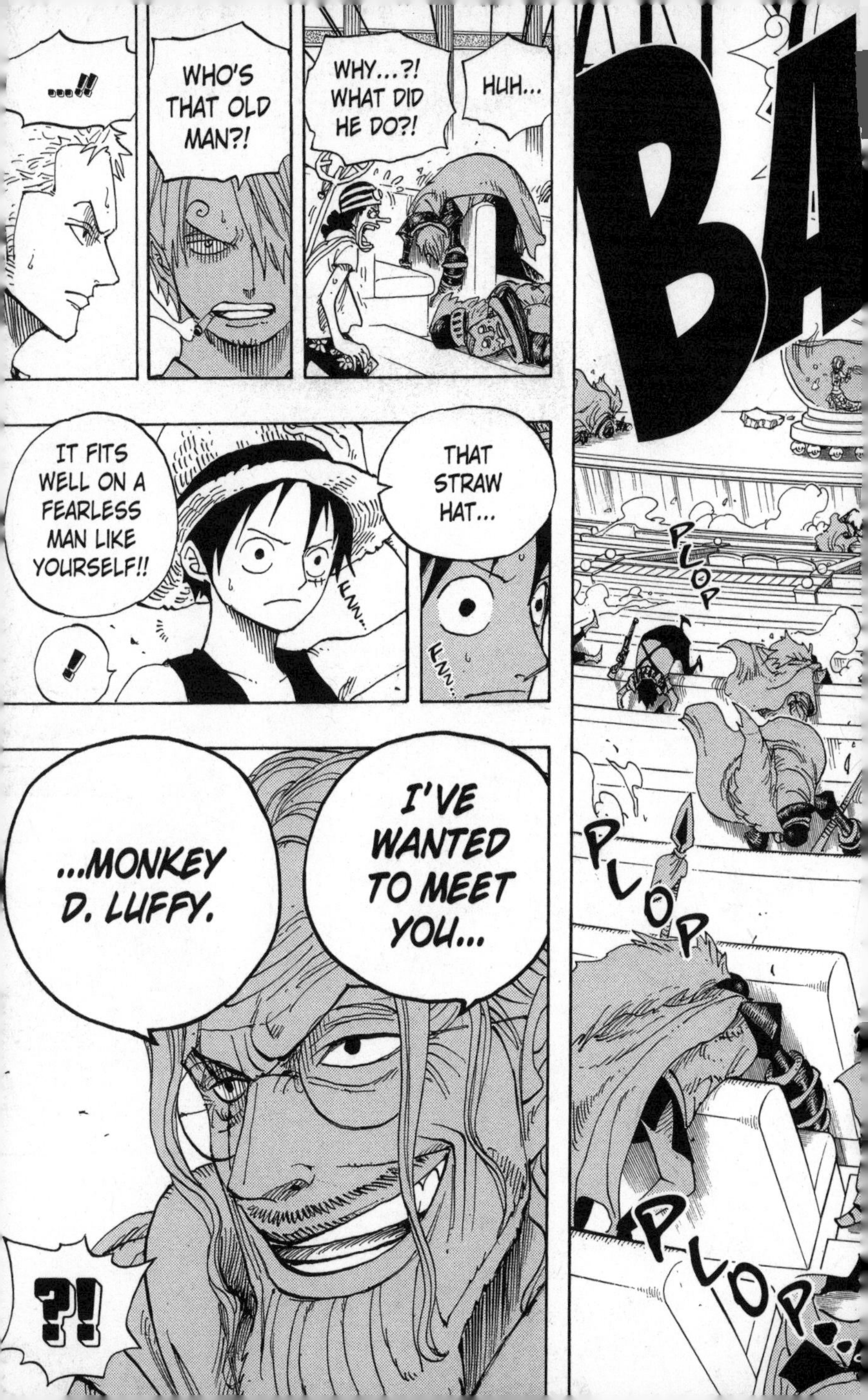
BA
PLOP
PLOP
PLOP...
HUH...
WHY...?! WHAT DID HE DO?!
WHO'S THAT OLD MAN?!
...!!
THAT STRAW HAT...
IT FITS WELL ON A FEARLESS MAN LIKE YOURSELF!!
!
I'VE WANTED TO MEET YOU...
...MONKEY D. LUFFY.
?!

SBS Question Corner

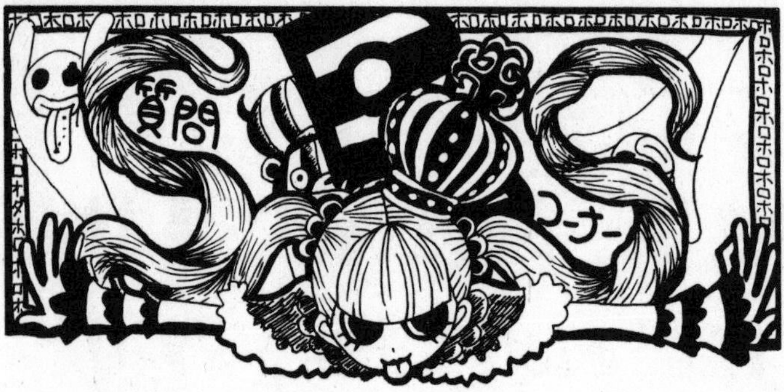
質問
コーナー

(Gifukko, Gifu)

Reader(Q): Oda Sensei, Hello. I really want to start SBS! Can I?! I won't do all of it! How about half? Huh?! Really?! Thank you! I'll say the first half and you can say the rest! Here I go… "Starting SBS!"

--Yusaku

Oda(A): You said the whole thing!
I thought I could say "SBS." Or at least "BS" or "S."

Q: If Camie had a friend named "Ochin," what would she call that friend?

--Marin

A: She adds a "chin" to everyone's name, so it'll be "Ochinchin" (in other words, "peepee"). Sigh. Why would you ask a question like this right from the start?! Actually, I got the exact same question from all over the country.

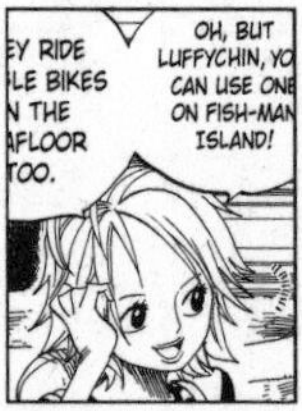
OH, BUT LUFFYCHIN, YO CAN USE ONE ON FISH-MAN ISLAND!
EY RIDE LE BIKES N THE AFLOOR TOO.

Q: Oda Sensei, in *One Piece* the male characters always refer to themselves as "ore" (I) with hiragana characters. Is there a reason for that?! There are many ways to write this, but you always do it that way. It's been bothering me!

--Rin (I have Luffy♥♥ as my wallpaper on my cell phone!)

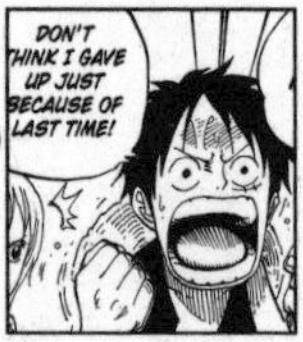
DON'T HINK I GAVE UP JUST BECAUSE OF LAST TIME!

A: You make an interesting point looking back from volume 52, for the last 11 years, you're right. There are many authors who spell "ore" with katakana or kanji characters to make sure they don't mix with the rest of the sentence, but I prefer to write it in hiragana. It's a little hard to explain why, but I plan to keep writing it like that.

Q: Am I a psychic?!

--No Seriously, I Moved the Cup with My Mind

A: I don't know!!

Chapter 504:
PIRATE FRONT LINE ON THE MOVE!!

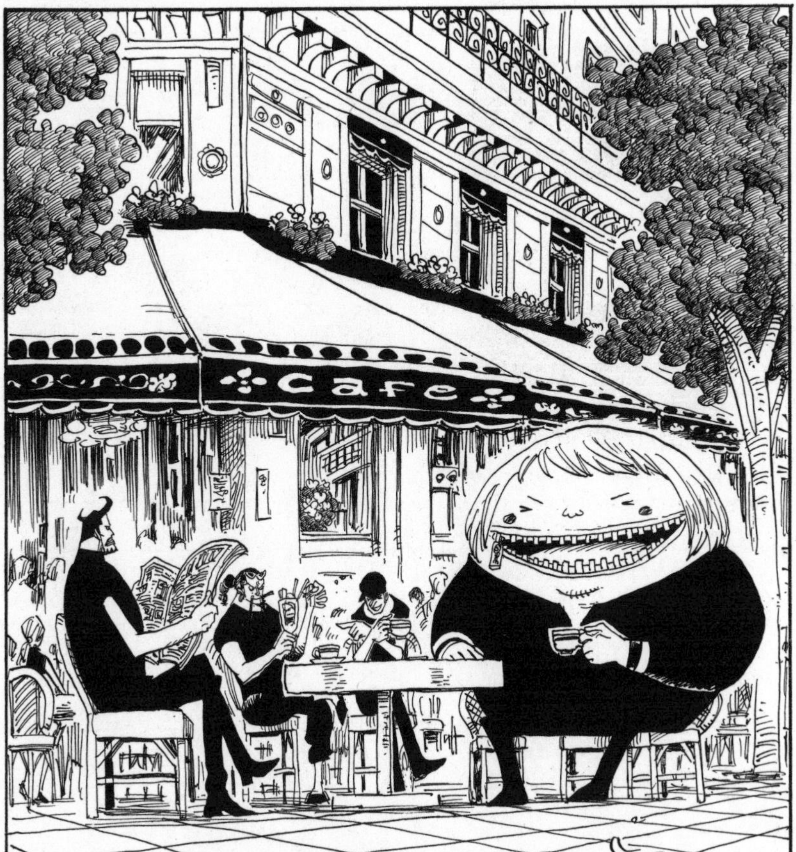
cafe

CP9'S INDEPENDENT REPORT, VOL. 13:
"WAITING FOR THEM TO FINISH SHOPPING"

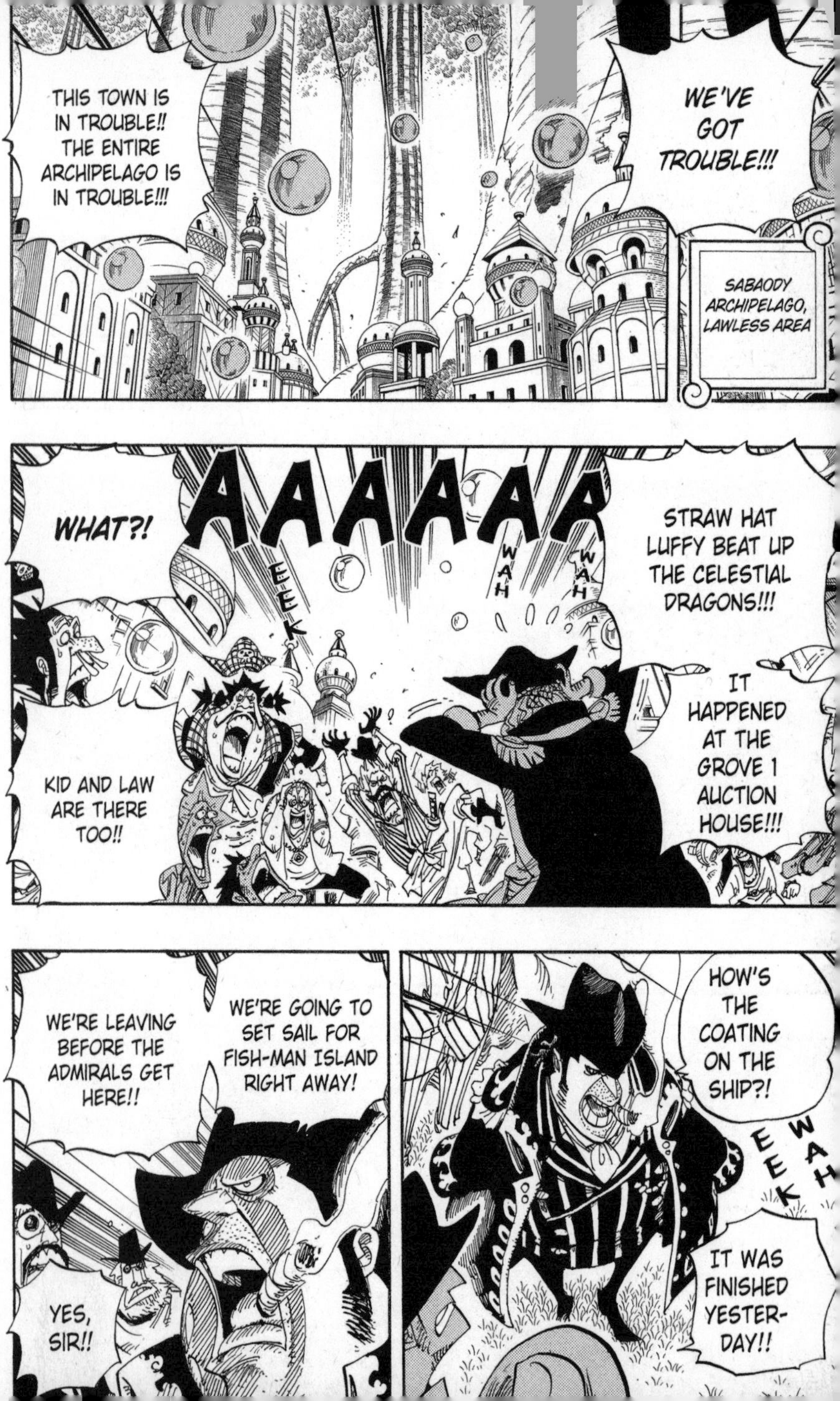
WE'VE GOT TROUBLE!!!
SABAODY ARCHIPELAGO, LAWLESS AREA
THIS TOWN IS IN TROUBLE!! THE ENTIRE ARCHIPELAGO IS IN TROUBLE!!!
STRAW HAT LUFFY BEAT UP THE CELESTIAL DRAGONS!!!
IT HAPPENED AT THE GROVE 1 AUCTION HOUSE!!!
AAAAAA
WAH
WAH
EEEK
WHAT?!
KID AND LAW ARE THERE TOO!!
HOW'S THE COATING ON THE SHIP?!
WAH
EEEK
IT WAS FINISHED YESTER-DAY!!
WE'RE GOING TO SET SAIL FOR FISH-MAN ISLAND RIGHT AWAY!
WE'RE LEAVING BEFORE THE ADMIRALS GET HERE!!
YES, SIR!!

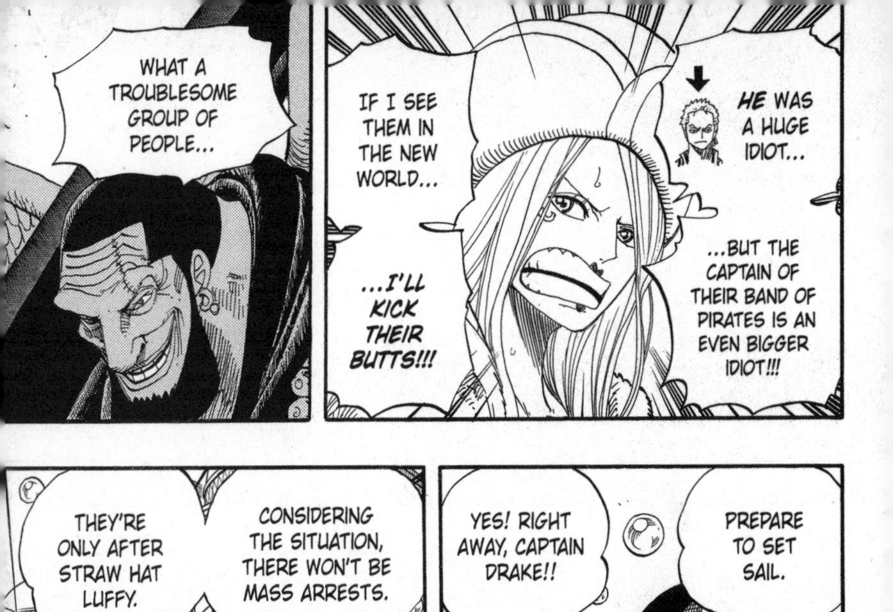
HE WAS A HUGE IDIOT...
...BUT THE CAPTAIN OF THEIR BAND OF PIRATES IS AN EVEN BIGGER IDIOT!!!
IF I SEE THEM IN THE NEW WORLD...
...I'LL KICK THEIR BUTTS!!!
WHAT A TROUBLESOME GROUP OF PEOPLE...
PREPARE TO SET SAIL.
YES! RIGHT AWAY, CAPTAIN DRAKE!!
NOW THEN, I WONDER WHO WILL COME...!
CONSIDERING THE SITUATION, THERE WON'T BE MASS ARRESTS.
THEY'RE ONLY AFTER STRAW HAT LUFFY.
WAH
WAH
音
I WANT TO STAY AND SEE WHAT THAT ADMIRAL IS LIKE.
APOO! PLEASE DON'T SAY THAT! LET'S RUN!

TEXT ON VEST READS "SOUND"--ED.

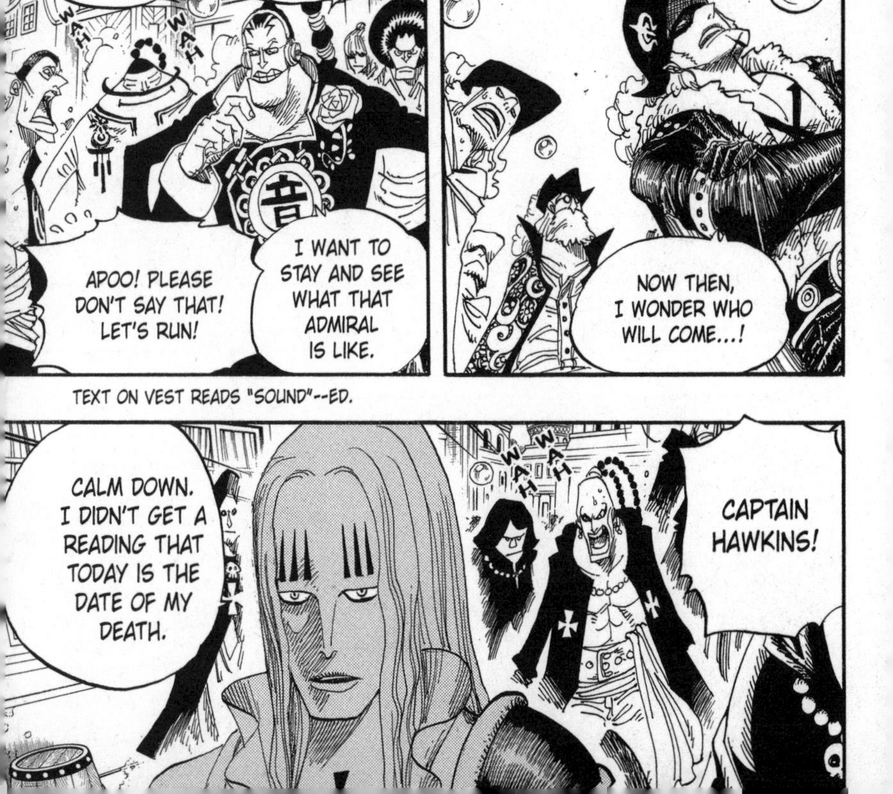
CAPTAIN HAWKINS!
WAH
WAH
CALM DOWN. I DIDN'T GET A READING THAT TODAY IS THE DATE OF MY DEATH.

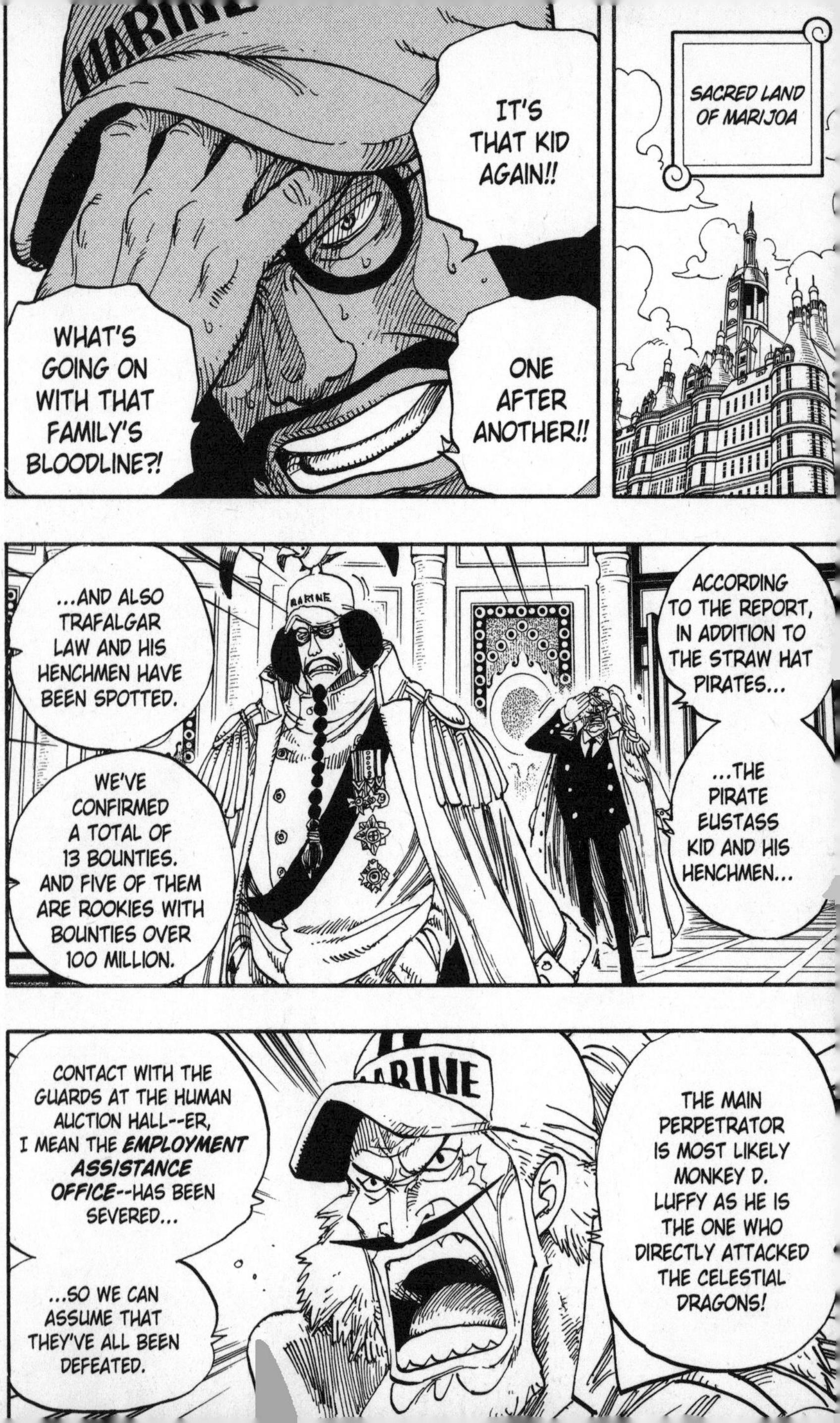
SACRED LAND OF MARIJOA
IT'S THAT KID AGAIN!!
ONE AFTER ANOTHER!!
WHAT'S GOING ON WITH THAT FAMILY'S BLOODLINE?!
ACCORDING TO THE REPORT, IN ADDITION TO THE STRAW HAT PIRATES...
...THE PIRATE EUSTASS KID AND HIS HENCHMEN...
...AND ALSO TRAFALGAR LAW AND HIS HENCHMEN HAVE BEEN SPOTTED.
WE'VE CONFIRMED A TOTAL OF 13 BOUNTIES. AND FIVE OF THEM ARE ROOKIES WITH BOUNTIES OVER 100 MILLION.
THE MAIN PERPETRATOR IS MOST LIKELY MONKEY D. LUFFY AS HE IS THE ONE WHO DIRECTLY ATTACKED THE CELESTIAL DRAGONS!
CONTACT WITH THE GUARDS AT THE HUMAN AUCTION HALL--ER, I MEAN THE *EMPLOYMENT ASSISTANCE OFFICE*--HAS BEEN SEVERED...
...SO WE CAN ASSUME THAT THEY'VE ALL BEEN DEFEATED.

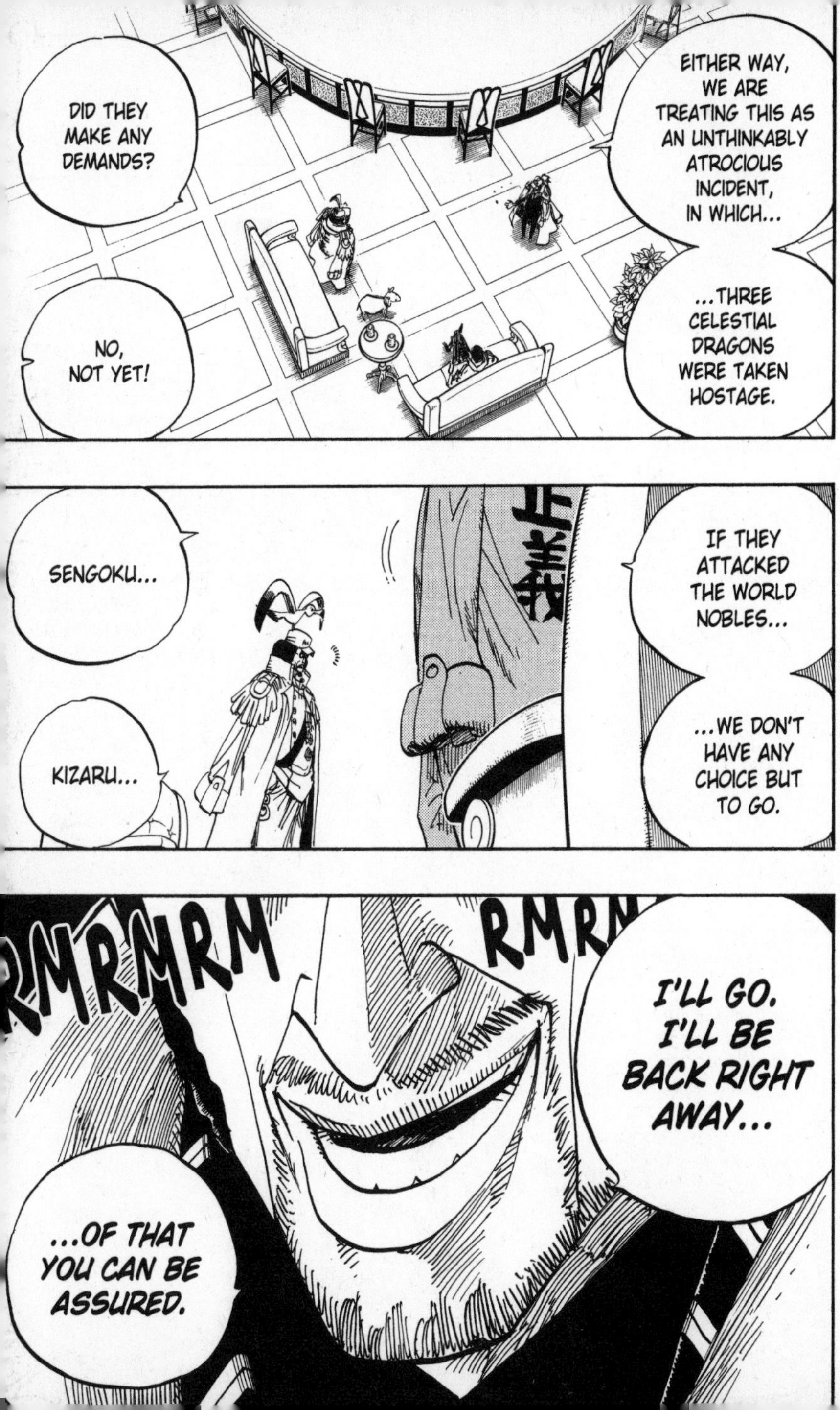
EITHER WAY, WE ARE TREATING THIS AS AN UNTHINKABLY ATROCIOUS INCIDENT, IN WHICH...
...THREE CELESTIAL DRAGONS WERE TAKEN HOSTAGE.
DID THEY MAKE ANY DEMANDS?
NO, NOT YET!
IF THEY ATTACKED THE WORLD NOBLES...
...WE DON'T HAVE ANY CHOICE BUT TO GO.
SENGOKU...
KIZARU...
I'LL GO. I'LL BE BACK RIGHT AWAY...
RMRM
RMRMRM
...OF THAT YOU CAN BE ASSURED.

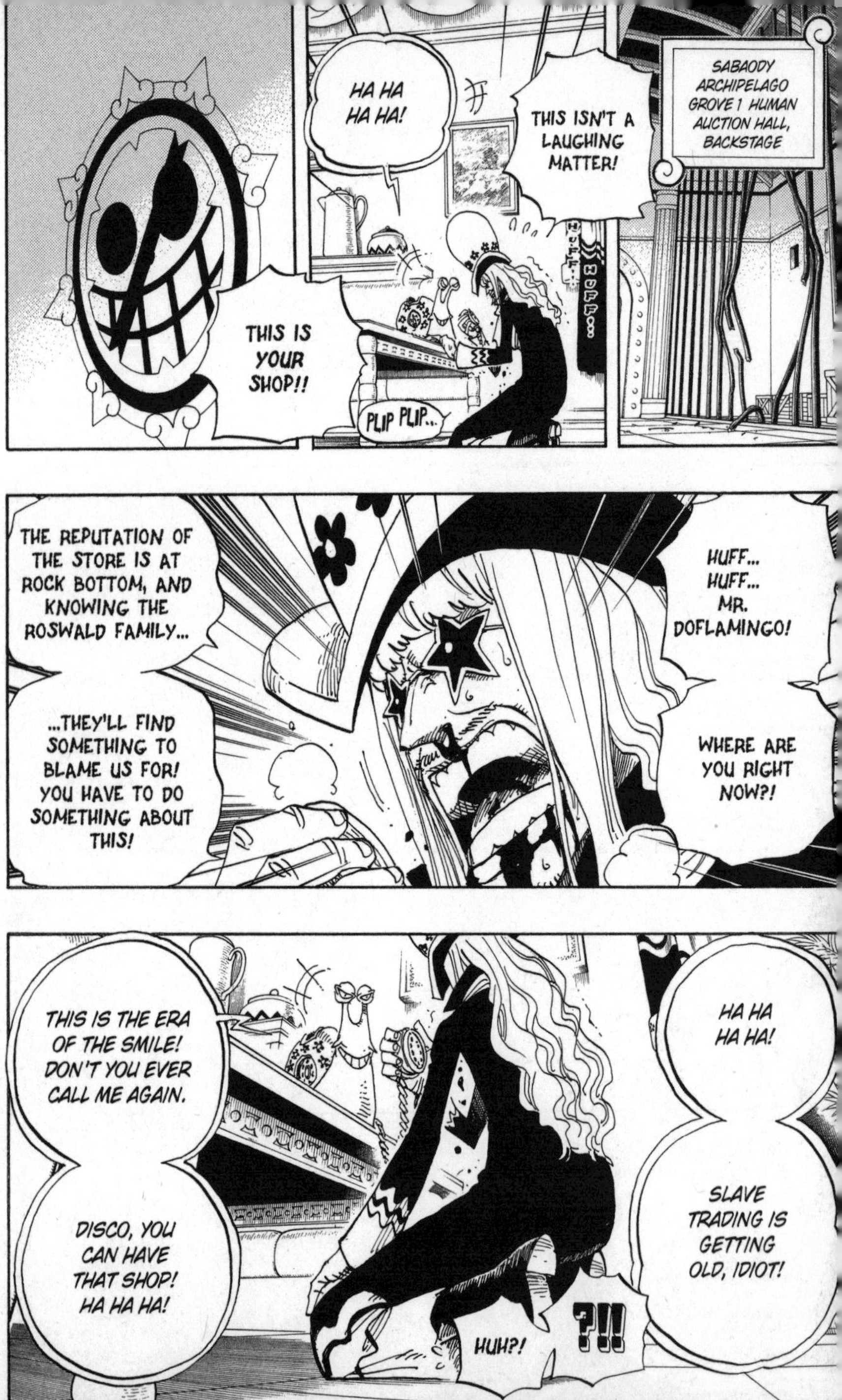
SABAODY ARCHIPELAGO GROVE 1 HUMAN AUCTION HALL, BACKSTAGE
THIS ISN'T A LAUGHING MATTER!
HA HA HA HA!
HUFF HUFF...
PLIP PLIP...
THIS IS YOUR SHOP!!
HUFF... HUFF... MR. DOFLAMINGO!
WHERE ARE YOU RIGHT NOW?!
THE REPUTATION OF THE STORE IS AT ROCK BOTTOM, AND KNOWING THE ROSWALD FAMILY...
...THEY'LL FIND SOMETHING TO BLAME US FOR! YOU HAVE TO DO SOMETHING ABOUT THIS!
HA HA HA HA!
SLAVE TRADING IS GETTING OLD, IDIOT!
?!!
HUH?!
THIS IS THE ERA OF THE SMILE! DON'T YOU EVER CALL ME AGAIN.
DISCO, YOU CAN HAVE THAT SHOP! HA HA HA!

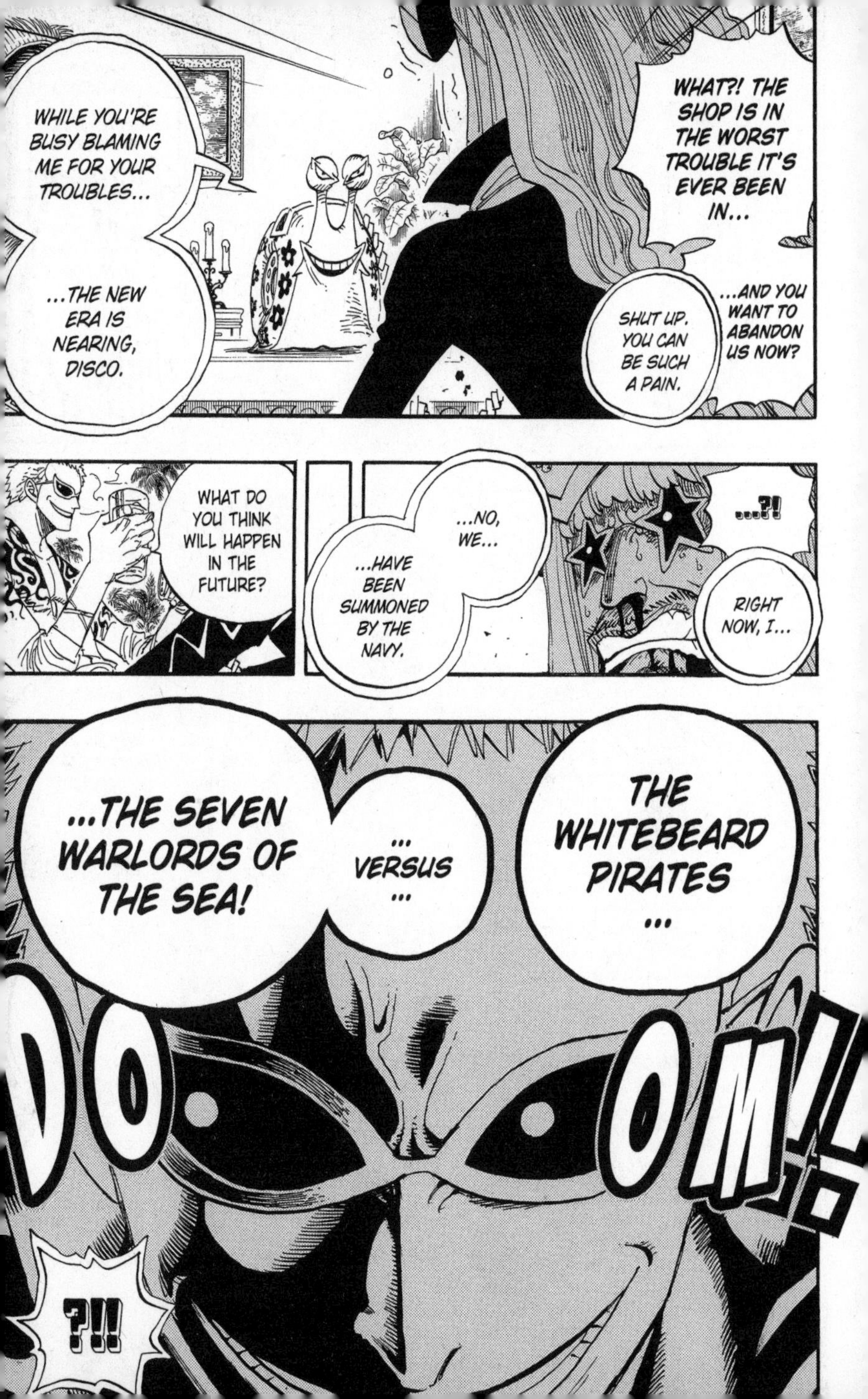
WHAT?! THE SHOP IS IN THE WORST TROUBLE IT'S EVER BEEN IN...
...AND YOU WANT TO ABANDON US NOW?
SHUT UP. YOU CAN BE SUCH A PAIN.
WHILE YOU'RE BUSY BLAMING ME FOR YOUR TROUBLES...
...THE NEW ERA IS NEARING, DISCO.
...?!
RIGHT NOW, I...
...NO, WE...
...HAVE BEEN SUMMONED BY THE NAVY.
WHAT DO YOU THINK WILL HAPPEN IN THE FUTURE?
THE WHITEBEARD PIRATES...
...VERSUS...
...THE SEVEN WARLORDS OF THE SEA!
DO-OM!!
?!!

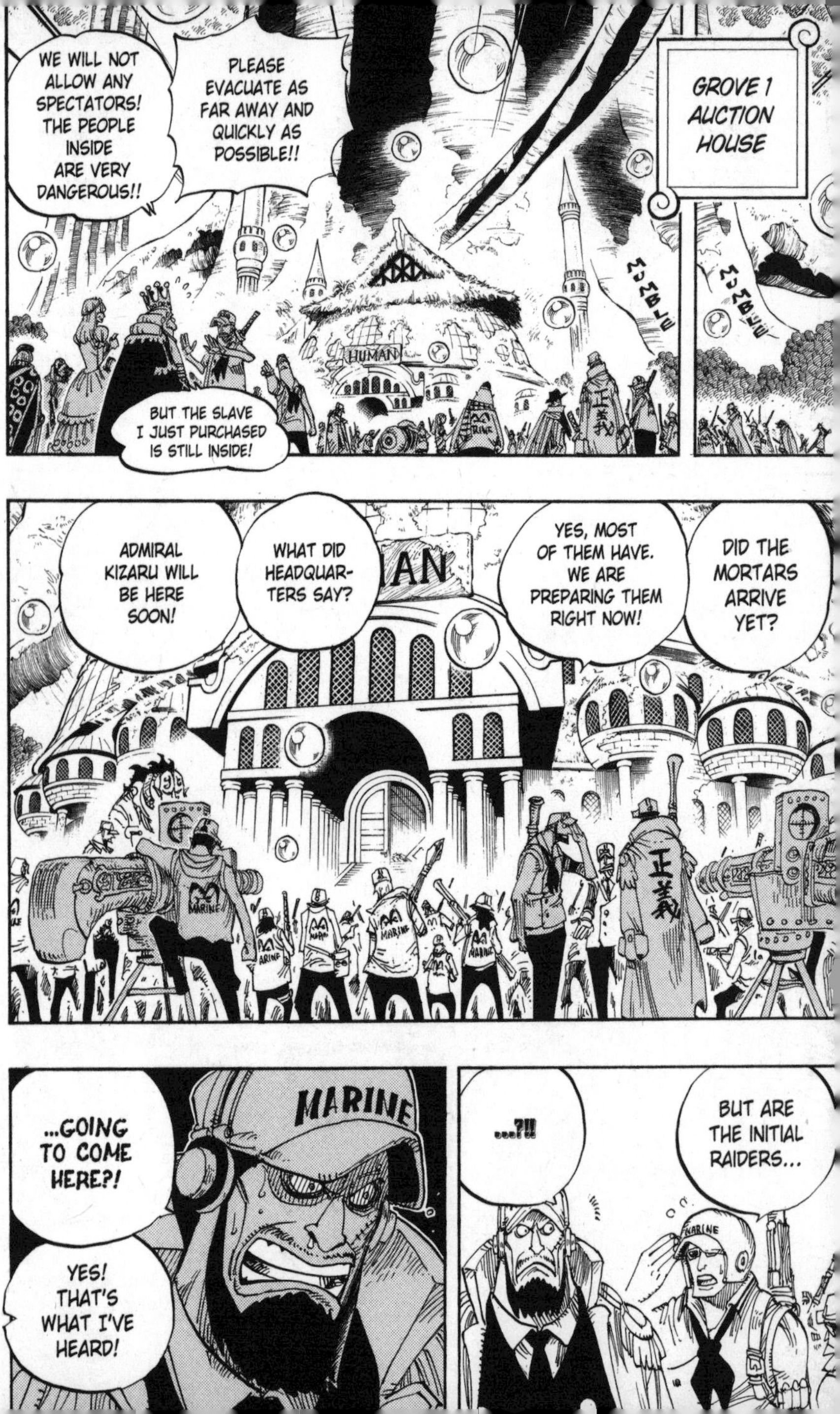
GROVE 1 AUCTION HOUSE
MUMBLE
MUMBLE
PLEASE EVACUATE AS FAR AWAY AND QUICKLY AS POSSIBLE!!
WE WILL NOT ALLOW ANY SPECTATORS! THE PEOPLE INSIDE ARE VERY DANGEROUS!!
HUMAN
BUT THE SLAVE I JUST PURCHASED IS STILL INSIDE!
DID THE MORTARS ARRIVE YET?
YES, MOST OF THEM HAVE. WE ARE PREPARING THEM RIGHT NOW!
WHAT DID HEADQUARTERS SAY?
ADMIRAL KIZARU WILL BE HERE SOON!
BUT ARE THE INITIAL RAIDERS...
...?!!
...GOING TO COME HERE?!
YES! THAT'S WHAT I'VE HEARD!

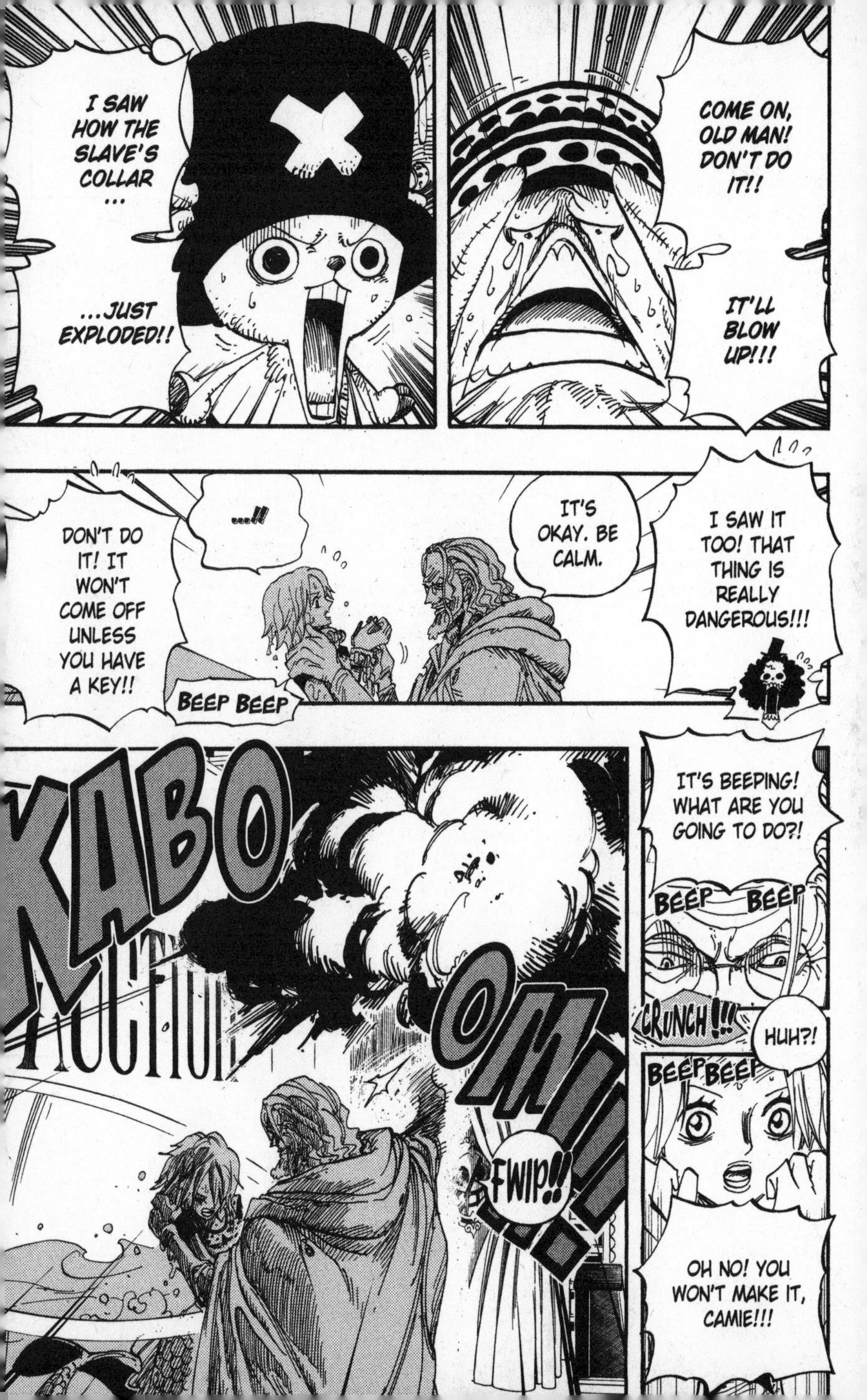
COME ON, OLD MAN! DON'T DO IT!!
IT'LL BLOW UP!!!
I SAW HOW THE SLAVE'S COLLAR ...
...JUST EXPLODED!!
I SAW IT TOO! THAT THING IS REALLY DANGEROUS!!!
IT'S OKAY. BE CALM.
...!!
DON'T DO IT! IT WON'T COME OFF UNLESS YOU HAVE A KEY!!
BEEP BEEP
IT'S BEEPING! WHAT ARE YOU GOING TO DO?!
BEEP BEEP
CRUNCH!!!
HUH?!
BEEP BEEP
OH NO! YOU WON'T MAKE IT, CAMIE!!!
KABOOM!!
FWIP!!

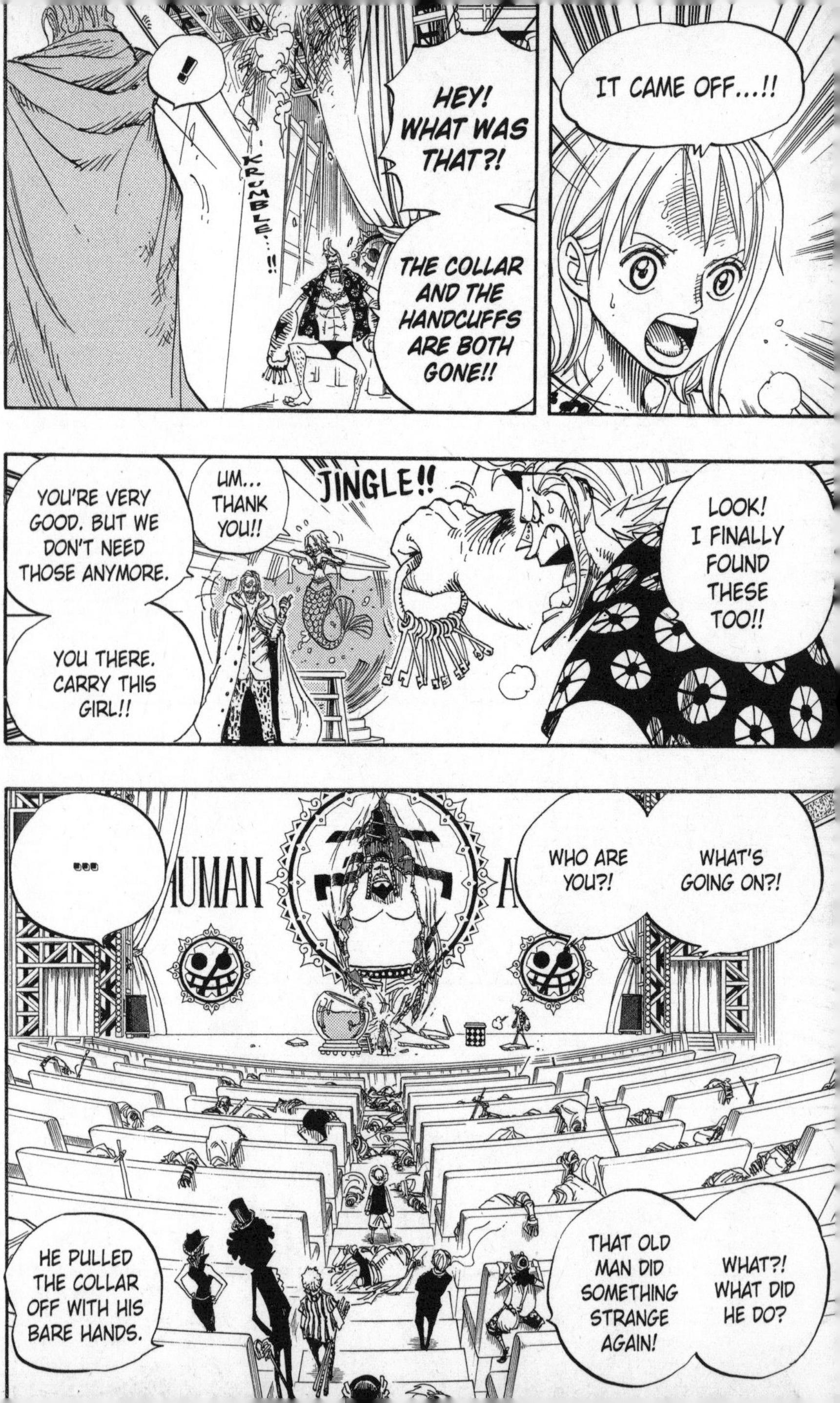
IT CAME OFF...!!
HEY! WHAT WAS THAT?!
THE COLLAR AND THE HANDCUFFS ARE BOTH GONE!!
!
KRUMBLE...!!
LOOK! I FINALLY FOUND THESE TOO!!
JINGLE!!
UM... THANK YOU!!
YOU'RE VERY GOOD. BUT WE DON'T NEED THOSE ANYMORE.
YOU THERE. CARRY THIS GIRL!!
WHAT'S GOING ON?!
WHO ARE YOU?!
HUMAN
...
WHAT?! WHAT DID HE DO?
THAT OLD MAN DID SOMETHING STRANGE AGAIN!
HE PULLED THE COLLAR OFF WITH HIS BARE HANDS.

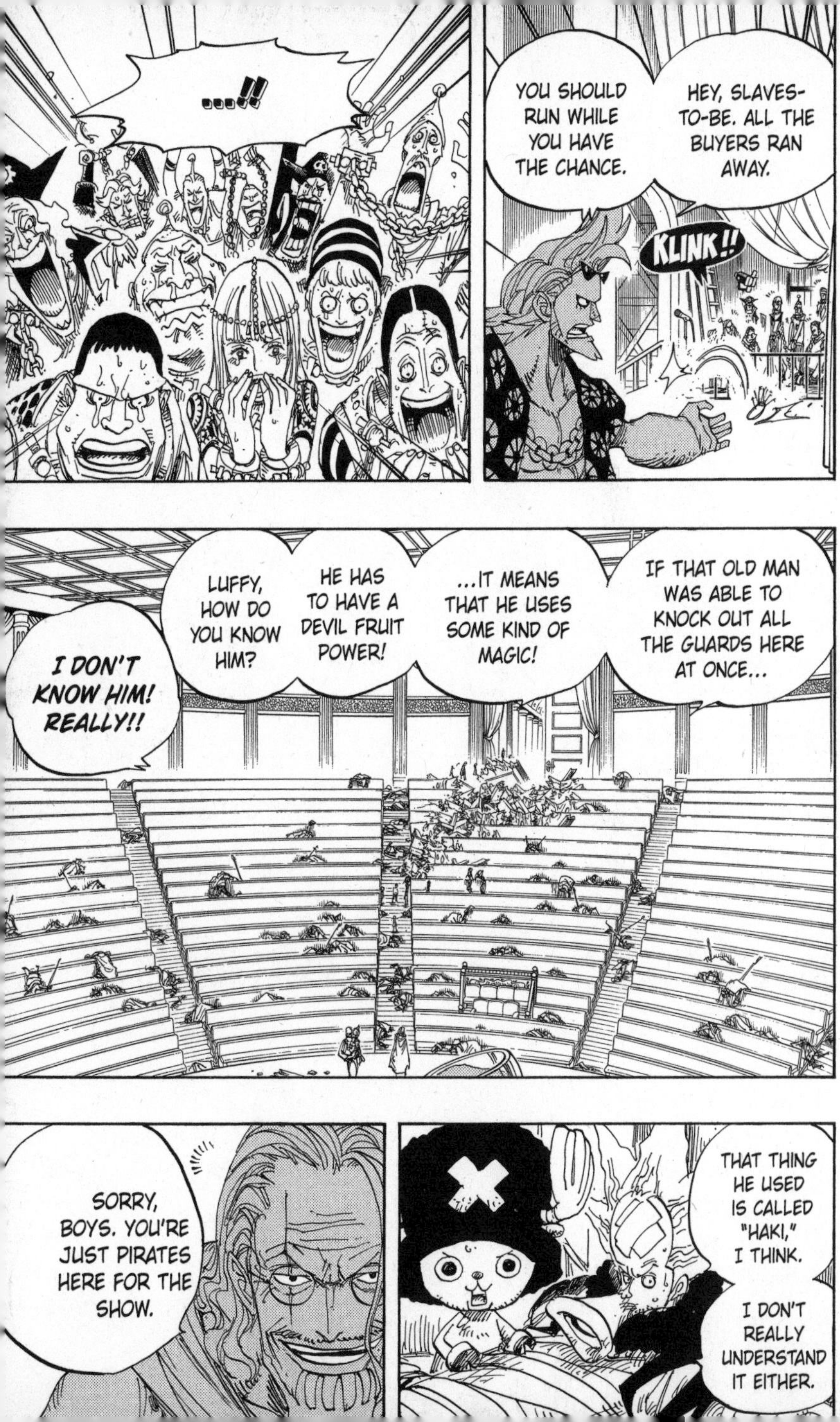
HEY, SLAVES-TO-BE. ALL THE BUYERS RAN AWAY.
YOU SHOULD RUN WHILE YOU HAVE THE CHANCE.
KLINK!!
...!!
IF THAT OLD MAN WAS ABLE TO KNOCK OUT ALL THE GUARDS HERE AT ONCE...
...IT MEANS THAT HE USES SOME KIND OF MAGIC!
HE HAS TO HAVE A DEVIL FRUIT POWER!
LUFFY, HOW DO YOU KNOW HIM?
I DON'T KNOW HIM! REALLY!!
THAT THING HE USED IS CALLED "HAKI," I THINK.
I DON'T REALLY UNDERSTAND IT EITHER.
SORRY, BOYS. YOU'RE JUST PIRATES HERE FOR THE SHOW.

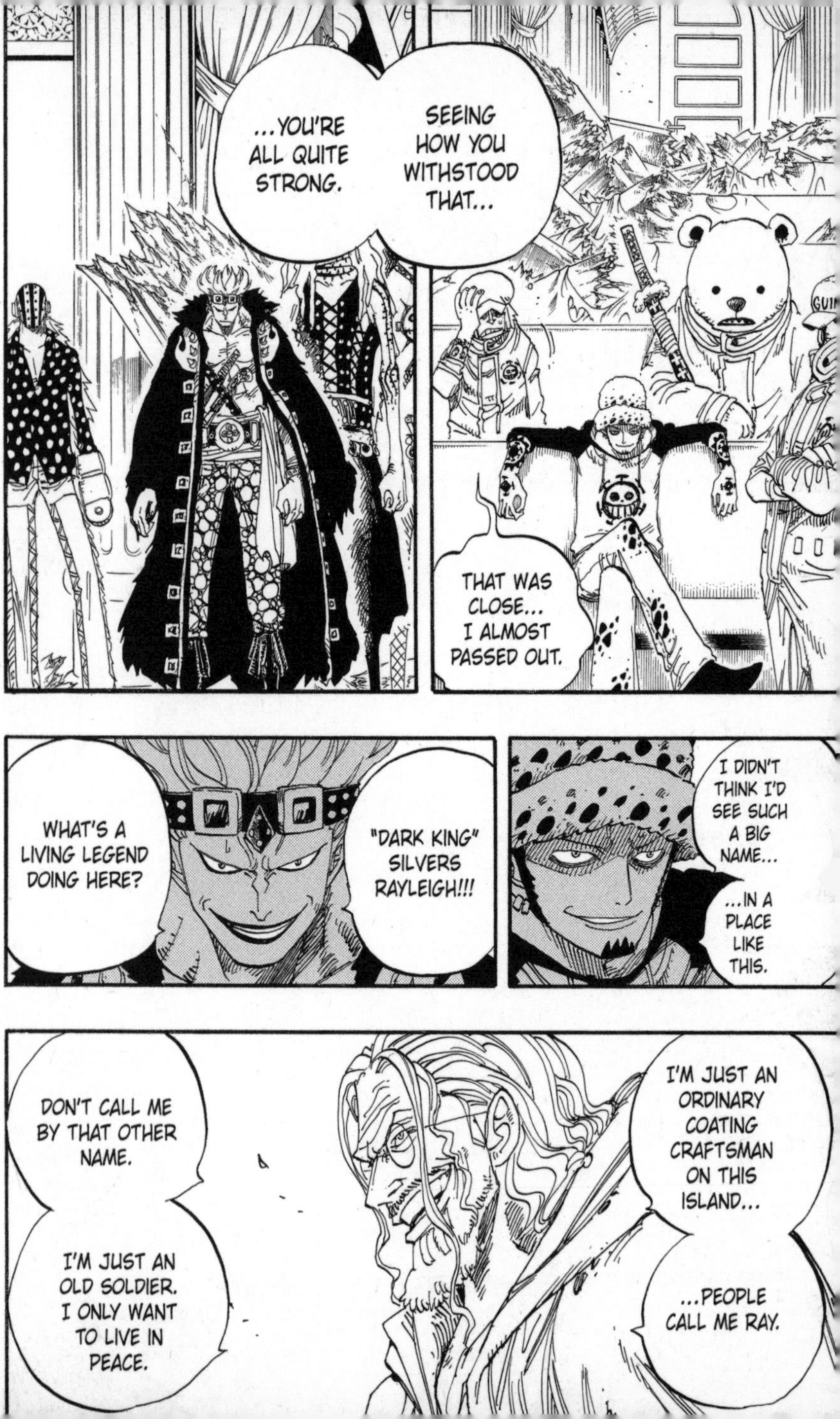
SEEING HOW YOU WITHSTOOD THAT...
...YOU'RE ALL QUITE STRONG.
THAT WAS CLOSE... I ALMOST PASSED OUT.
I DIDN'T THINK I'D SEE SUCH A BIG NAME...
...IN A PLACE LIKE THIS.
"DARK KING" SILVERS RAYLEIGH!!!
WHAT'S A LIVING LEGEND DOING HERE?
I'M JUST AN ORDINARY COATING CRAFTSMAN ON THIS ISLAND...
...PEOPLE CALL ME RAY.
DON'T CALL ME BY THAT OTHER NAME.
I'M JUST AN OLD SOLDIER. I ONLY WANT TO LIVE IN PEACE.

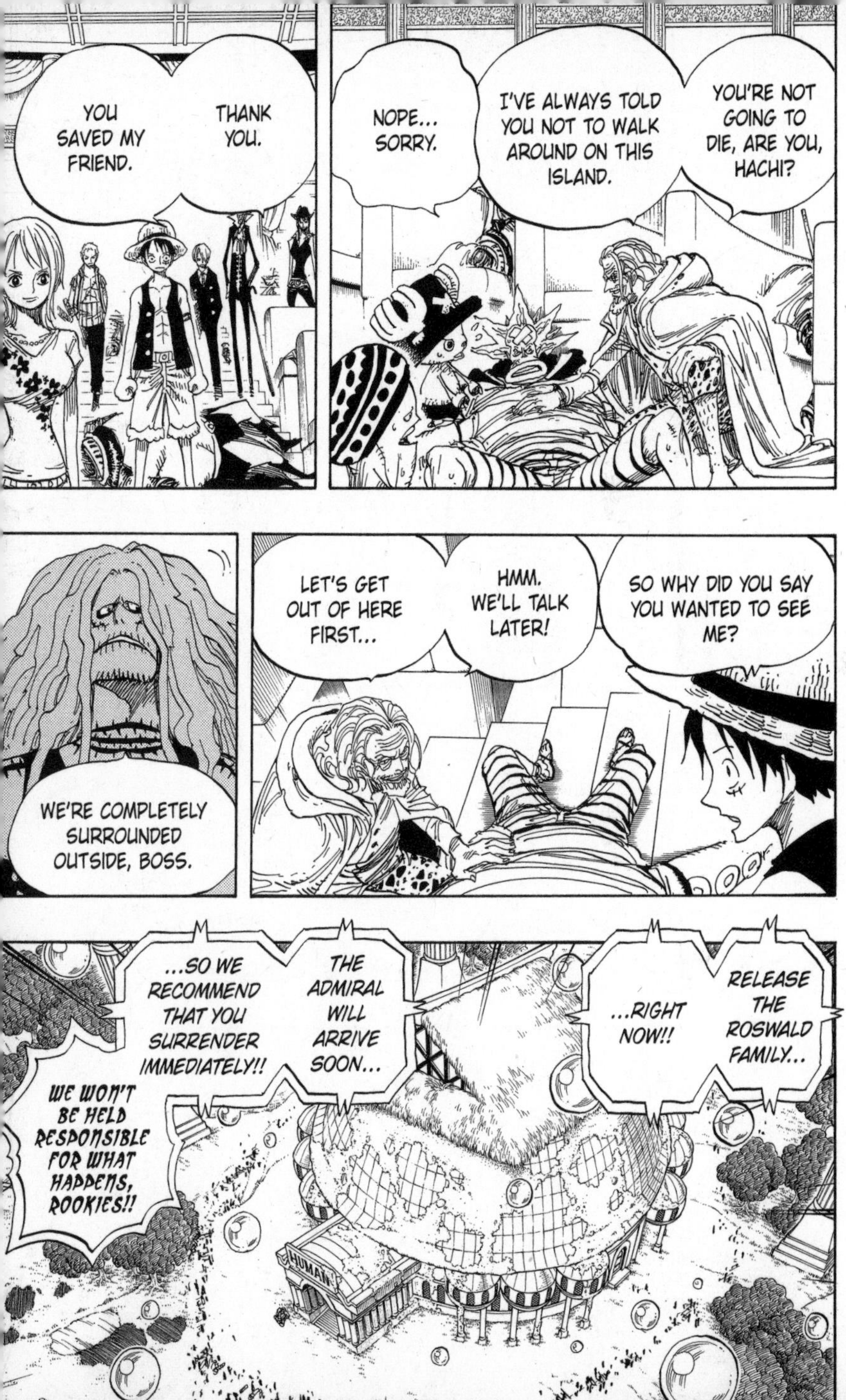
YOU'RE NOT GOING TO DIE, ARE YOU, HACHI?
I'VE ALWAYS TOLD YOU NOT TO WALK AROUND ON THIS ISLAND.
NOPE... SORRY.
THANK YOU.
YOU SAVED MY FRIEND.
SO WHY DID YOU SAY YOU WANTED TO SEE ME?
HMM. WE'LL TALK LATER!
LET'S GET OUT OF HERE FIRST...
WE'RE COMPLETELY SURROUNDED OUTSIDE, BOSS.
RELEASE THE ROSWALD FAMILY...
...RIGHT NOW!!
THE ADMIRAL WILL ARRIVE SOON...
...SO WE RECOMMEND THAT YOU SURRENDER IMMEDIATELY!!
WE WON'T BE HELD RESPONSIBLE FOR WHAT HAPPENS, ROOKIES!!
HUMAN

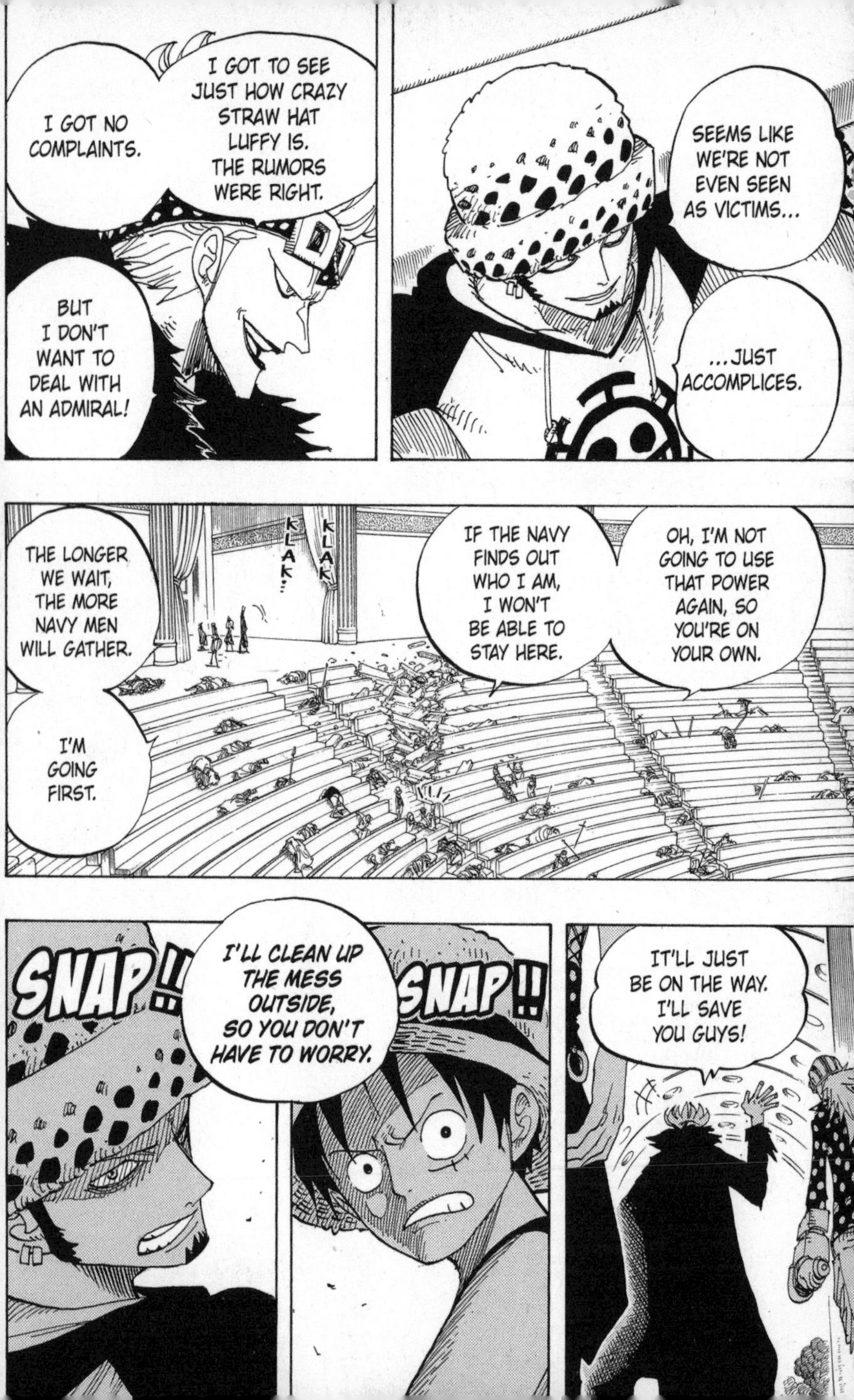

SEEMS LIKE WE'RE NOT EVEN SEEN AS VICTIMS...
...JUST ACCOMPLICES.
I GOT TO SEE JUST HOW CRAZY STRAW HAT LUFFY IS. THE RUMORS WERE RIGHT.
I GOT NO COMPLAINTS.
BUT I DON'T WANT TO DEAL WITH AN ADMIRAL!
OH, I'M NOT GOING TO USE THAT POWER AGAIN, SO YOU'RE ON YOUR OWN.
IF THE NAVY FINDS OUT WHO I AM, I WON'T BE ABLE TO STAY HERE.
KLAK
KLAK...
THE LONGER WE WAIT, THE MORE NAVY MEN WILL GATHER.
I'M GOING FIRST.
IT'LL JUST BE ON THE WAY. I'LL SAVE YOU GUYS!
SNAP!!
I'LL CLEAN UP THE MESS OUTSIDE, SO YOU DON'T HAVE TO WORRY.
SNAP!!

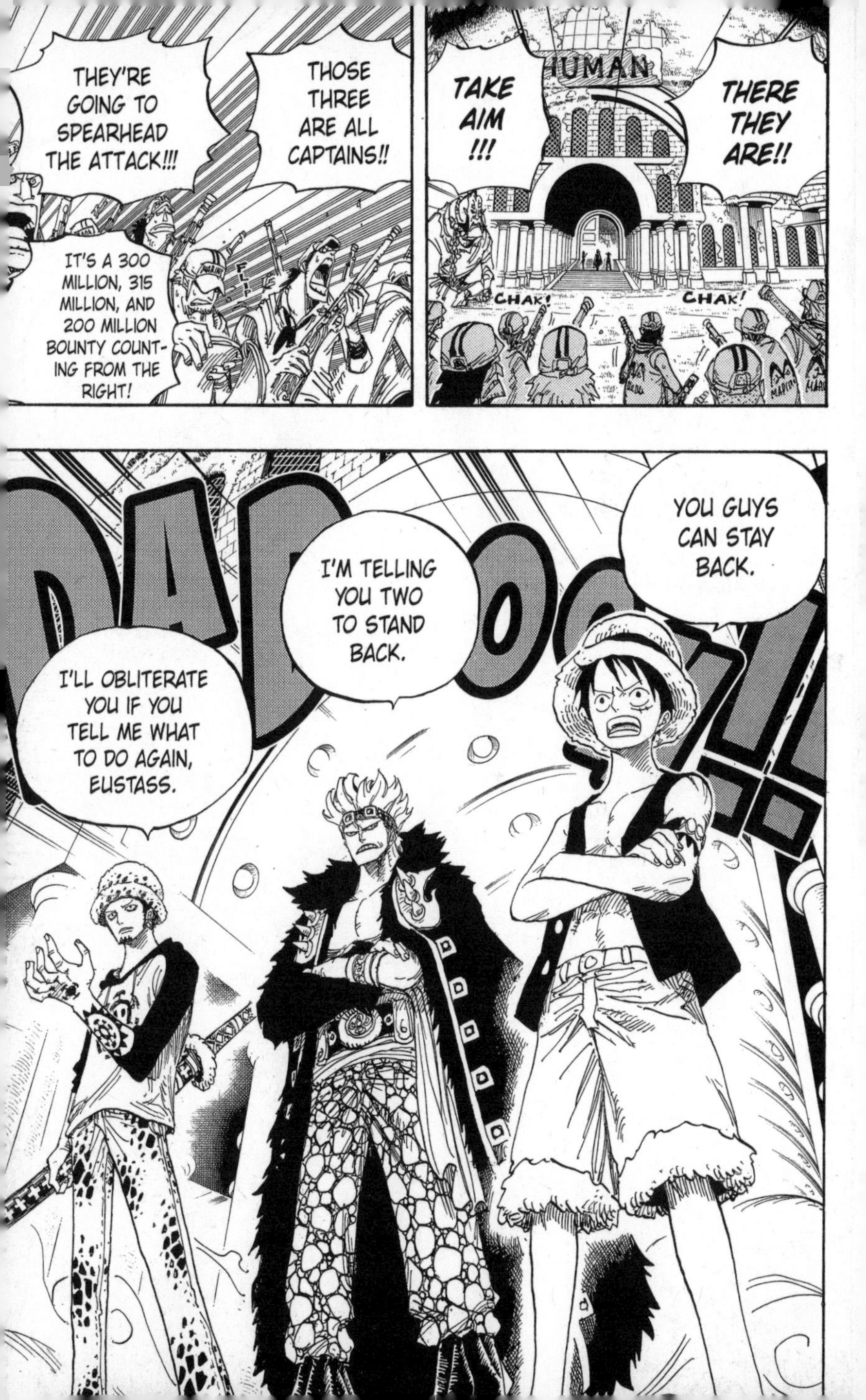
HUMAN
THERE THEY ARE!!
TAKE AIM!!!
CHAK!
CHAK!
THOSE THREE ARE ALL CAPTAINS!!
THEY'RE GOING TO SPEARHEAD THE ATTACK!!!
IT'S A 300 MILLION, 315 MILLION, AND 200 MILLION BOUNTY COUNTING FROM THE RIGHT!
YOU GUYS CAN STAY BACK.
I'M TELLING YOU TWO TO STAND BACK.
I'LL OBLITERATE YOU IF YOU TELL ME WHAT TO DO AGAIN, EUSTASS.

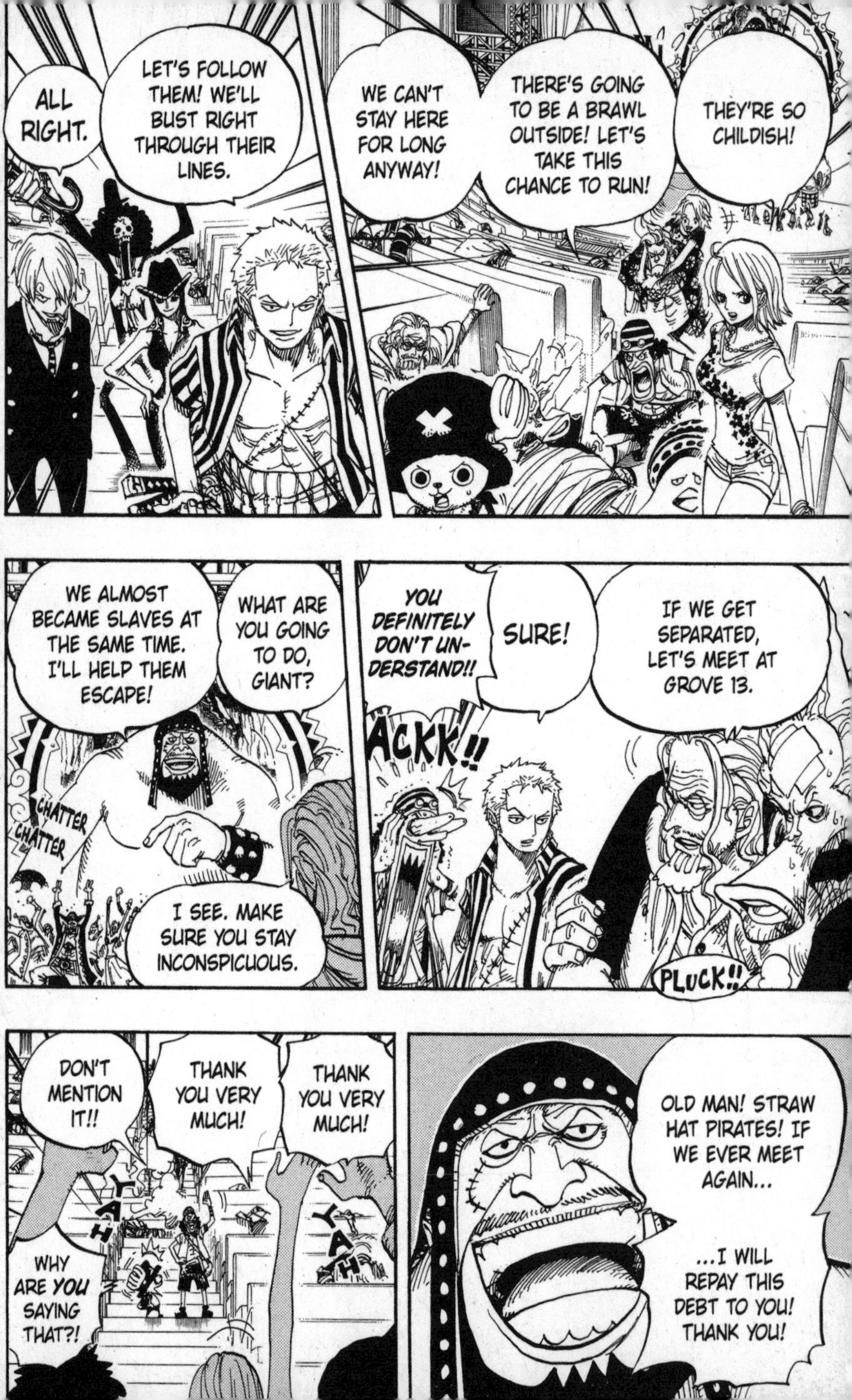

THEY'RE SO CHILDISH!
THERE'S GOING TO BE A BRAWL OUTSIDE! LET'S TAKE THIS CHANCE TO RUN!
WE CAN'T STAY HERE FOR LONG ANYWAY!
LET'S FOLLOW THEM! WE'LL BUST RIGHT THROUGH THEIR LINES.
ALL RIGHT.
IF WE GET SEPARATED, LET'S MEET AT GROVE 13.
SURE!
YOU DEFINITELY DON'T UN-DERSTAND!!
ACKK!!
PLUCK!!
WHAT ARE YOU GOING TO DO, GIANT?
WE ALMOST BECAME SLAVES AT THE SAME TIME. I'LL HELP THEM ESCAPE!
CHATTER CHATTER
I SEE. MAKE SURE YOU STAY INCONSPICUOUS.
OLD MAN! STRAW HAT PIRATES! IF WE EVER MEET AGAIN...
...I WILL REPAY THIS DEBT TO YOU! THANK YOU!
THANK YOU VERY MUCH!
THANK YOU VERY MUCH!
DON'T MENTION IT!!
YAH
YAH
WHY ARE *YOU* SAYING THAT?!

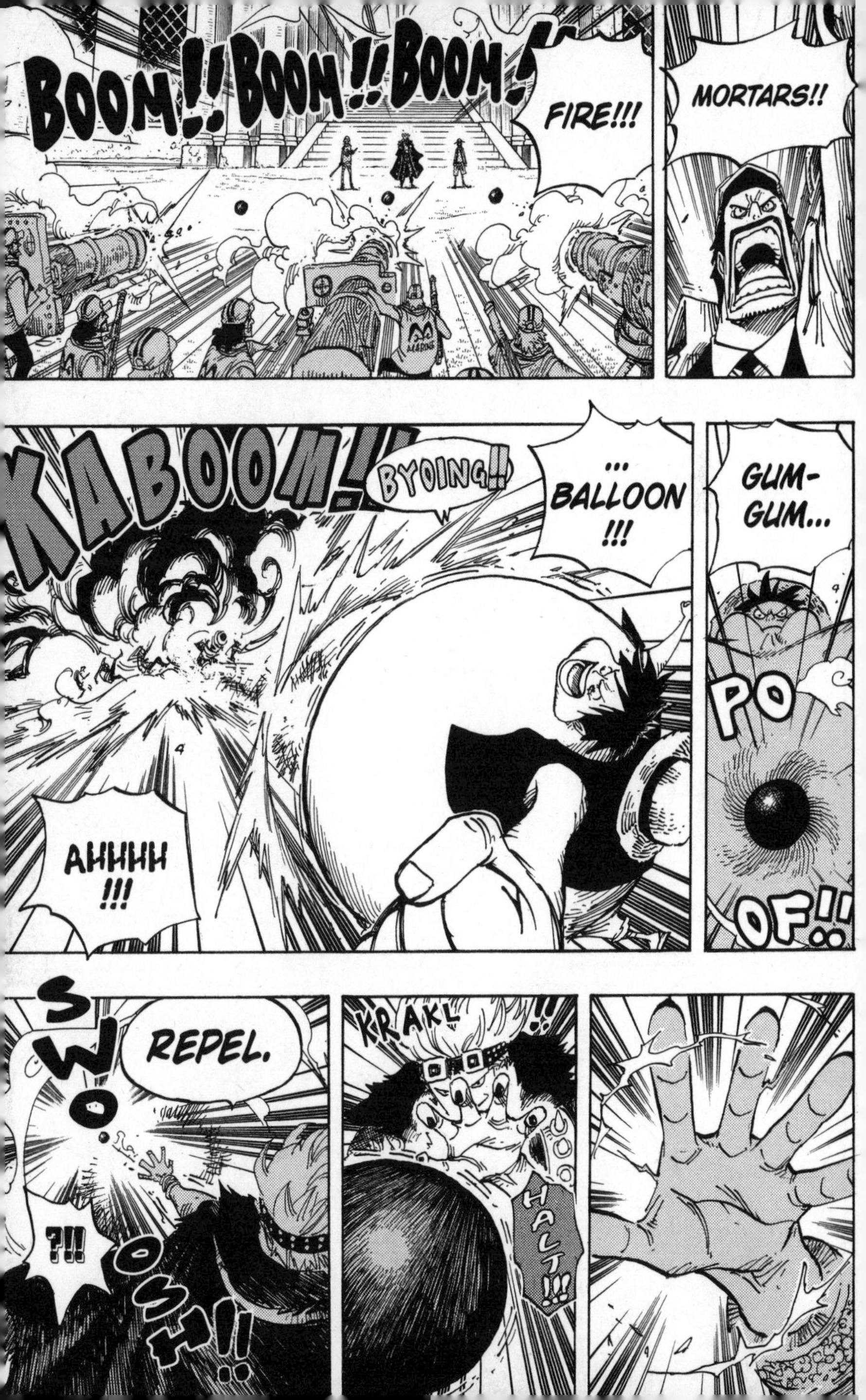
MORTARS!!
FIRE!!!
BOOM!! BOOM!! BOOM!!
GUM-GUM...
POOF!!
... BALLOON !!!
BYOING!!
KABOOM!!
AHHHH !!!
KRAKL
!!
HALT!!!
REPEL.
SWOOSH!!
?!!

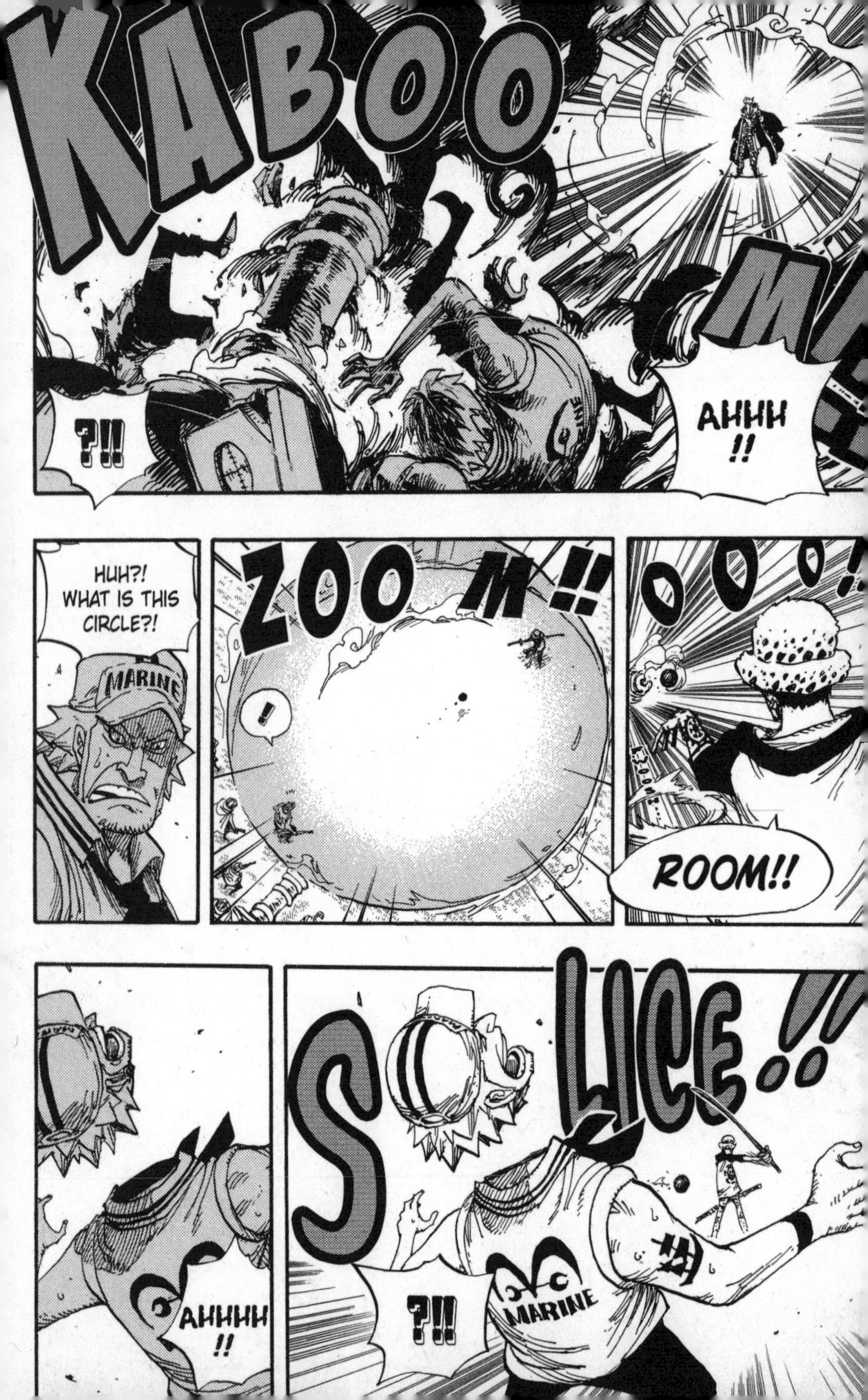
KABOOM
AHHH !!
?!!
OOO!!
ROOM!!
ZOOM!!
!
HUH?! WHAT IS THIS CIRCLE?!
MARINE
SLICE!!
?!!
MARINE
AHHHH !!

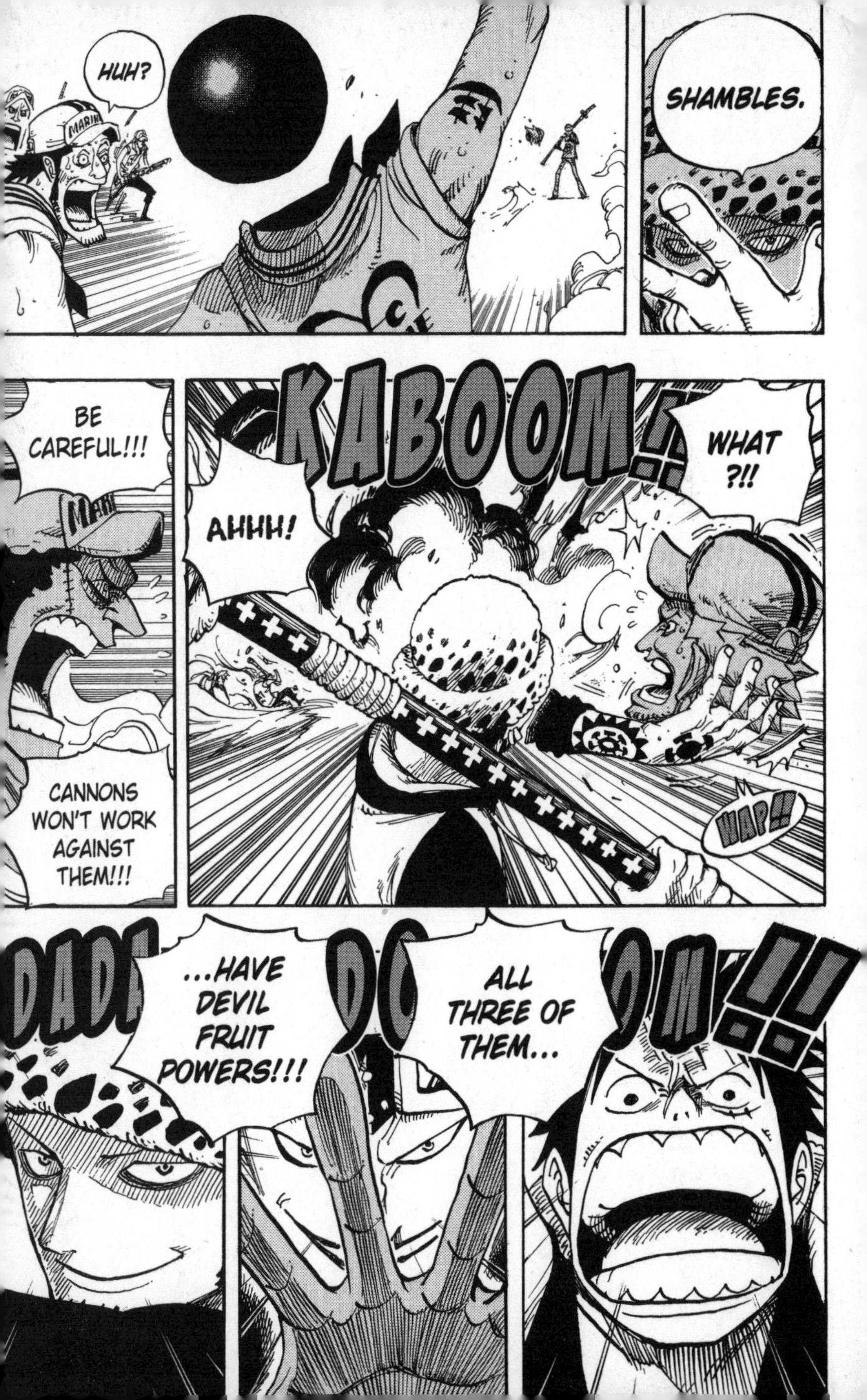
SHAMBLES.
HUH?
KABOOM!!
WHAT ?!!
AHHH!
WAP!!
BE CAREFUL!!!
CANNONS WON'T WORK AGAINST THEM!!!
ALL THREE OF THEM...
...HAVE DEVIL FRUIT POWERS!!!

SBS Question Corner

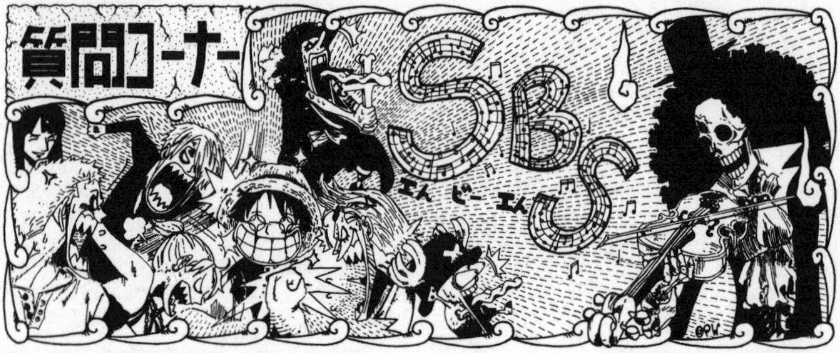
質問コーナー
SBS

(Valter, Italy)

Q: Hey, Odacchi! There's something moving around in my kitchen lately that's dressed in black and has mastered the art of Shave! Is it what I think it is?! Is it a newcomer to CP9?! I'm always scared that it'll learn Moon Walk next! Please do something about it, Odacchi!

--Farewell! Coun Cast

A: That's probably the one in the roach order, roach family...the cockroach. It flies. They can use Moon Walk. There was a time when one flew straight at me from the front and I was traumatized by it. It definitely knows how to use the Six Powers. Good luck!

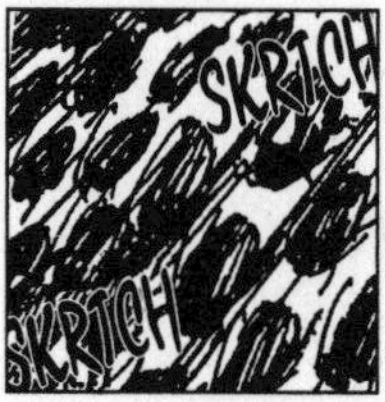
SKRITCH
SKRITCH

Q: Boss! Boss Oda! I got a question for you! In chapter 502, how did stupid Charlos pick his nose?! I get it! It's the same as the bubble bike!

--Kinta

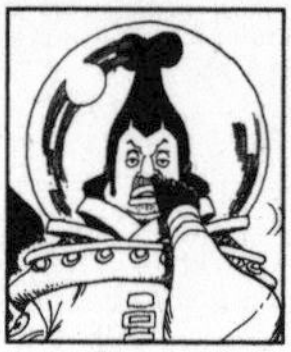

A: Aye aye. That's right. It's a bubble. That means you can go through it. In the Sabaody Archipelago towns, amusement park attractions, home life, and all sorts of other places, bubbles are used in many ways. I hope you can see that as something fun.

Q: In volume 51, on page 95, Brook made Nami mad again. What did he say? Please tell me.

--Ari

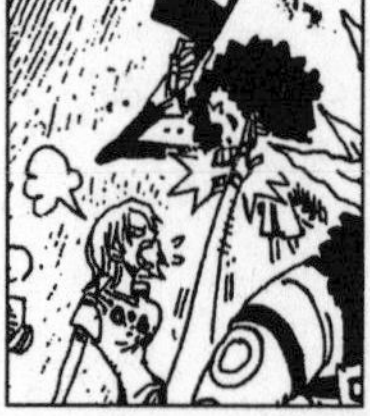

A: Nice catch. Here's the conversation:
Brook: Excuse me, Nami. For dessert may I see your underwear...?
Nami: THWAK! No!
Same as always.

Chapter 505: KUMA

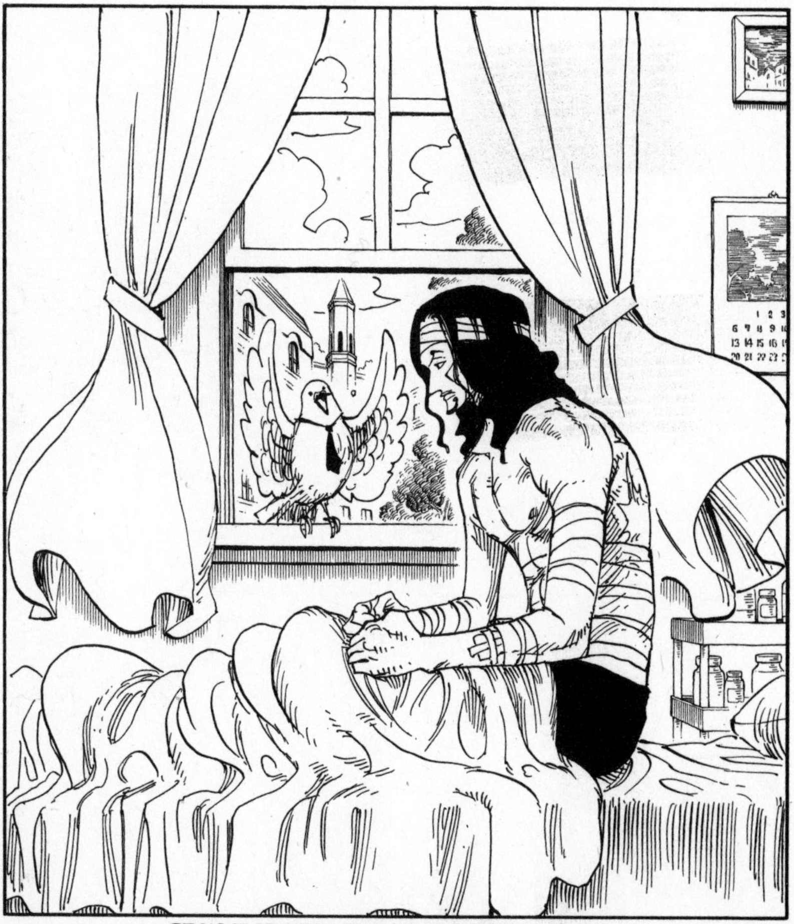

CP9'S INDEPENDENT REPORT, VOL. 14:
"WAKING UP"

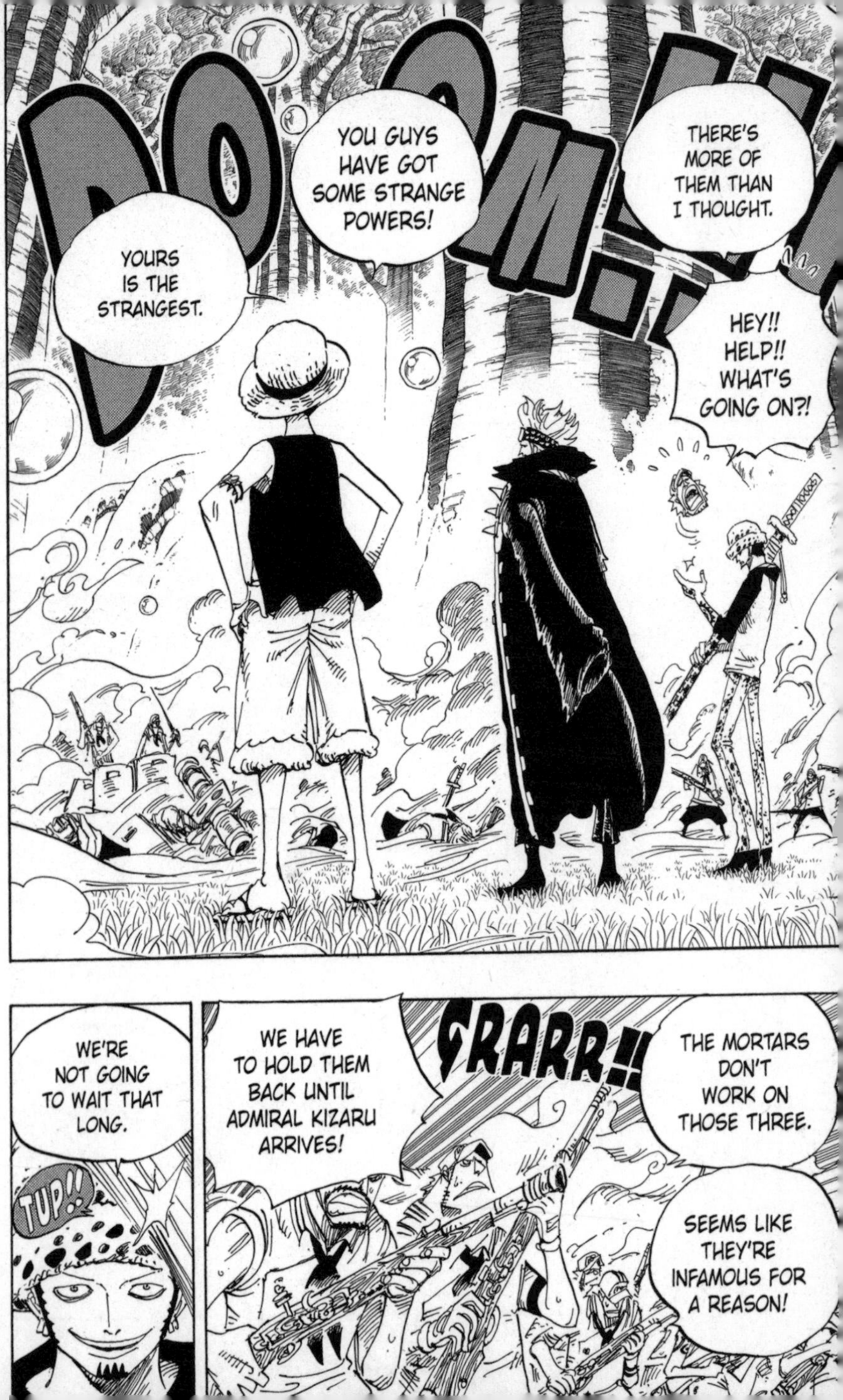
THERE'S MORE OF THEM THAN I THOUGHT.
HEY!! HELP!! WHAT'S GOING ON?!
YOU GUYS HAVE GOT SOME STRANGE POWERS!
YOURS IS THE STRANGEST.
THE MORTARS DON'T WORK ON THOSE THREE.
GRARR!!
WE HAVE TO HOLD THEM BACK UNTIL ADMIRAL KIZARU ARRIVES!
SEEMS LIKE THEY'RE INFAMOUS FOR A REASON!
WE'RE NOT GOING TO WAIT THAT LONG.
TUP!!

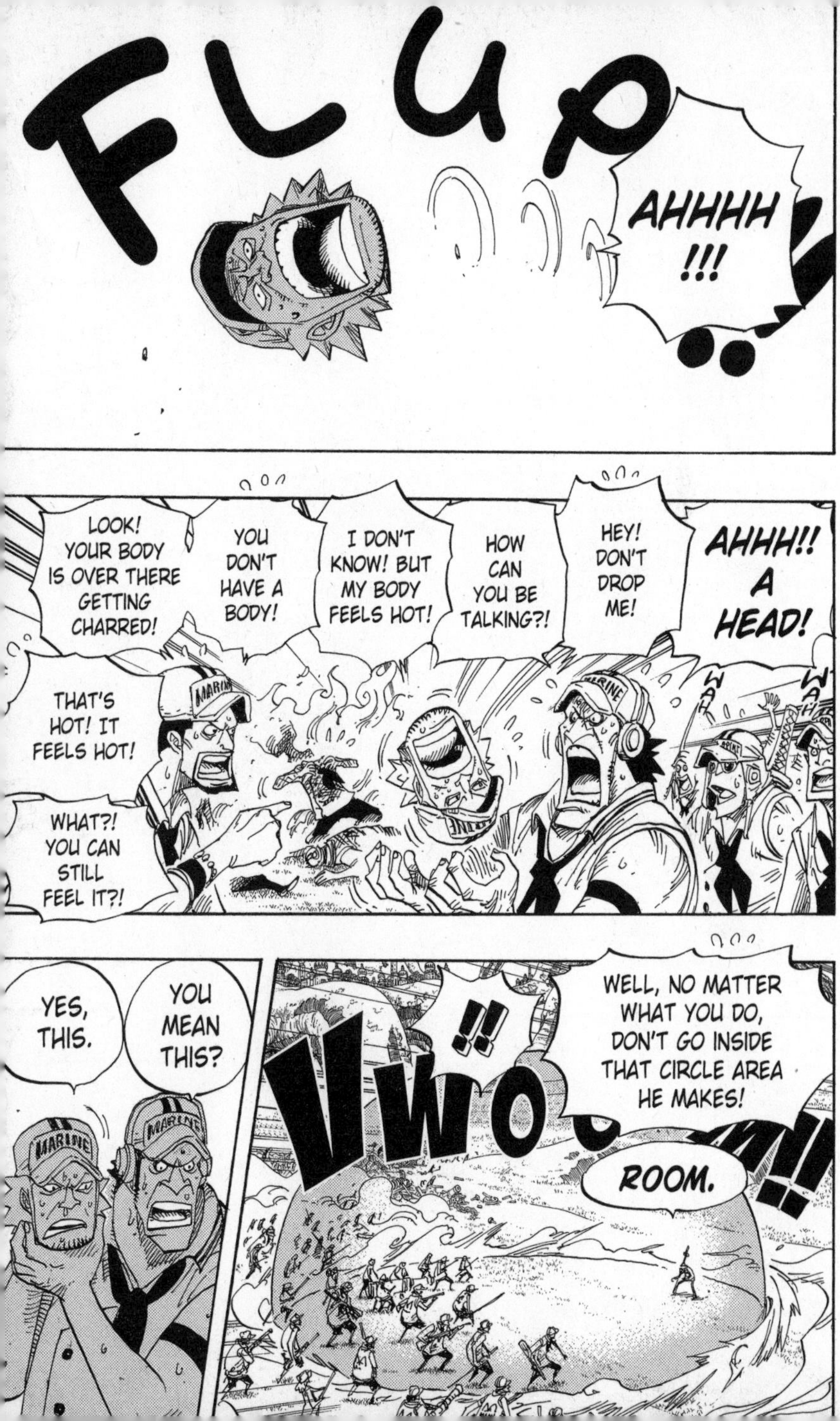
FLUP
AHHHH!!!
AHHH!! A HEAD!
HEY! DON'T DROP ME!
HOW CAN YOU BE TALKING?!
I DON'T KNOW! BUT MY BODY FEELS HOT!
YOU DON'T HAVE A BODY!
LOOK! YOUR BODY IS OVER THERE GETTING CHARRED!
WAH
WAH
THAT'S HOT! IT FEELS HOT!
WHAT?! YOU CAN STILL FEEL IT?!
WELL, NO MATTER WHAT YOU DO, DON'T GO INSIDE THAT CIRCLE AREA HE MAKES!
VWO...M!!
ROOM.
YOU MEAN THIS?
YES, THIS.

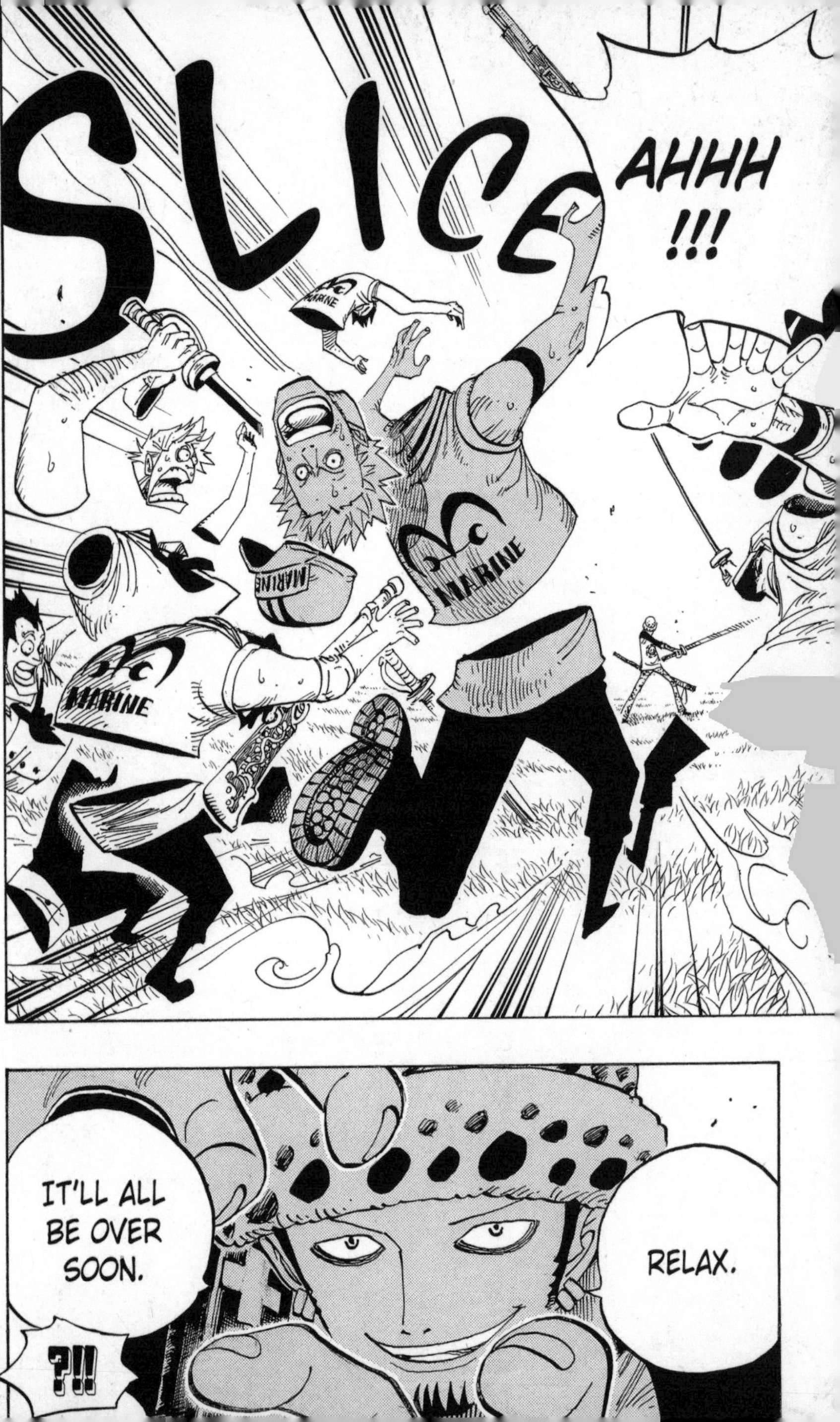

SLICE
AHHH !!!
MARINE
MARINE
MARINE
MARINE
RELAX.
IT'LL ALL BE OVER SOON.
?!!

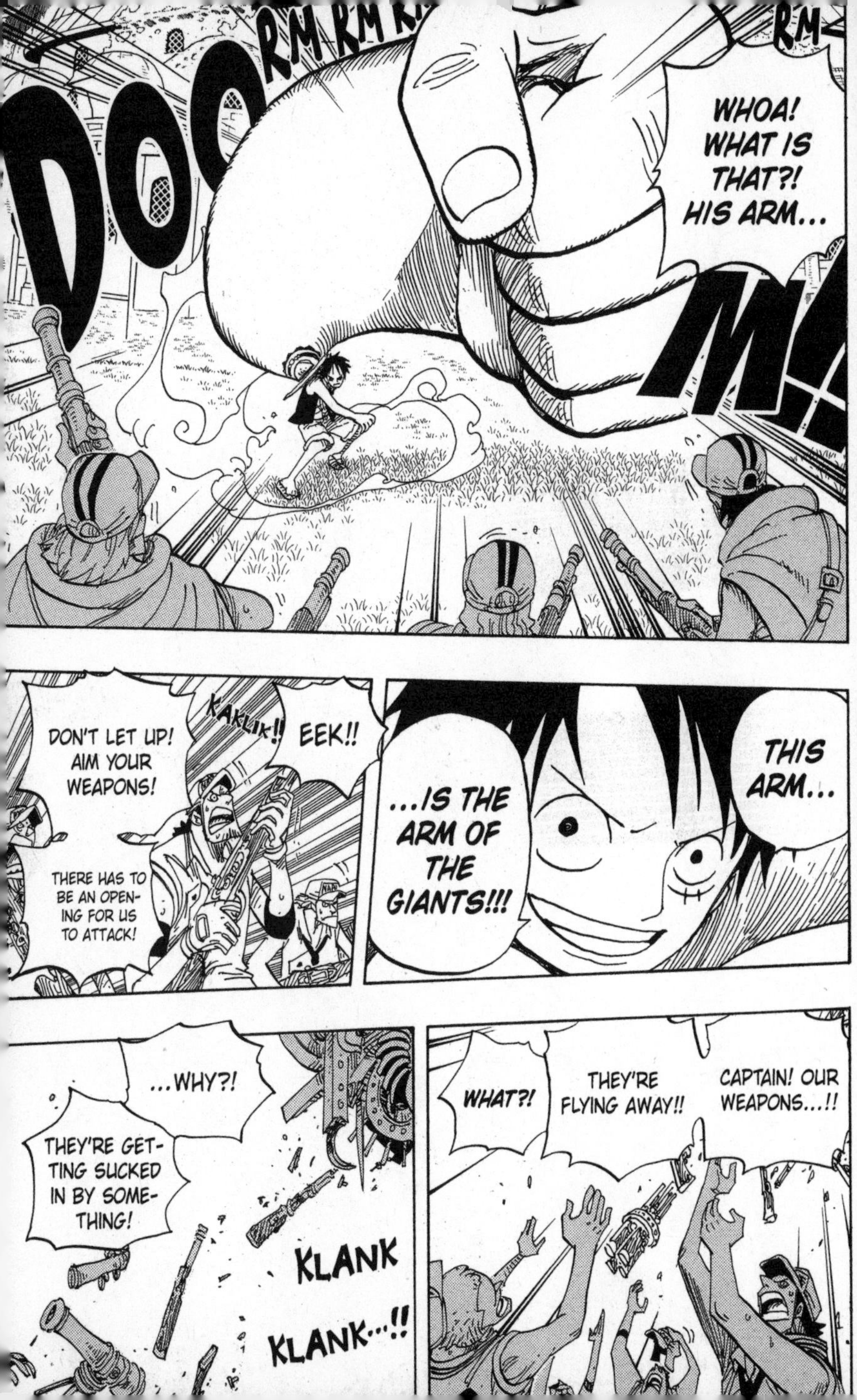
RM
WHOA! WHAT IS THAT?! HIS ARM...
RM RM
DOO
THIS ARM...
...IS THE ARM OF THE GIANTS!!!
EEK!!
KAKLIK!!
DON'T LET UP! AIM YOUR WEAPONS!
THERE HAS TO BE AN OPENING FOR US TO ATTACK!
CAPTAIN! OUR WEAPONS...!!
THEY'RE FLYING AWAY!!
WHAT?!
...WHY?!
THEY'RE GETTING SUCKED IN BY SOMETHING!
KLANK
KLANK...!!

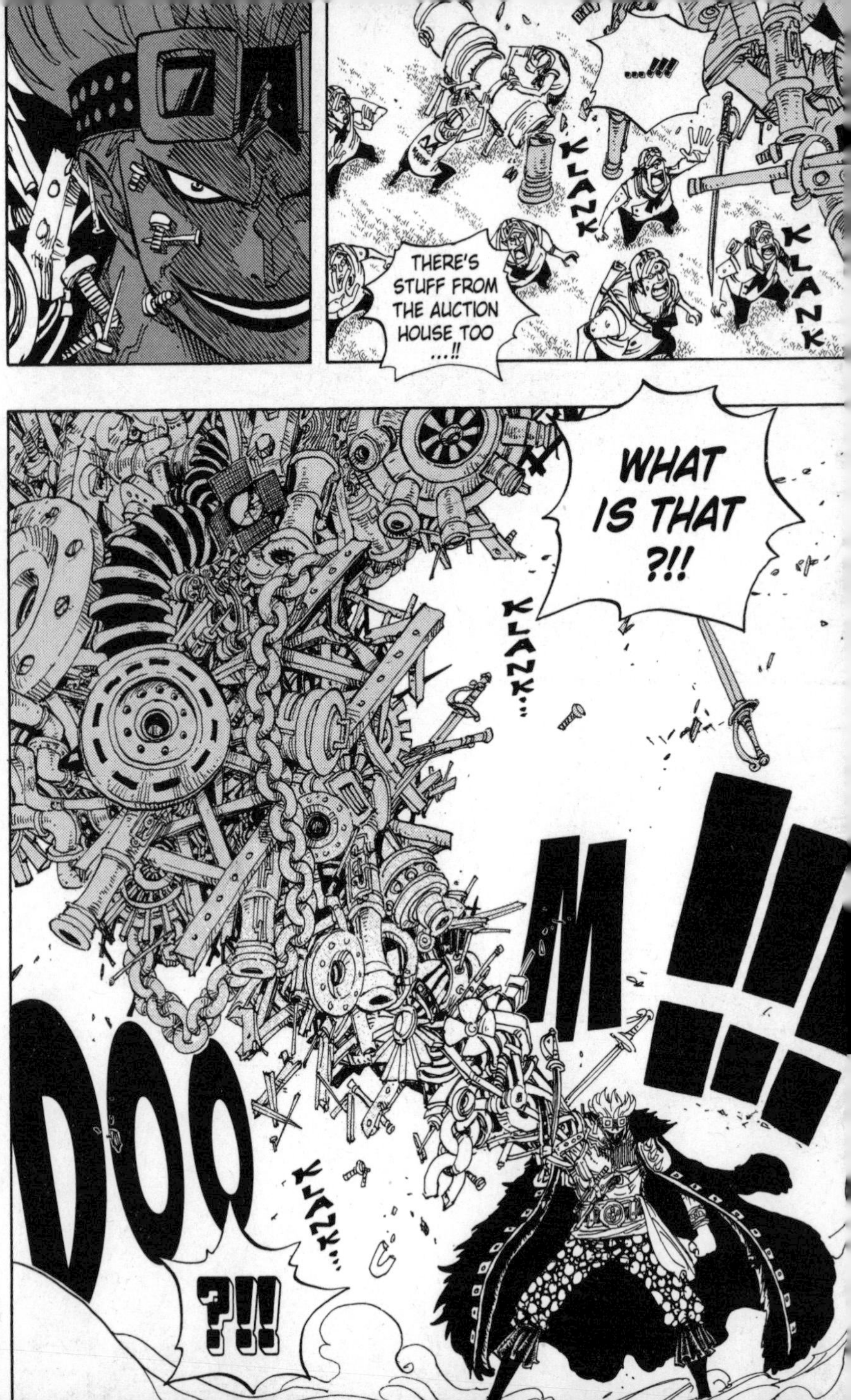
...!!!
KLANK
KLANK
THERE'S STUFF FROM THE AUCTION HOUSE TOO ...!!
WHAT IS THAT ?!!
KLANK...
DOOM!!!
KLANK...
?!!

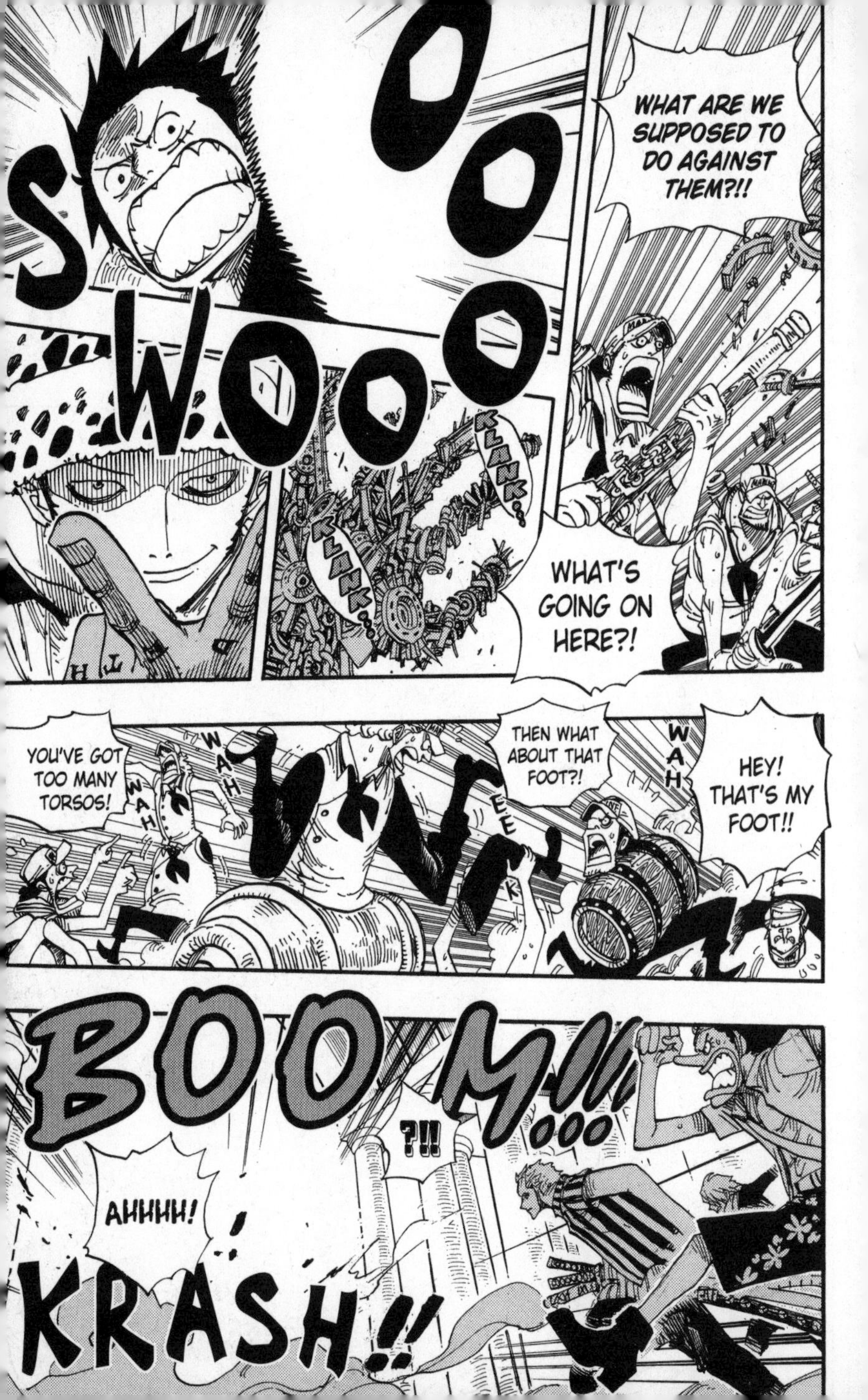
WHAT ARE WE SUPPOSED TO DO AGAINST THEM?!!
WHAT'S GOING ON HERE?!
KLANK...
KLANK...
SWOOOOO
HEY! THAT'S MY FOOT!!
WAH
THEN WHAT ABOUT THAT FOOT?!
EEK
YOU'VE GOT TOO MANY TORSOS!
WAH
WAH
BOOM!!
?!!
AHHHH!
KRASH!!

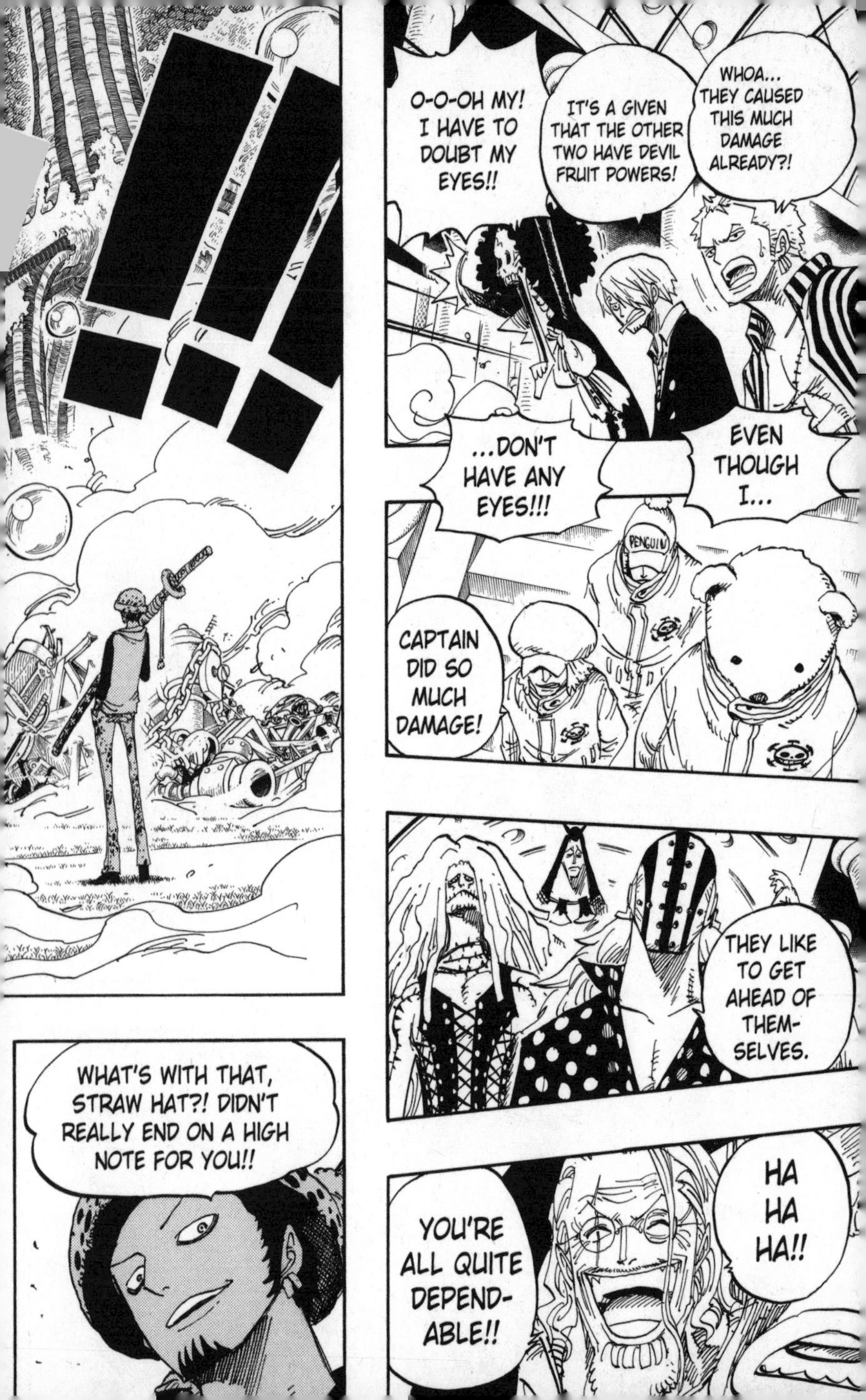
WHOA... THEY CAUSED THIS MUCH DAMAGE ALREADY?!
IT'S A GIVEN THAT THE OTHER TWO HAVE DEVIL FRUIT POWERS!
O-O-OH MY! I HAVE TO DOUBT MY EYES!!
EVEN THOUGH I...
...DON'T HAVE ANY EYES!!!
PENGUIN
CAPTAIN DID SO MUCH DAMAGE!
!!!
THEY LIKE TO GET AHEAD OF THEM-SELVES.
HA HA HA!!
YOU'RE ALL QUITE DEPEND-ABLE!!
WHAT'S WITH THAT, STRAW HAT?! DIDN'T REALLY END ON A HIGH NOTE FOR YOU!!

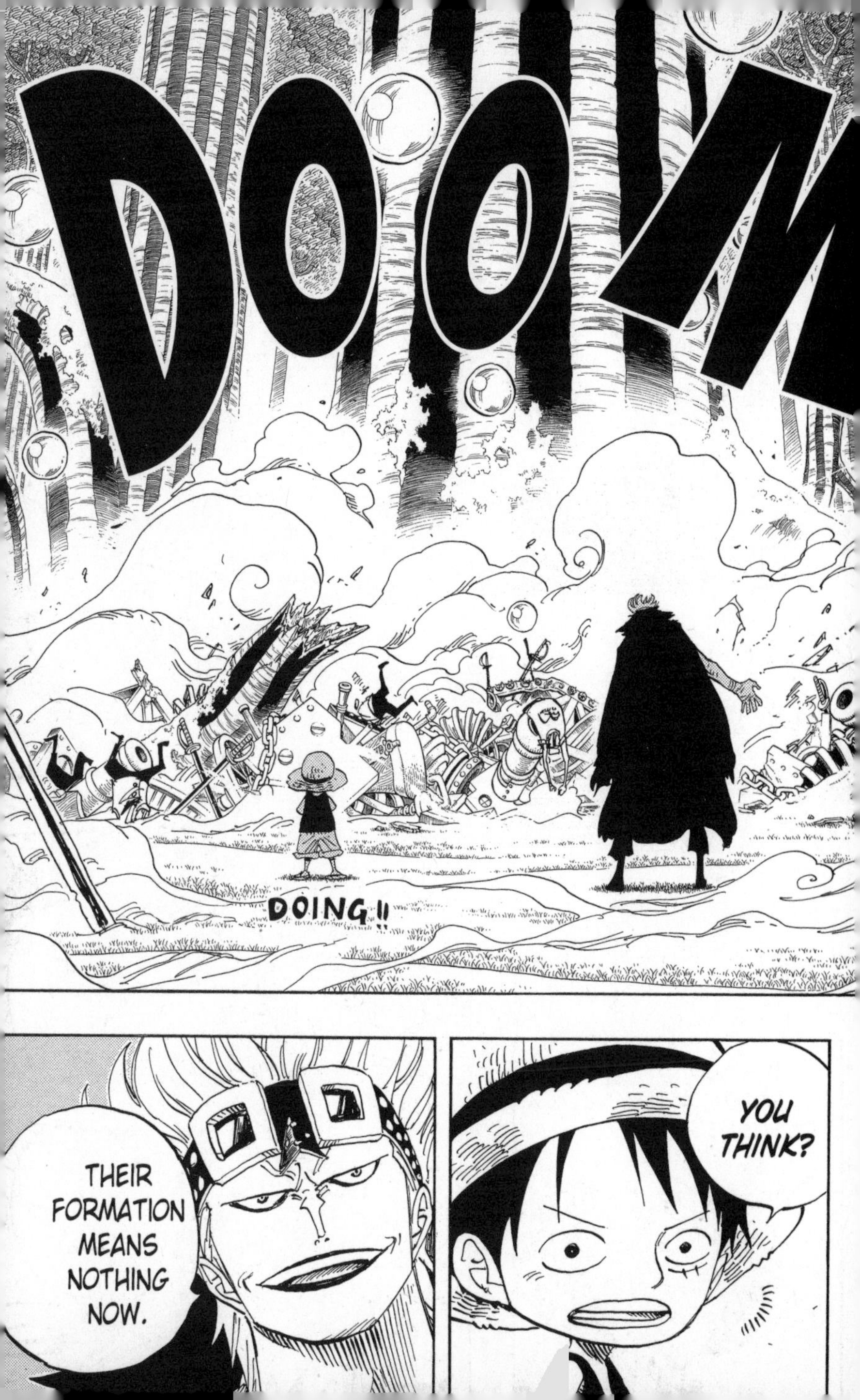
DOOOM
DOING!!
YOU THINK?
THEIR FORMATION MEANS NOTHING NOW.

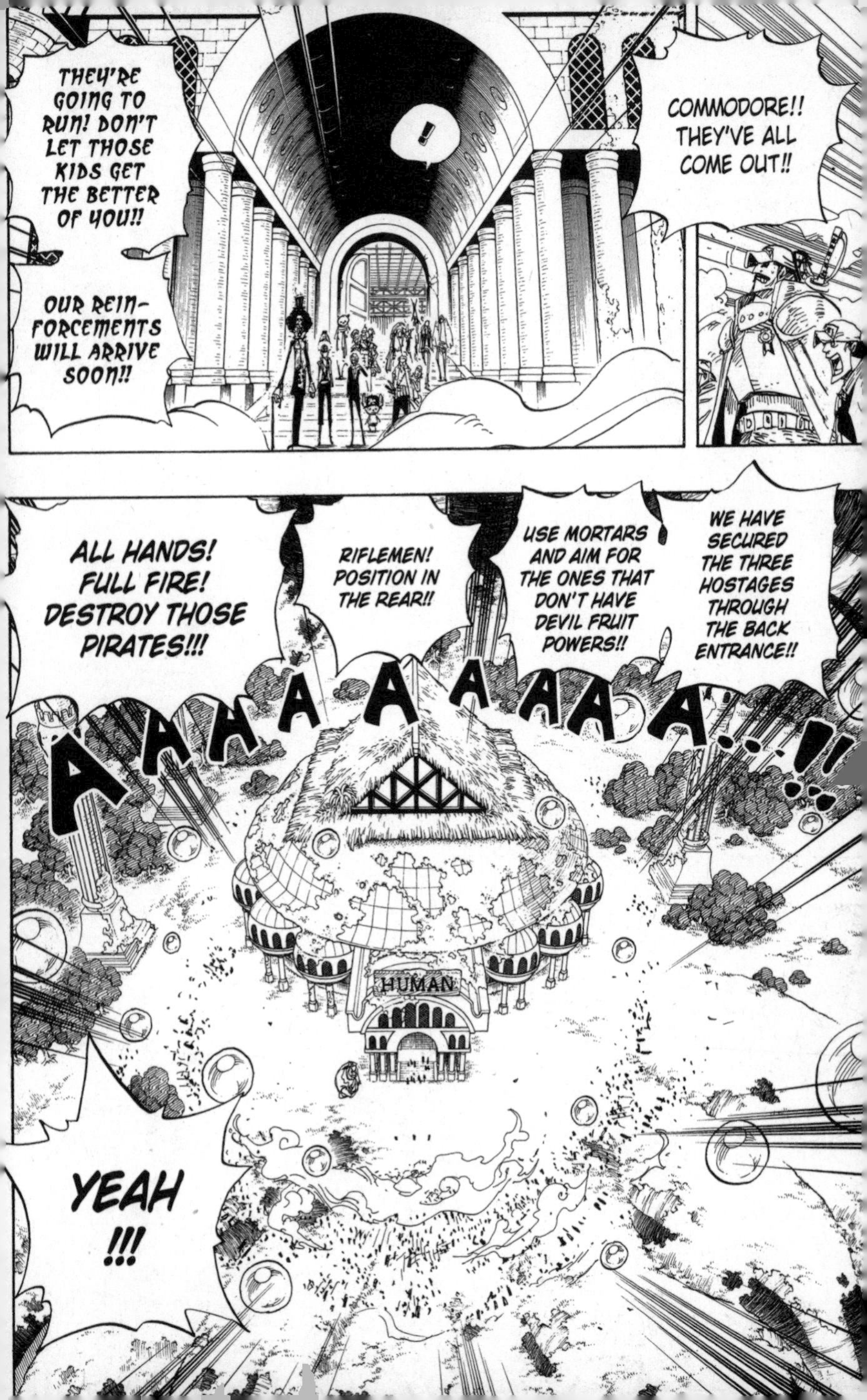
COMMODORE!! THEY'VE ALL COME OUT!!
!
THEY'RE GOING TO RUN! DON'T LET THOSE KIDS GET THE BETTER OF YOU!!
OUR REIN-FORCEMENTS WILL ARRIVE SOON!!
WE HAVE SECURED THE THREE HOSTAGES THROUGH THE BACK ENTRANCE!!
USE MORTARS AND AIM FOR THE ONES THAT DON'T HAVE DEVIL FRUIT POWERS!!
RIFLEMEN! POSITION IN THE REAR!!
ALL HANDS! FULL FIRE! DESTROY THOSE PIRATES!!!
AAAAAAAAAAA...!!
HUMAN
YEAH !!!

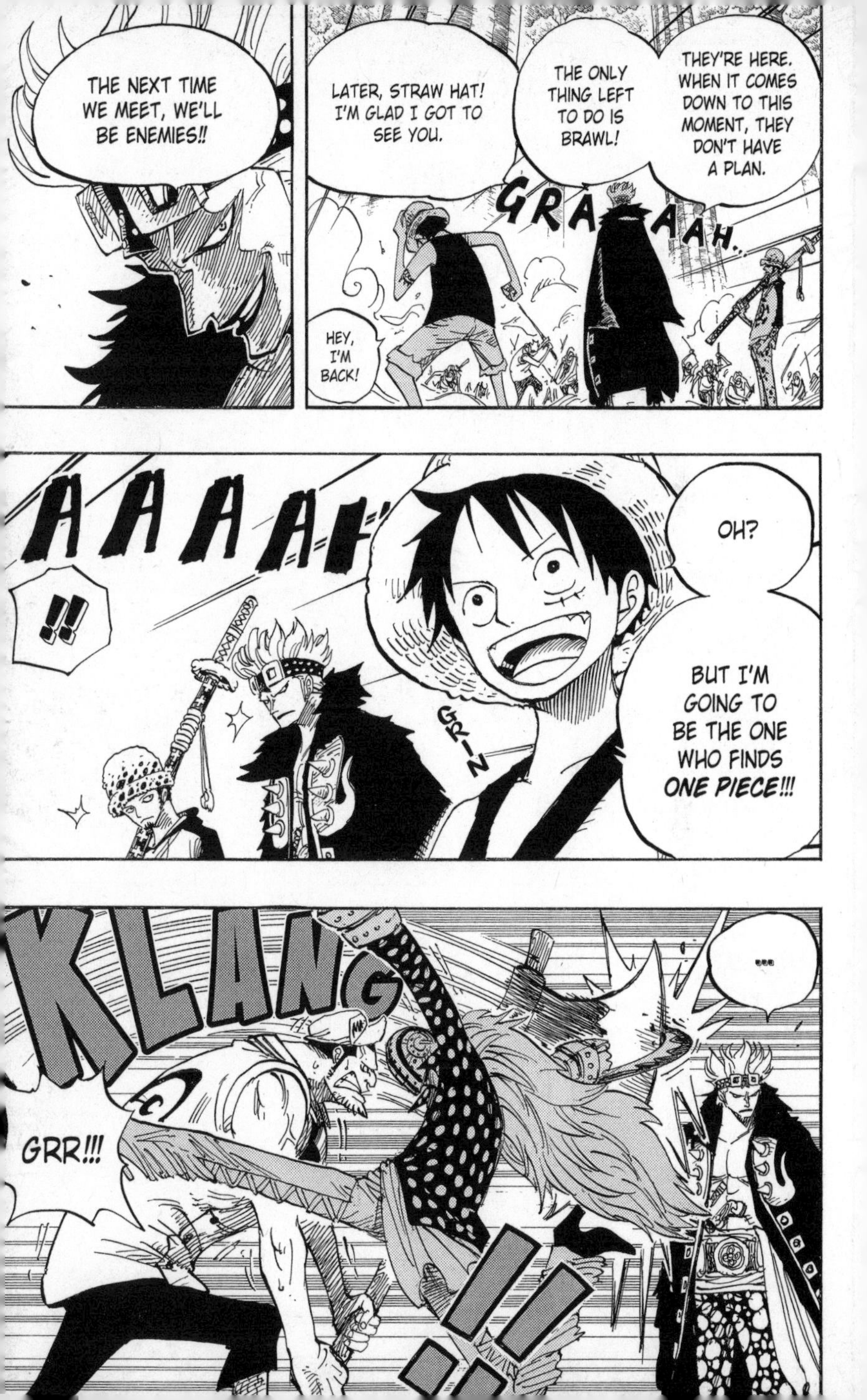
THEY'RE HERE. WHEN IT COMES DOWN TO THIS MOMENT, THEY DON'T HAVE A PLAN.
THE ONLY THING LEFT TO DO IS BRAWL!
LATER, STRAW HAT! I'M GLAD I GOT TO SEE YOU.
GRAAAH...
HEY, I'M BACK!
THE NEXT TIME WE MEET, WE'LL BE ENEMIES!!
OH?
BUT I'M GOING TO BE THE ONE WHO FINDS ONE PIECE!!!
GRIN
AAAAH
!!
...
KLANG
GRR!!!
!!

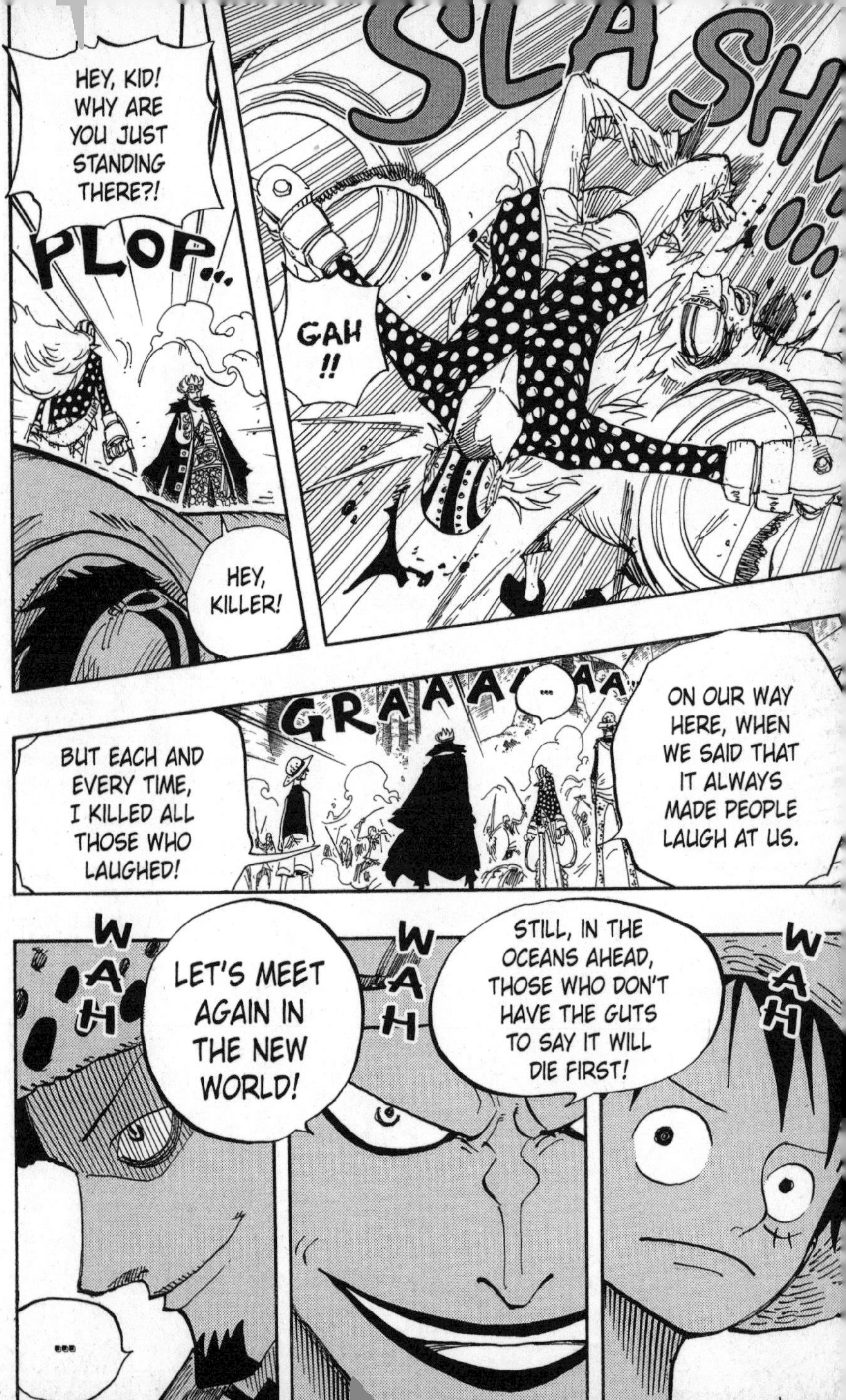
SLASH...
GAH!!
HEY, KID! WHY ARE YOU JUST STANDING THERE?!
PLOP...
HEY, KILLER!
ON OUR WAY HERE, WHEN WE SAID THAT IT ALWAYS MADE PEOPLE LAUGH AT US.
GRAAAAAAA
...
BUT EACH AND EVERY TIME, I KILLED ALL THOSE WHO LAUGHED!
WAH
STILL, IN THE OCEANS AHEAD, THOSE WHO DON'T HAVE THE GUTS TO SAY IT WILL DIE FIRST!
WAH
LET'S MEET AGAIN IN THE NEW WORLD!
WAH
...

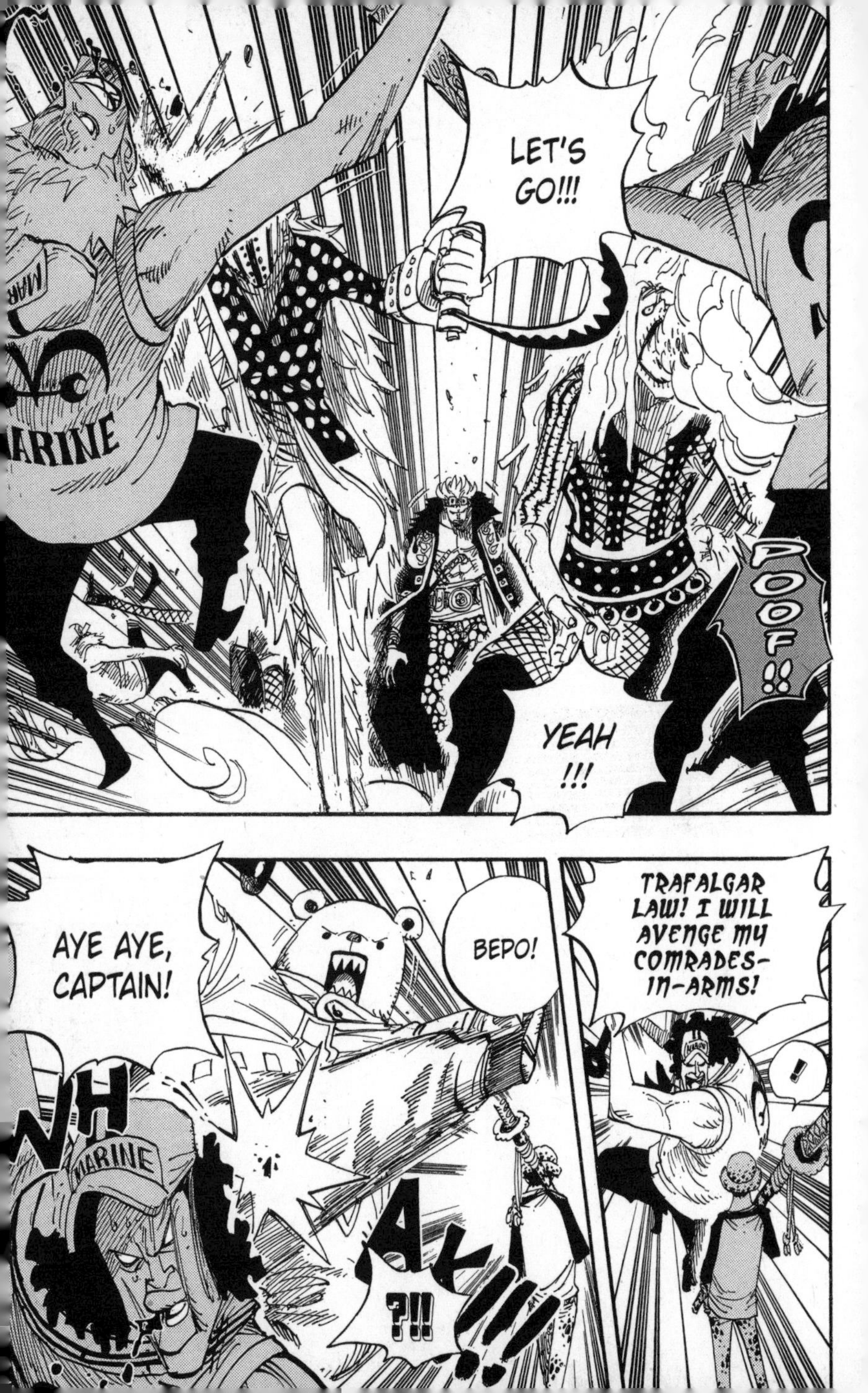
LET'S GO!!!
POOF!!
YEAH !!!
TRAFALGAR LAW! I WILL AVENGE MY COMRADES-IN-ARMS!
!
BEPO!
AYE AYE, CAPTAIN!
WHAK!!
?!!

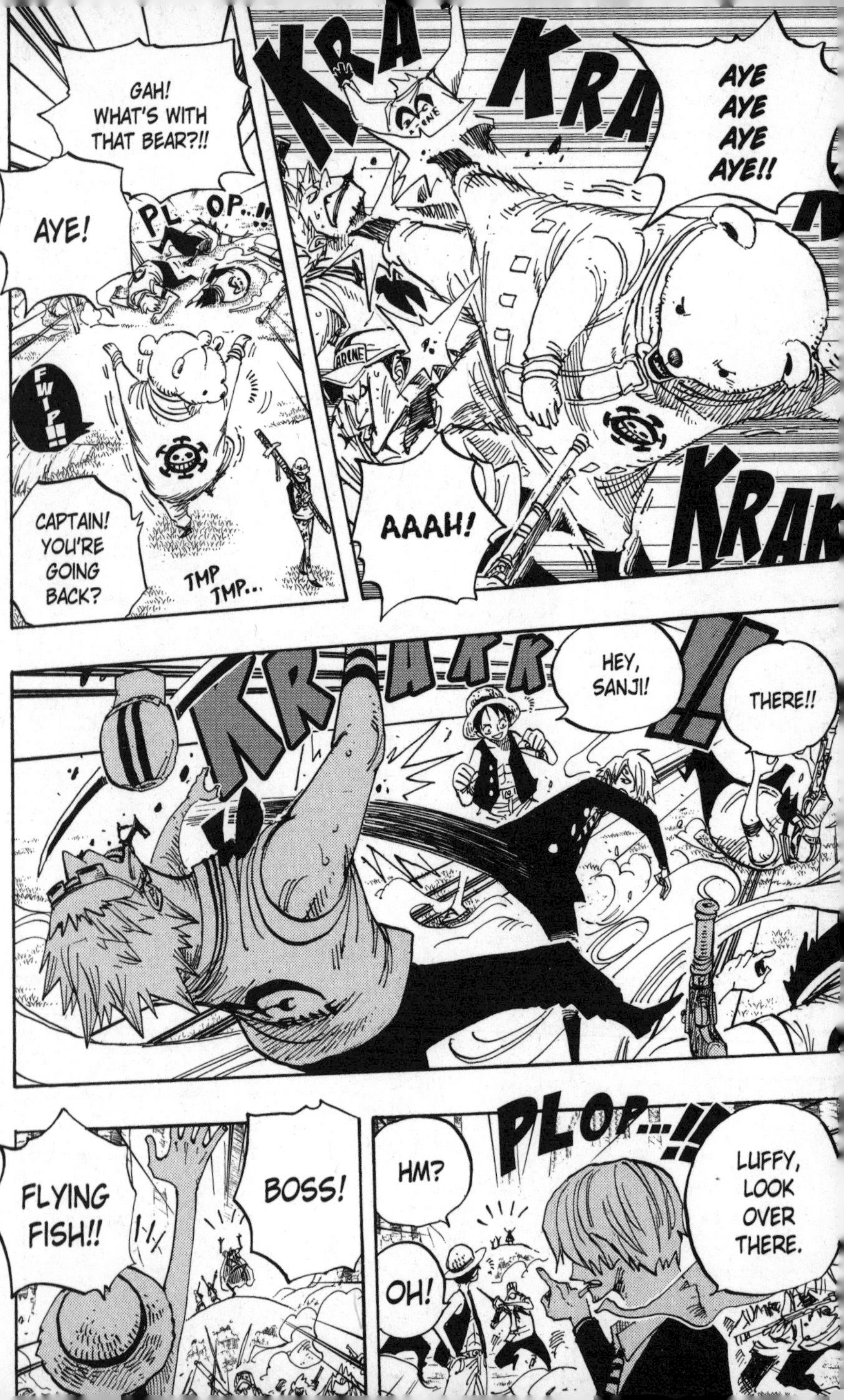
KRA
KRA
AYE AYE AYE AYE!!
AAAH!
KRAK
GAH! WHAT'S WITH THAT BEAR?!!
AYE!
PLOP...!!
FWIP!!
CAPTAIN! YOU'RE GOING BACK?
TMP TMP...
KRAKK!!
HEY, SANJI!
THERE!!
PLOP...!!
LUFFY, LOOK OVER THERE.
HM?
OH!
BOSS!
FLYING FISH!!

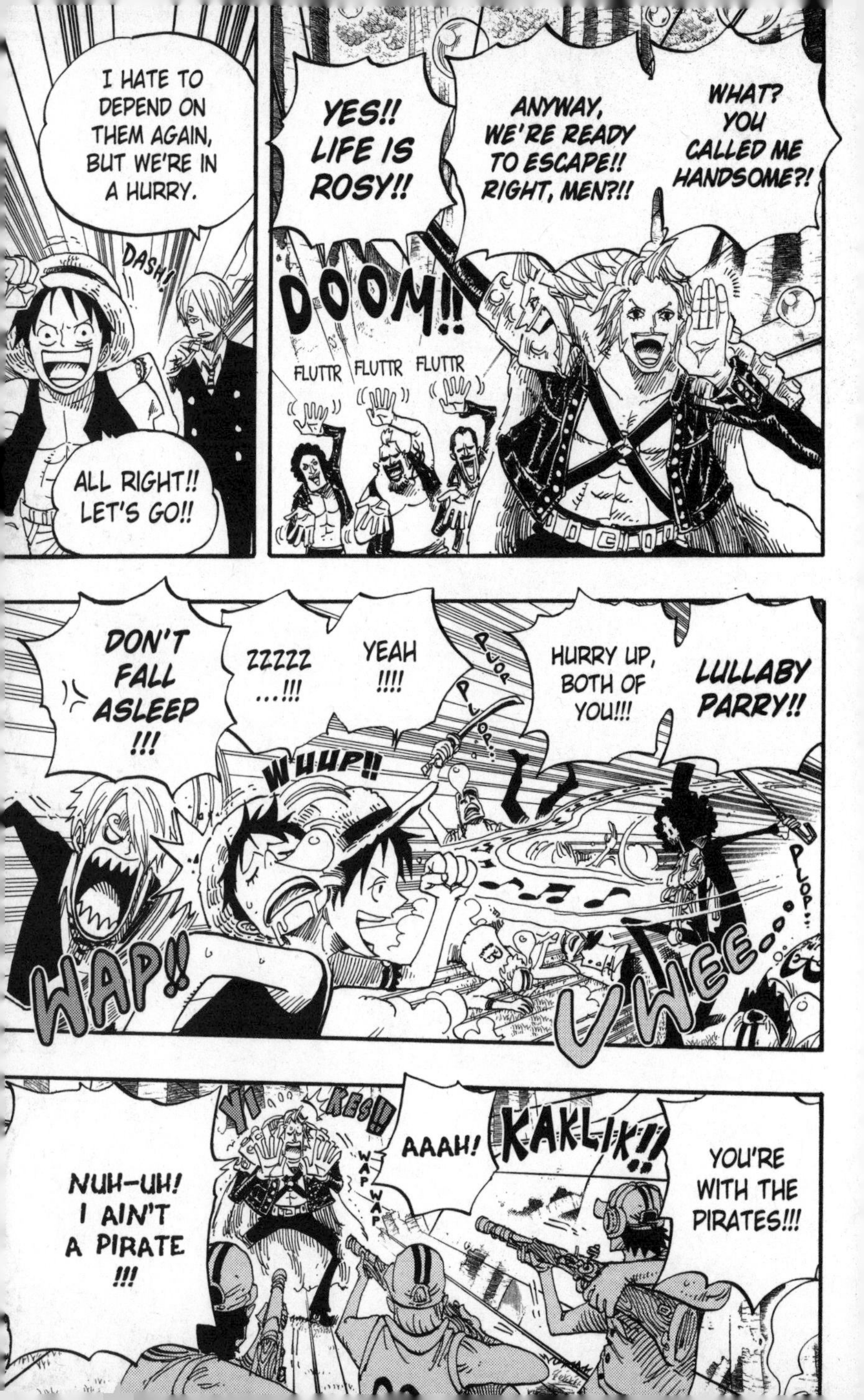
WHAT? YOU CALLED ME HANDSOME?!
ANYWAY, WE'RE READY TO ESCAPE!! RIGHT, MEN?!!
YES!! LIFE IS ROSY!!
DOOM!!
FLUTTR
FLUTTR
FLUTTR
I HATE TO DEPEND ON THEM AGAIN, BUT WE'RE IN A HURRY.
DASH!
ALL RIGHT!! LET'S GO!!
LULLABY PARRY!!
HURRY UP, BOTH OF YOU!!!
PLOP
PLOP...
YEAH !!!!
ZZZZZ ...!!!
DON'T FALL ASLEEP !!!
WUUP!!
PLOP...
UWEE...
WAP!!
YOU'RE WITH THE PIRATES!!!
KAKLIK!!
AAAH!
YIKES!!
WAP
WAP
NUH-UH! I AIN'T A PIRATE !!!

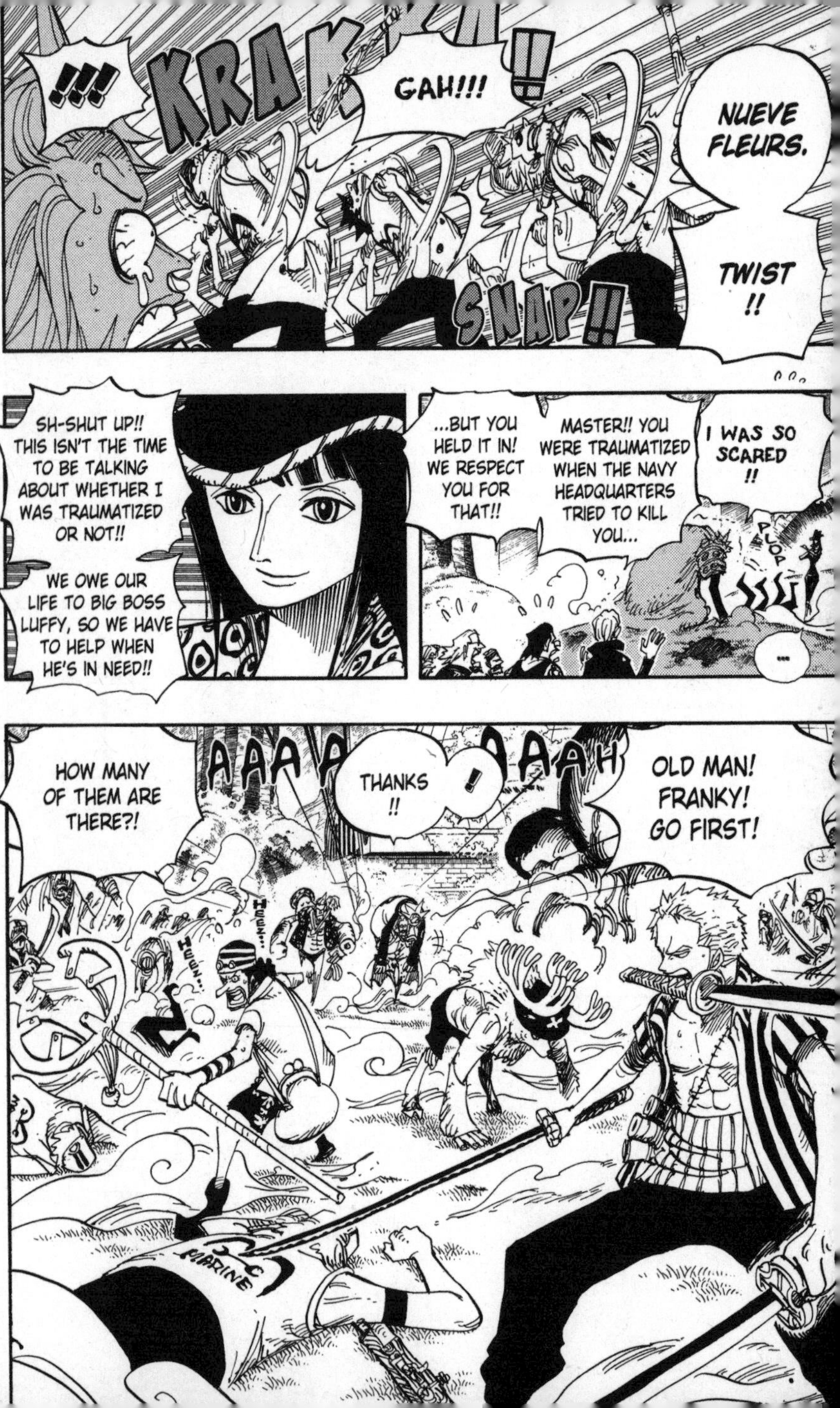
NUEVE FLEURS.
TWIST !!
GAH!!!
KRAK !!
SNAP !!
!!!
I WAS SO SCARED !!
MASTER!! YOU WERE TRAUMATIZED WHEN THE NAVY HEADQUARTERS TRIED TO KILL YOU...
...BUT YOU HELD IT IN! WE RESPECT YOU FOR THAT!!
PUOP
...
SH-SHUT UP!! THIS ISN'T THE TIME TO BE TALKING ABOUT WHETHER I WAS TRAUMATIZED OR NOT!!
WE OWE OUR LIFE TO BIG BOSS LUFFY, SO WE HAVE TO HELP WHEN HE'S IN NEED!!
OLD MAN! FRANKY! GO FIRST!
!
AAAAAAH
THANKS !!
HOW MANY OF THEM ARE THERE?!
HEEZ...
HEEZ...
MARINE

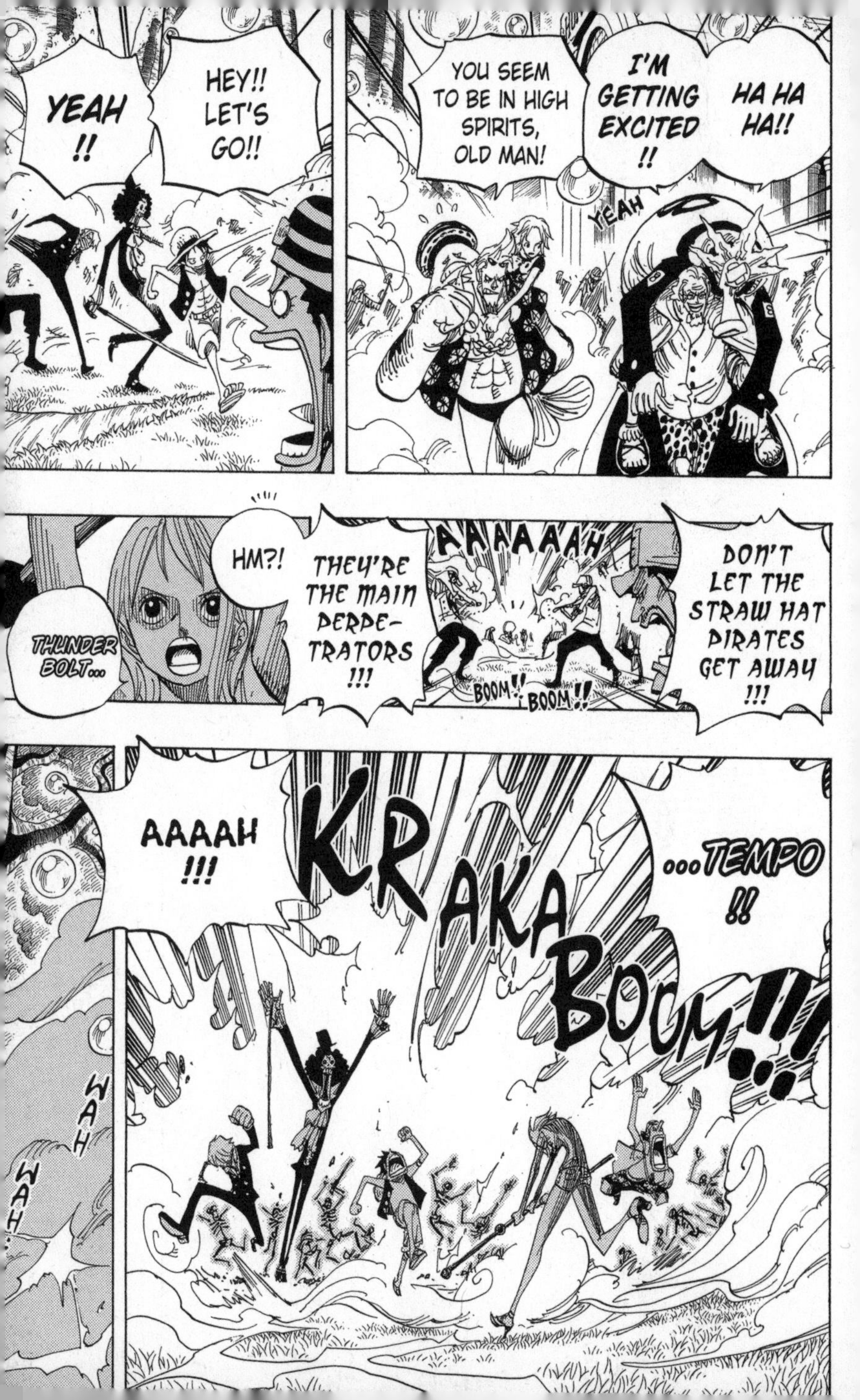
HA HA HA!!
I'M GETTING EXCITED!!
YOU SEEM TO BE IN HIGH SPIRITS, OLD MAN!
YEAH
HEY!! LET'S GO!!
YEAH!!
DON'T LET THE STRAW HAT PIRATES GET AWAY!!!
AAAAAAH
BOOM!! BOOM!!
THEY'RE THE MAIN PERPE-TRATORS!!!
HM?!
THUNDER BOLT...
...TEMPO!!
KRAKABOOM!!!
AAAAH!!!
WAH WAH...

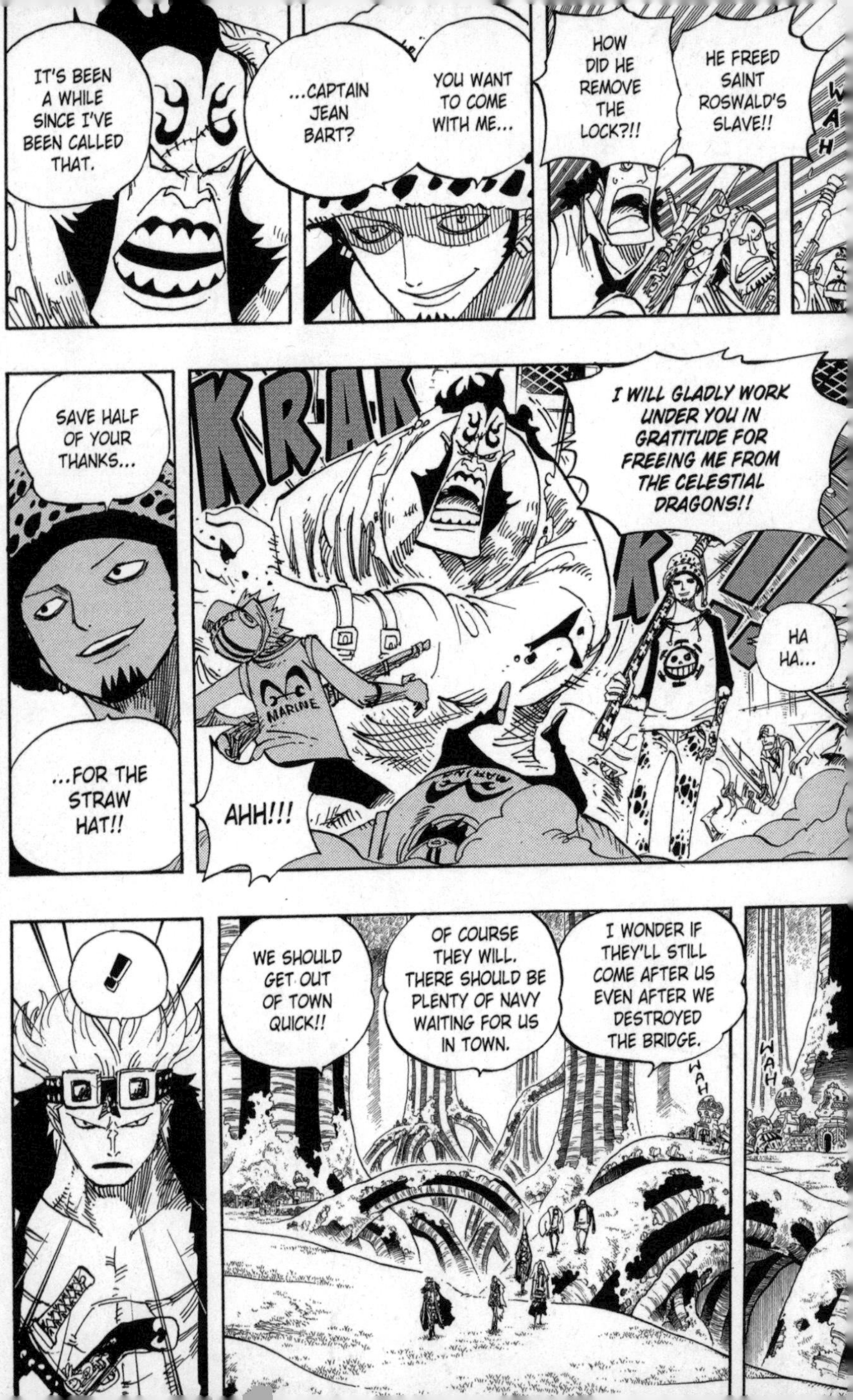
WAH
HE FREED SAINT ROSWALD'S SLAVE!!
HOW DID HE REMOVE THE LOCK?!!
YOU WANT TO COME WITH ME...
...CAPTAIN JEAN BART?
IT'S BEEN A WHILE SINCE I'VE BEEN CALLED THAT.
I WILL GLADLY WORK UNDER YOU IN GRATITUDE FOR FREEING ME FROM THE CELESTIAL DRAGONS!!
KRAK
HA HA...
AHH!!!
SAVE HALF OF YOUR THANKS...
...FOR THE STRAW HAT!!
WAH
I WONDER IF THEY'LL STILL COME AFTER US EVEN AFTER WE DESTROYED THE BRIDGE.
WAH
OF COURSE THEY WILL. THERE SHOULD BE PLENTY OF NAVY WAITING FOR US IN TOWN.
WE SHOULD GET OUT OF TOWN QUICK!!
!

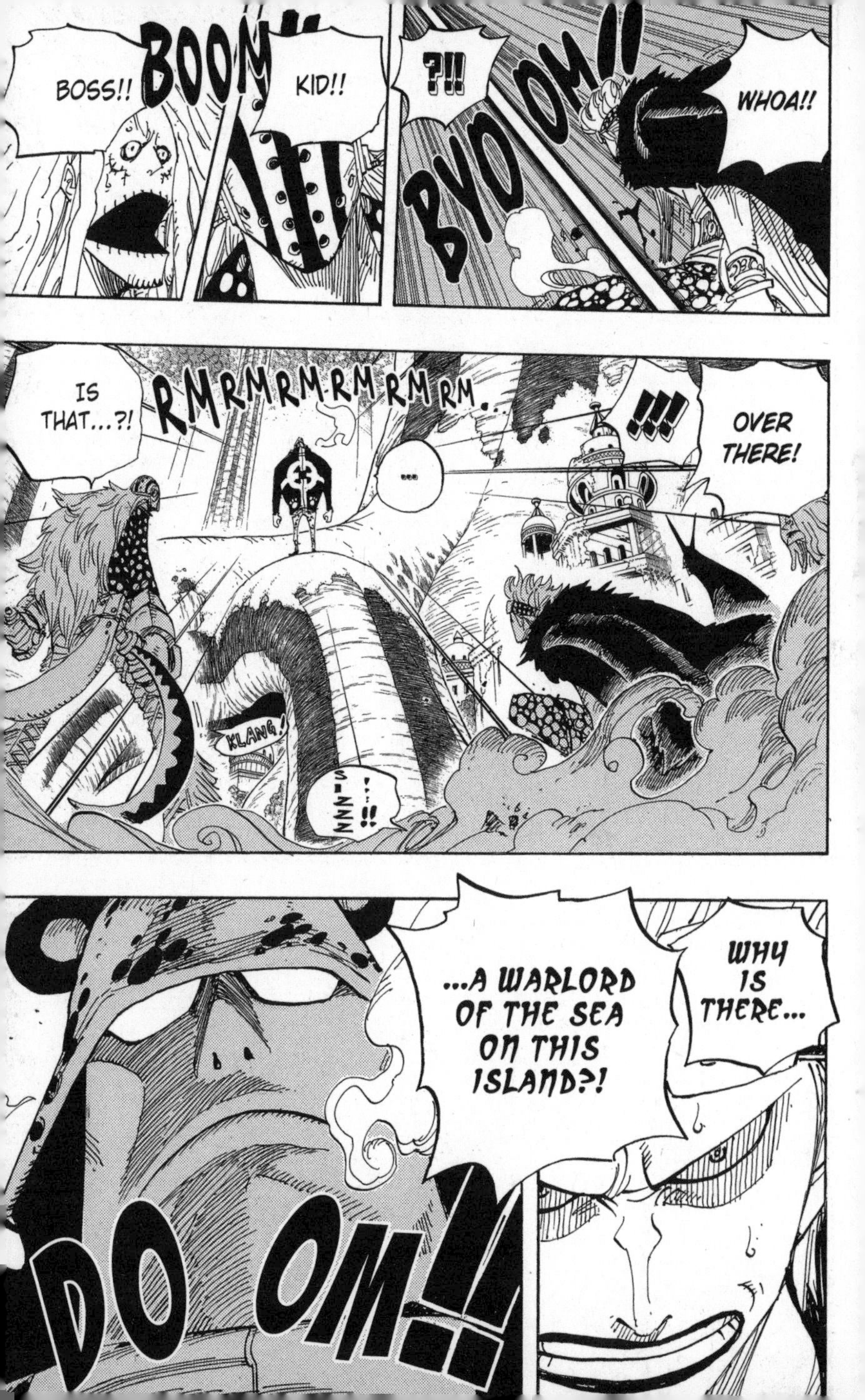
WHOA!!
?!!
BYO OM!!
KID!!
BOOM!!
BOSS!!
OVER THERE!
!!!
...
RMRMRM RM RM RM RM.
IS THAT...?!
KLANG!
SIZZZ
!!
WHY IS THERE...
...A WARLORD OF THE SEA ON THIS ISLAND?!
DO OM!!

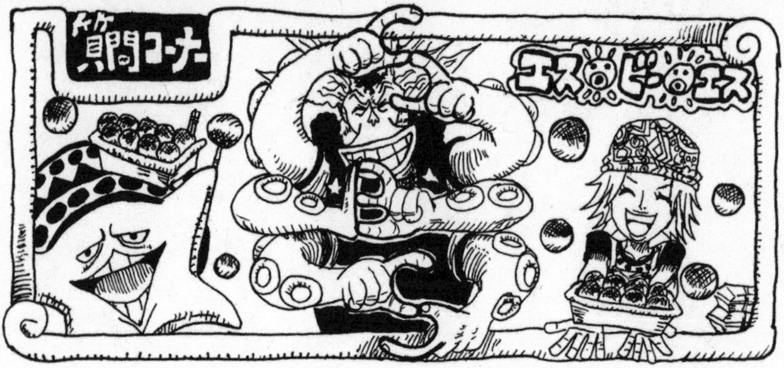
質問コーナー
エスビーエス

(Ponio, Aichi)

Q: I'm a young maiko from Kyoto. Is the rumored (S)illy (B)utt (S)chool here? Oh, come on, Oda Sensei. You shouldn't call people silly butts. Also, in chapter 494, I find Franky really adorable when he keeps reacting to the word "formation." I hope we can make a "formation" someday too.

--Maiko-han

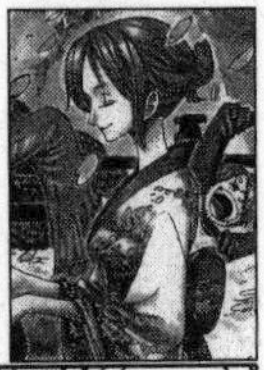

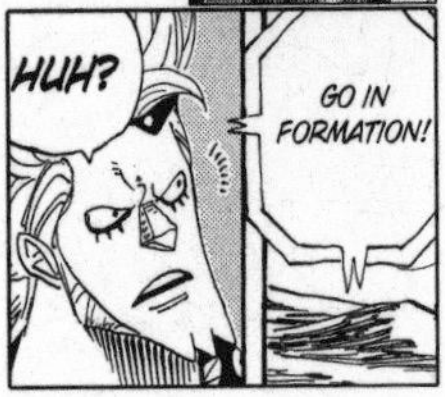
GO IN FORMATION!
HUH?

A: Oh, wow! Are you a real Geisha? You mistook the meaning of SBS, But I don't care! Oh, and Franky? Yes, that's right. He's an idiot, so he thought "formation" meant something else! He's a Bit too much of a pervert sometimes. Please send me letters again.

Chapter 506:

ROGER AND RAYLEIGH

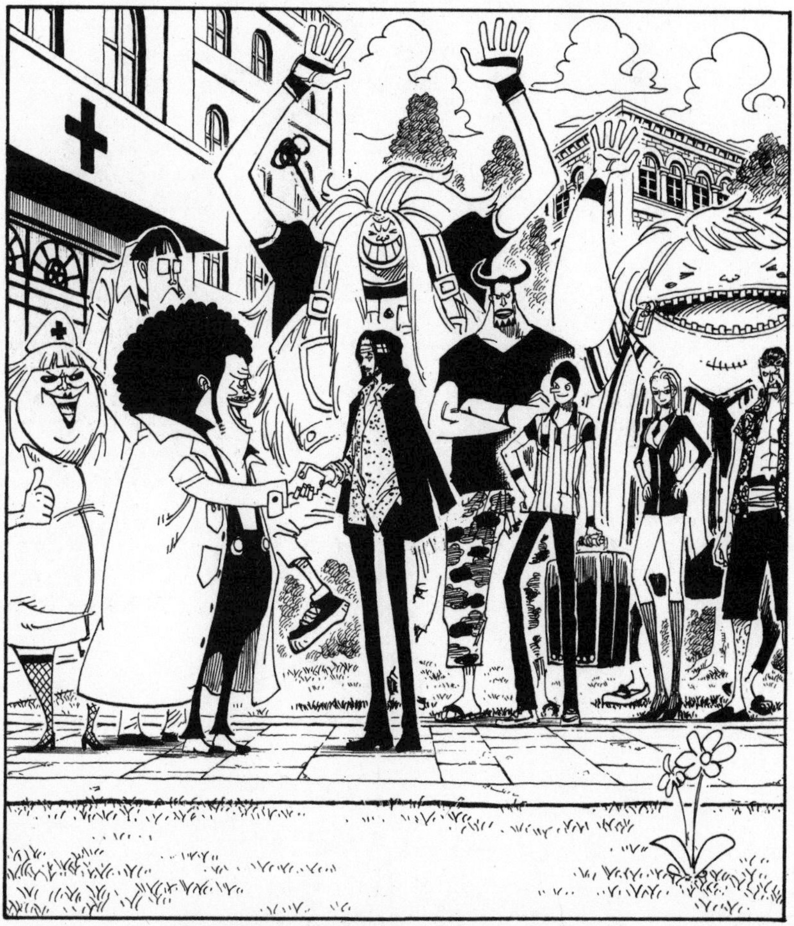

CP9'S INDEPENDENT REPORT, VOL. 15:
"DISCHARGED FROM THE HOSPITAL"

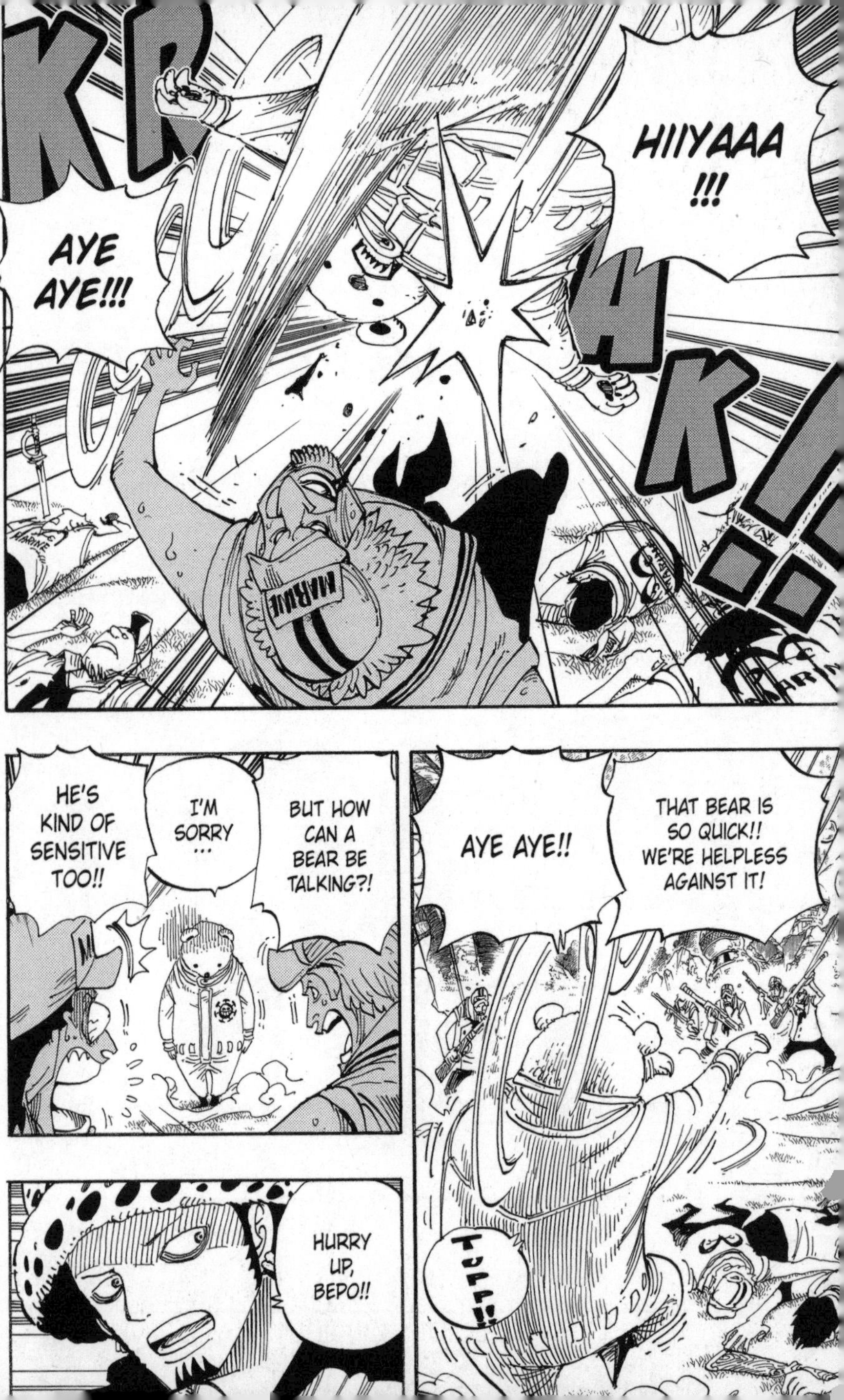
HIIYAAA !!!
AYE AYE!!!
THAT BEAR IS SO QUICK!! WE'RE HELPLESS AGAINST IT!
AYE AYE!!
TUPP!!
BUT HOW CAN A BEAR BE TALKING?!
I'M SORRY ...
HE'S KIND OF SENSITIVE TOO!!
HURRY UP, BEPO!!

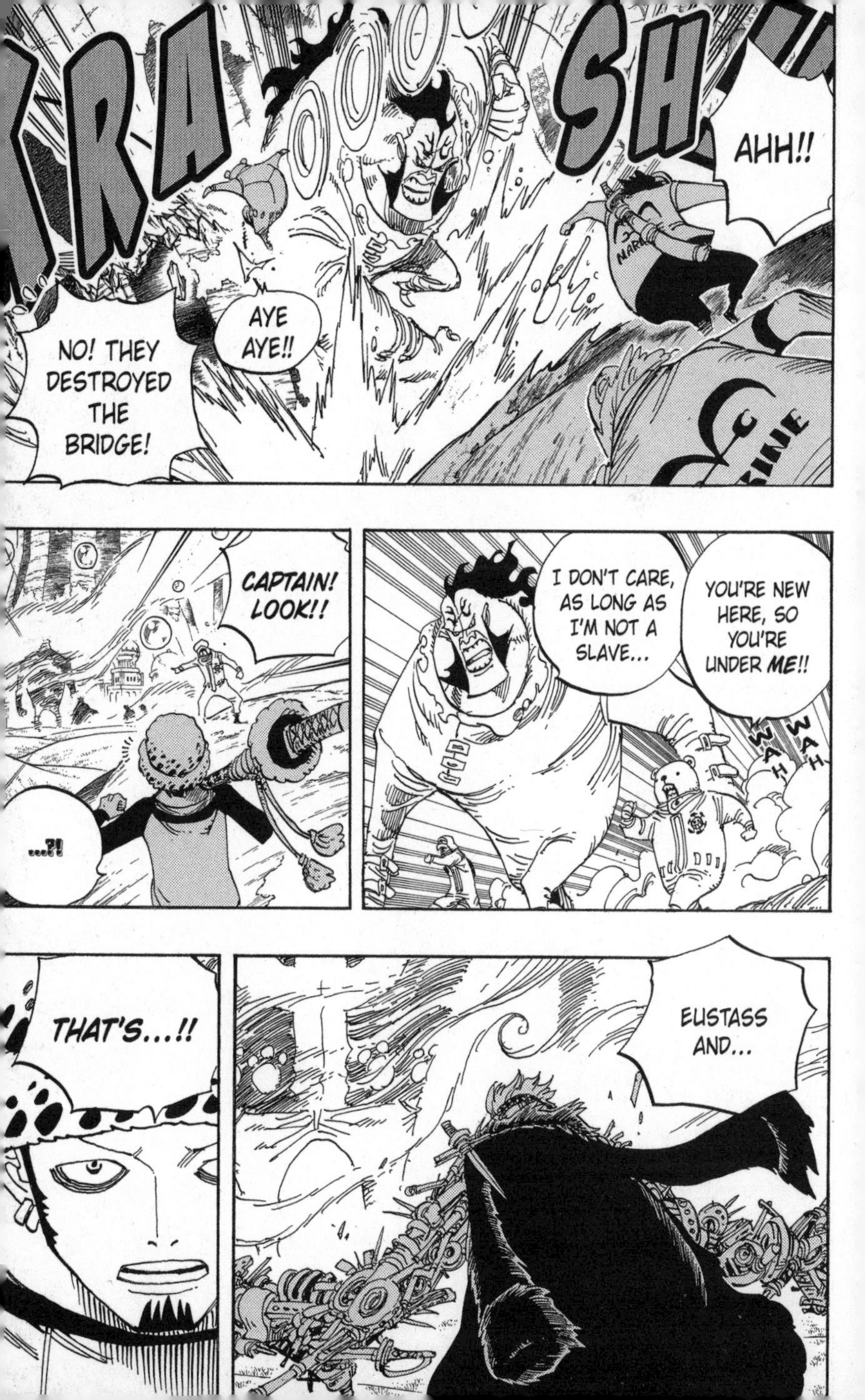
SH
AHH!!
AYE AYE!!
RA
NO! THEY DESTROYED THE BRIDGE!
YOU'RE NEW HERE, SO YOU'RE UNDER ME!!
I DON'T CARE, AS LONG AS I'M NOT A SLAVE...
WAH WAH
CAPTAIN! LOOK!!
...?!
EUSTASS AND...
THAT'S...!!

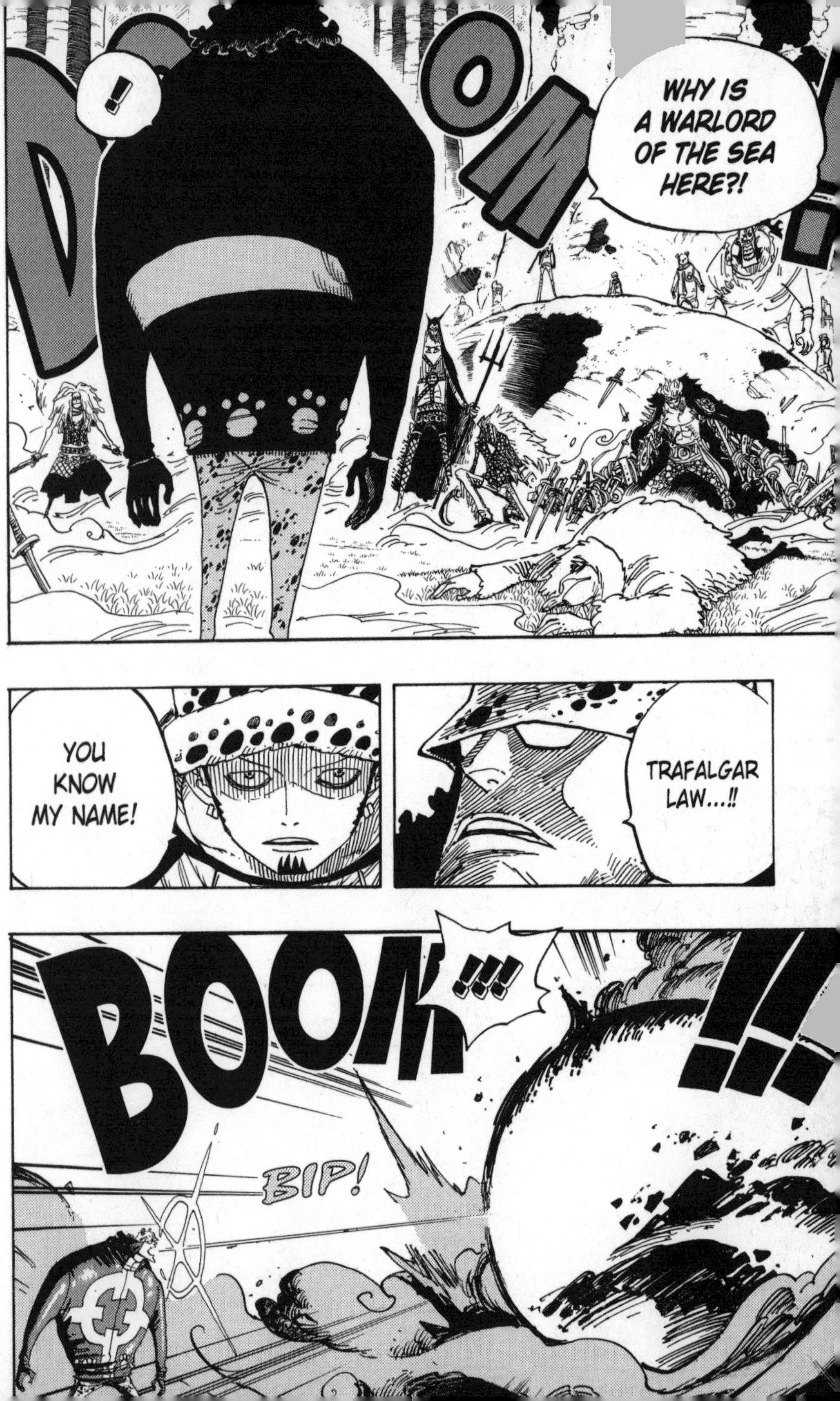
WHY IS A WARLORD OF THE SEA HERE?!
!
TRAFALGAR LAW...!!
YOU KNOW MY NAME!
BOOM!!!
!!
BIP!

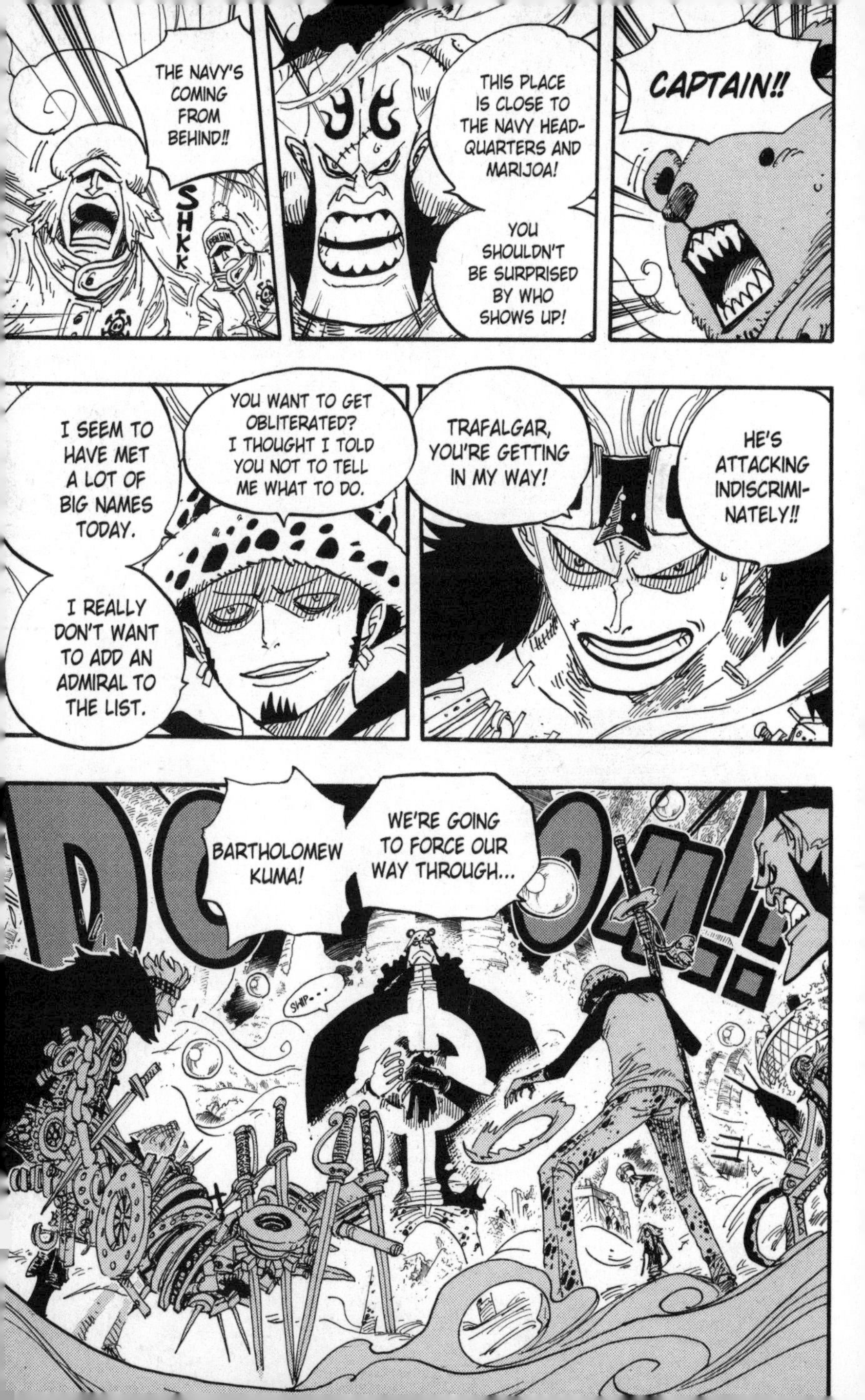
CAPTAIN!!
THIS PLACE IS CLOSE TO THE NAVY HEAD-QUARTERS AND MARIJOA!
YOU SHOULDN'T BE SURPRISED BY WHO SHOWS UP!
THE NAVY'S COMING FROM BEHIND!!
SHKK
HE'S ATTACKING INDISCRIMI-NATELY!!
TRAFALGAR, YOU'RE GETTING IN MY WAY!
YOU WANT TO GET OBLITERATED? I THOUGHT I TOLD YOU NOT TO TELL ME WHAT TO DO.
I SEEM TO HAVE MET A LOT OF BIG NAMES TODAY.
I REALLY DON'T WANT TO ADD AN ADMIRAL TO THE LIST.
WE'RE GOING TO FORCE OUR WAY THROUGH...
BARTHOLOMEW KUMA!
DOOM!!

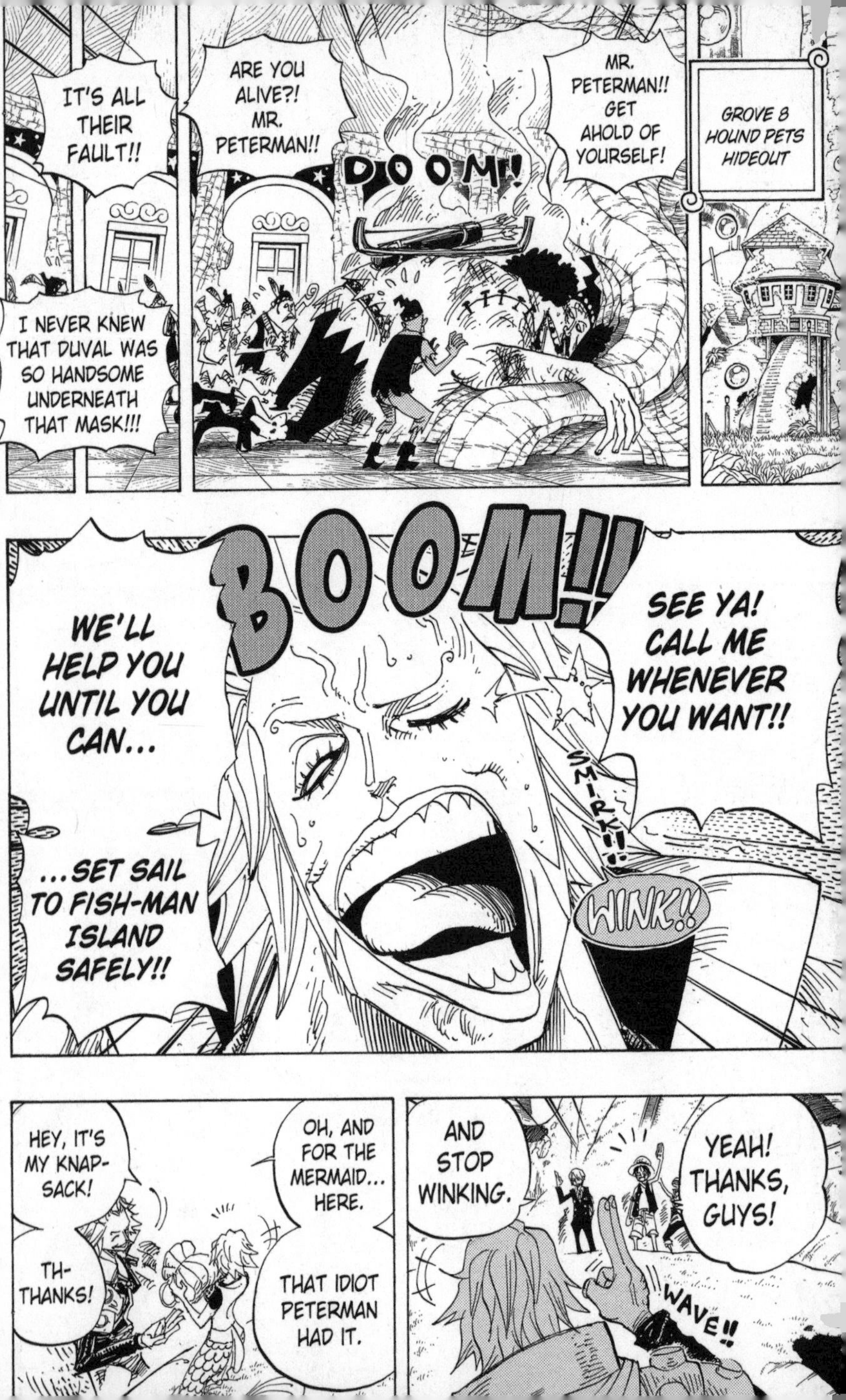
GROVE 8 HOUND PETS HIDEOUT
MR. PETERMAN!! GET AHOLD OF YOURSELF!
ARE YOU ALIVE?! MR. PETERMAN!!
DOOM!!
IT'S ALL THEIR FAULT!!
I NEVER KNEW THAT DUVAL WAS SO HANDSOME UNDERNEATH THAT MASK!!!
BOOM!!
SEE YA! CALL ME WHENEVER YOU WANT!!
SMIRK!!
WINK!!
WE'LL HELP YOU UNTIL YOU CAN...
...SET SAIL TO FISH-MAN ISLAND SAFELY!!
YEAH! THANKS, GUYS!
AND STOP WINKING.
WAVE!!
OH, AND FOR THE MERMAID... HERE.
THAT IDIOT PETERMAN HAD IT.
HEY, IT'S MY KNAP-SACK!
TH-THANKS!

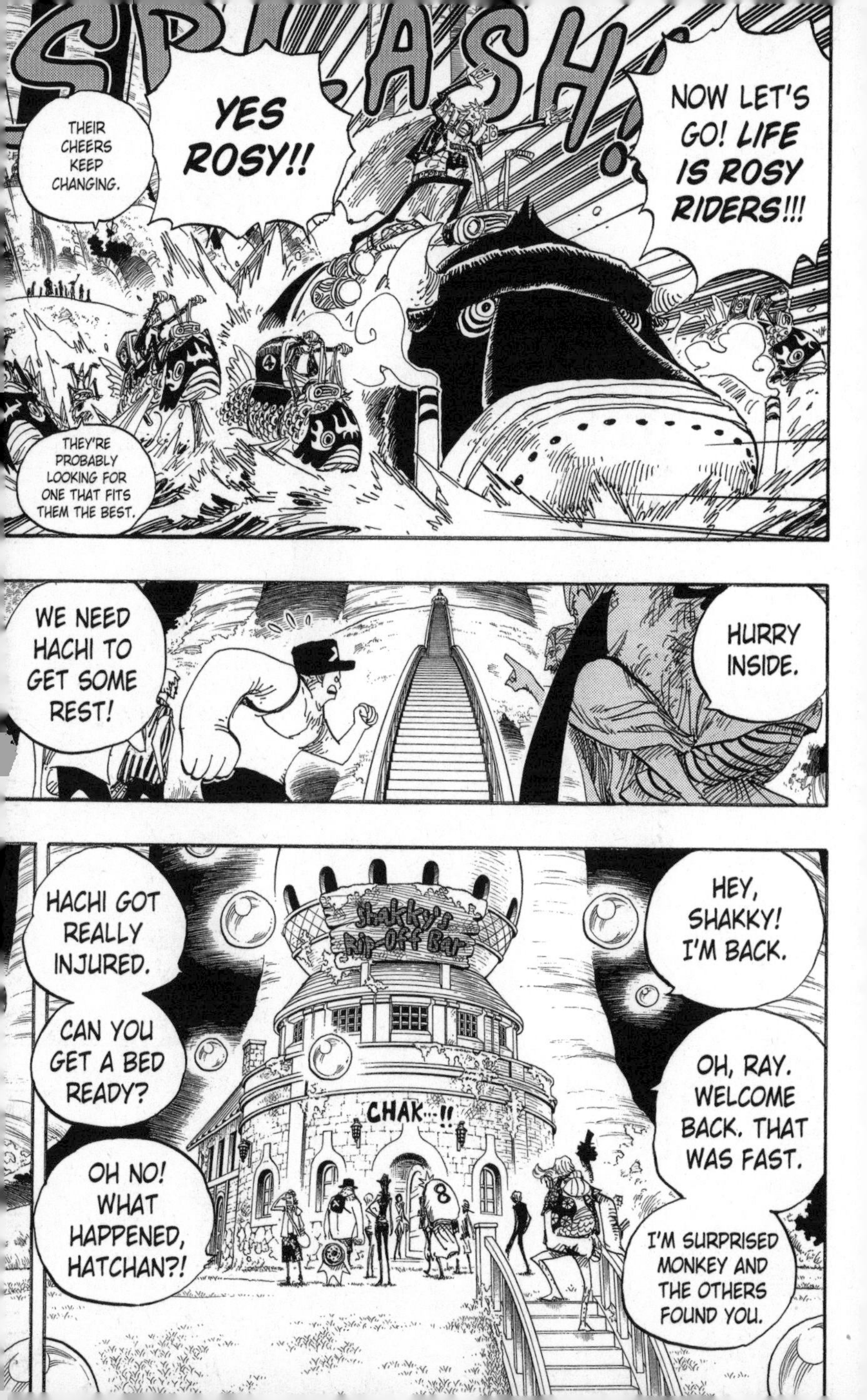
SPLASH!
NOW LET'S GO! LIFE IS ROSY RIDERS!!!
YES ROSY!!
THEIR CHEERS KEEP CHANGING.
THEY'RE PROBABLY LOOKING FOR ONE THAT FITS THEM THE BEST.
HURRY INSIDE.
WE NEED HACHI TO GET SOME REST!
HEY, SHAKKY! I'M BACK.
OH, RAY. WELCOME BACK. THAT WAS FAST.
I'M SURPRISED MONKEY AND THE OTHERS FOUND YOU.
Shakky's Rip-Off Bar
CHAK...!!
HACHI GOT REALLY INJURED.
CAN YOU GET A BED READY?
OH NO! WHAT HAPPENED, HATCHAN?!

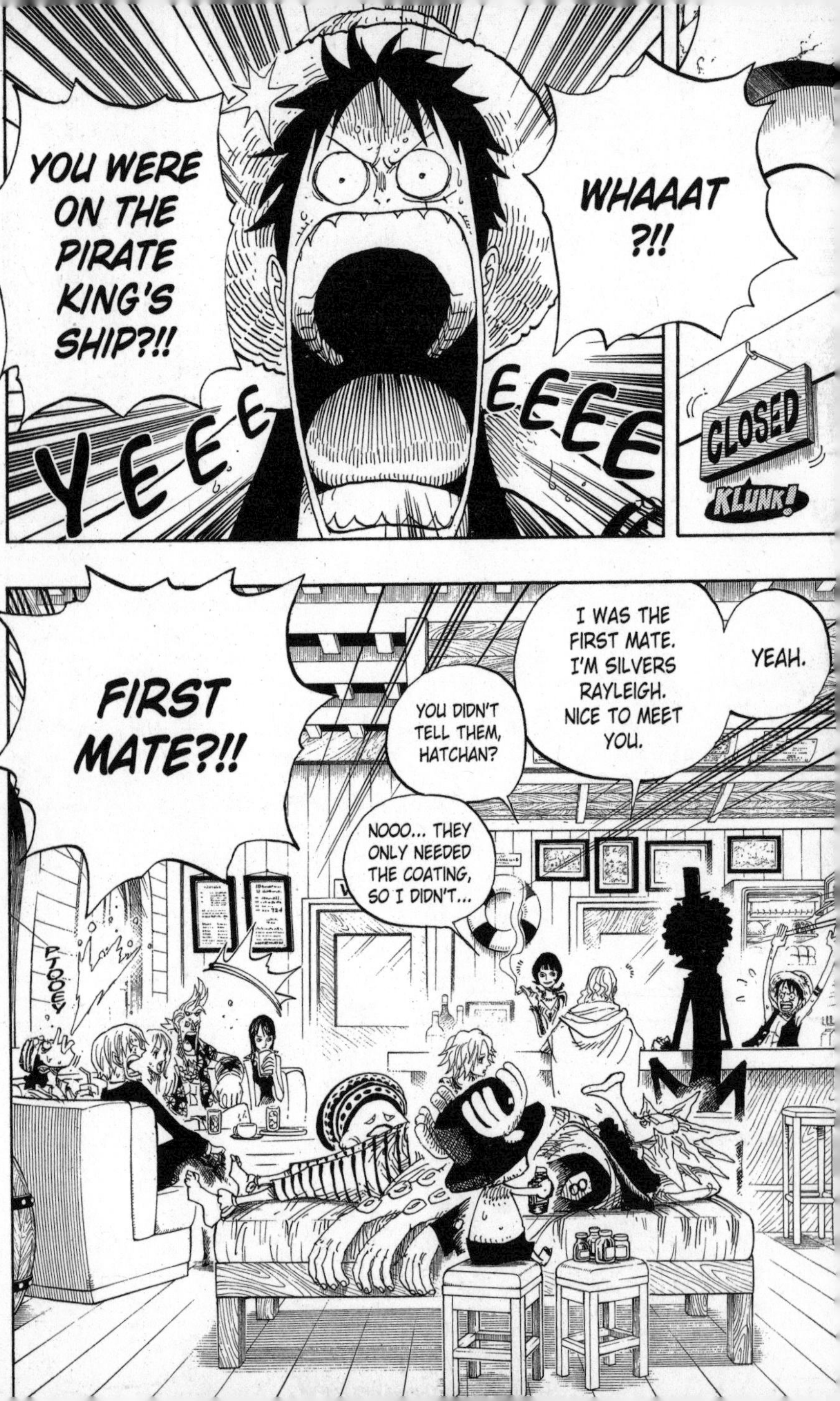
CLOSED
KLUNK!
WHAAAT ?!!
YOU WERE ON THE PIRATE KING'S SHIP?!!
YEEEEEEEE
YEAH.
I WAS THE FIRST MATE. I'M SILVERS RAYLEIGH. NICE TO MEET YOU.
FIRST MATE?!!
YOU DIDN'T TELL THEM, HATCHAN?
NOOO... THEY ONLY NEEDED THE COATING, SO I DIDN'T...
P-TOOEY

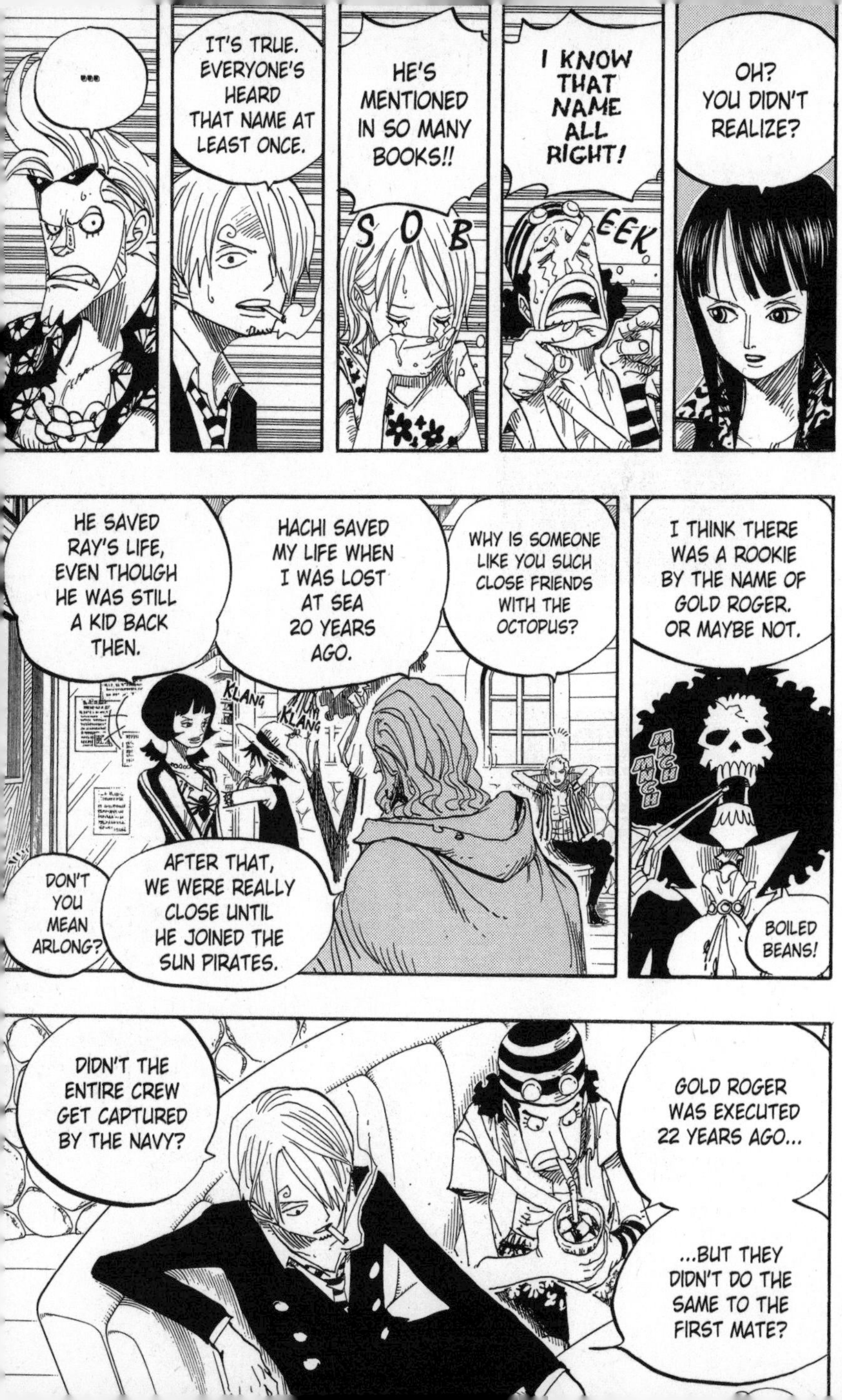
OH? YOU DIDN'T REALIZE?
I KNOW THAT NAME ALL RIGHT!
EEK
HE'S MENTIONED IN SO MANY BOOKS!!
SOB
IT'S TRUE. EVERYONE'S HEARD THAT NAME AT LEAST ONCE.
...
I THINK THERE WAS A ROOKIE BY THE NAME OF GOLD ROGER. OR MAYBE NOT.
MNCH
MNCH
BOILED BEANS!
WHY IS SOMEONE LIKE YOU SUCH CLOSE FRIENDS WITH THE OCTOPUS?
HACHI SAVED MY LIFE WHEN I WAS LOST AT SEA 20 YEARS AGO.
HE SAVED RAY'S LIFE, EVEN THOUGH HE WAS STILL A KID BACK THEN.
KLANG
KLANG
AFTER THAT, WE WERE REALLY CLOSE UNTIL HE JOINED THE SUN PIRATES.
DON'T YOU MEAN ARLONG?
GOLD ROGER WAS EXECUTED 22 YEARS AGO...
DIDN'T THE ENTIRE CREW GET CAPTURED BY THE NAVY?
...BUT THEY DIDN'T DO THE SAME TO THE FIRST MATE?

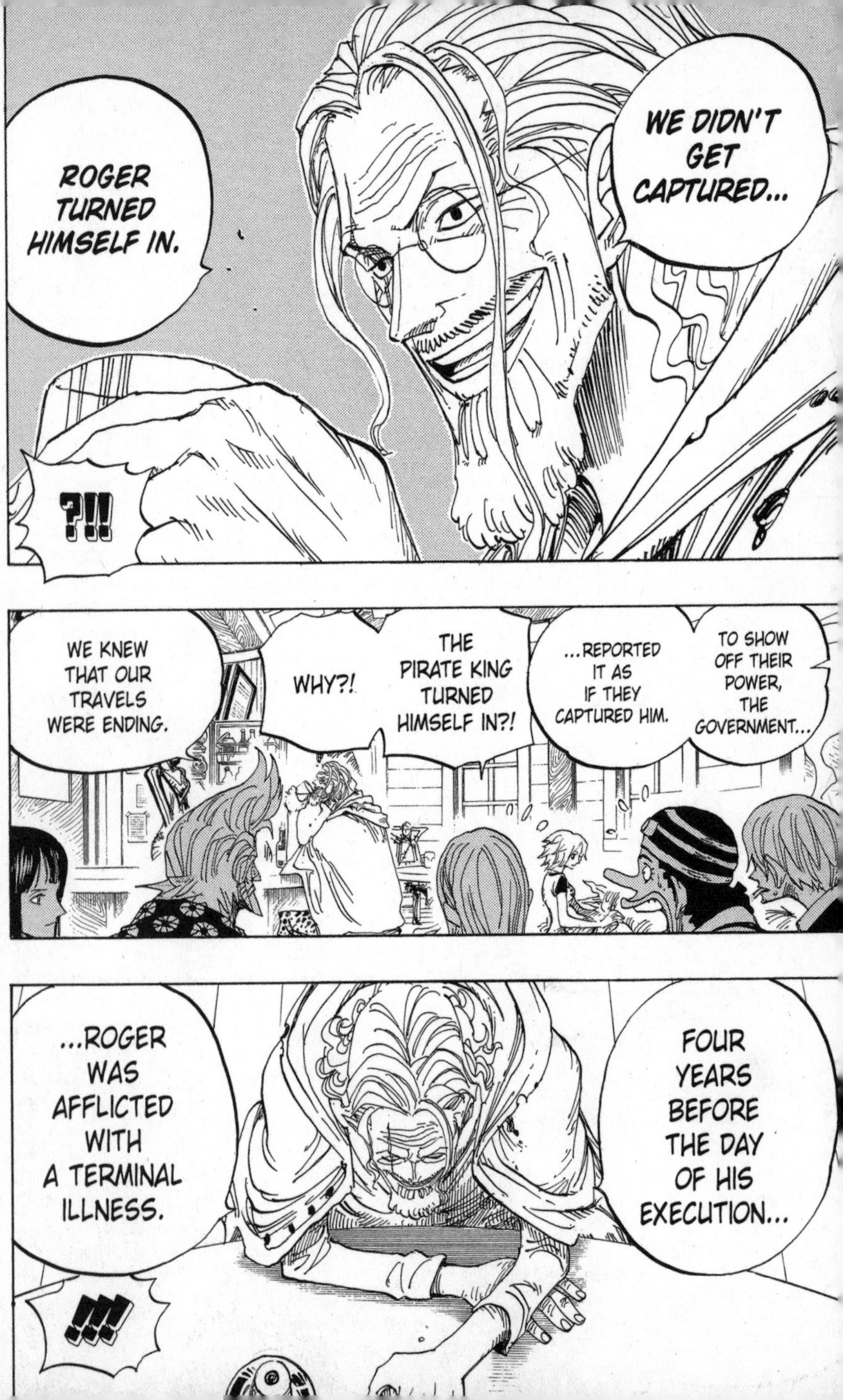
WE DIDN'T GET CAPTURED...
ROGER TURNED HIMSELF IN.
?!!
TO SHOW OFF THEIR POWER, THE GOVERNMENT...
...REPORTED IT AS IF THEY CAPTURED HIM.
THE PIRATE KING TURNED HIMSELF IN?!
WHY?!
WE KNEW THAT OUR TRAVELS WERE ENDING.
FOUR YEARS BEFORE THE DAY OF HIS EXECUTION...
...ROGER WAS AFFLICTED WITH A TERMINAL ILLNESS.
!!!

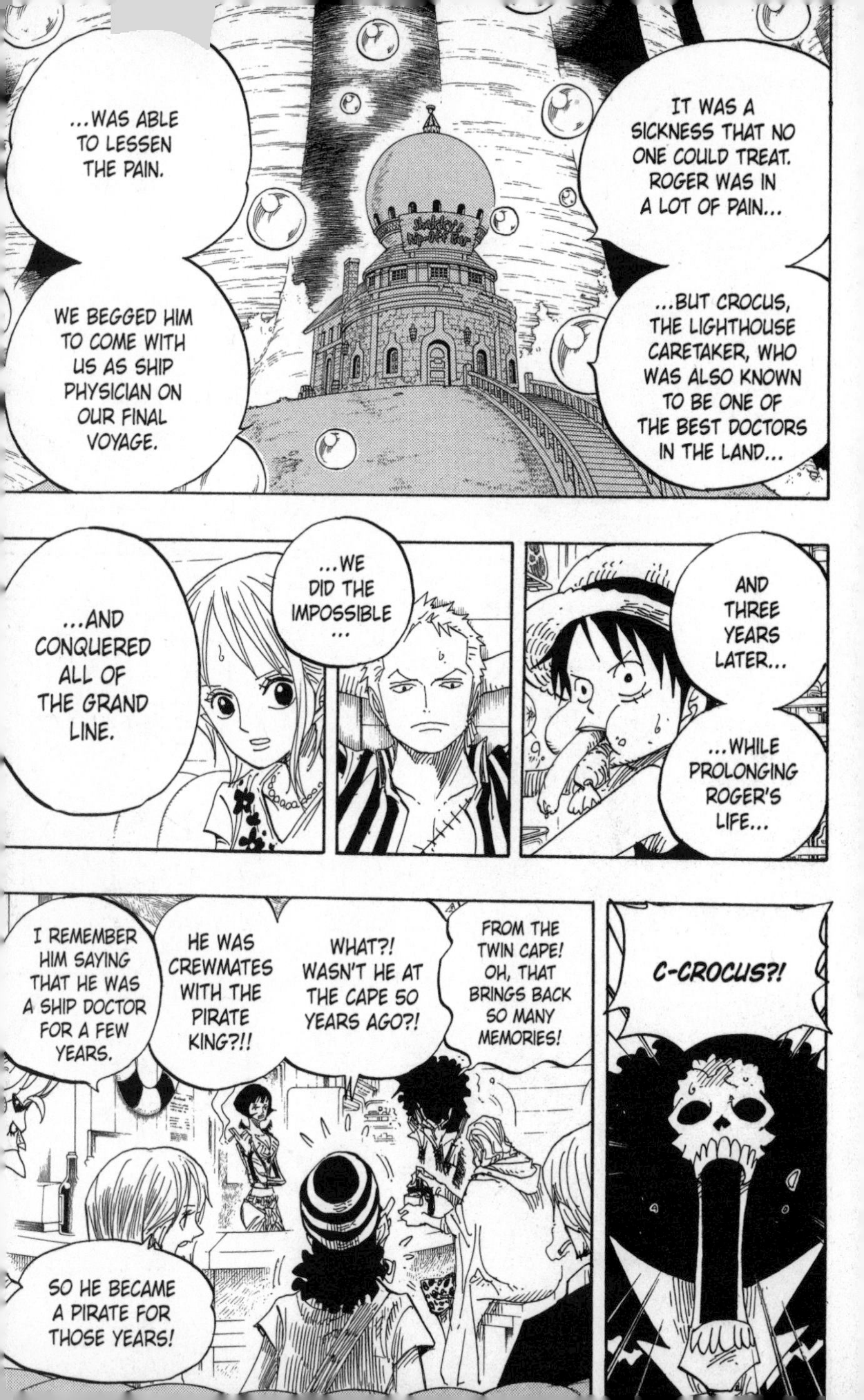
IT WAS A SICKNESS THAT NO ONE COULD TREAT. ROGER WAS IN A LOT OF PAIN...
...BUT CROCUS, THE LIGHTHOUSE CARETAKER, WHO WAS ALSO KNOWN TO BE ONE OF THE BEST DOCTORS IN THE LAND...
...WAS ABLE TO LESSEN THE PAIN.
WE BEGGED HIM TO COME WITH US AS SHIP PHYSICIAN ON OUR FINAL VOYAGE.
AND THREE YEARS LATER...
...WHILE PROLONGING ROGER'S LIFE...
...WE DID THE IMPOSSIBLE...
...AND CONQUERED ALL OF THE GRAND LINE.
C-CROCUS?!
FROM THE TWIN CAPE! OH, THAT BRINGS BACK SO MANY MEMORIES!
WHAT?! WASN'T HE AT THE CAPE 50 YEARS AGO?!
HE WAS CREWMATES WITH THE PIRATE KING?!!
I REMEMBER HIM SAYING THAT HE WAS A SHIP DOCTOR FOR A FEW YEARS.
SO HE BECAME A PIRATE FOR THOSE YEARS!

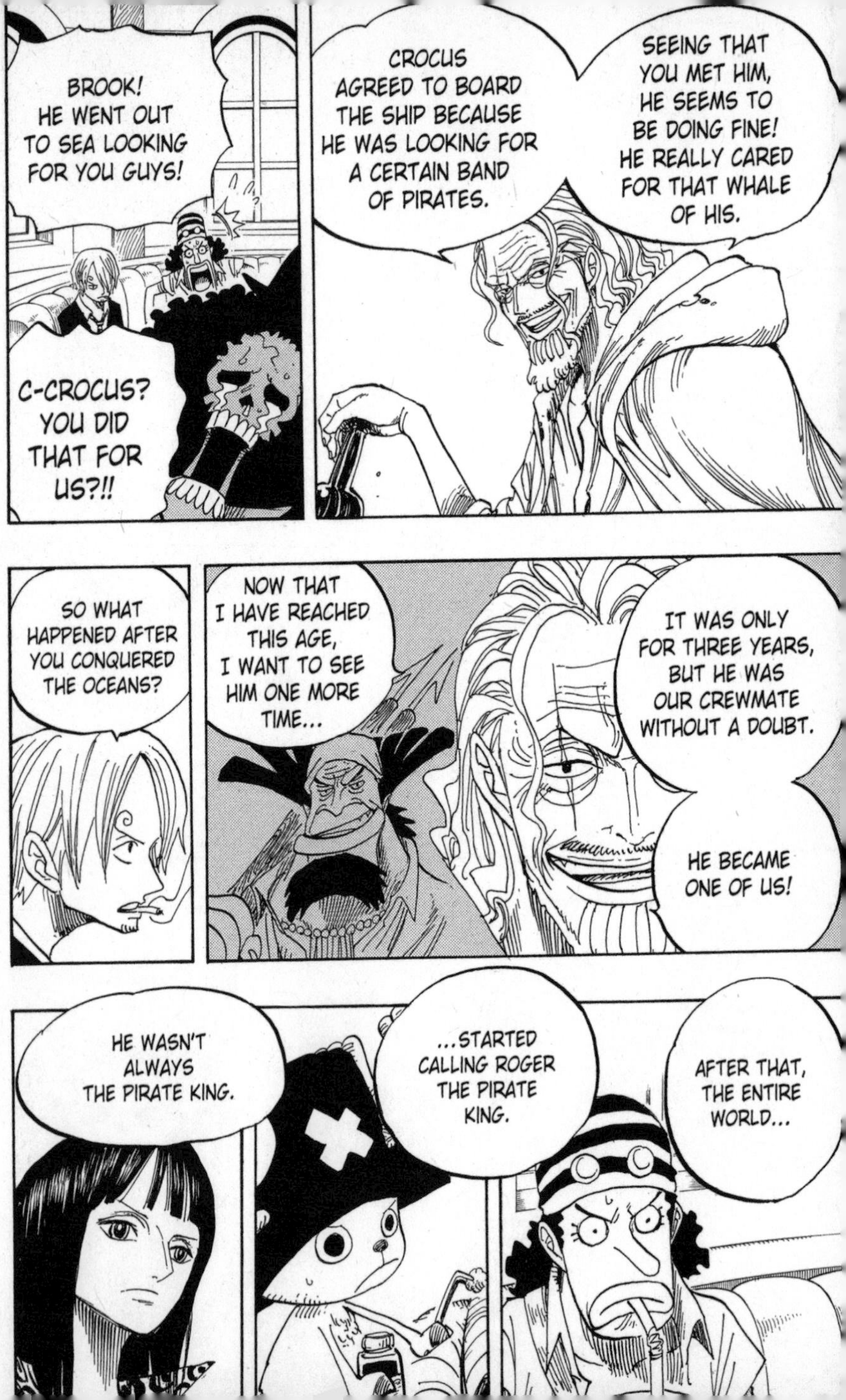
SEEING THAT YOU MET HIM, HE SEEMS TO BE DOING FINE! HE REALLY CARED FOR THAT WHALE OF HIS.
CROCUS AGREED TO BOARD THE SHIP BECAUSE HE WAS LOOKING FOR A CERTAIN BAND OF PIRATES.
BROOK! HE WENT OUT TO SEA LOOKING FOR YOU GUYS!
C-CROCUS? YOU DID THAT FOR US?!!
IT WAS ONLY FOR THREE YEARS, BUT HE WAS OUR CREWMATE WITHOUT A DOUBT.
HE BECAME ONE OF US!
NOW THAT I HAVE REACHED THIS AGE, I WANT TO SEE HIM ONE MORE TIME...
SO WHAT HAPPENED AFTER YOU CONQUERED THE OCEANS?
AFTER THAT, THE ENTIRE WORLD...
...STARTED CALLING ROGER THE PIRATE KING.
HE WASN'T ALWAYS THE PIRATE KING.

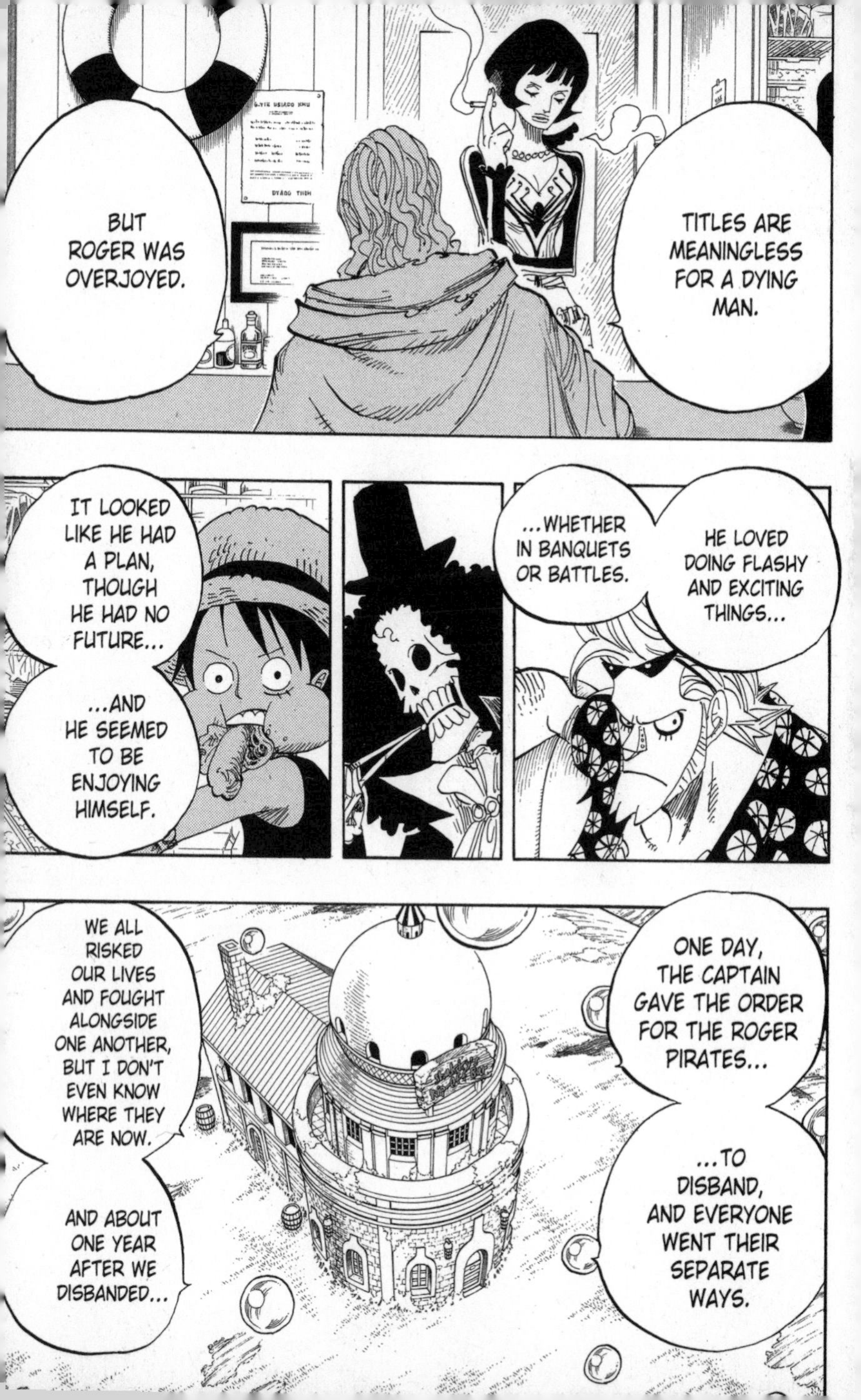
TITLES ARE MEANINGLESS FOR A DYING MAN.
BUT ROGER WAS OVERJOYED.
HE LOVED DOING FLASHY AND EXCITING THINGS...
...WHETHER IN BANQUETS OR BATTLES.
IT LOOKED LIKE HE HAD A PLAN, THOUGH HE HAD NO FUTURE...
...AND HE SEEMED TO BE ENJOYING HIMSELF.
ONE DAY, THE CAPTAIN GAVE THE ORDER FOR THE ROGER PIRATES...
...TO DISBAND, AND EVERYONE WENT THEIR SEPARATE WAYS.
WE ALL RISKED OUR LIVES AND FOUGHT ALONGSIDE ONE ANOTHER, BUT I DON'T EVEN KNOW WHERE THEY ARE NOW.
AND ABOUT ONE YEAR AFTER WE DISBANDED...

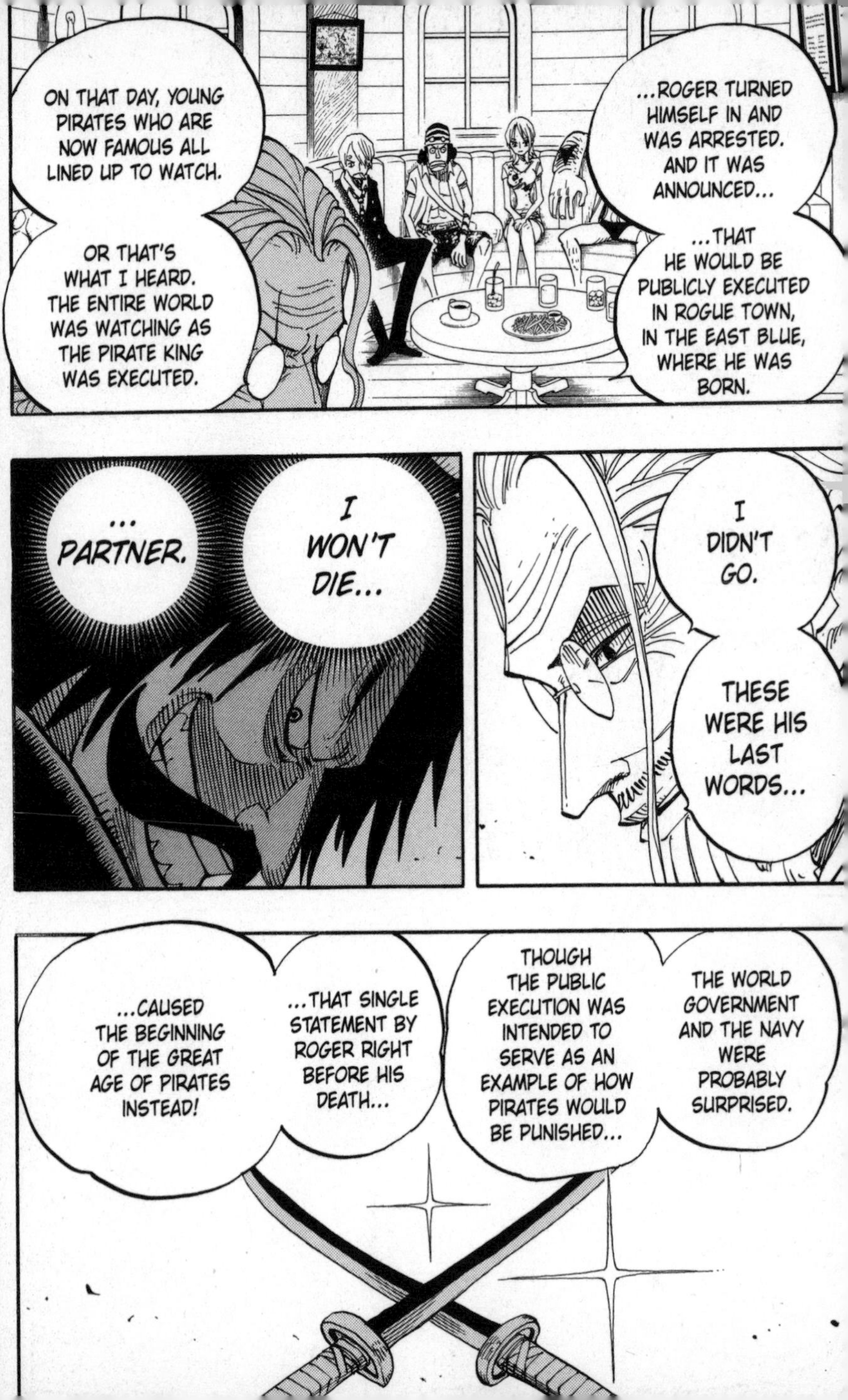
...ROGER TURNED HIMSELF IN AND WAS ARRESTED. AND IT WAS ANNOUNCED...
...THAT HE WOULD BE PUBLICLY EXECUTED IN ROGUE TOWN, IN THE EAST BLUE, WHERE HE WAS BORN.
ON THAT DAY, YOUNG PIRATES WHO ARE NOW FAMOUS ALL LINED UP TO WATCH.
OR THAT'S WHAT I HEARD. THE ENTIRE WORLD WAS WATCHING AS THE PIRATE KING WAS EXECUTED.
I DIDN'T GO.
THESE WERE HIS LAST WORDS...
I WON'T DIE...
... PARTNER.
THE WORLD GOVERNMENT AND THE NAVY WERE PROBABLY SURPRISED.
THOUGH THE PUBLIC EXECUTION WAS INTENDED TO SERVE AS AN EXAMPLE OF HOW PIRATES WOULD BE PUNISHED...
...THAT SINGLE STATEMENT BY ROGER RIGHT BEFORE HIS DEATH...
...CAUSED THE BEGINNING OF THE GREAT AGE OF PIRATES INSTEAD!

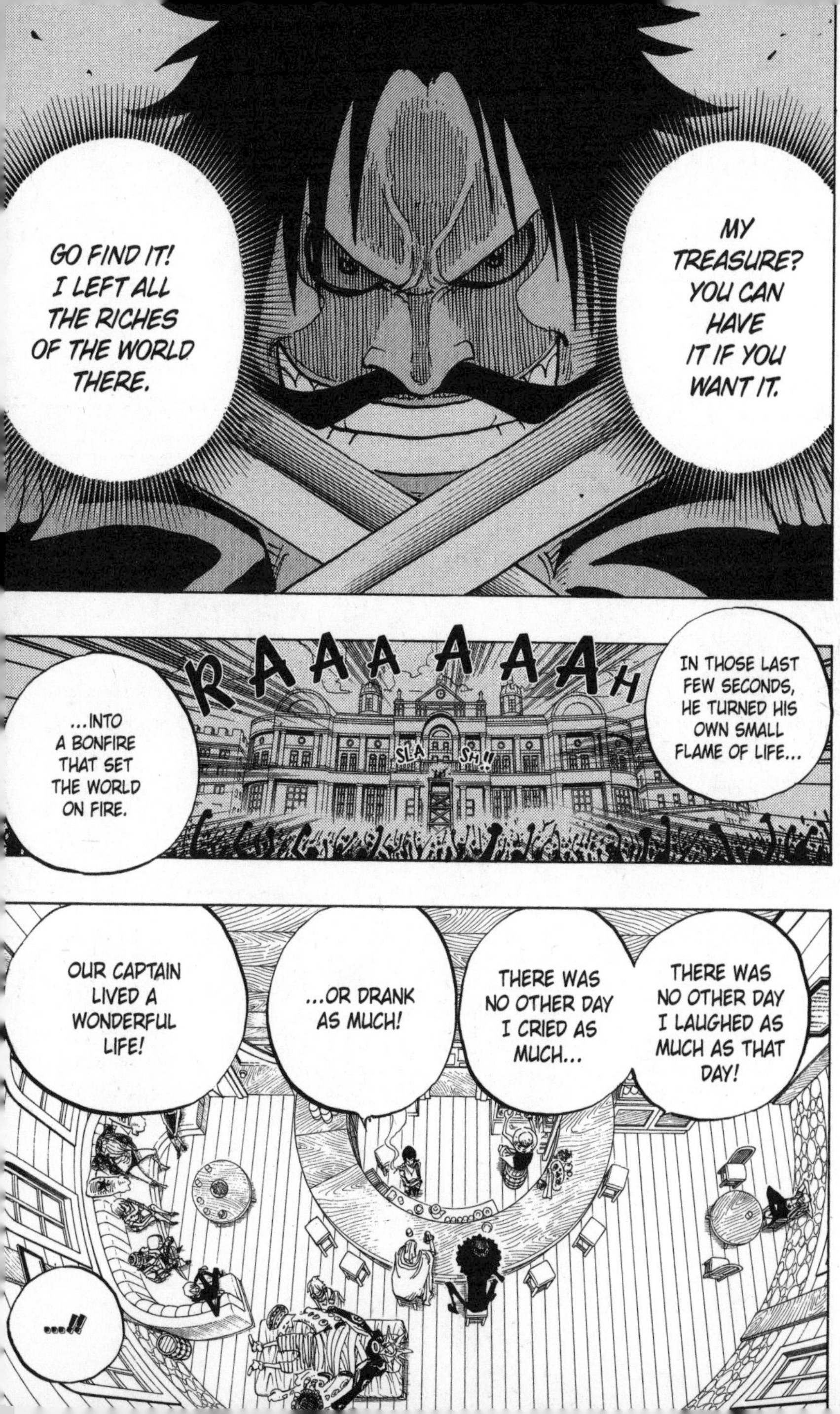

MY TREASURE? YOU CAN HAVE IT IF YOU WANT IT.
GO FIND IT! I LEFT ALL THE RICHES OF THE WORLD THERE.
IN THOSE LAST FEW SECONDS, HE TURNED HIS OWN SMALL FLAME OF LIFE...
RAAAAAAH
SLASH!!
...INTO A BONFIRE THAT SET THE WORLD ON FIRE.
THERE WAS NO OTHER DAY I LAUGHED AS MUCH AS THAT DAY!
THERE WAS NO OTHER DAY I CRIED AS MUCH...
...OR DRANK AS MUCH!
OUR CAPTAIN LIVED A WONDERFUL LIFE!
...!!

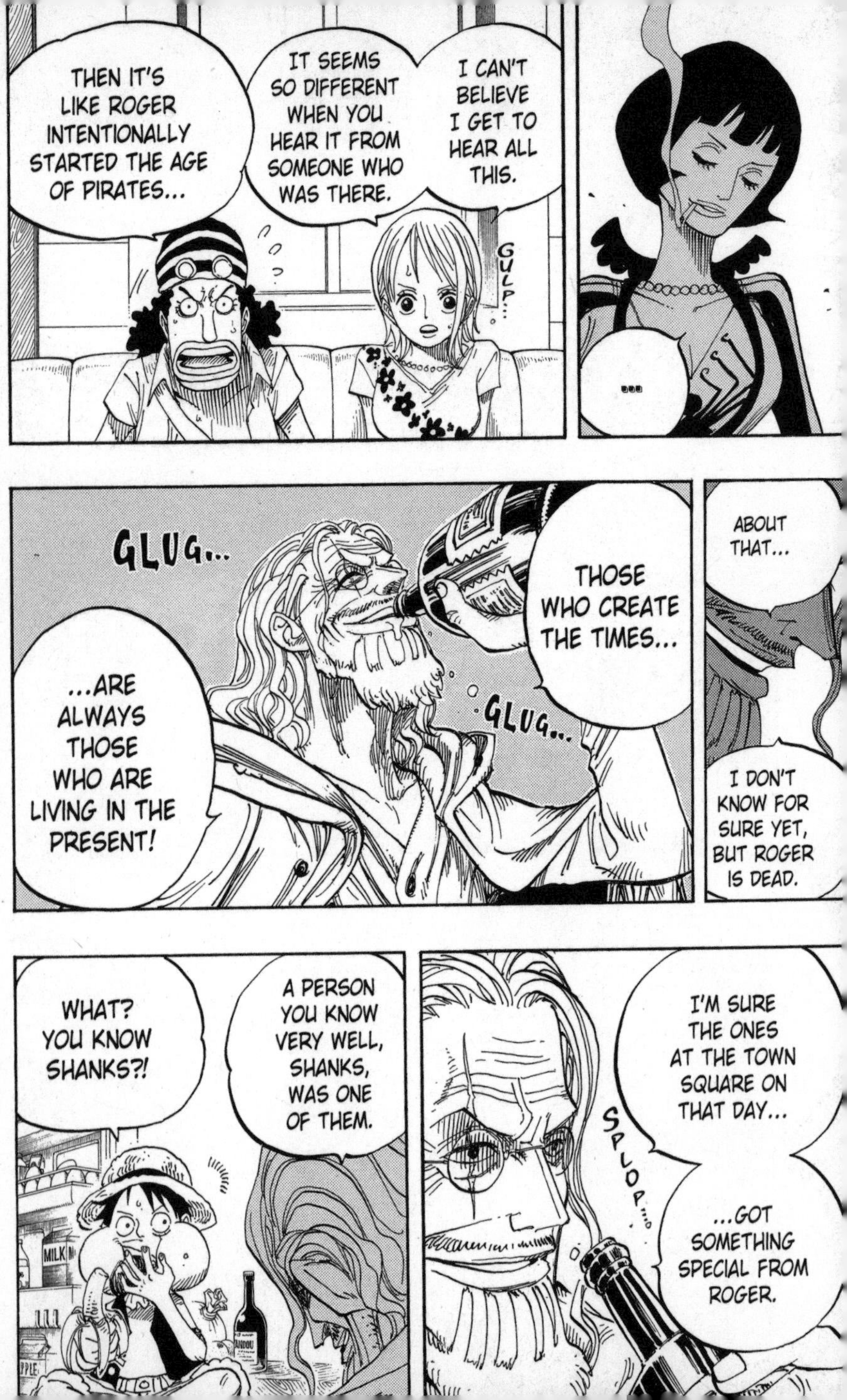
...
I CAN'T BELIEVE I GET TO HEAR ALL THIS.
GULP...
IT SEEMS SO DIFFERENT WHEN YOU HEAR IT FROM SOMEONE WHO WAS THERE.
THEN IT'S LIKE ROGER INTENTIONALLY STARTED THE AGE OF PIRATES...
ABOUT THAT...
I DON'T KNOW FOR SURE YET, BUT ROGER IS DEAD.
THOSE WHO CREATE THE TIMES...
GLUG...
GLUG...
...ARE ALWAYS THOSE WHO ARE LIVING IN THE PRESENT!
I'M SURE THE ONES AT THE TOWN SQUARE ON THAT DAY...
SPLOOP...
...GOT SOMETHING SPECIAL FROM ROGER.
A PERSON YOU KNOW VERY WELL, SHANKS, WAS ONE OF THEM.
WHAT? YOU KNOW SHANKS?!
MILK

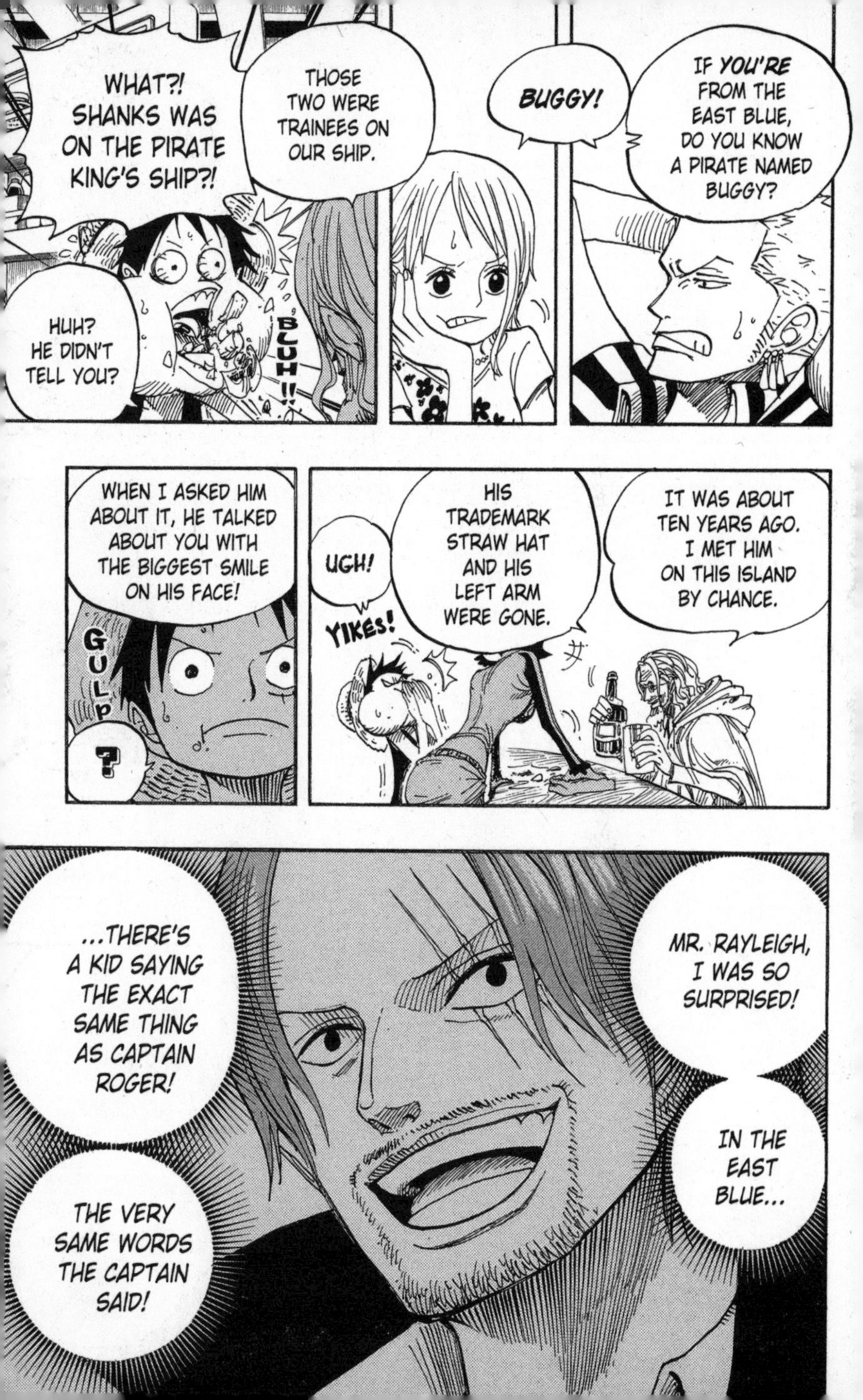
IF YOU'RE FROM THE EAST BLUE, DO YOU KNOW A PIRATE NAMED BUGGY?
BUGGY!
THOSE TWO WERE TRAINEES ON OUR SHIP.
WHAT?! SHANKS WAS ON THE PIRATE KING'S SHIP?!
BLUH!!
HUH? HE DIDN'T TELL YOU?
IT WAS ABOUT TEN YEARS AGO. I MET HIM ON THIS ISLAND BY CHANCE.
HIS TRADEMARK STRAW HAT AND HIS LEFT ARM WERE GONE.
UGH!
YIKES!
WHEN I ASKED HIM ABOUT IT, HE TALKED ABOUT YOU WITH THE BIGGEST SMILE ON HIS FACE!
GULP
?
MR. RAYLEIGH, I WAS SO SURPRISED!
IN THE EAST BLUE...
...THERE'S A KID SAYING THE EXACT SAME THING AS CAPTAIN ROGER!
THE VERY SAME WORDS THE CAPTAIN SAID!

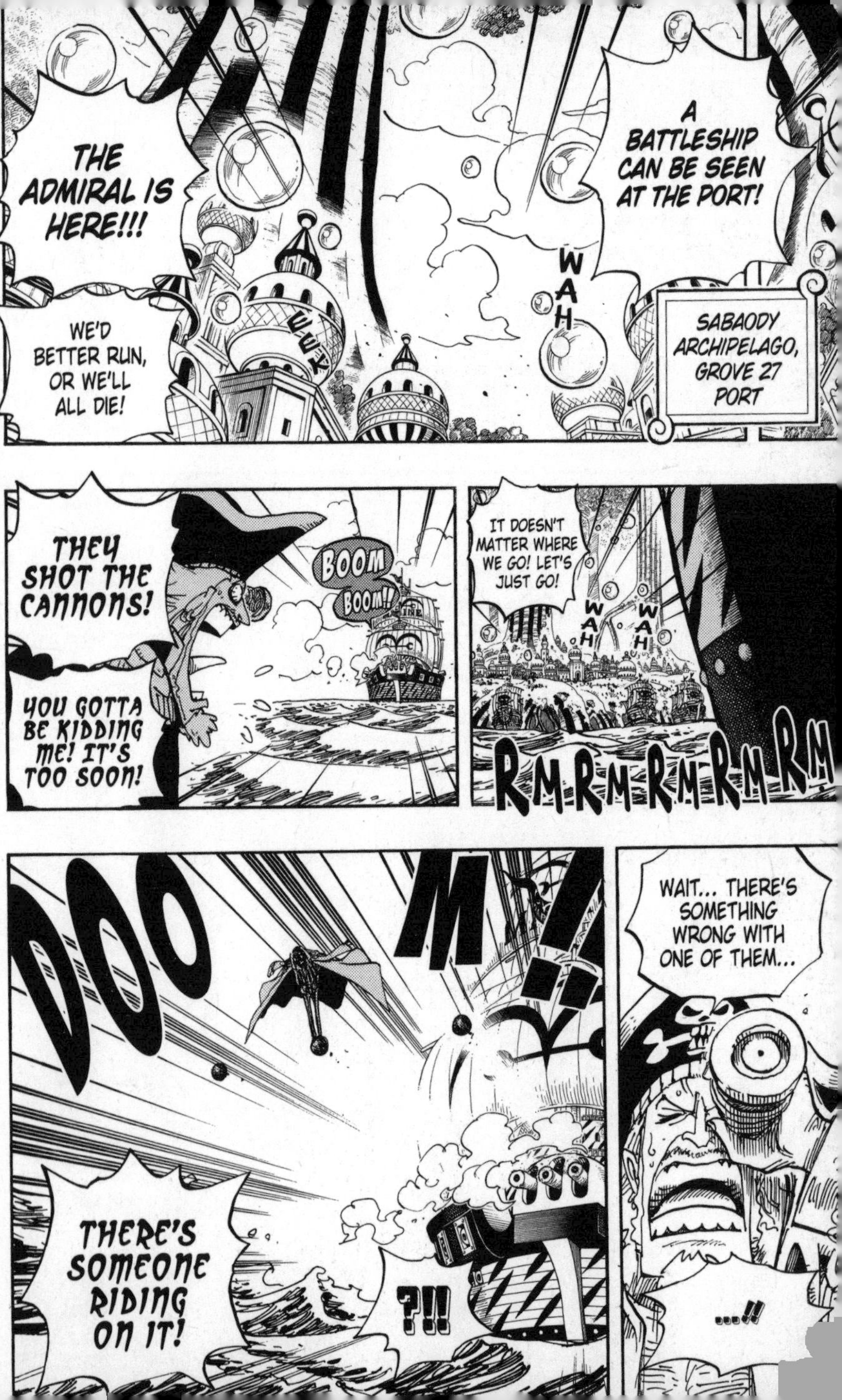
A BATTLESHIP CAN BE SEEN AT THE PORT!
WAH
SABAODY ARCHIPELAGO, GROVE 27 PORT
THE ADMIRAL IS HERE!!!
WE'D BETTER RUN, OR WE'LL ALL DIE!
IT DOESN'T MATTER WHERE WE GO! LET'S JUST GO!
WAH
WAH
RMRMRMRMRMRM
THEY SHOT THE CANNONS!
BOOM
BOOM!!
YOU GOTTA BE KIDDING ME! IT'S TOO SOON!
WAIT... THERE'S SOMETHING WRONG WITH ONE OF THEM...
...!!
DOOM!!
THERE'S SOMEONE RIDING ON IT!
?!!

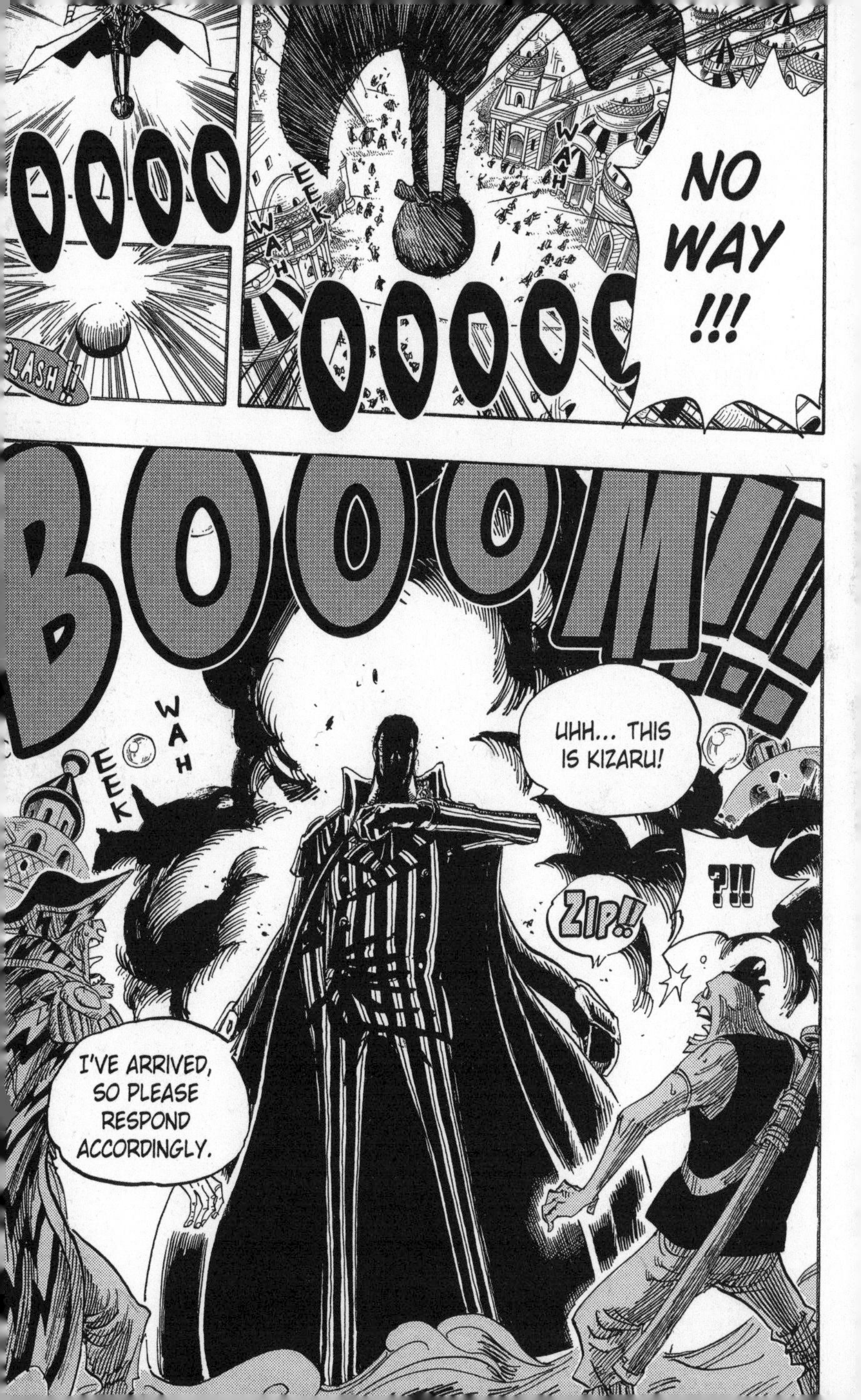
NO WAY!!!
WAH
EEK
WAH
OOOOO
OOOO
FLASH!!
BOOOM!!
UHH... THIS IS KIZARU!
?!!
ZIP!!
WAH
EEK
I'VE ARRIVED, SO PLEASE RESPOND ACCORDINGLY.

Chapter 507: KIZARU ARRIVES

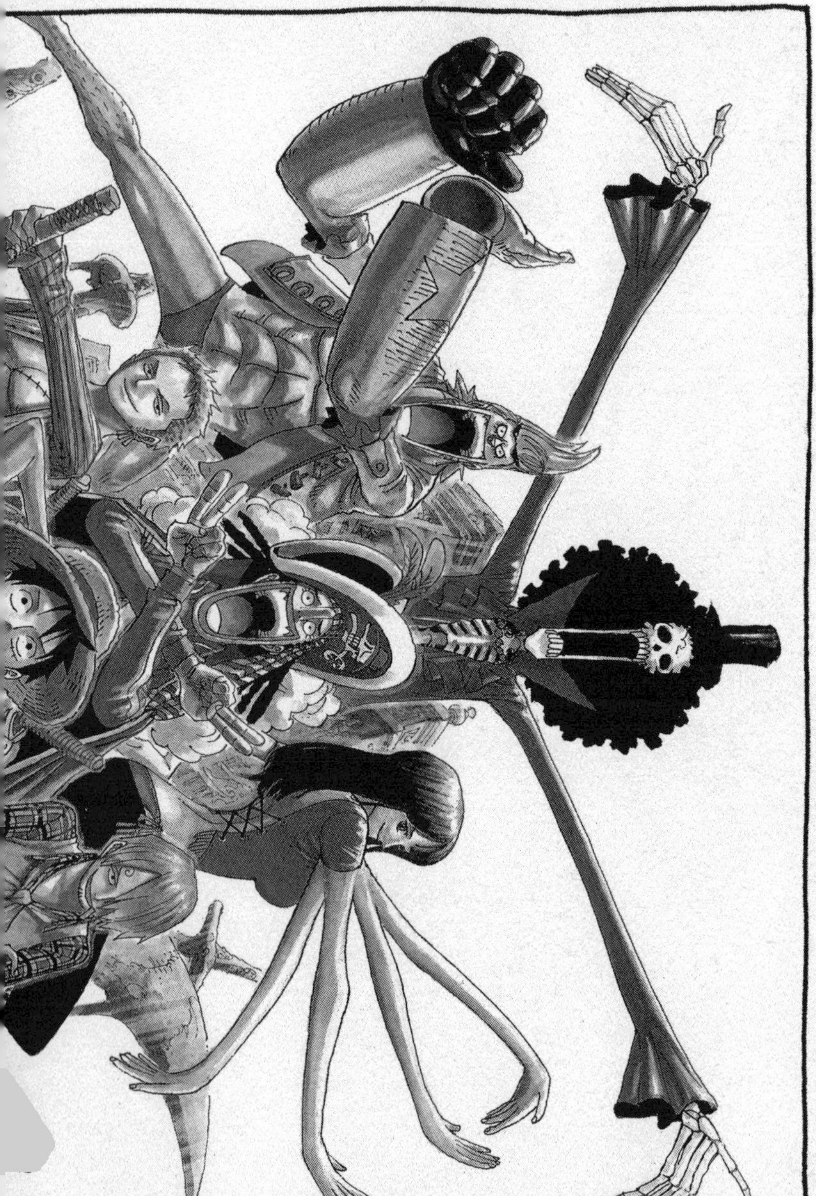

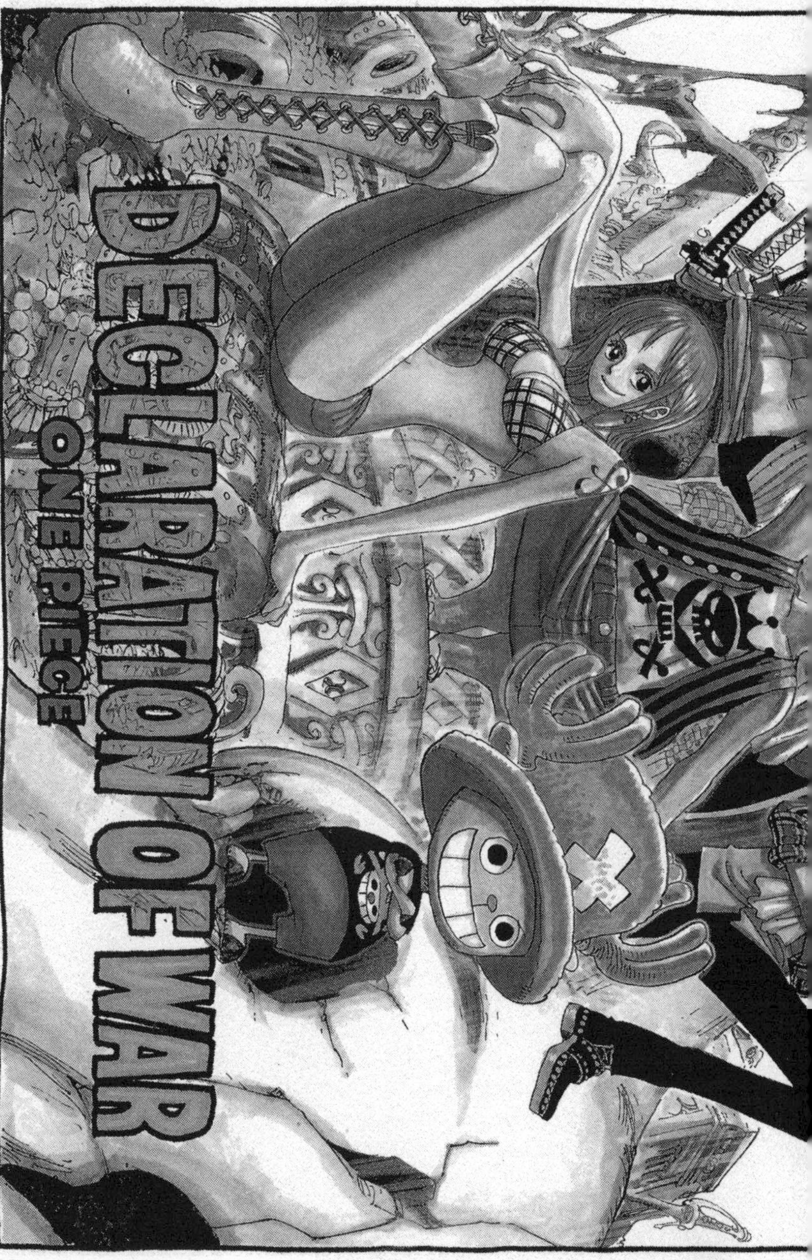
DECLARATION OF WAR
ONE PIECE

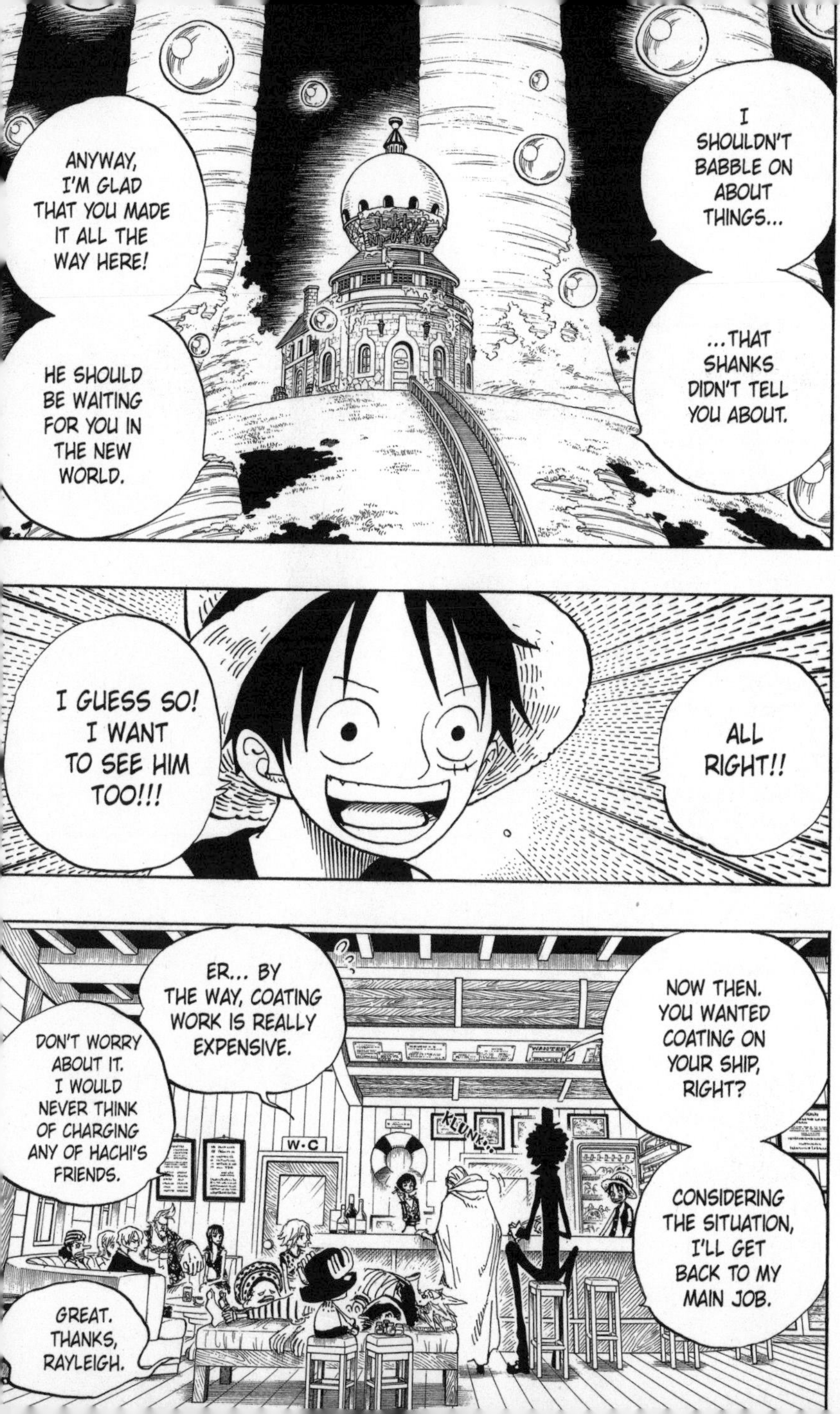
I SHOULDN'T BABBLE ON ABOUT THINGS...
...THAT SHANKS DIDN'T TELL YOU ABOUT.
ANYWAY, I'M GLAD THAT YOU MADE IT ALL THE WAY HERE!
HE SHOULD BE WAITING FOR YOU IN THE NEW WORLD.
ALL RIGHT!!
I GUESS SO! I WANT TO SEE HIM TOO!!!
NOW THEN. YOU WANTED COATING ON YOUR SHIP, RIGHT?
CONSIDERING THE SITUATION, I'LL GET BACK TO MY MAIN JOB.
ER... BY THE WAY, COATING WORK IS REALLY EXPENSIVE.
DON'T WORRY ABOUT IT. I WOULD NEVER THINK OF CHARGING ANY OF HACHI'S FRIENDS.
KLUNK!!
W·C
GREAT. THANKS, RAYLEIGH.

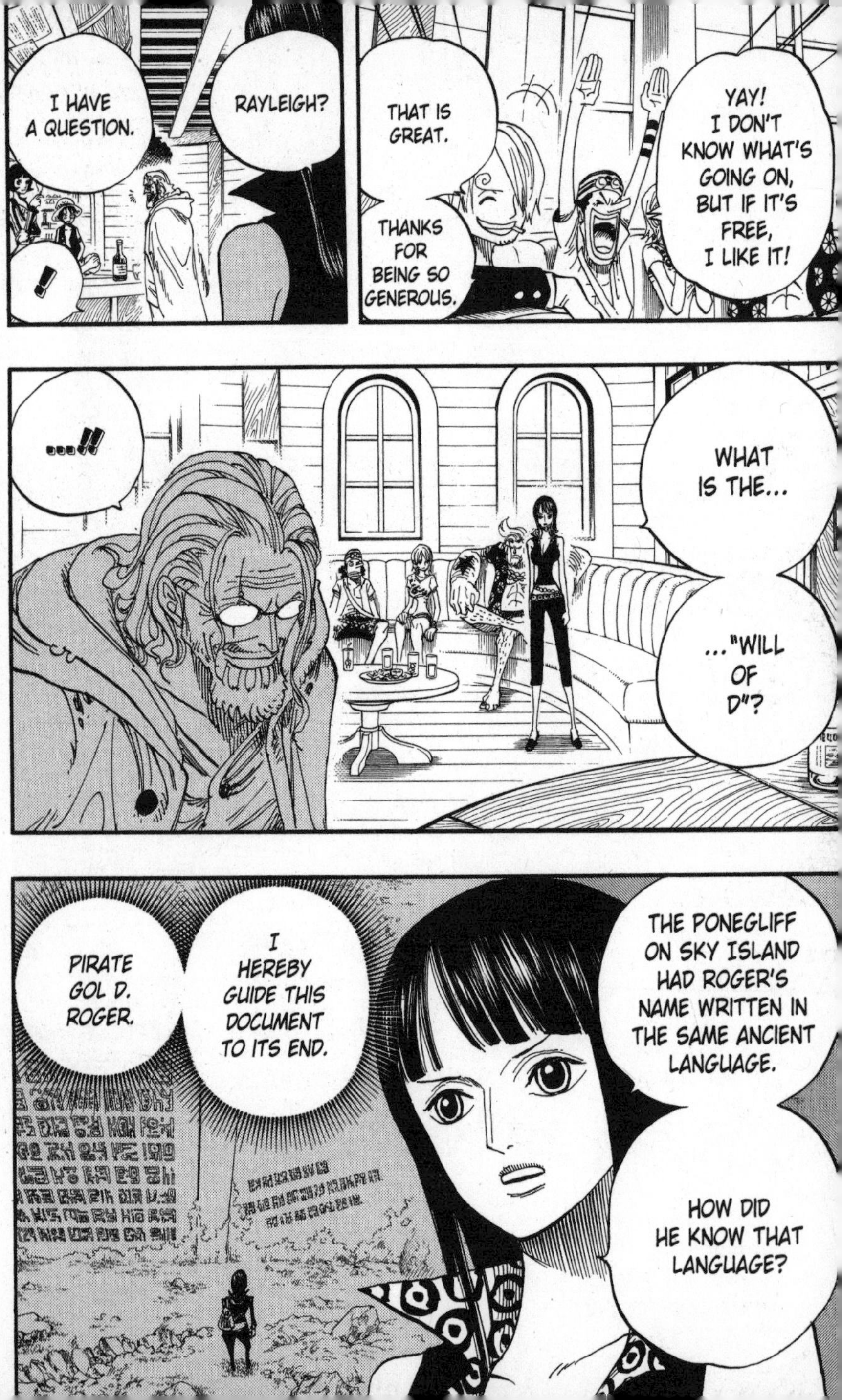
YAY! I DON'T KNOW WHAT'S GOING ON, BUT IF IT'S FREE, I LIKE IT!
THAT IS GREAT.
THANKS FOR BEING SO GENEROUS.
RAYLEIGH?
I HAVE A QUESTION.
!
WHAT IS THE...
..."WILL OF D"?
...!!
THE PONEGLIFF ON SKY ISLAND HAD ROGER'S NAME WRITTEN IN THE SAME ANCIENT LANGUAGE.
HOW DID HE KNOW THAT LANGUAGE?
I HEREBY GUIDE THIS DOCUMENT TO ITS END.
PIRATE GOL D. ROGER.

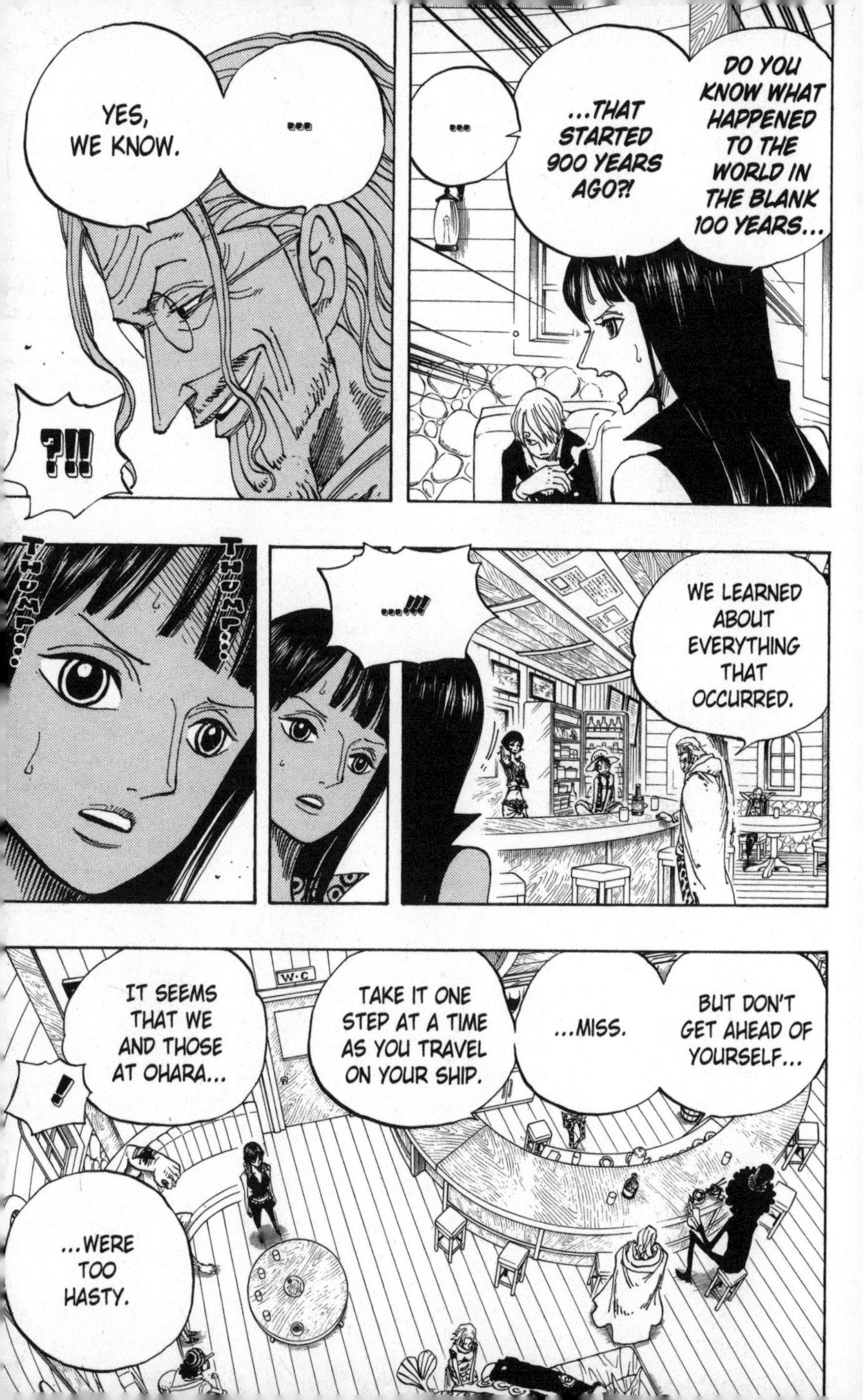
DO YOU KNOW WHAT HAPPENED TO THE WORLD IN THE BLANK 100 YEARS...
...THAT STARTED 900 YEARS AGO?!
...
...
YES, WE KNOW.
?!!
WE LEARNED ABOUT EVERYTHING THAT OCCURRED.
...!!!
THUMP...
THUMP...
BUT DON'T GET AHEAD OF YOURSELF...
...MISS.
TAKE IT ONE STEP AT A TIME AS YOU TRAVEL ON YOUR SHIP.
W·C
IT SEEMS THAT WE AND THOSE AT OHARA...
!
...WERE TOO HASTY.

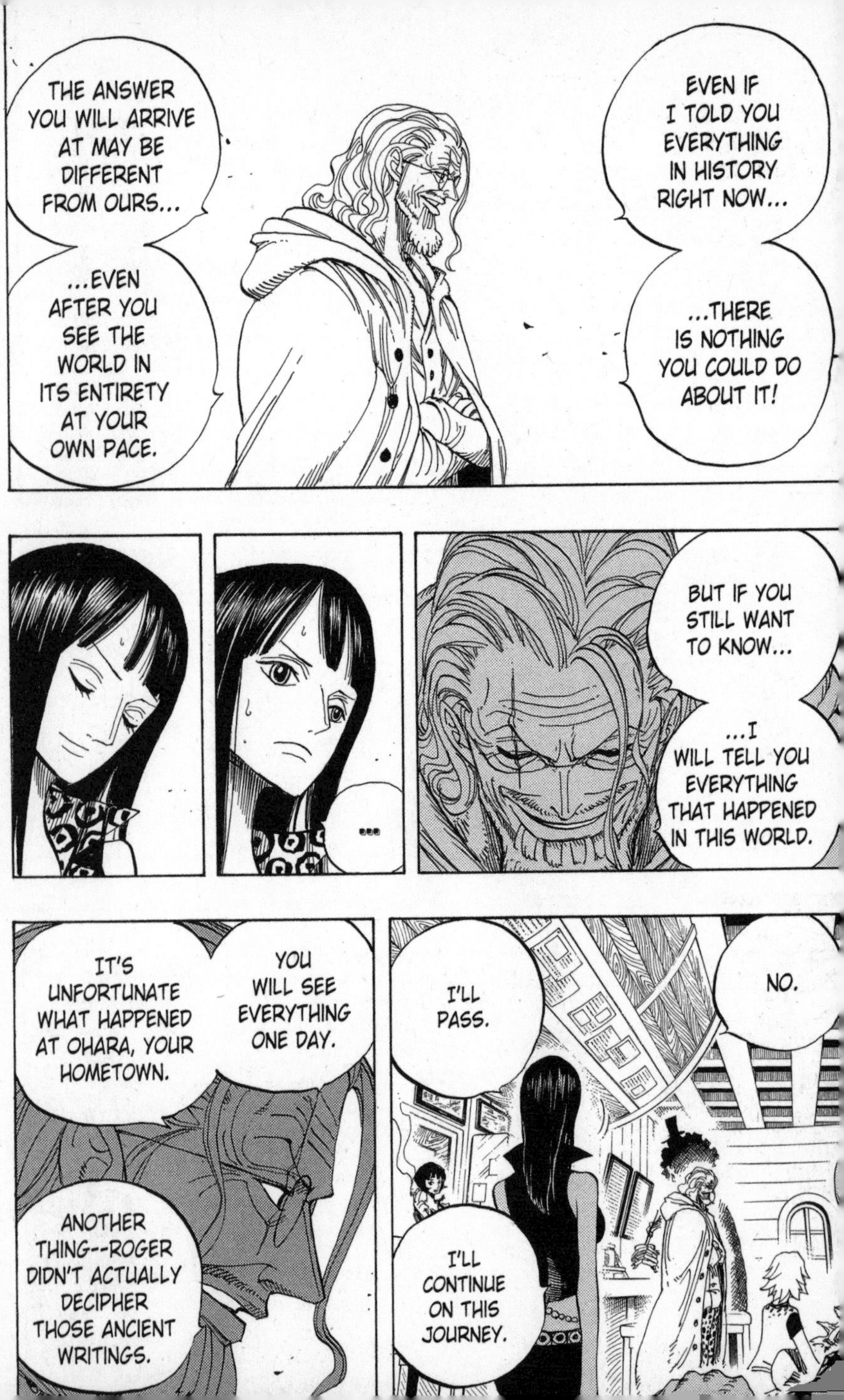
EVEN IF I TOLD YOU EVERYTHING IN HISTORY RIGHT NOW...
...THERE IS NOTHING YOU COULD DO ABOUT IT!
THE ANSWER YOU WILL ARRIVE AT MAY BE DIFFERENT FROM OURS...
...EVEN AFTER YOU SEE THE WORLD IN ITS ENTIRETY AT YOUR OWN PACE.
BUT IF YOU STILL WANT TO KNOW...
...I WILL TELL YOU EVERYTHING THAT HAPPENED IN THIS WORLD.
...
NO.
I'LL PASS.
I'LL CONTINUE ON THIS JOURNEY.
YOU WILL SEE EVERYTHING ONE DAY.
IT'S UNFORTUNATE WHAT HAPPENED AT OHARA, YOUR HOMETOWN.
ANOTHER THING--ROGER DIDN'T ACTUALLY DECIPHER THOSE ANCIENT WRITINGS.

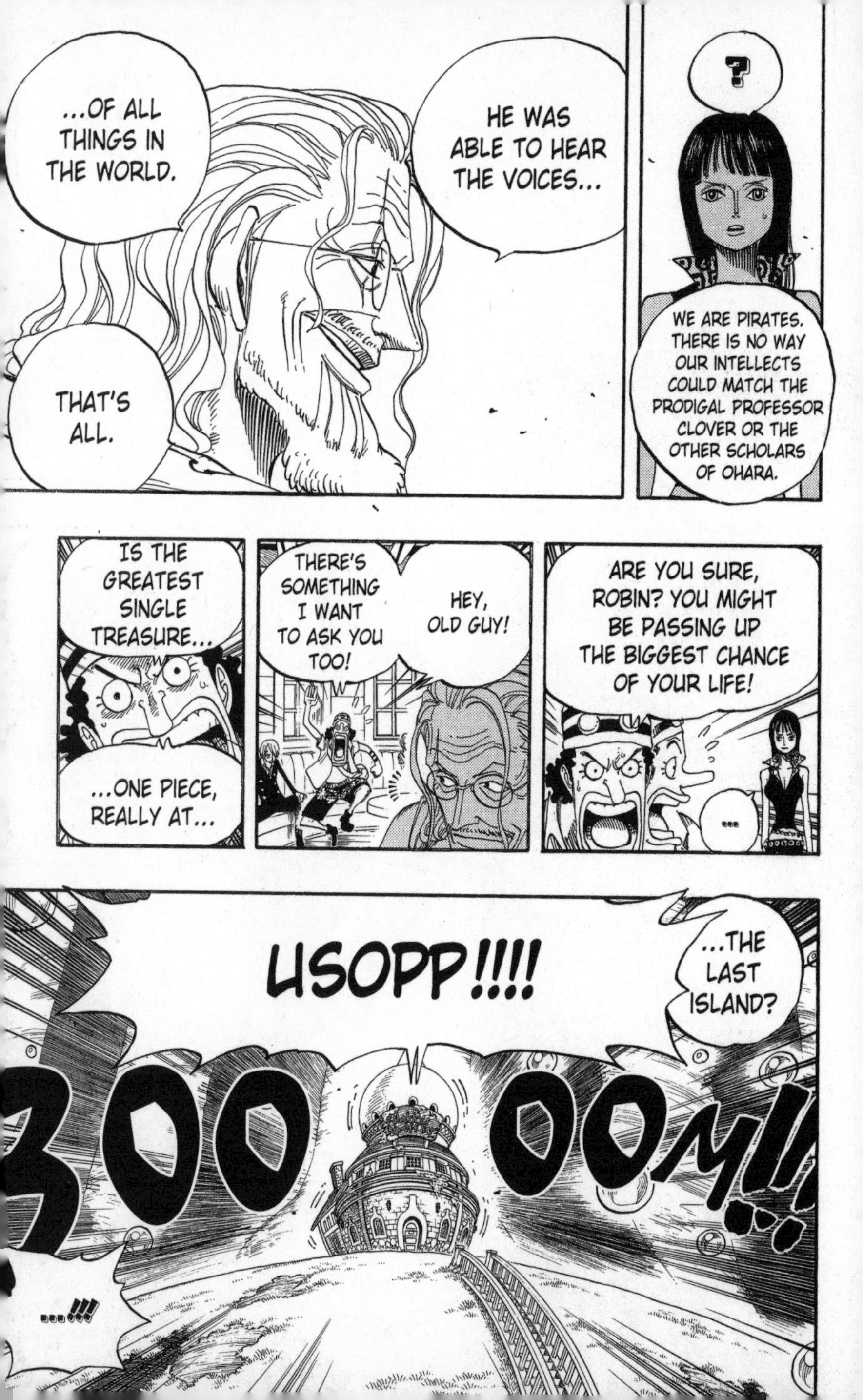
?
WE ARE PIRATES. THERE IS NO WAY OUR INTELLECTS COULD MATCH THE PRODIGAL PROFESSOR CLOVER OR THE OTHER SCHOLARS OF OHARA.
HE WAS ABLE TO HEAR THE VOICES...
...OF ALL THINGS IN THE WORLD.
THAT'S ALL.
ARE YOU SURE, ROBIN? YOU MIGHT BE PASSING UP THE BIGGEST CHANCE OF YOUR LIFE!
...
HEY, OLD GUY!
THERE'S SOMETHING I WANT TO ASK YOU TOO!
IS THE GREATEST SINGLE TREASURE...
...ONE PIECE, REALLY AT...
...THE LAST ISLAND?
USOPP!!!!
BOOOOM!!
...!!!

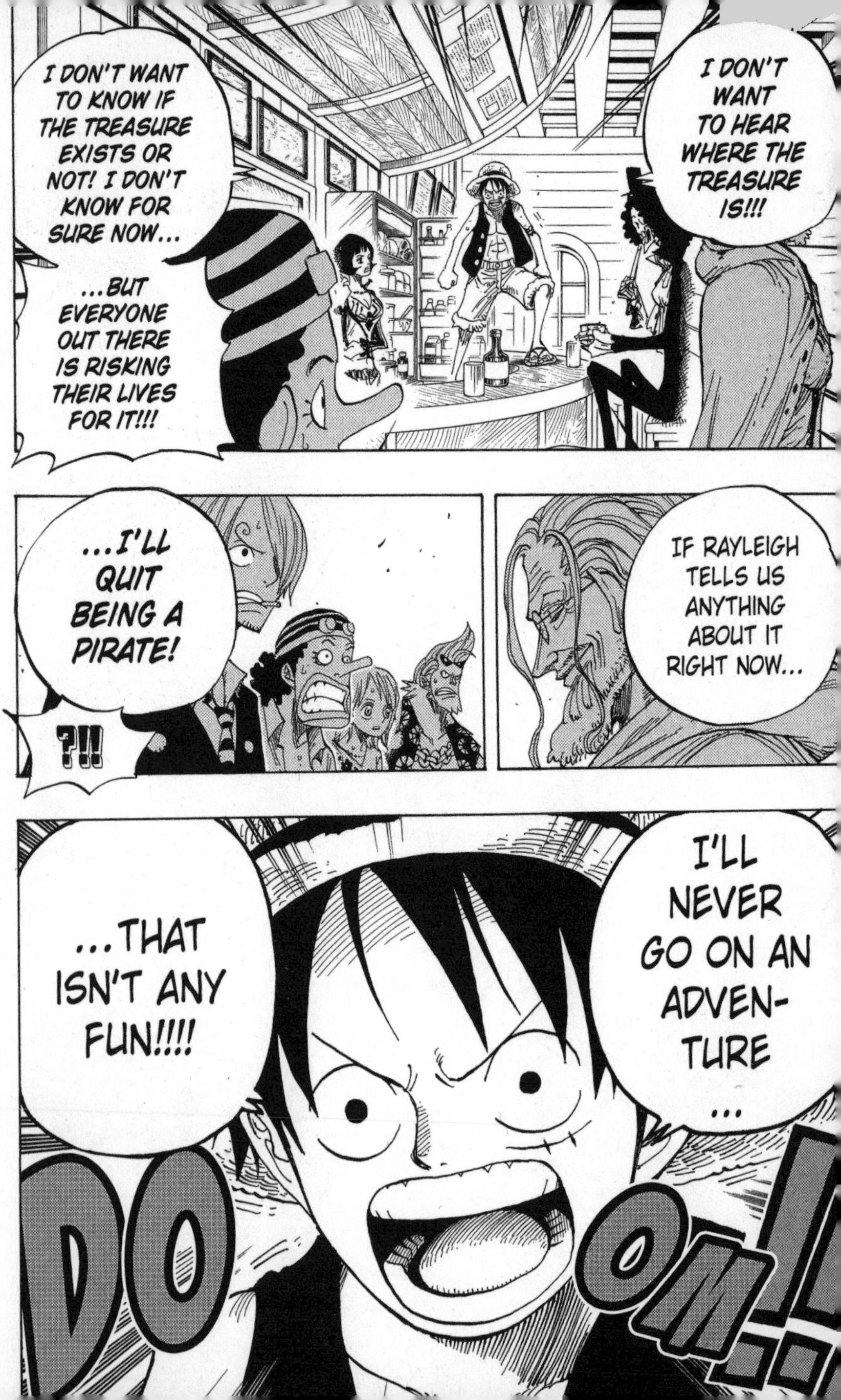
I DON'T WANT TO HEAR WHERE THE TREASURE IS!!!
I DON'T WANT TO KNOW IF THE TREASURE EXISTS OR NOT! I DON'T KNOW FOR SURE NOW...
...BUT EVERYONE OUT THERE IS RISKING THEIR LIVES FOR IT!!!
IF RAYLEIGH TELLS US ANYTHING ABOUT IT RIGHT NOW...
...I'LL QUIT BEING A PIRATE!
?!!
I'LL NEVER GO ON AN ADVEN-TURE ...
...THAT ISN'T ANY FUN!!!!
DO
ON!!

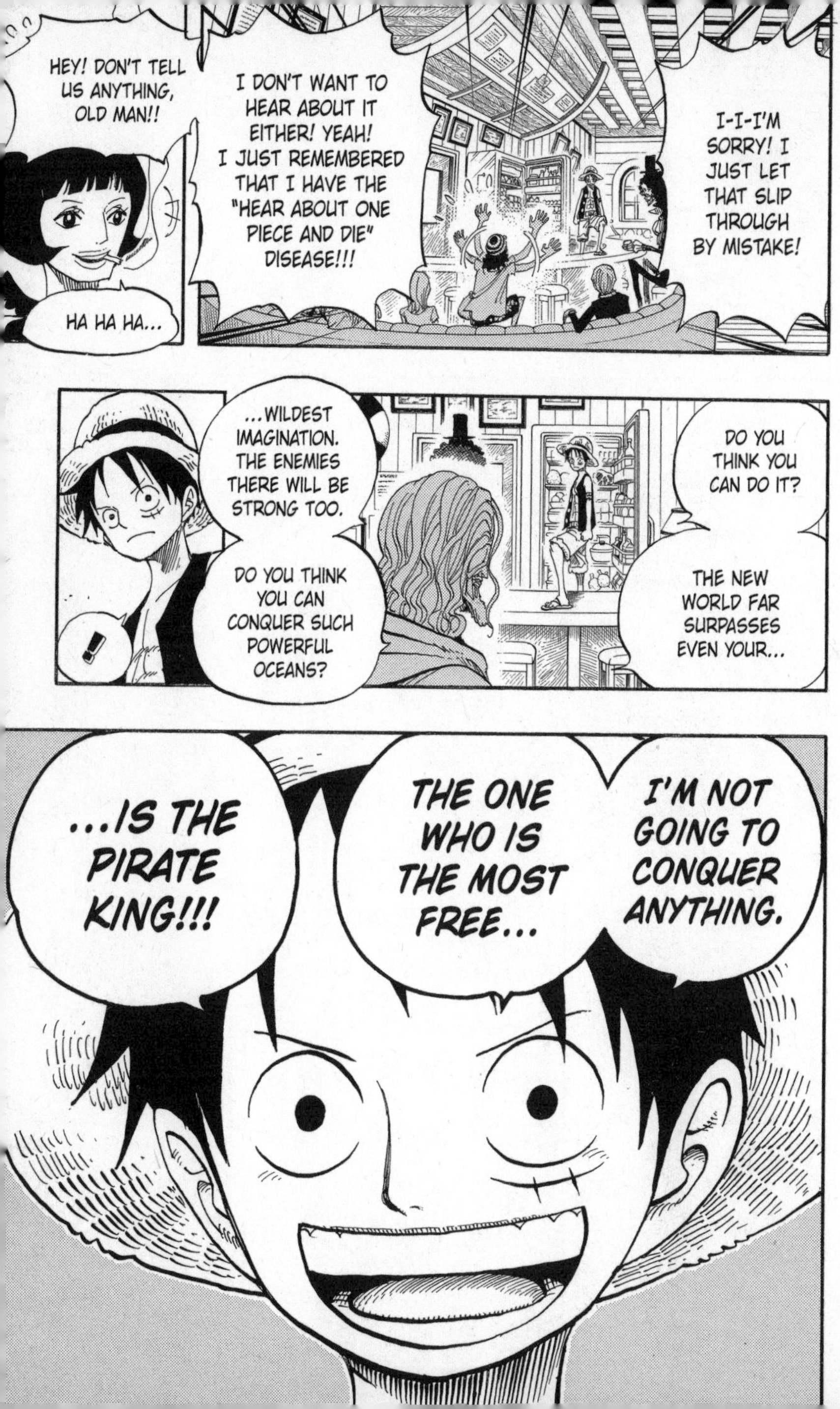
HEY! DON'T TELL US ANYTHING, OLD MAN!!
I DON'T WANT TO HEAR ABOUT IT EITHER! YEAH! I JUST REMEMBERED THAT I HAVE THE "HEAR ABOUT ONE PIECE AND DIE" DISEASE!!!
I-I-I'M SORRY! I JUST LET THAT SLIP THROUGH BY MISTAKE!
HA HA HA...
DO YOU THINK YOU CAN DO IT?
THE NEW WORLD FAR SURPASSES EVEN YOUR...
...WILDEST IMAGINATION. THE ENEMIES THERE WILL BE STRONG TOO.
DO YOU THINK YOU CAN CONQUER SUCH POWERFUL OCEANS?
!
I'M NOT GOING TO CONQUER ANYTHING.
THE ONE WHO IS THE MOST FREE...
...IS THE PIRATE KING!!!

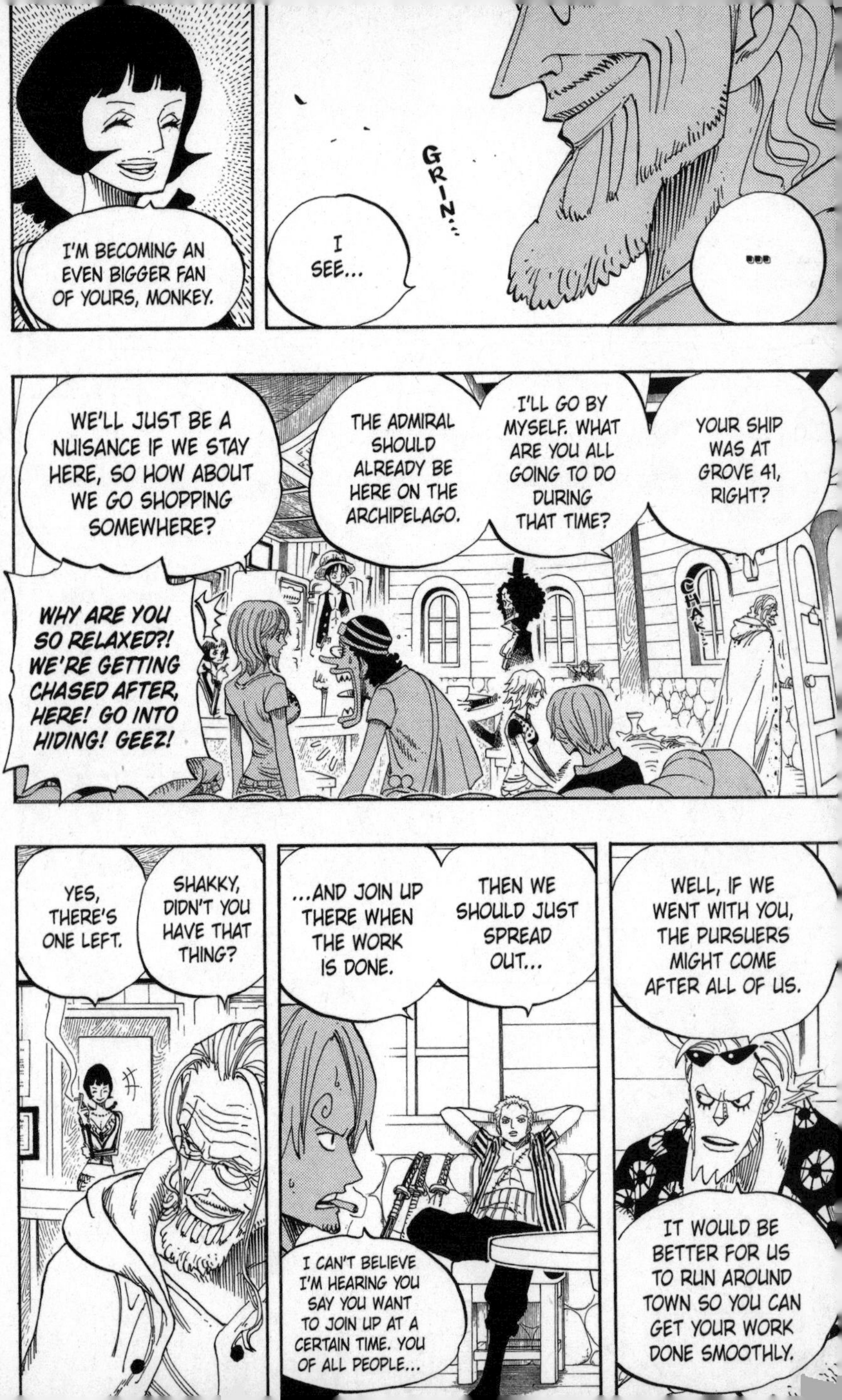
...
GRIN...
I SEE...
I'M BECOMING AN EVEN BIGGER FAN OF YOURS, MONKEY.
YOUR SHIP WAS AT GROVE 41, RIGHT?
I'LL GO BY MYSELF. WHAT ARE YOU ALL GOING TO DO DURING THAT TIME?
THE ADMIRAL SHOULD ALREADY BE HERE ON THE ARCHIPELAGO.
WE'LL JUST BE A NUISANCE IF WE STAY HERE, SO HOW ABOUT WE GO SHOPPING SOMEWHERE?
CHAK...
WHY ARE YOU SO RELAXED?! WE'RE GETTING CHASED AFTER, HERE! GO INTO HIDING! GEEZ!
WELL, IF WE WENT WITH YOU, THE PURSUERS MIGHT COME AFTER ALL OF US.
IT WOULD BE BETTER FOR US TO RUN AROUND TOWN SO YOU CAN GET YOUR WORK DONE SMOOTHLY.
THEN WE SHOULD JUST SPREAD OUT...
...AND JOIN UP THERE WHEN THE WORK IS DONE.
I CAN'T BELIEVE I'M HEARING YOU SAY YOU WANT TO JOIN UP AT A CERTAIN TIME. YOU OF ALL PEOPLE...
SHAKKY, DIDN'T YOU HAVE THAT THING?
YES, THERE'S ONE LEFT.

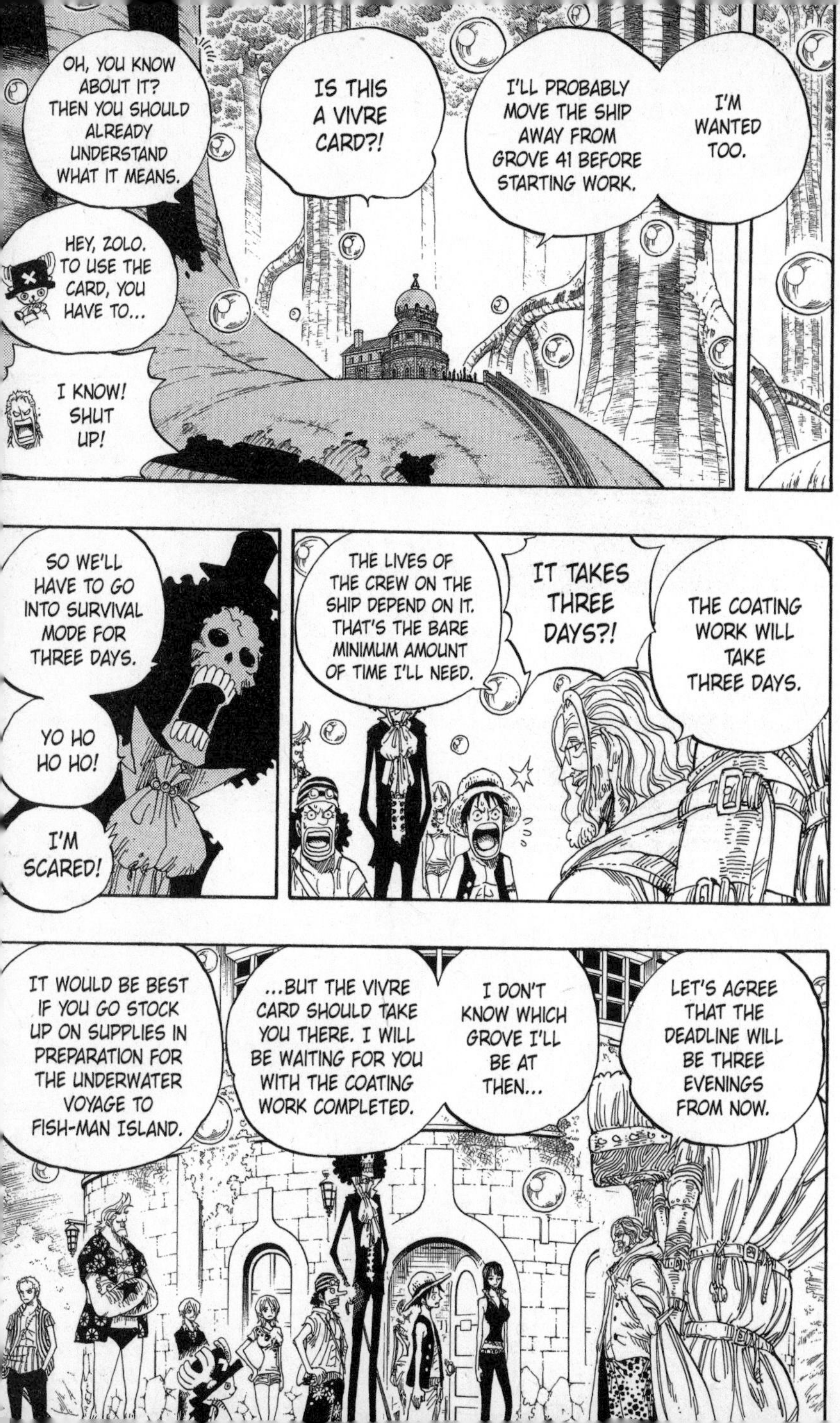
I'M WANTED TOO.
I'LL PROBABLY MOVE THE SHIP AWAY FROM GROVE 41 BEFORE STARTING WORK.
IS THIS A VIVRE CARD?!
OH, YOU KNOW ABOUT IT? THEN YOU SHOULD ALREADY UNDERSTAND WHAT IT MEANS.
HEY, ZOLO. TO USE THE CARD, YOU HAVE TO...
I KNOW! SHUT UP!
THE COATING WORK WILL TAKE THREE DAYS.
IT TAKES THREE DAYS?!
THE LIVES OF THE CREW ON THE SHIP DEPEND ON IT. THAT'S THE BARE MINIMUM AMOUNT OF TIME I'LL NEED.
SO WE'LL HAVE TO GO INTO SURVIVAL MODE FOR THREE DAYS.
YO HO HO HO!
I'M SCARED!
LET'S AGREE THAT THE DEADLINE WILL BE THREE EVENINGS FROM NOW.
I DON'T KNOW WHICH GROVE I'LL BE AT THEN...
...BUT THE VIVRE CARD SHOULD TAKE YOU THERE. I WILL BE WAITING FOR YOU WITH THE COATING WORK COMPLETED.
IT WOULD BE BEST IF YOU GO STOCK UP ON SUPPLIES IN PREPARATION FOR THE UNDERWATER VOYAGE TO FISH-MAN ISLAND.

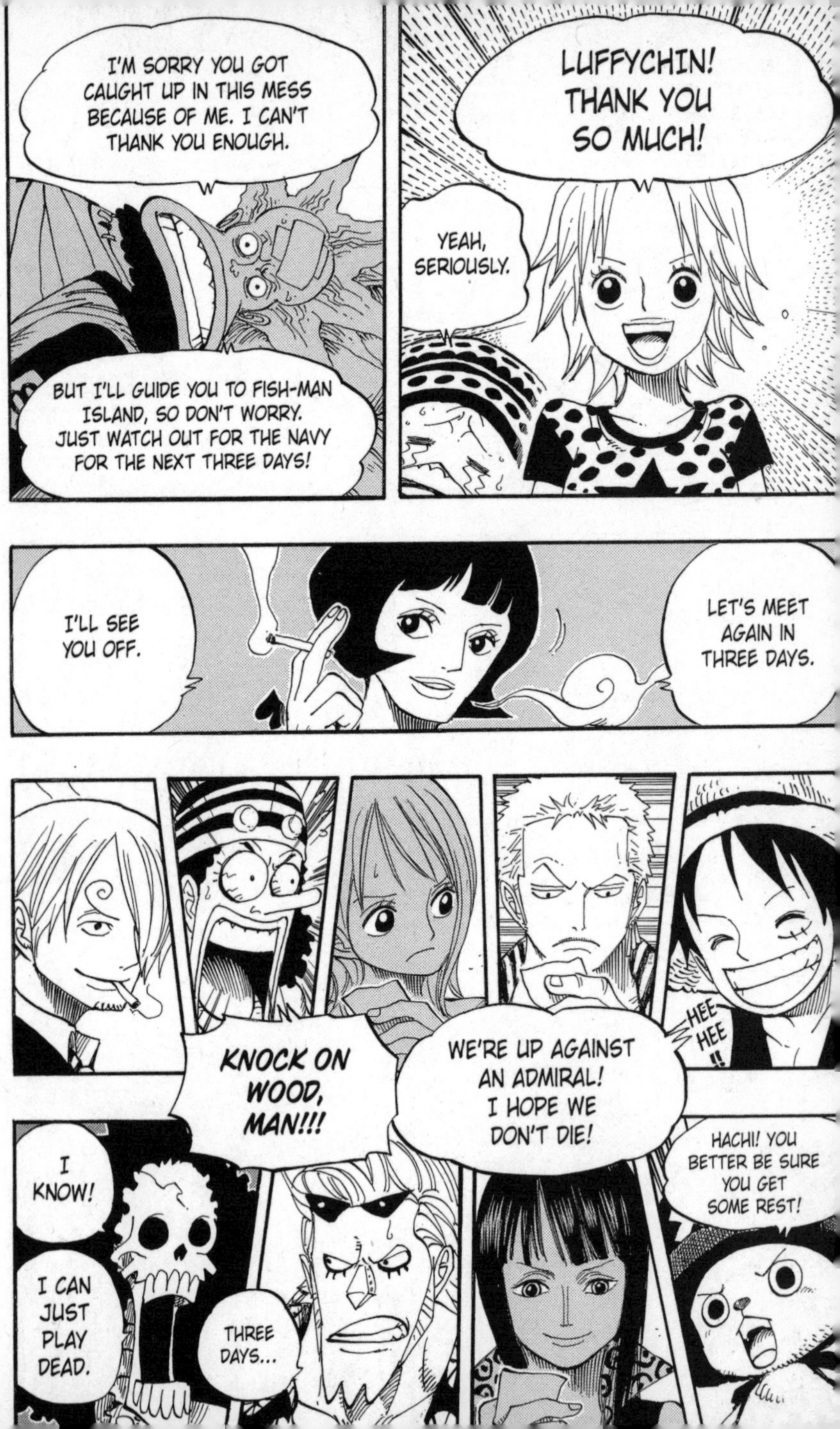
LUFFYCHIN! THANK YOU SO MUCH!
YEAH, SERIOUSLY.
I'M SORRY YOU GOT CAUGHT UP IN THIS MESS BECAUSE OF ME. I CAN'T THANK YOU ENOUGH.
BUT I'LL GUIDE YOU TO FISH-MAN ISLAND, SO DON'T WORRY. JUST WATCH OUT FOR THE NAVY FOR THE NEXT THREE DAYS!
LET'S MEET AGAIN IN THREE DAYS.
I'LL SEE YOU OFF.
HEE HEE!!
WE'RE UP AGAINST AN ADMIRAL! I HOPE WE DON'T DIE!
KNOCK ON WOOD, MAN!!!
HACHI! YOU BETTER BE SURE YOU GET SOME REST!
THREE DAYS...
I KNOW!
I CAN JUST PLAY DEAD.

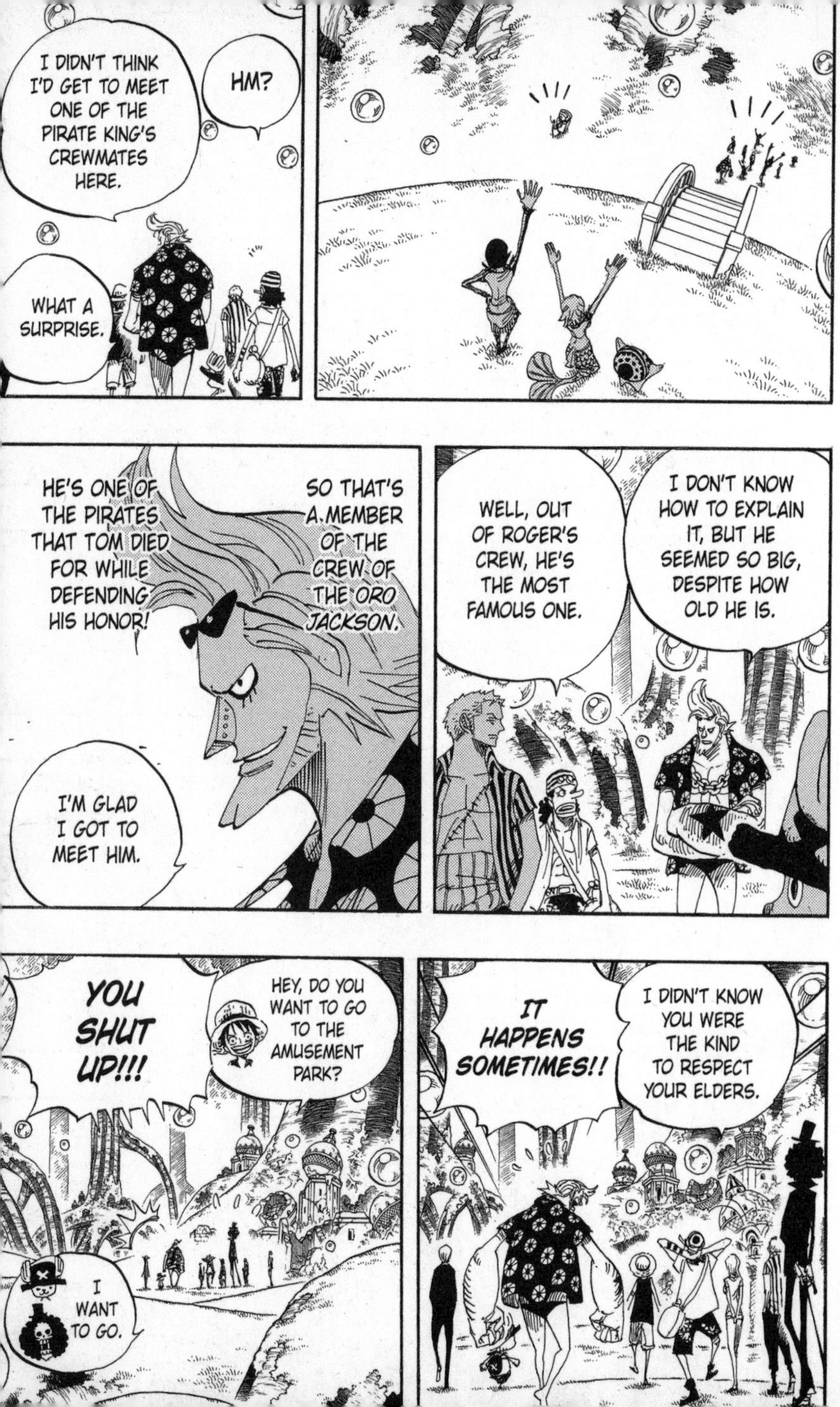
HM?
I DIDN'T THINK I'D GET TO MEET ONE OF THE PIRATE KING'S CREWMATES HERE.
WHAT A SURPRISE.
I DON'T KNOW HOW TO EXPLAIN IT, BUT HE SEEMED SO BIG, DESPITE HOW OLD HE IS.
WELL, OUT OF ROGER'S CREW, HE'S THE MOST FAMOUS ONE.
SO THAT'S A MEMBER OF THE CREW OF THE ORO JACKSON.
HE'S ONE OF THE PIRATES THAT TOM DIED FOR WHILE DEFENDING HIS HONOR!
I'M GLAD I GOT TO MEET HIM.
I DIDN'T KNOW YOU WERE THE KIND TO RESPECT YOUR ELDERS.
IT HAPPENS SOMETIMES!!
HEY, DO YOU WANT TO GO TO THE AMUSEMENT PARK?
YOU SHUT UP!!!
I WANT TO GO.

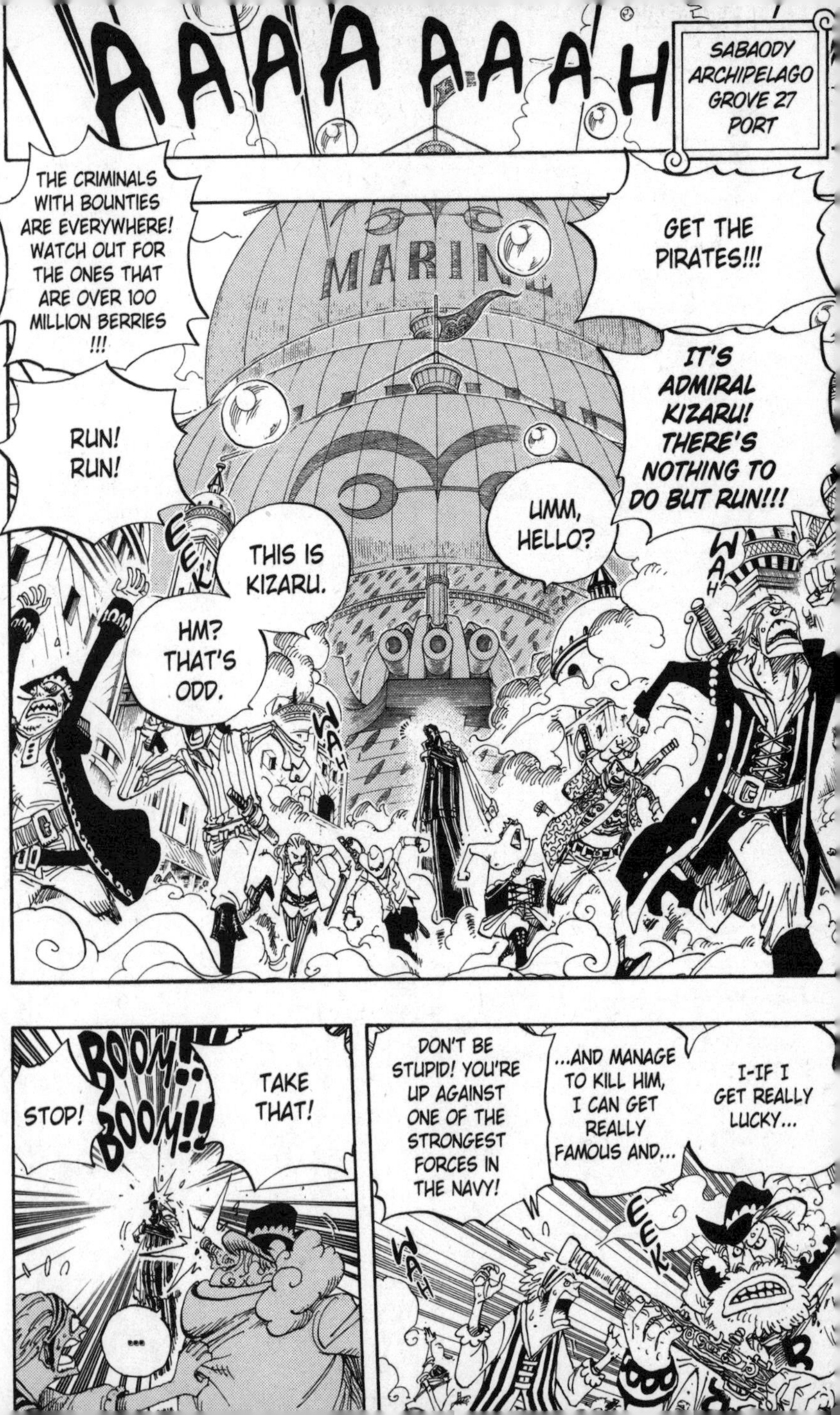
SABAODY ARCHIPELAGO GROVE 27 PORT
AAAAAAAH
GET THE PIRATES!!!
THE CRIMINALS WITH BOUNTIES ARE EVERYWHERE! WATCH OUT FOR THE ONES THAT ARE OVER 100 MILLION BERRIES !!!
IT'S ADMIRAL KIZARU! THERE'S NOTHING TO DO BUT RUN!!!
RUN! RUN!
WAH
UMM, HELLO?
THIS IS KIZARU.
EEK
HM? THAT'S ODD.
WAH
I-IF I GET REALLY LUCKY...
...AND MANAGE TO KILL HIM, I CAN GET REALLY FAMOUS AND...
DON'T BE STUPID! YOU'RE UP AGAINST ONE OF THE STRONGEST FORCES IN THE NAVY!
EEK
WAH
R
TAKE THAT!
BOOM!! BOOM!!
STOP!
...

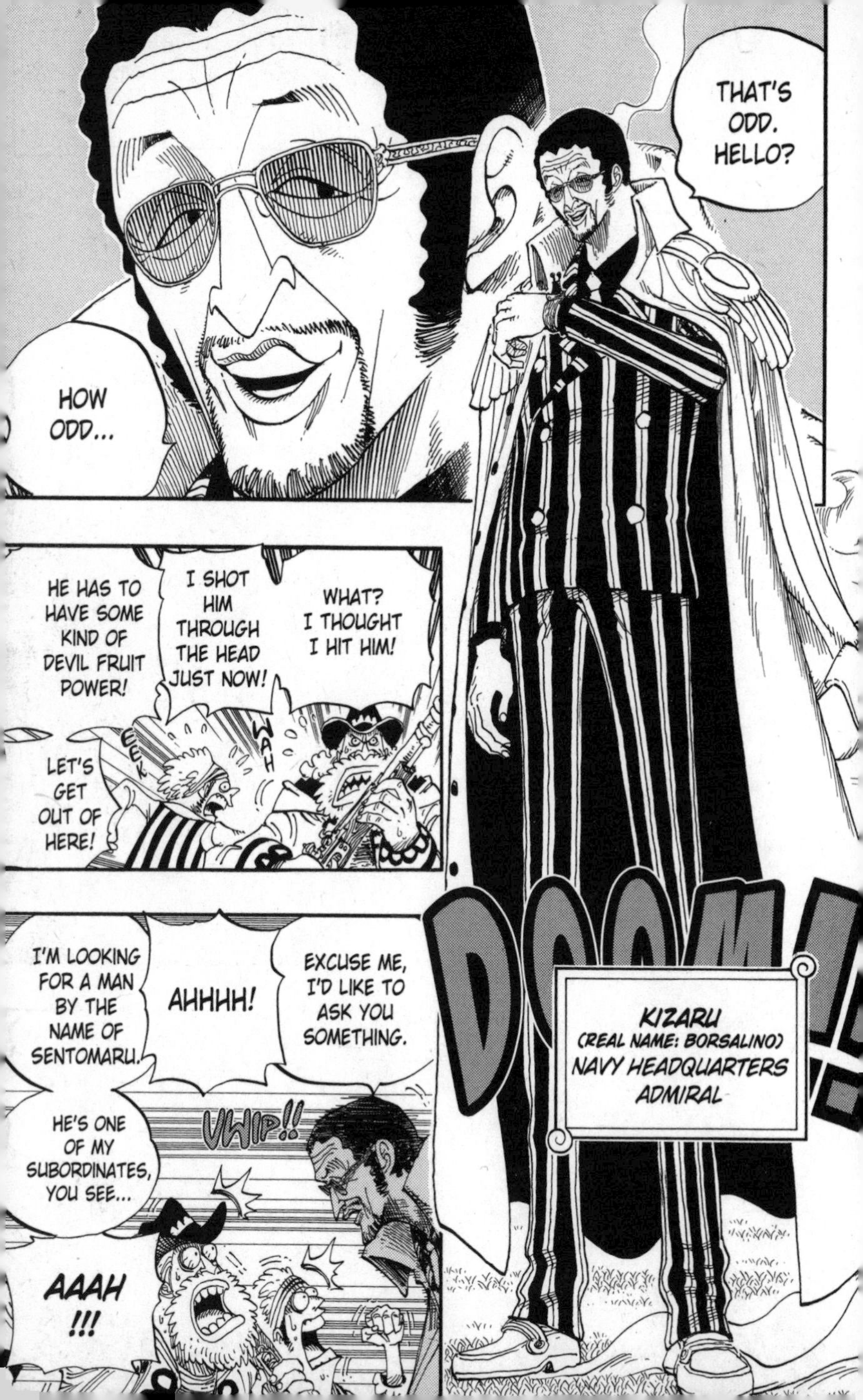
THAT'S ODD. HELLO?
DOOM!!
KIZARU (REAL NAME: BORSALINO) NAVY HEADQUARTERS ADMIRAL
HOW ODD...
WHAT? I THOUGHT I HIT HIM!
I SHOT HIM THROUGH THE HEAD JUST NOW!
HE HAS TO HAVE SOME KIND OF DEVIL FRUIT POWER!
WAH
EEK
LET'S GET OUT OF HERE!
EXCUSE ME, I'D LIKE TO ASK YOU SOMETHING.
AHHHH!
I'M LOOKING FOR A MAN BY THE NAME OF SENTOMARU.
WHIP!!
HE'S ONE OF MY SUBORDINATES, YOU SEE...
AAAH!!!

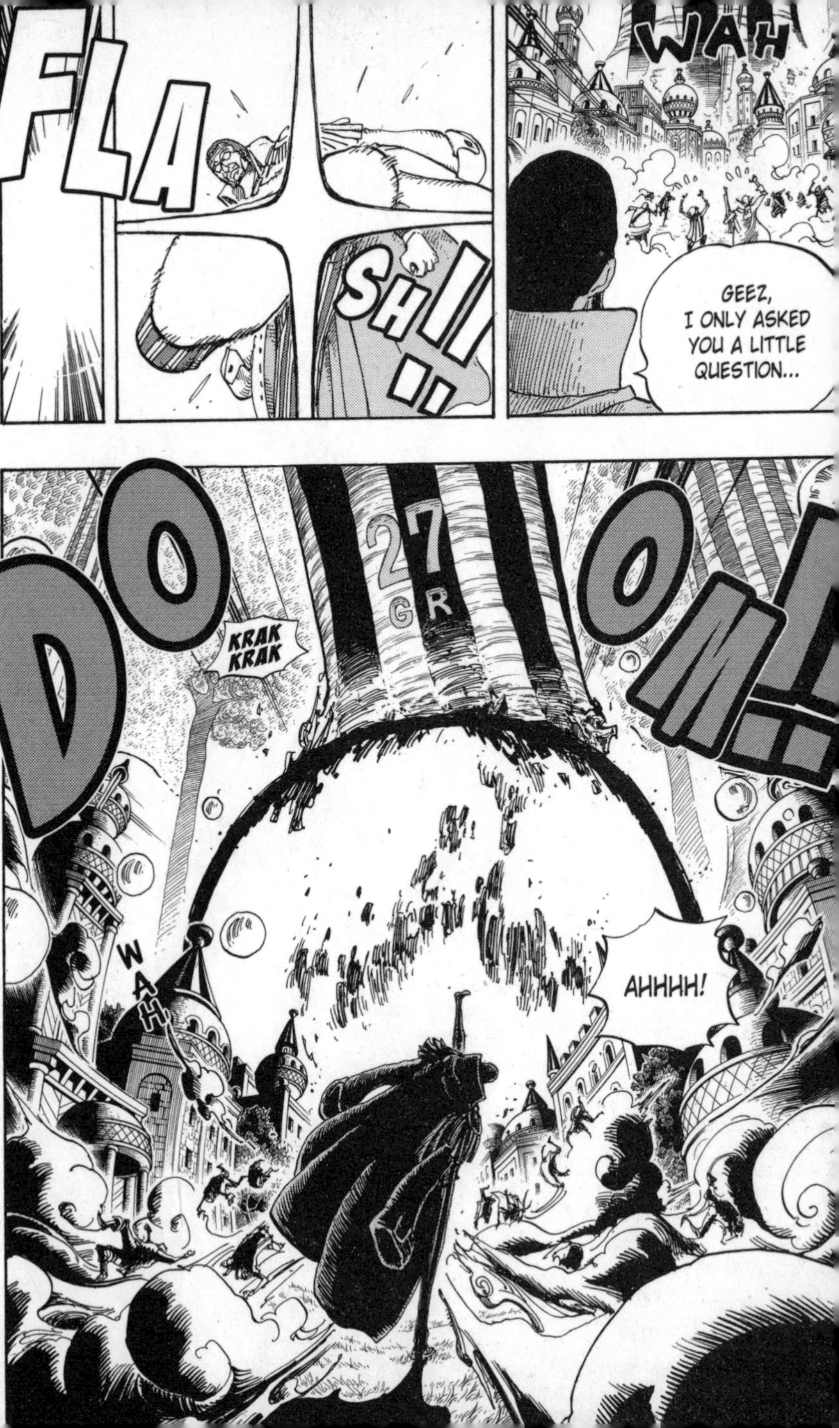
WAH
GEEZ, I ONLY ASKED YOU A LITTLE QUESTION...
SH!!
FLA
DOOM!!
27 GR
KRAK KRAK
AHHHH!
WAH

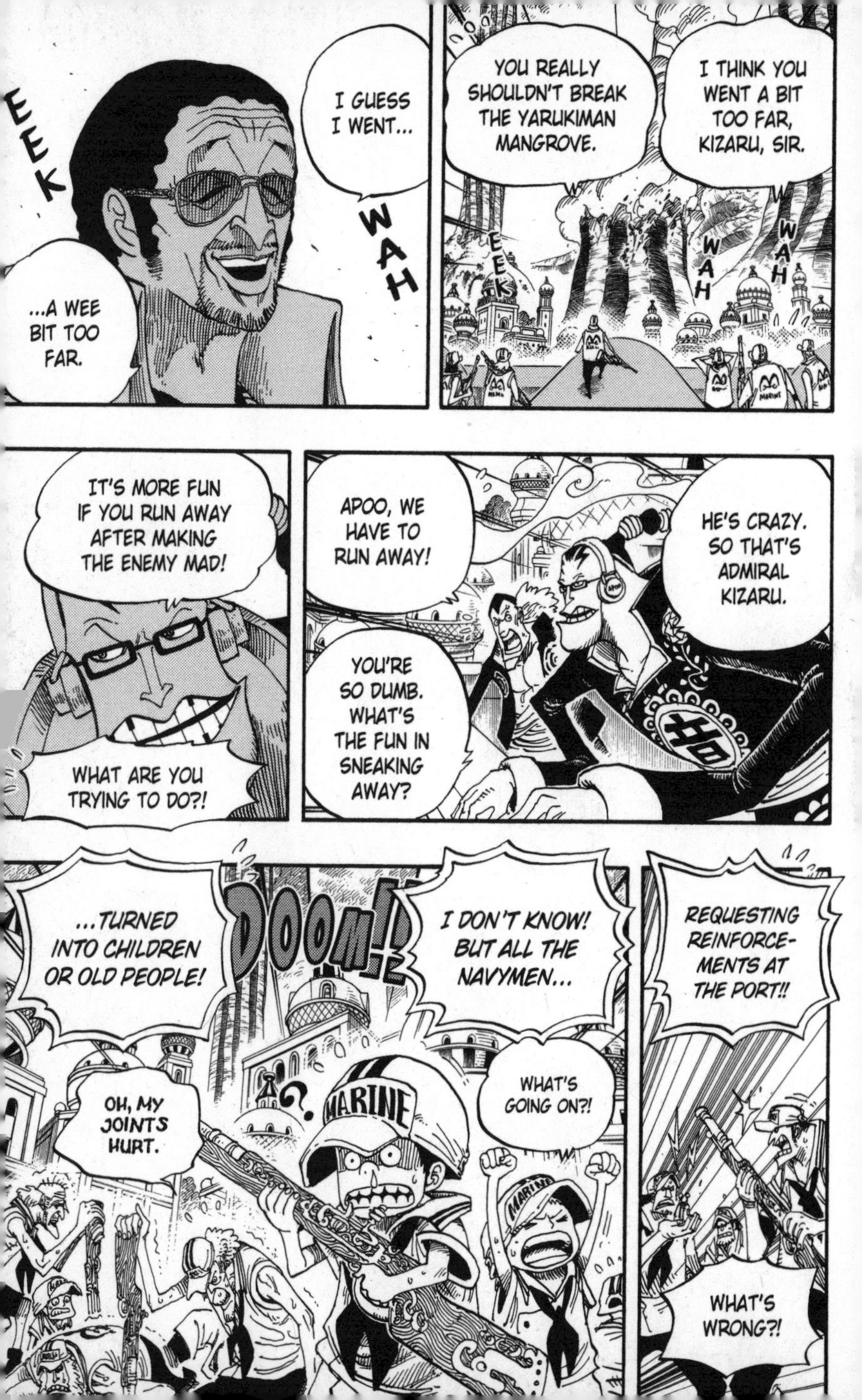
I THINK YOU WENT A BIT TOO FAR, KIZARU, SIR.
YOU REALLY SHOULDN'T BREAK THE YARUKIMAN MANGROVE.
WAH
WAH
EEK
EEK
I GUESS I WENT...
WAH
...A WEE BIT TOO FAR.
HE'S CRAZY. SO THAT'S ADMIRAL KIZARU.
APOO, WE HAVE TO RUN AWAY!
YOU'RE SO DUMB. WHAT'S THE FUN IN SNEAKING AWAY?
IT'S MORE FUN IF YOU RUN AWAY AFTER MAKING THE ENEMY MAD!
WHAT ARE YOU TRYING TO DO?!
REQUESTING REINFORCE-MENTS AT THE PORT!!
WHAT'S WRONG?!
I DON'T KNOW! BUT ALL THE NAVYMEN...
...TURNED INTO CHILDREN OR OLD PEOPLE!
DOOM!!
MARINE
WHAT'S GOING ON?!
OH, MY JOINTS HURT.

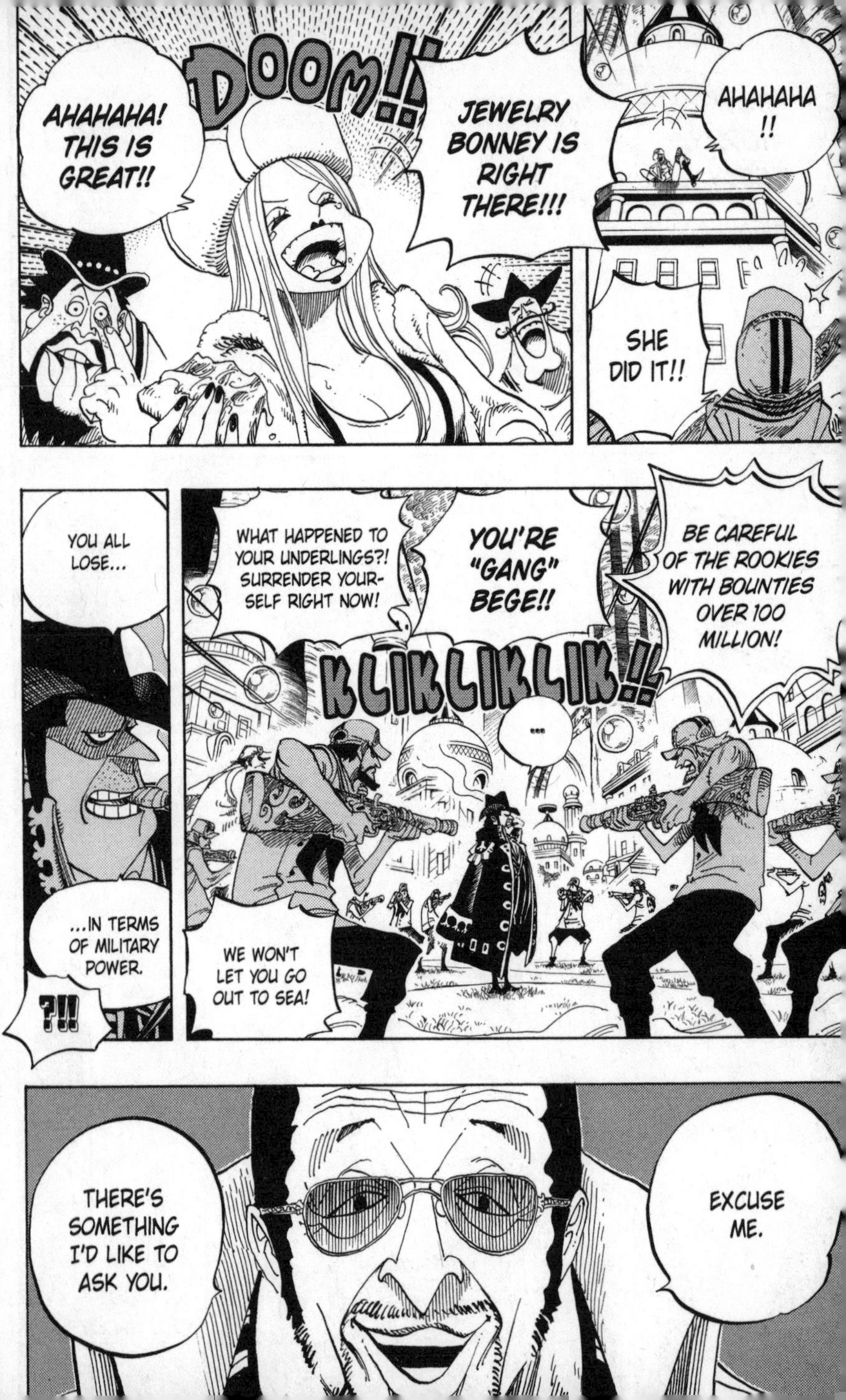
AHAHAHA !!
SHE DID IT!!
JEWELRY BONNEY IS RIGHT THERE!!!
DOOM!!
AHAHAHA! THIS IS GREAT!!
BE CAREFUL OF THE ROOKIES WITH BOUNTIES OVER 100 MILLION!
YOU'RE "GANG" BEGE!!
WHAT HAPPENED TO YOUR UNDERLINGS?! SURRENDER YOURSELF RIGHT NOW!
KLIKLIKLIK!!
...
WE WON'T LET YOU GO OUT TO SEA!
YOU ALL LOSE...
...IN TERMS OF MILITARY POWER.
?!!
EXCUSE ME.
THERE'S SOMETHING I'D LIKE TO ASK YOU.

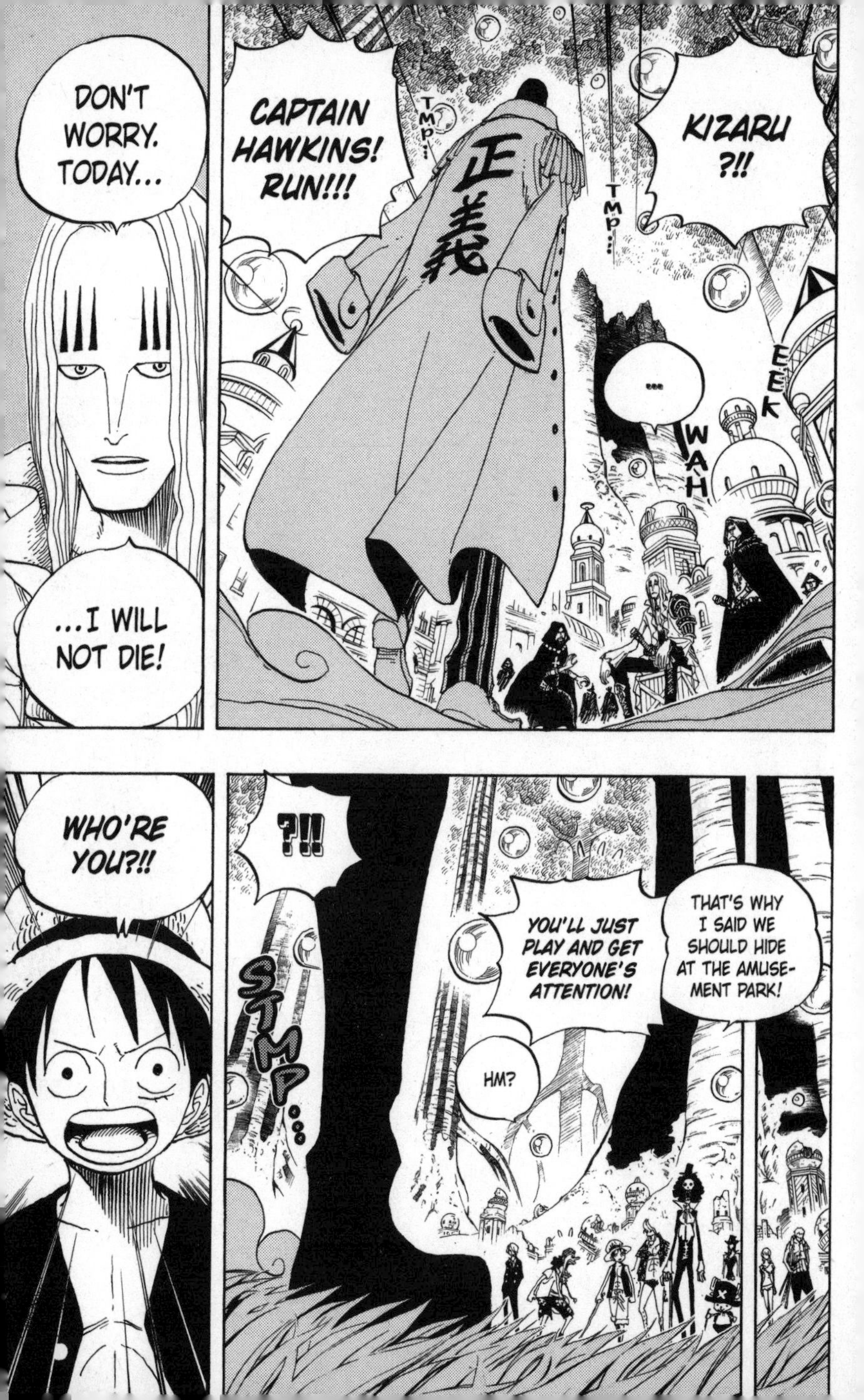
KIZARU ?!!
TMP...
CAPTAIN HAWKINS! RUN!!!
TMP...
EEK
...
WAH
DON'T WORRY. TODAY...
...I WILL NOT DIE!
?!!
THAT'S WHY I SAID WE SHOULD HIDE AT THE AMUSEMENT PARK!
YOU'LL JUST PLAY AND GET EVERYONE'S ATTENTION!
STMP...
HM?
WHO'RE YOU?!!

SBS Question Corner

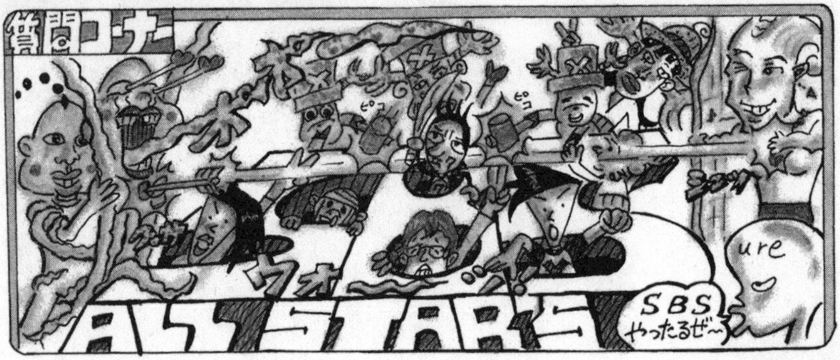
SBS
やったるぜ〜

(T.M. Luffy, Aomori)

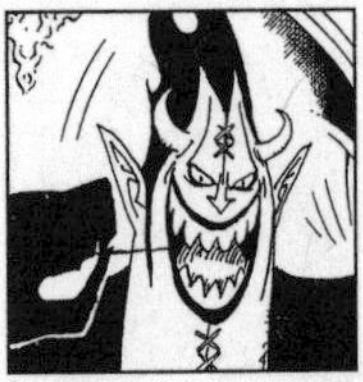

Q: Please hear me out! Yesterday, when I got out of the bath, I was about to wear my favorite tighty-whities. I then realized that my shadow was gone! When did that happen? And what kind of marionette did my shadow turn into? Please ask Moria for me!

-- Iwashi-chan

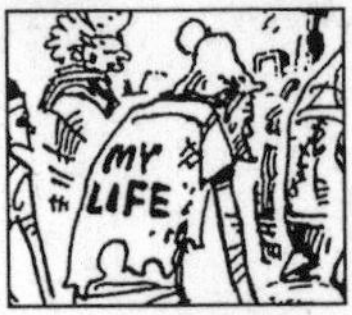
MY
LIFE

Oda: Well, Moria?
Moria: Ki shi shi! Shut up! You answer him!
Oda: Okay, I found him. It's this guy (→).
He was getting lectured by Luffy.

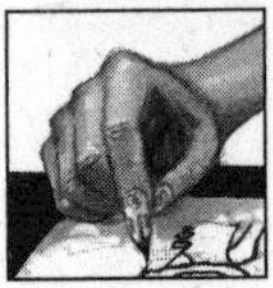

Q: Oda Sensei, you have assistants, don't you? With other comics, it's pretty obvious which drawings are done by the assistants, but I can't tell with *One Piece* even from the first volume! Do you draw the sketches for everything?

--Woman Who Re-read from Volume 1

A: It would be impossible for me to do everything. My staff draws the backgrounds for me. They look at my rough sketches and groundwork, then draw everything up very carefully. My staff is really filled with many great people. The difference with other comics is probably that things like crowds, animals, smoke, clouds, oceans and anything that "lives and moves" are all drawn by me. When you depend on other people to draw moving things, the presentation becomes a little off sometimes. A little awkward, even. But with this, it's more like something that I refuse to let others do because I'm stubborn.

Chapter 508:
ISLAND OF CARNAGE

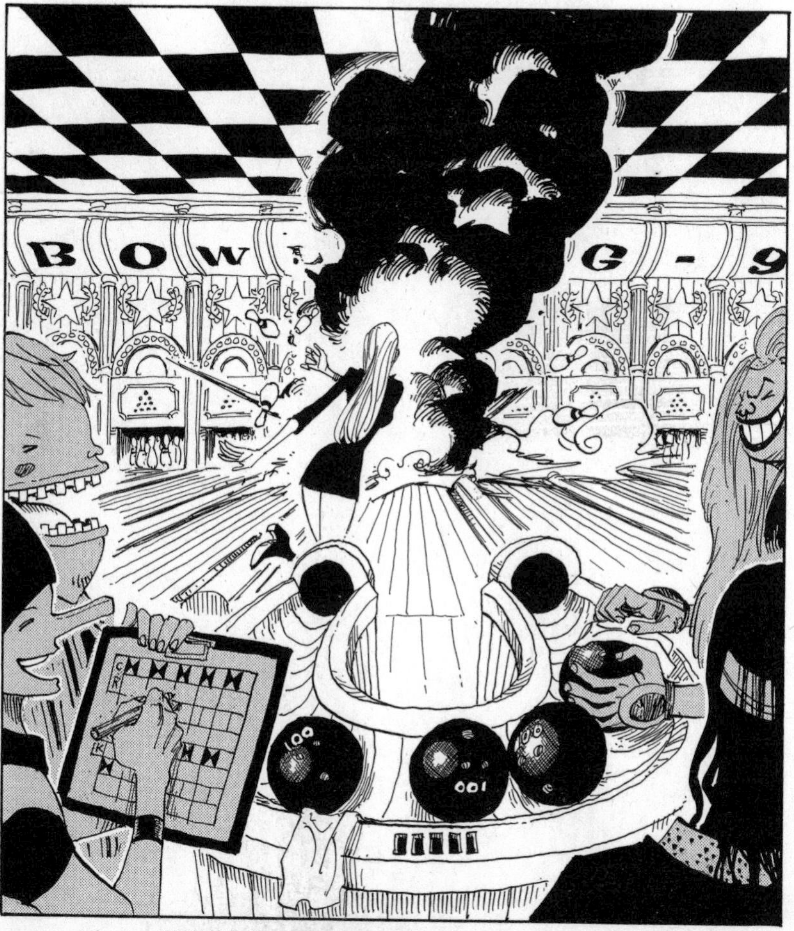

CP9'S INDEPENDENT REPORT, VOL. 16:
"FUN BOWLING EXCURSION"

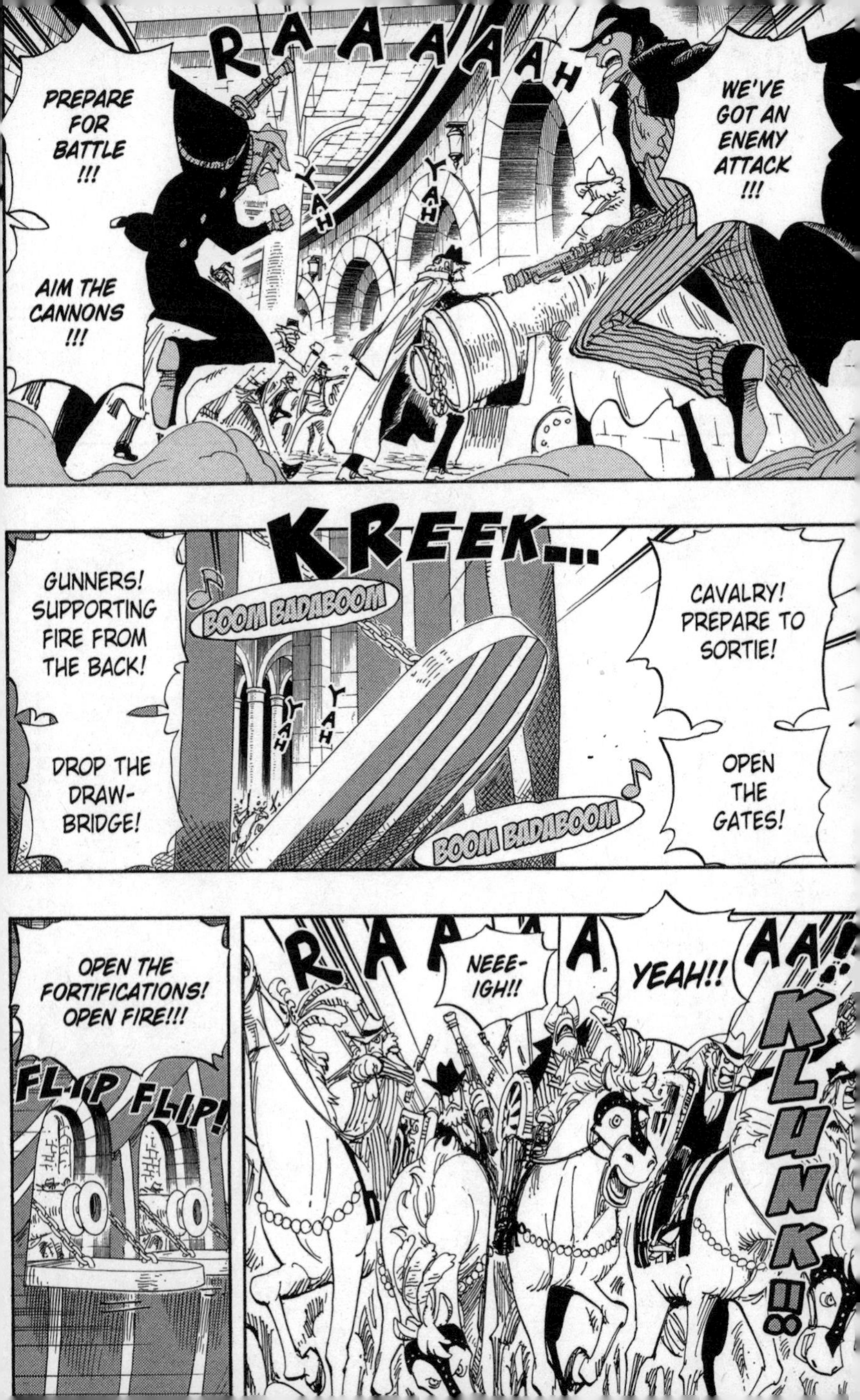
WE'VE GOT AN ENEMY ATTACK!!!
RAAAAAH
YAH
YAH
PREPARE FOR BATTLE!!!
AIM THE CANNONS!!!
CAVALRY! PREPARE TO SORTIE!
OPEN THE GATES!
KREEK...
BOOM BADABOOM
BOOM BADABOOM
YAH
YAH
GUNNERS! SUPPORTING FIRE FROM THE BACK!
DROP THE DRAW-BRIDGE!
KLUNK!!
RAAAAAA!!
YEAH!!
NEEE-IGH!!
OPEN THE FORTIFICATIONS! OPEN FIRE!!!
FLIP FLIP!

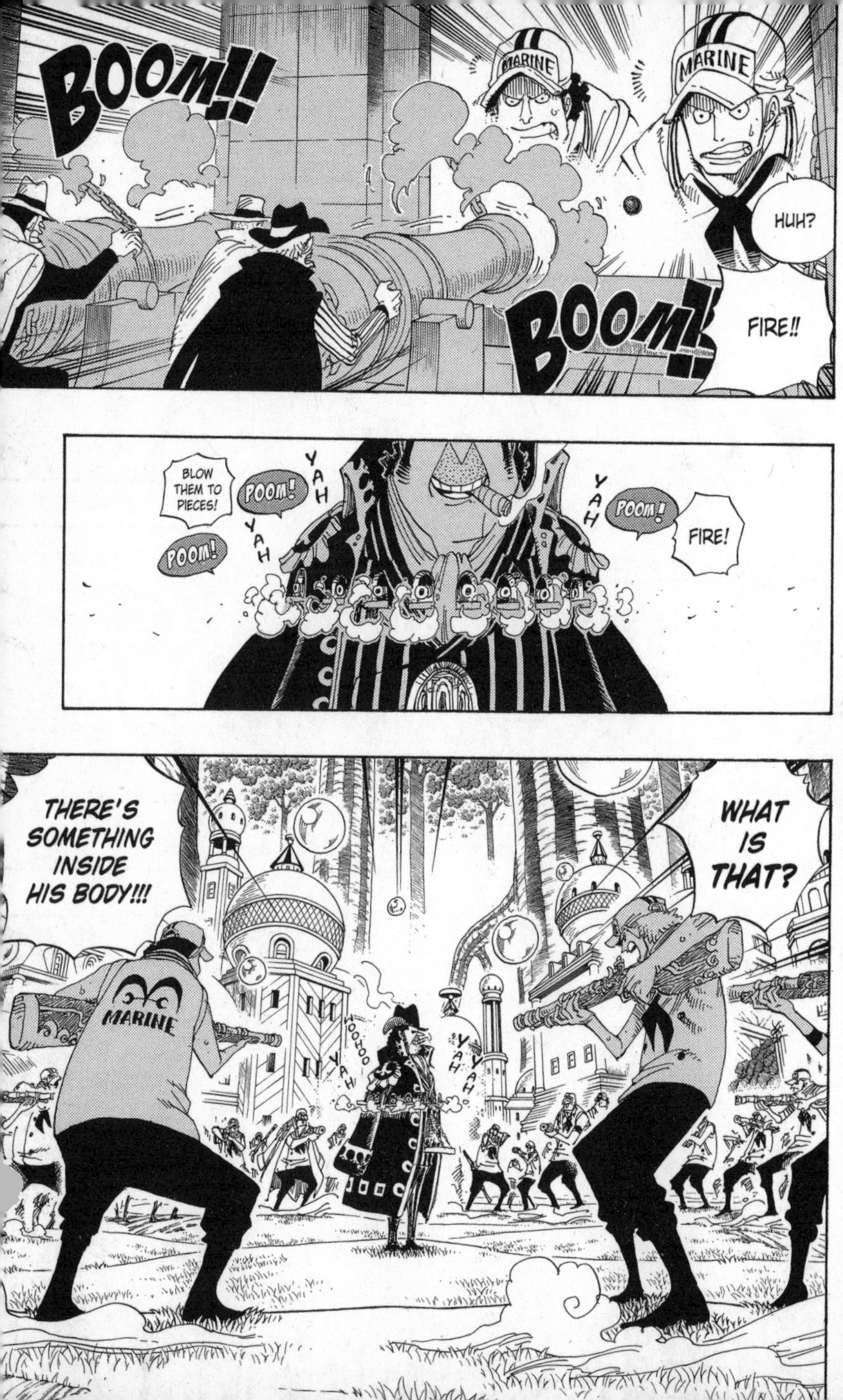
HUH?
FIRE!!
BOOM!!
BOOM!!
FIRE!
YAH
POOM!
YAH
BLOW THEM TO PIECES!
POOM!
YAH
POOM!
WHAT IS THAT?
YAH YAH
WOOHOO YAH
THERE'S SOMETHING INSIDE HIS BODY!!!

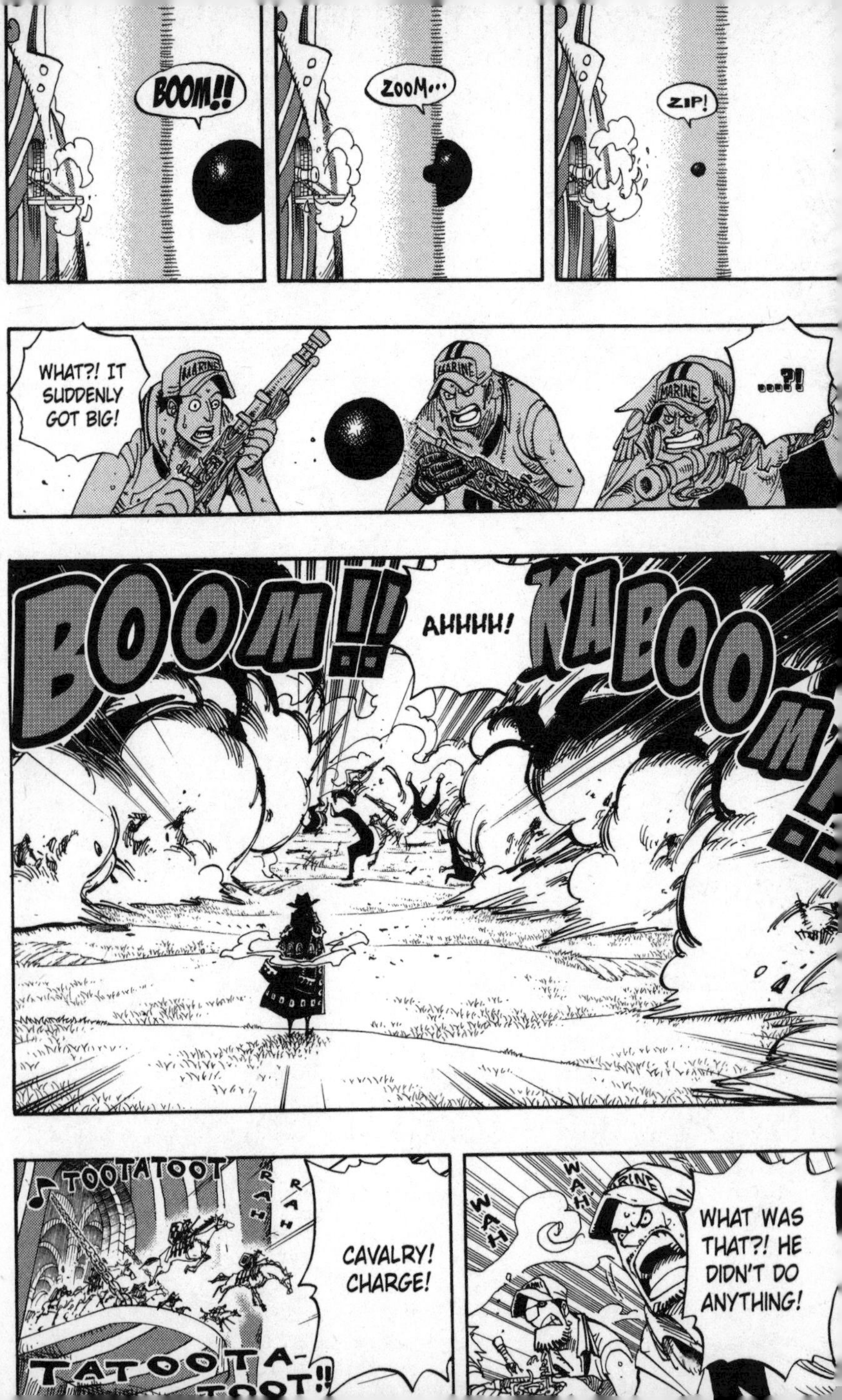
ZIP!
ZOOM...
BOOM!!
...?!
WHAT?! IT SUDDENLY GOT BIG!
KABOOM!!
AHHHH!
BOOM!!
WAH WAH
WHAT WAS THAT?! HE DIDN'T DO ANYTHING!
RAH RAH
CAVALRY! CHARGE!
TOOTATOOT
TATOOTA-TOOT!!

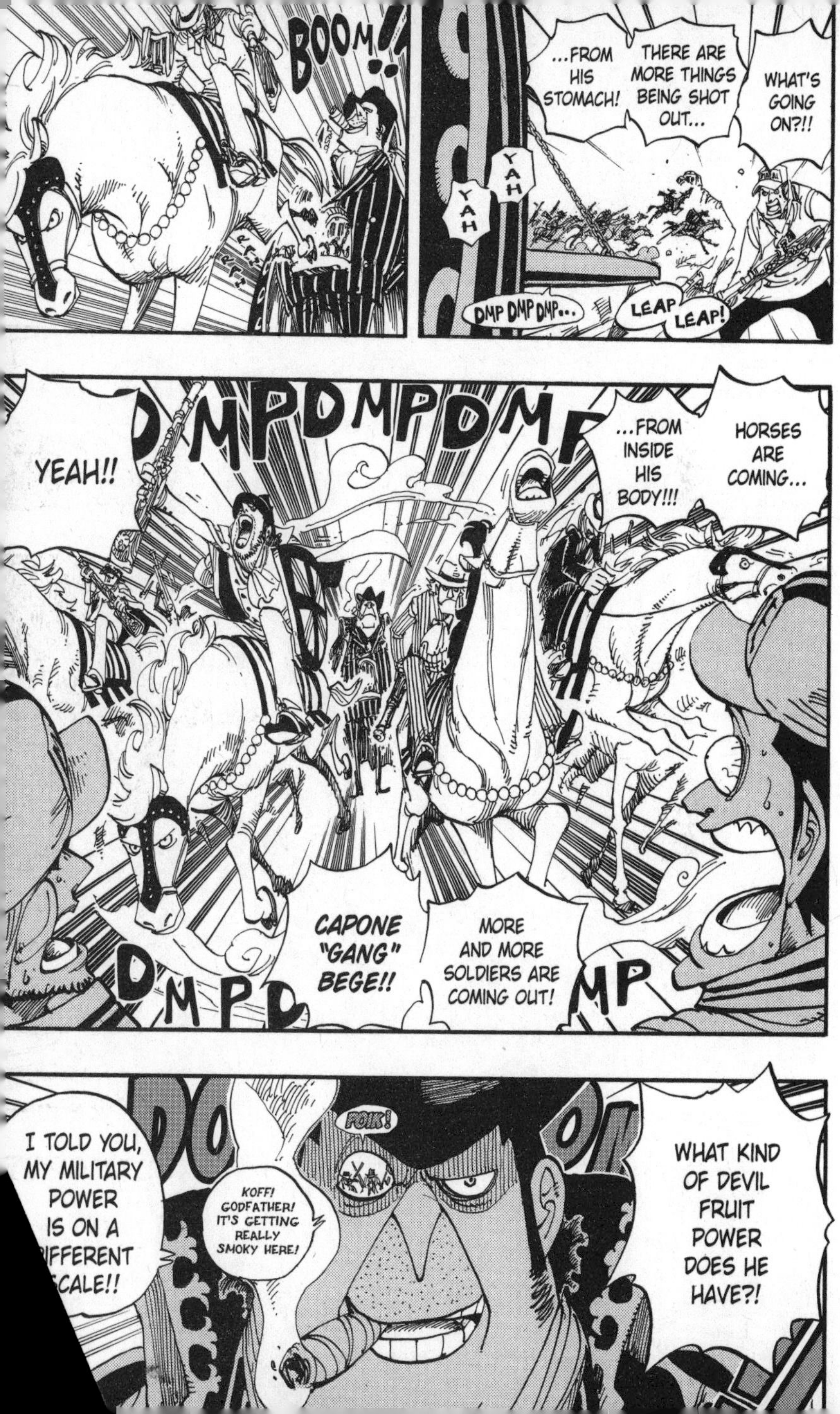

WHAT'S GOING ON?!!
THERE ARE MORE THINGS BEING SHOT OUT...
...FROM HIS STOMACH!
YAH
YAH
LEAP LEAP!
DMP DMP DMP...
BOOM!!
HORSES ARE COMING...
...FROM INSIDE HIS BODY!!!
DMPDMPDMP
YEAH!!
MORE AND MORE SOLDIERS ARE COMING OUT!
CAPONE "GANG" BEGE!!
DMPD
MP
WHAT KIND OF DEVIL FRUIT POWER DOES HE HAVE?!
POIK!
KOFF! GODFATHER! IT'S GETTING REALLY SMOKY HERE!
I TOLD YOU, MY MILITARY POWER IS ON A IFFERENT CALE!!

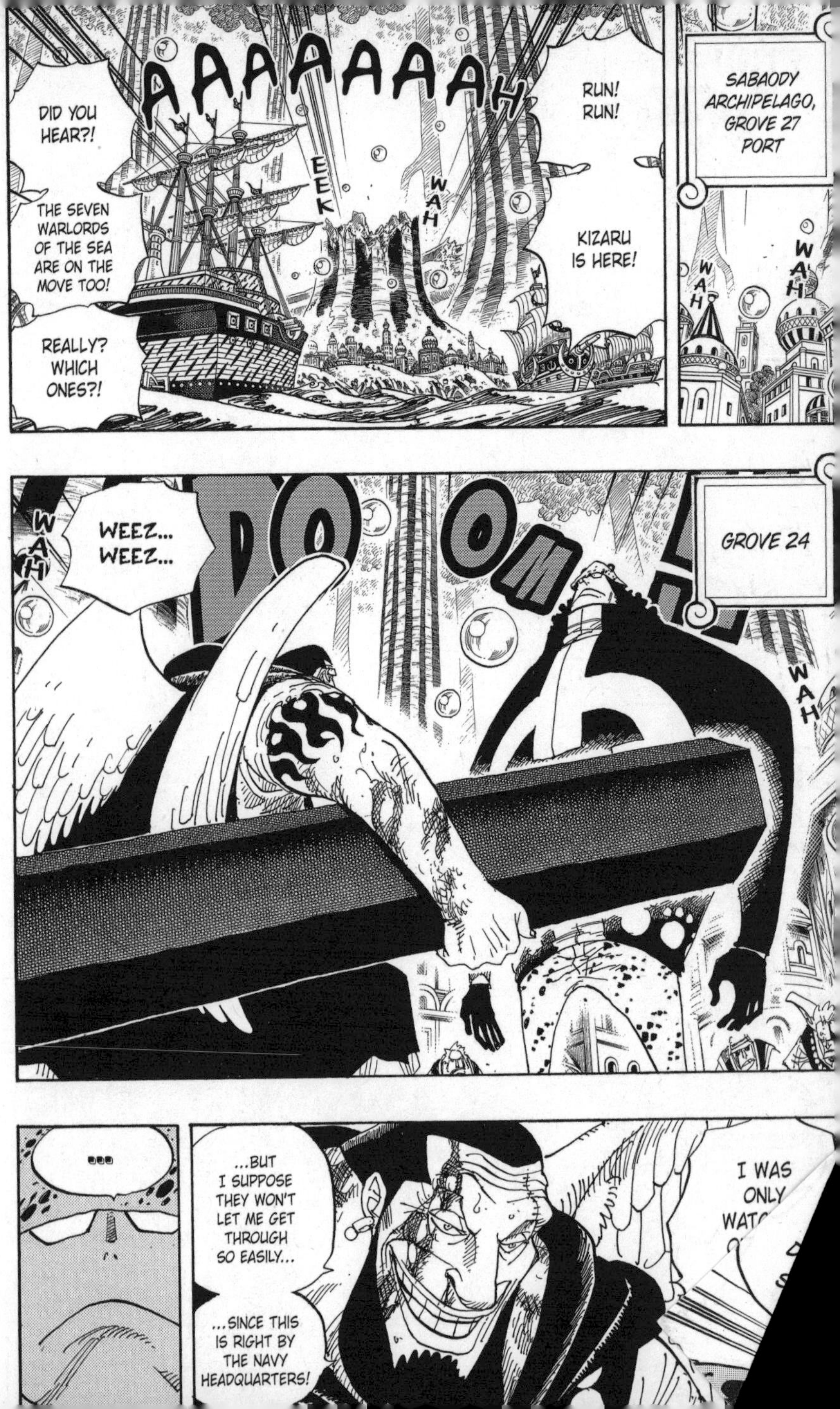
SABAODY ARCHIPELAGO, GROVE 27 PORT
WAH
WAH
AAAAAAAAH
RUN! RUN!
KIZARU IS HERE!
WAH
EEK
DID YOU HEAR?!
THE SEVEN WARLORDS OF THE SEA ARE ON THE MOVE TOO!
REALLY? WHICH ONES?!
GROVE 24
WAH
DOOM
WEEZ... WEEZ...
WAH
I WAS ONLY
...BUT I SUPPOSE THEY WON'T LET ME GET THROUGH SO EASILY...
...SINCE THIS IS RIGHT BY THE NAVY HEADQUARTERS!
...

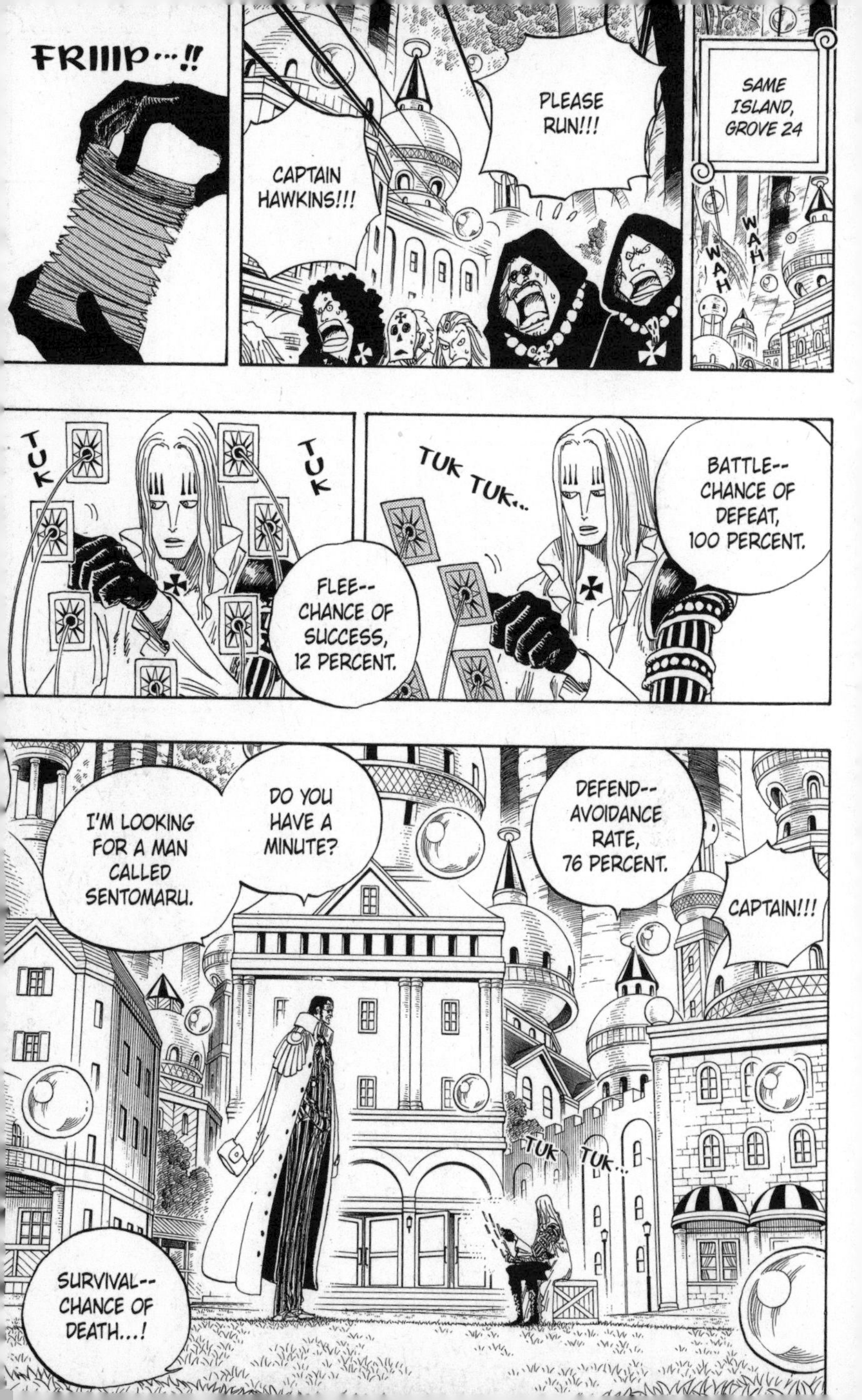
SAME ISLAND, GROVE 24
WAH WAH
PLEASE RUN!!!
CAPTAIN HAWKINS!!!
FRIIIP…!!
BATTLE-- CHANCE OF DEFEAT, 100 PERCENT.
TUK TUK..
FLEE-- CHANCE OF SUCCESS, 12 PERCENT.
TUK TUK
CAPTAIN!!!
DEFEND-- AVOIDANCE RATE, 76 PERCENT.
DO YOU HAVE A MINUTE?
I'M LOOKING FOR A MAN CALLED SENTOMARU.
TUK TUK..
SURVIVAL-- CHANCE OF DEATH...!

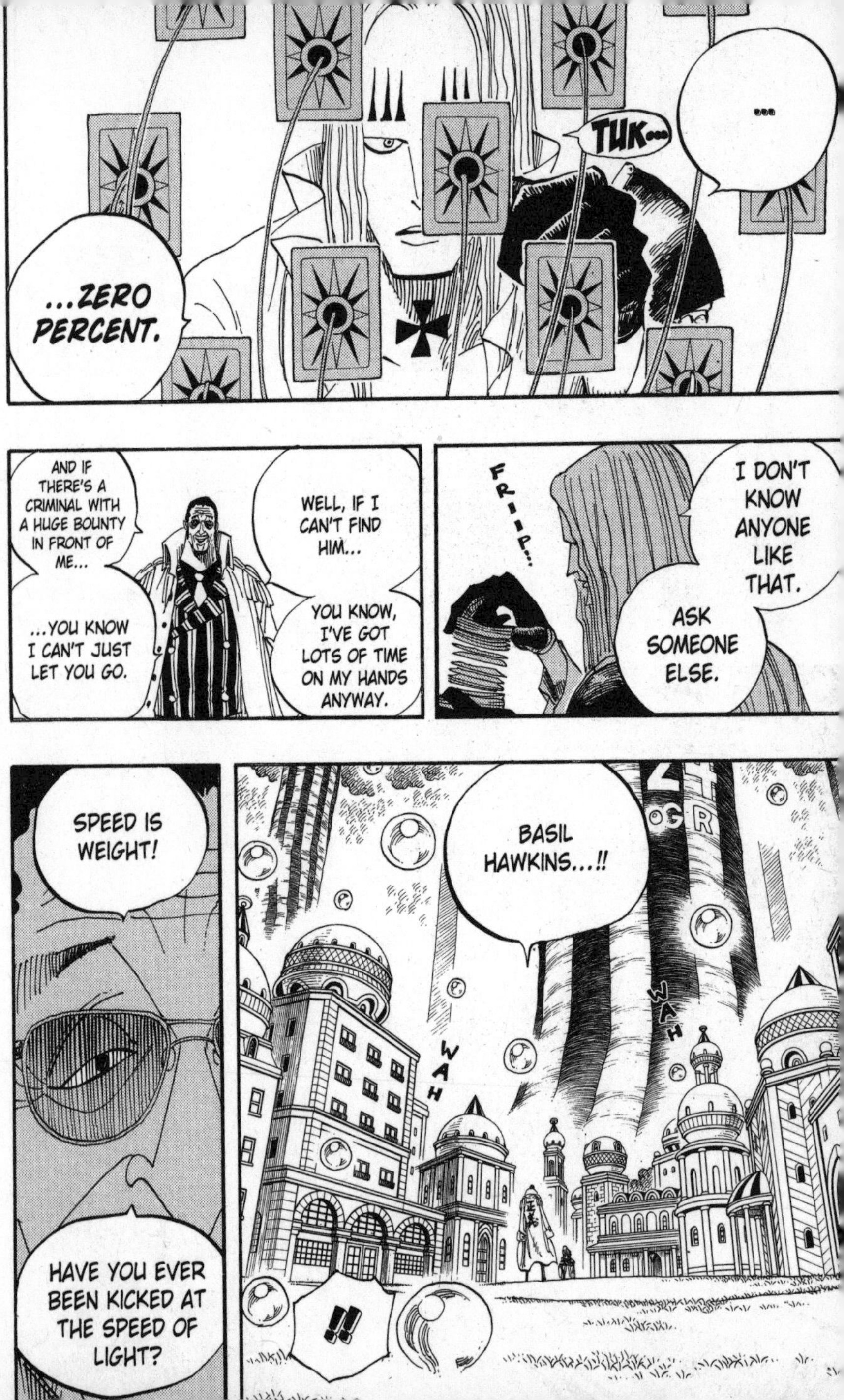
...
TUK...
...ZERO PERCENT.
FRIIP!!
I DON'T KNOW ANYONE LIKE THAT.
ASK SOMEONE ELSE.
WELL, IF I CAN'T FIND HIM...
YOU KNOW, I'VE GOT LOTS OF TIME ON MY HANDS ANYWAY.
AND IF THERE'S A CRIMINAL WITH A HUGE BOUNTY IN FRONT OF ME...
...YOU KNOW I CAN'T JUST LET YOU GO.
BASIL HAWKINS...!!
WAH
WAH
!!
SPEED IS WEIGHT!
HAVE YOU EVER BEEN KICKED AT THE SPEED OF LIGHT?

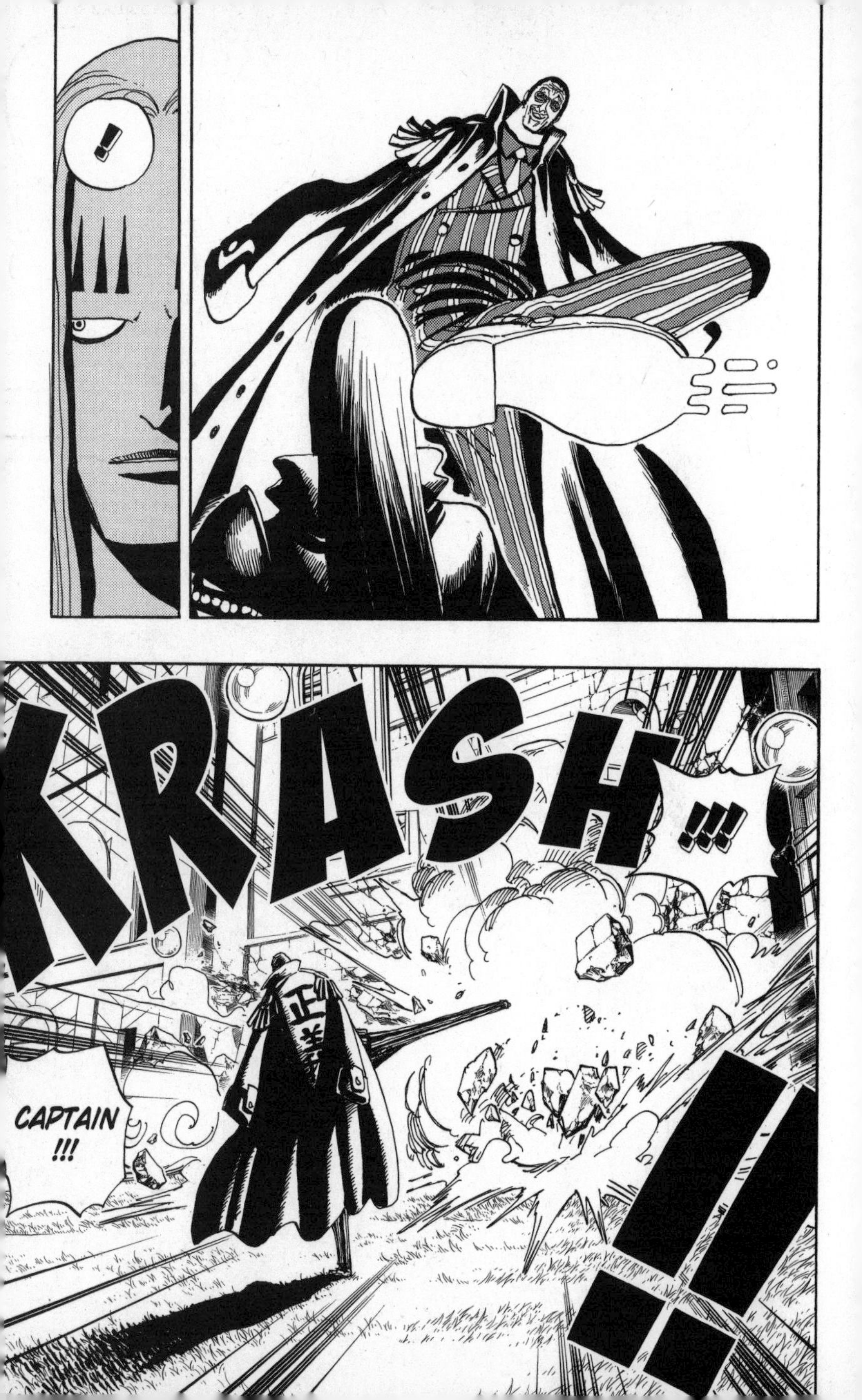
!
KRASH!!!
CAPTAIN !!!
!!

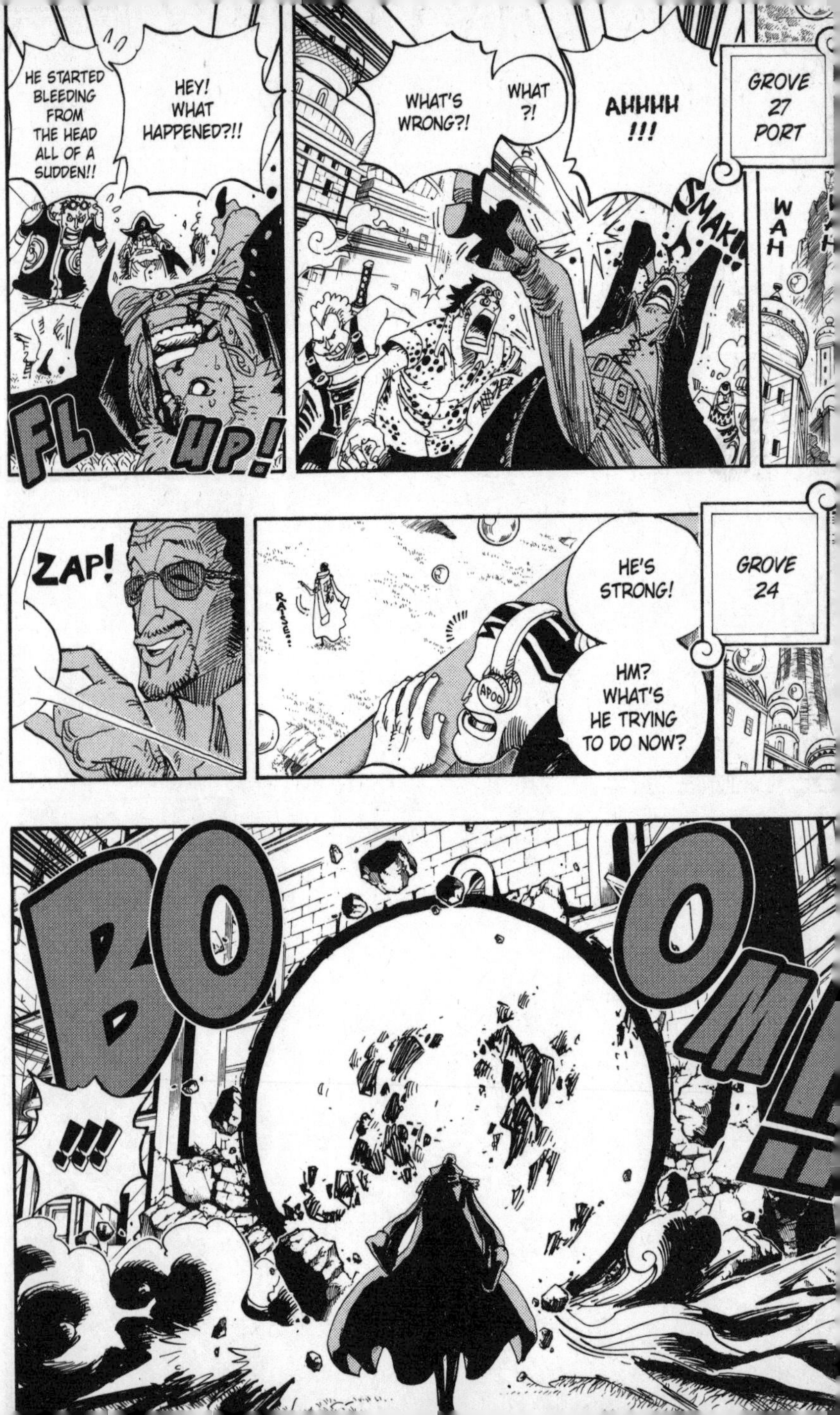
GROVE 27 PORT
WAH
AHHHH !!!
WHAT ?!
WHAT'S WRONG?!
SMAK!!
HEY! WHAT HAPPENED?!!
HE STARTED BLEEDING FROM THE HEAD ALL OF A SUDDEN!!
FLUP!
GROVE 24
HE'S STRONG!
HM? WHAT'S HE TRYING TO DO NOW?
RAISE...
APOO
ZAP!
BOOM!!
!!!

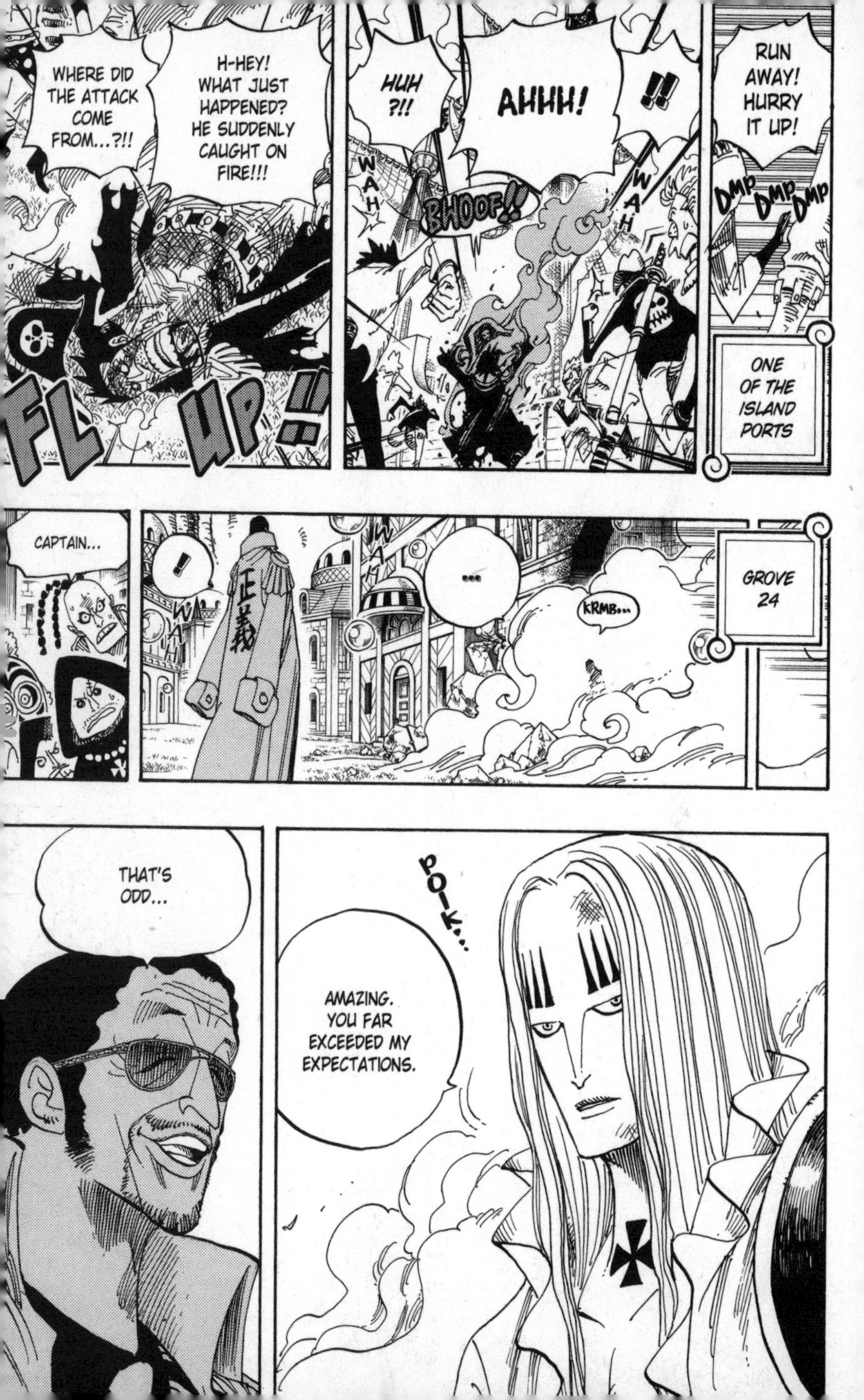
ONE OF THE ISLAND PORTS
RUN AWAY! HURRY IT UP!
DMP DMP DMP
!!
AHHH!
HUH ?!!
WAH
BWOOF!!
WAH
H-HEY! WHAT JUST HAPPENED? HE SUDDENLY CAUGHT ON FIRE!!!
WHERE DID THE ATTACK COME FROM...?!!
FL UP!!
GROVE 24
KRMB...
...
WAH
!
WAH
CAPTAIN...
POIK...
AMAZING. YOU FAR EXCEEDED MY EXPECTATIONS.
THAT'S ODD...

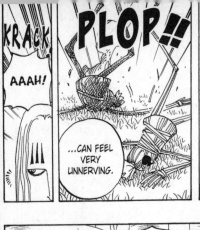

ONLY HAVING TEN AGAINST AN ADMIRAL...
SKRIP...!!
SKRIP
SLITH...SLITH...
PLOP!!
...CAN FEEL VERY UNNERVING.
KRACK
AAAH!
?!
WUD...!!!
UGH!!!
TH
THAT'S "MAD MONK" UROUGE!
AND BAR-THOLOMEW KUMA!
MURMUR!!
HUFF... HUFF...
HE'S TOO STRONG ...!!
TMP...
TMP...
?!
IS THAT... KIZARU?!!

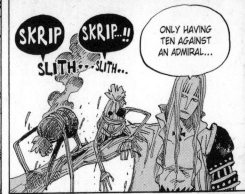

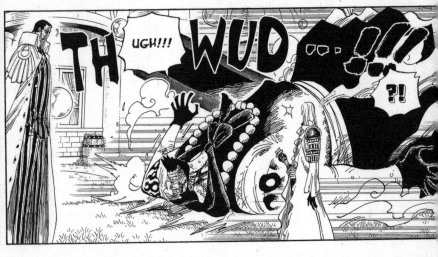

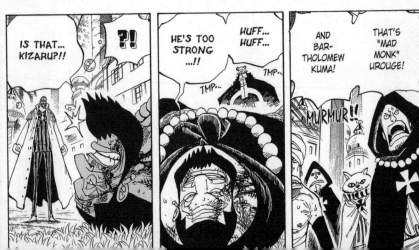

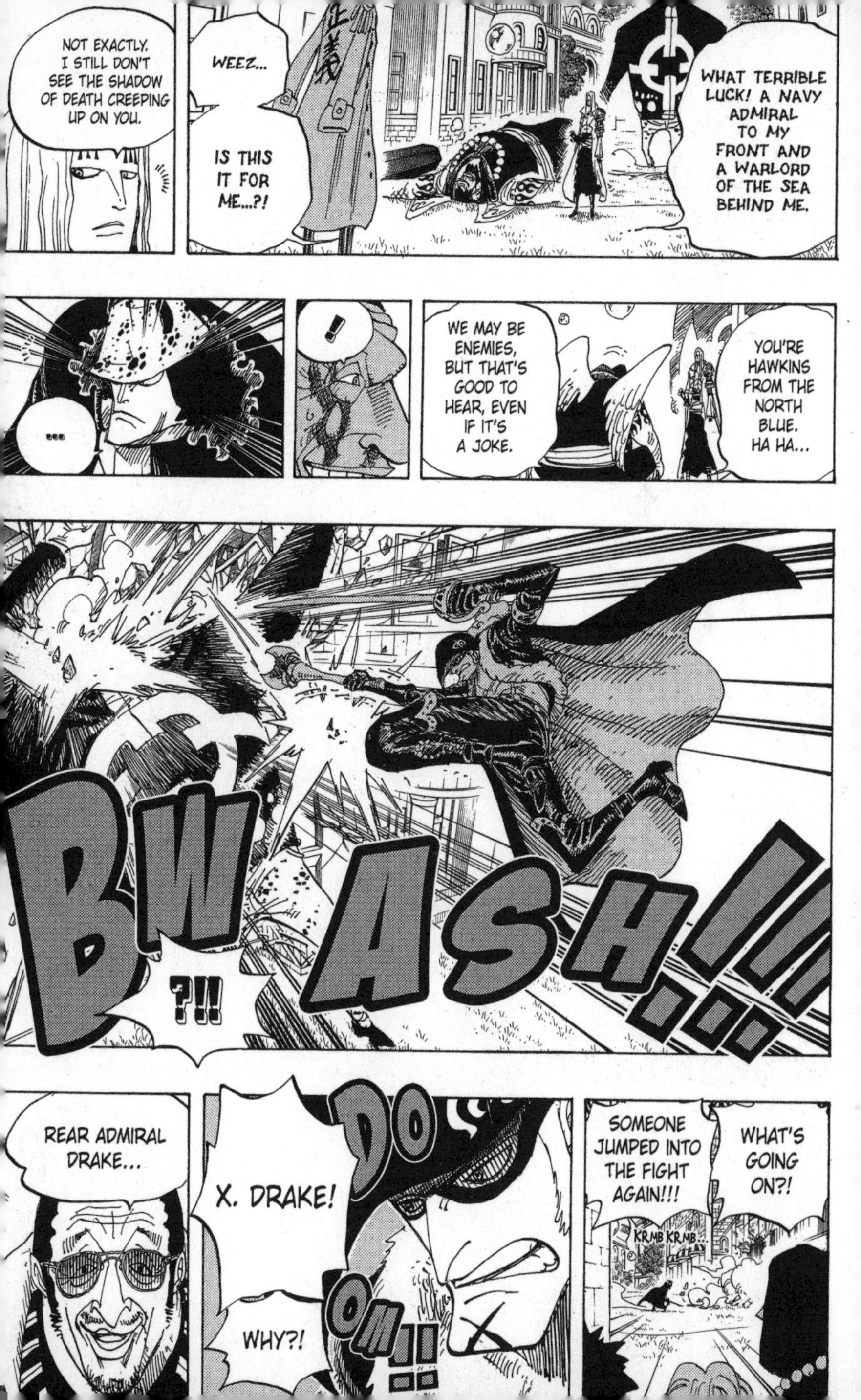
WHAT TERRIBLE LUCK! A NAVY ADMIRAL TO MY FRONT AND A WARLORD OF THE SEA BEHIND ME.
WEEZ...
IS THIS IT FOR ME...?!
NOT EXACTLY. I STILL DON'T SEE THE SHADOW OF DEATH CREEPING UP ON YOU.
YOU'RE HAWKINS FROM THE NORTH BLUE. HA HA...
WE MAY BE ENEMIES, BUT THAT'S GOOD TO HEAR, EVEN IF IT'S A JOKE.
!
...
BWASH!!!
?!!
WHAT'S GOING ON?!
SOMEONE JUMPED INTO THE FIGHT AGAIN!!!
KRMB KRMB...
DOOM!!
X. DRAKE!
WHY?!
REAR ADMIRAL DRAKE...

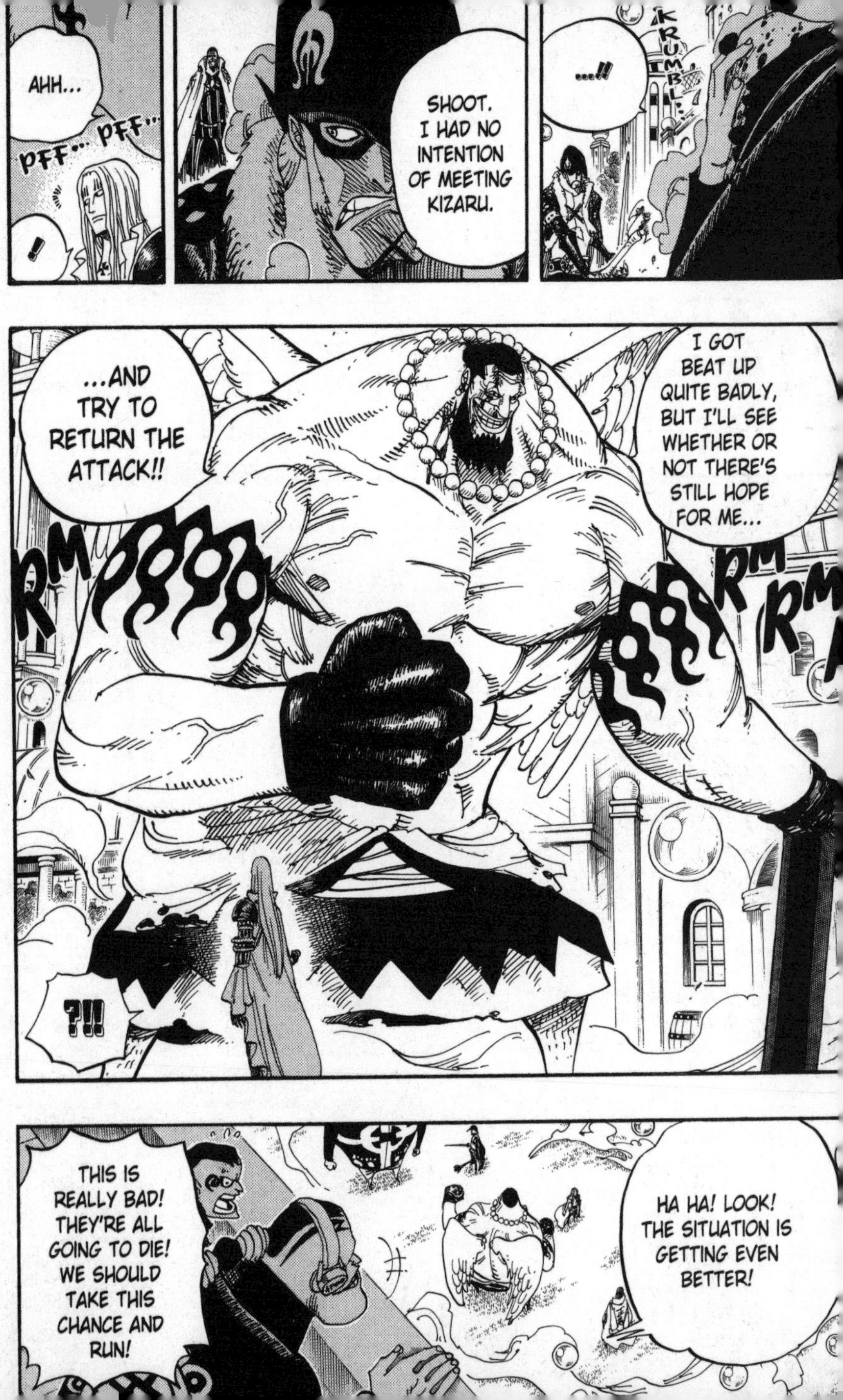
KRUMBL...
...!!
SHOOT. I HAD NO INTENTION OF MEETING KIZARU.
AHH...
PFF... PFF...
!
I GOT BEAT UP QUITE BADLY, BUT I'LL SEE WHETHER OR NOT THERE'S STILL HOPE FOR ME...
...AND TRY TO RETURN THE ATTACK!!
RM
RM
RM
?!!
HA HA! LOOK! THE SITUATION IS GETTING EVEN BETTER!
THIS IS REALLY BAD! THEY'RE ALL GOING TO DIE! WE SHOULD TAKE THIS CHANCE AND RUN!

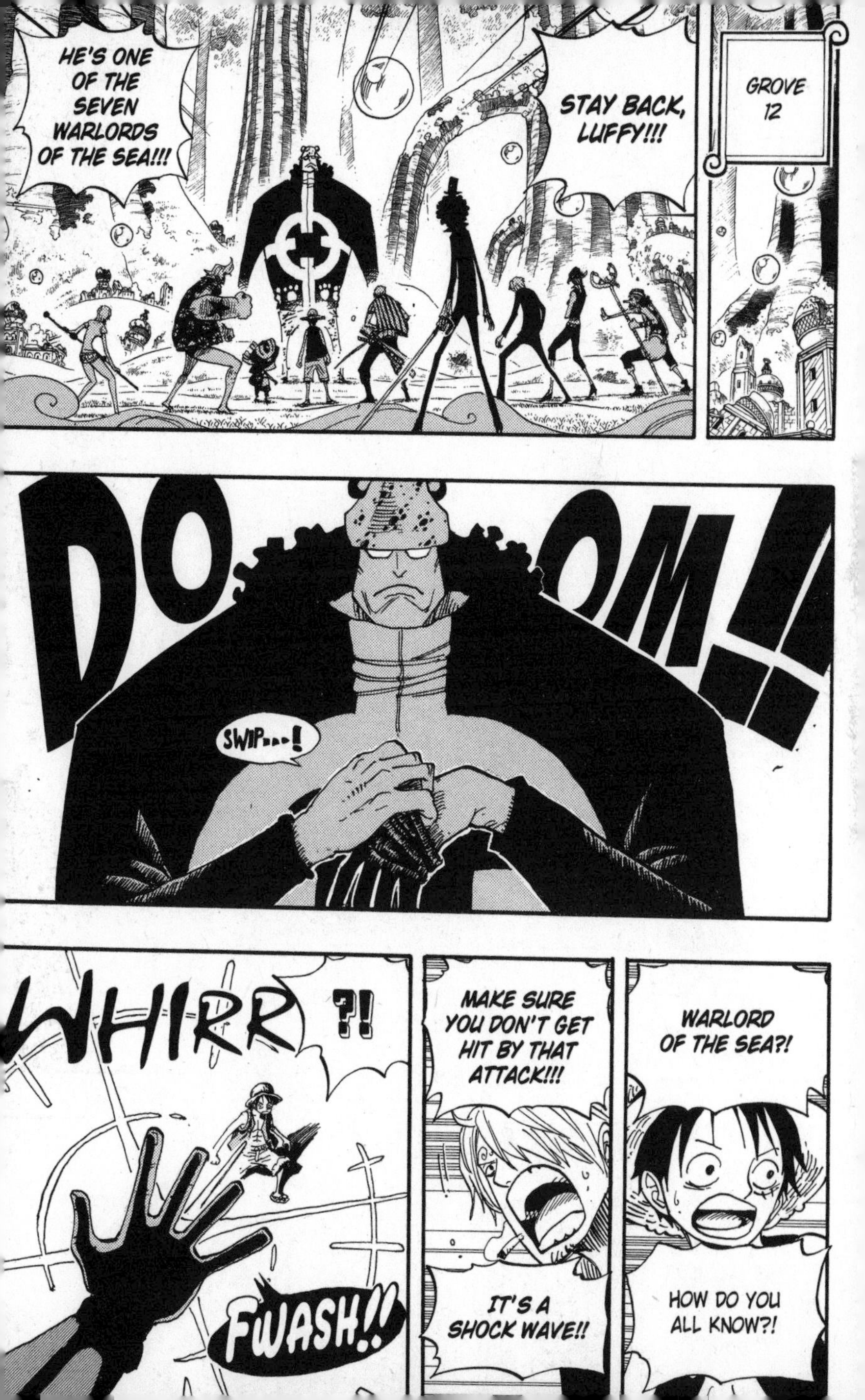

GROVE 12
STAY BACK, LUFFY!!!
HE'S ONE OF THE SEVEN WARLORDS OF THE SEA!!!
DO OM!!
SWIP...!
WARLORD OF THE SEA?!
HOW DO YOU ALL KNOW?!
MAKE SURE YOU DON'T GET HIT BY THAT ATTACK!!!
IT'S A SHOCK WAVE!!
?!
WHIRR
FWASH!!

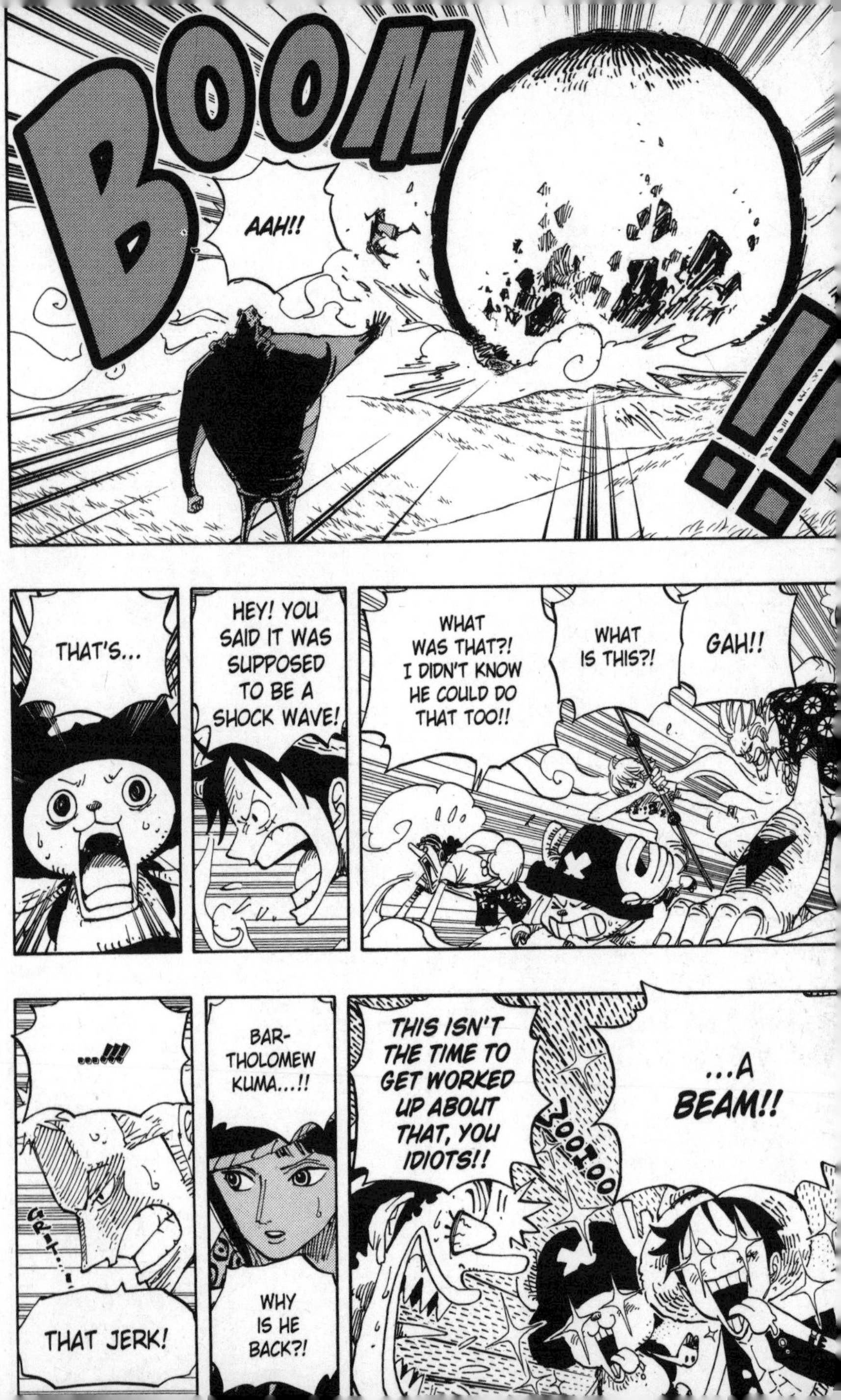
BOOM
AAH!!
GAH!!
WHAT IS THIS?!
WHAT WAS THAT?! I DIDN'T KNOW HE COULD DO THAT TOO!!
HEY! YOU SAID IT WAS SUPPOSED TO BE A SHOCK WAVE!
THAT'S...
...A BEAM!!
THIS ISN'T THE TIME TO GET WORKED UP ABOUT THAT, YOU IDIOTS!!
BAR-THOLOMEW KUMA...!!
WHY IS HE BACK?!
...!!!
GRIT...
THAT JERK!

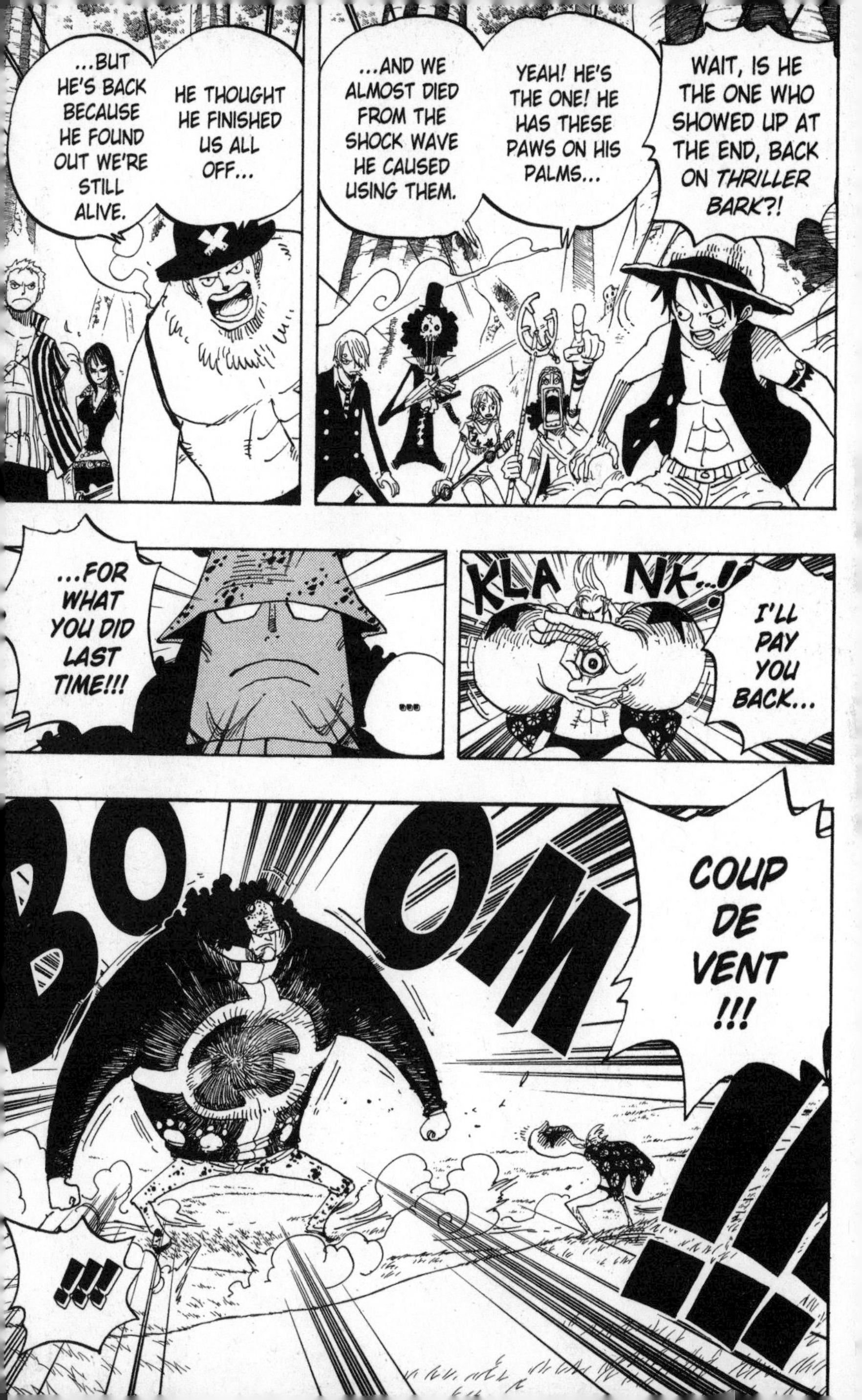
WAIT, IS HE THE ONE WHO SHOWED UP AT THE END, BACK ON *THRILLER BARK*?!
YEAH! HE'S THE ONE! HE HAS THESE PAWS ON HIS PALMS...
...AND WE ALMOST DIED FROM THE SHOCK WAVE HE CAUSED USING THEM.
HE THOUGHT HE FINISHED US ALL OFF...
...BUT HE'S BACK BECAUSE HE FOUND OUT WE'RE STILL ALIVE.
KLANK...!
I'LL PAY YOU BACK...
...
...FOR WHAT YOU DID LAST TIME!!!
COUP DE VENT!!!
BOOM
!!!

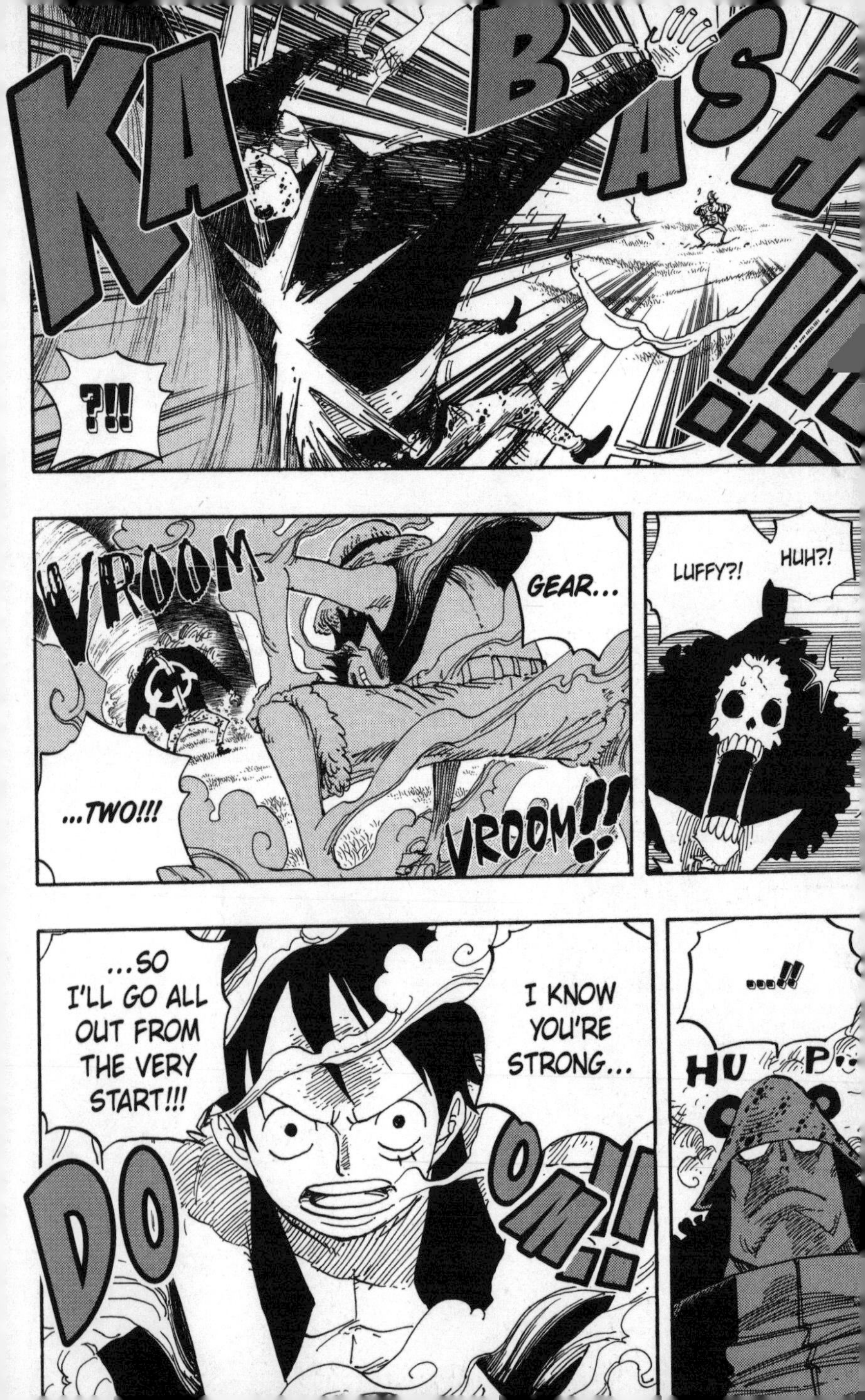
KABASH!!
?!!
HUH?!
LUFFY?!
GEAR...
VROOM
VROOM!!
...TWO!!!
...!!
HUP
I KNOW YOU'RE STRONG...
...SO I'LL GO ALL OUT FROM THE VERY START!!!
DOOM!!

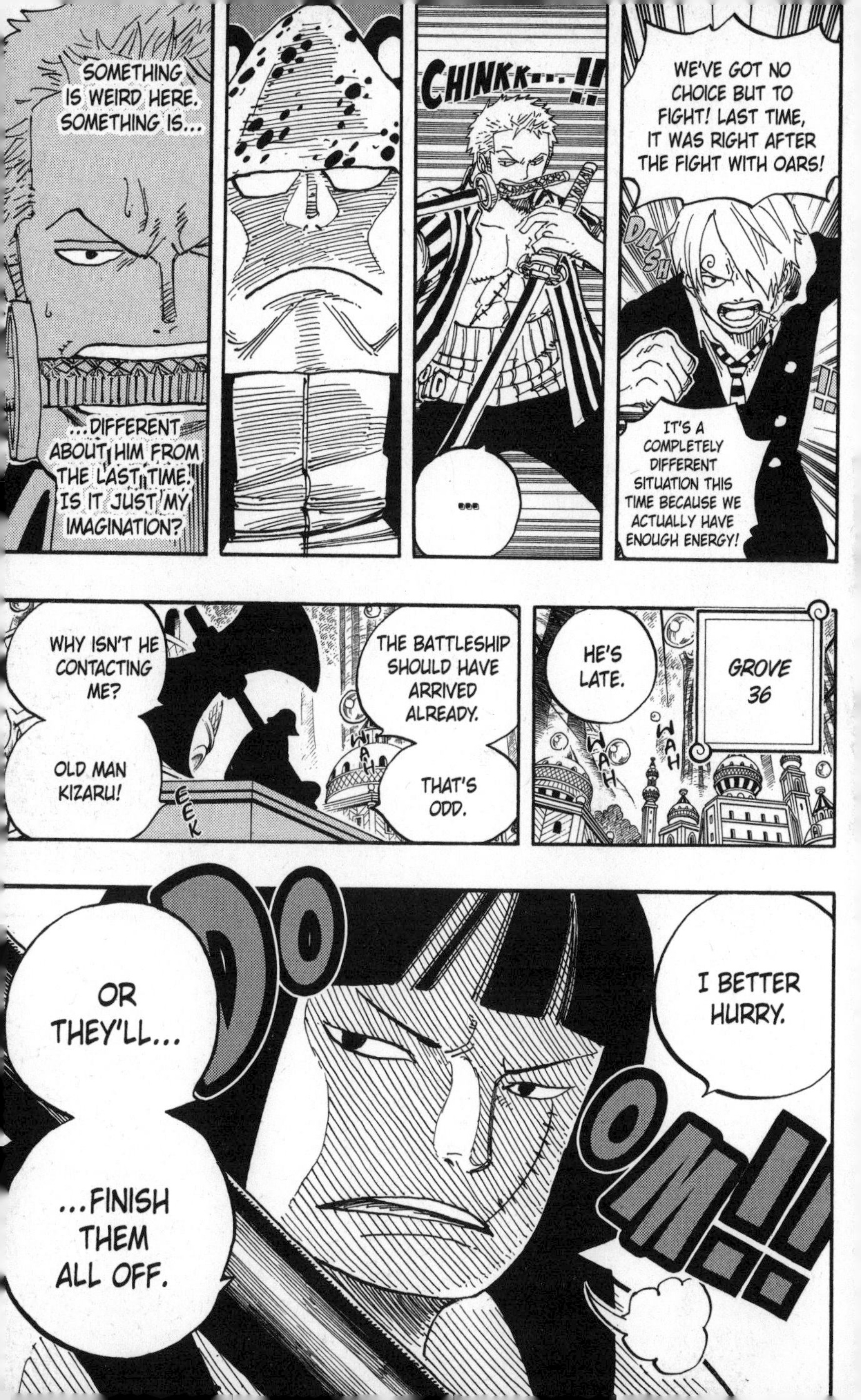
WE'VE GOT NO CHOICE BUT TO FIGHT! LAST TIME, IT WAS RIGHT AFTER THE FIGHT WITH OARS!
DASH
IT'S A COMPLETELY DIFFERENT SITUATION THIS TIME BECAUSE WE ACTUALLY HAVE ENOUGH ENERGY!
CHINKK...!!
...
SOMETHING IS WEIRD HERE. SOMETHING IS...
...DIFFERENT ABOUT HIM FROM THE LAST TIME. IS IT JUST MY IMAGINATION?
GROVE 36
HE'S LATE.
WAH
WAH
THE BATTLESHIP SHOULD HAVE ARRIVED ALREADY.
THAT'S ODD.
WAH
WHY ISN'T HE CONTACTING ME?
OLD MAN KIZARU!
EEK
I BETTER HURRY.
OR THEY'LL...
...FINISH THEM ALL OFF.
DOOM!!

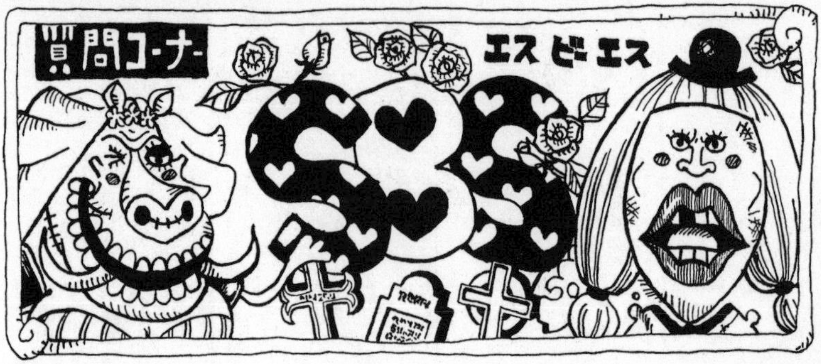
質問コーナー
エスビーエス
SBS

(Usopper, Gunma)

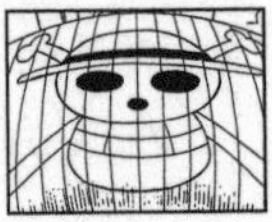

Q: Oda Sensei, hello. I have a question. I sometimes read up on the history of pirates, and I've been wondering about the "Supernova" rookies. I made a list below of where I think their names come from. What do you think of it?

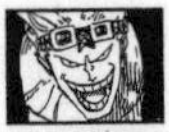	Eustass "Captain" Kid	=	13th century pirate monk Eustace + 17th century Scottish pirate William Kid
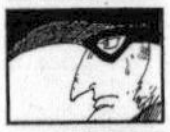	X. Drake	=	16th century English explorer, privateer and knight Francis Drake
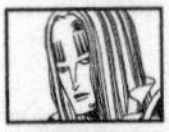	Basil Hawkins	=	Same as above John Hawkins + 17th century pirate ship doctor Basil Ringrose
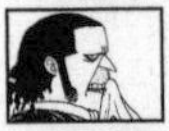	Capone "Gang" Bege	=	Same as above, Thomas Cavendish
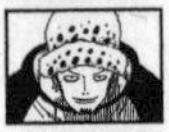	Trafalgar Law	=	18th century English pirate Edward Low
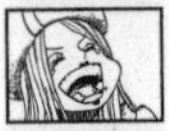	Jewelry Bonney	=	18th century female pirate Anne Bonny
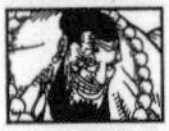	Urouge	=	16th century Turkish pirate Aruj Barbarossa
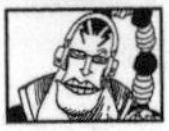	Scratchmen Apoo	=	19th century Chinese pirate Chui Apoo

I don't know about "Killer," but please correct me if I'm wrong!

--Chii-yan Mii-yan SP

A: Wonderful! Thank you so much! You saved me the trouble of explaining everything. But there is one thing I have to correct. Capone "Gang" Bege comes from the famous American gangster "Al Capone" and the English privateer William le Sauvage. You can think of privateers as pirates that are like the Seven Warlords of the Sea. Oh, and the name Killer is just made up. So yes, the rookies all have names taken from real pirates. But just the names. I think this should get a lot of pirate lovers really excited. Oh, and my Question Corner ends here! The special Question Corner section will start on page 148!

Chapter 509:
KIZARU VS. FOUR CAPTAINS

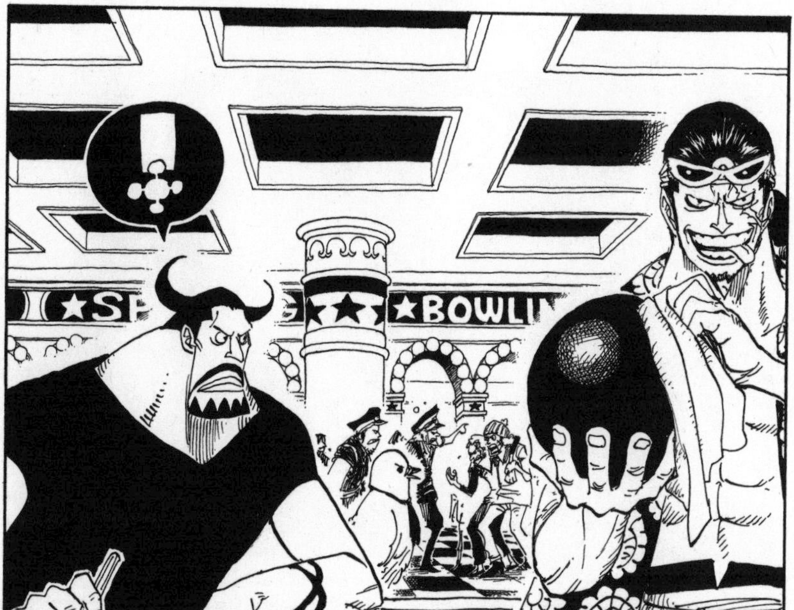
!
BOWLI
★S

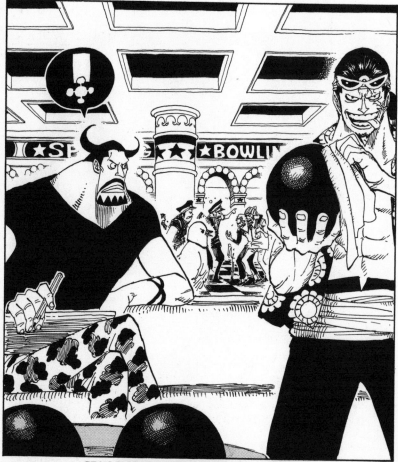

CP9'S INDEPENDENT REPORT, VOL. 17:
"COMMOTION IN TOWN"

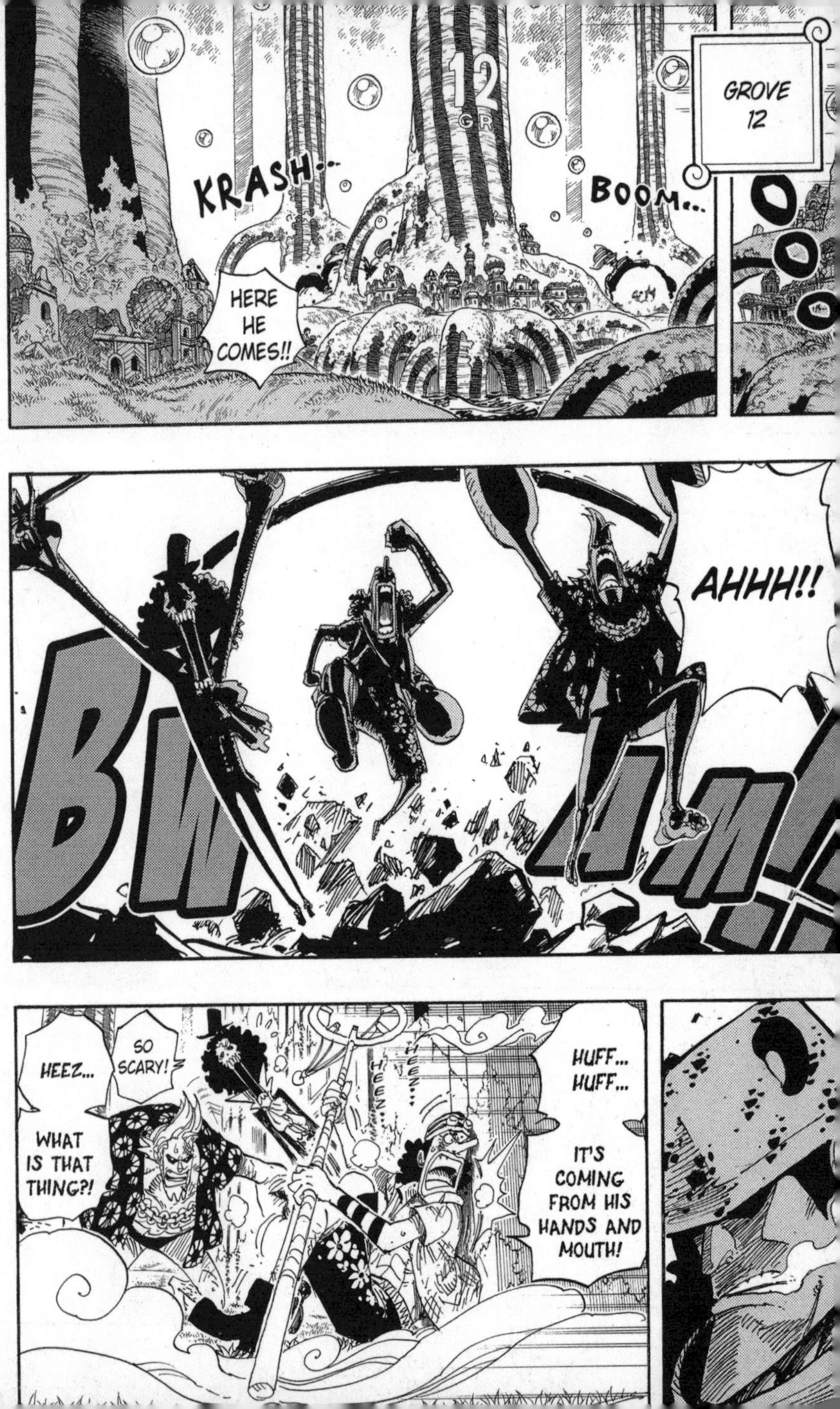
GROVE 12
BOOM...
KRASH...
HERE HE COMES!!
AHHH!!
HUFF... HUFF...
IT'S COMING FROM HIS HANDS AND MOUTH!
HEEZ...
SO SCARY!
HEEZ...
WHAT IS THAT THING?!

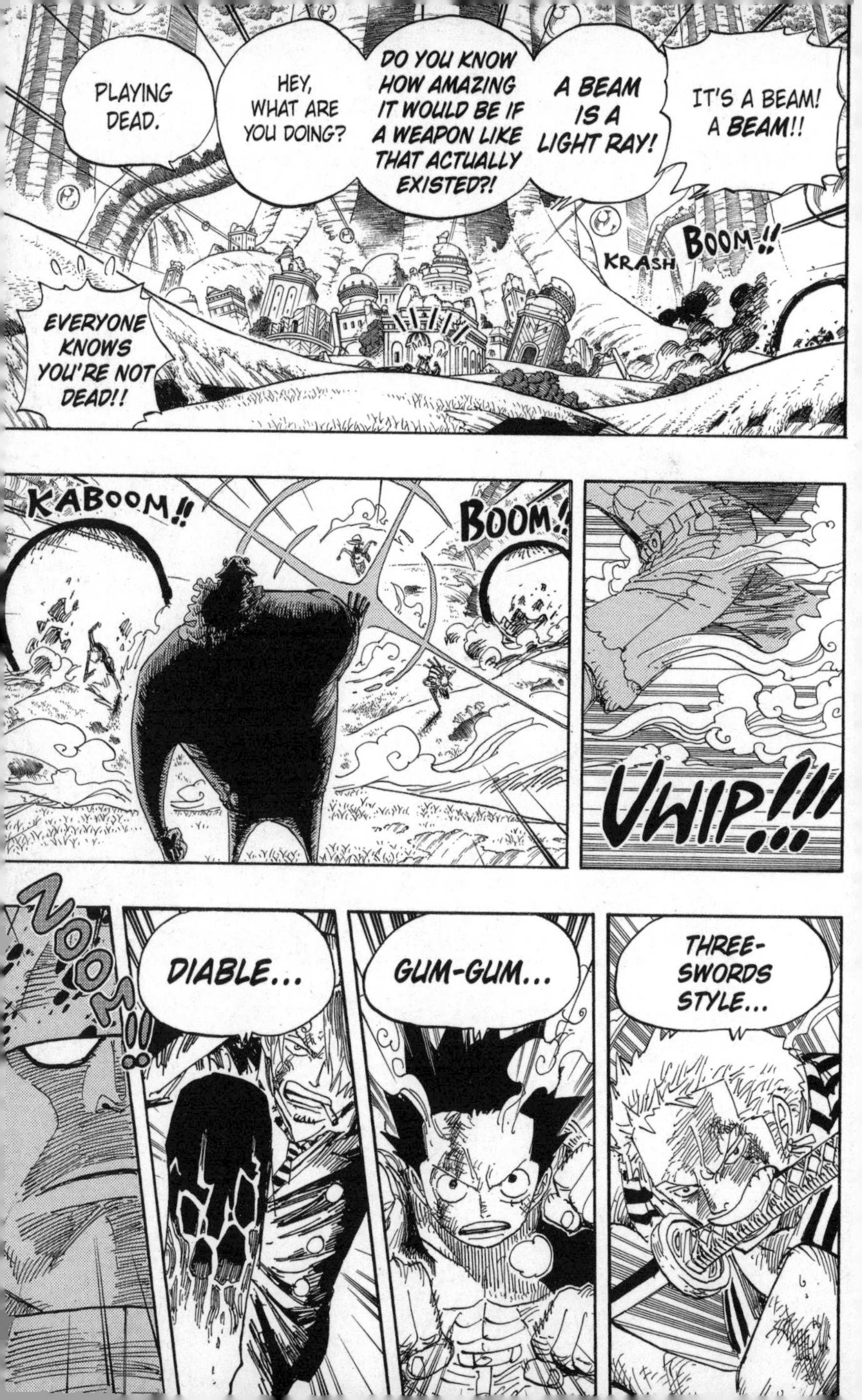
IT'S A BEAM! A BEAM!!
A BEAM IS A LIGHT RAY!
DO YOU KNOW HOW AMAZING IT WOULD BE IF A WEAPON LIKE THAT ACTUALLY EXISTED?!
HEY, WHAT ARE YOU DOING?
PLAYING DEAD.
BOOM!!
KRASH
EVERYONE KNOWS YOU'RE NOT DEAD!!
UWIP!!!
BOOM!!
KABOOM!!
THREE-SWORDS STYLE...
GUM-GUM...
DIABLE...
NOOM!!

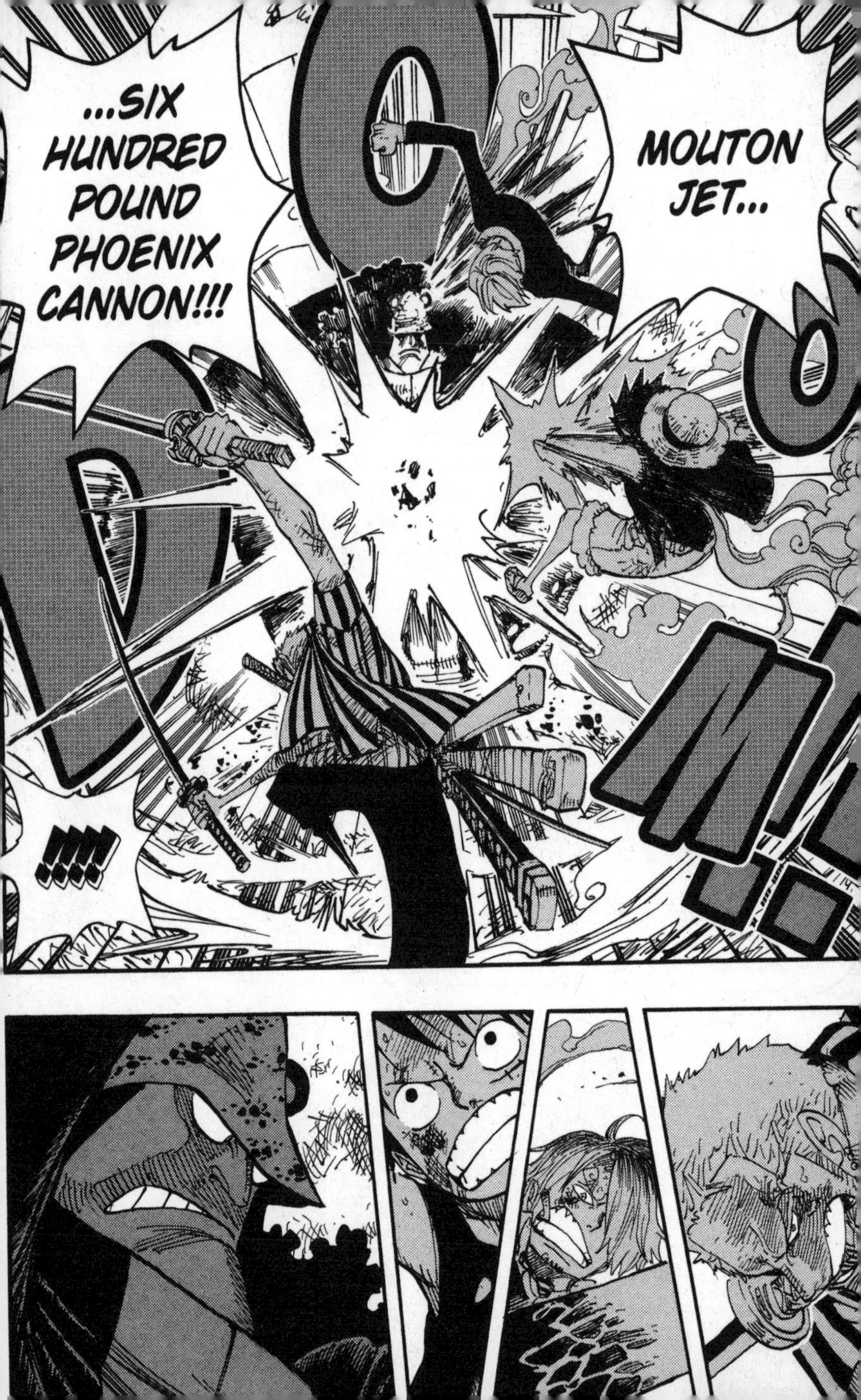
MOUTON JET...
...SIX HUNDRED POUND PHOENIX CANNON!!!
!!!!

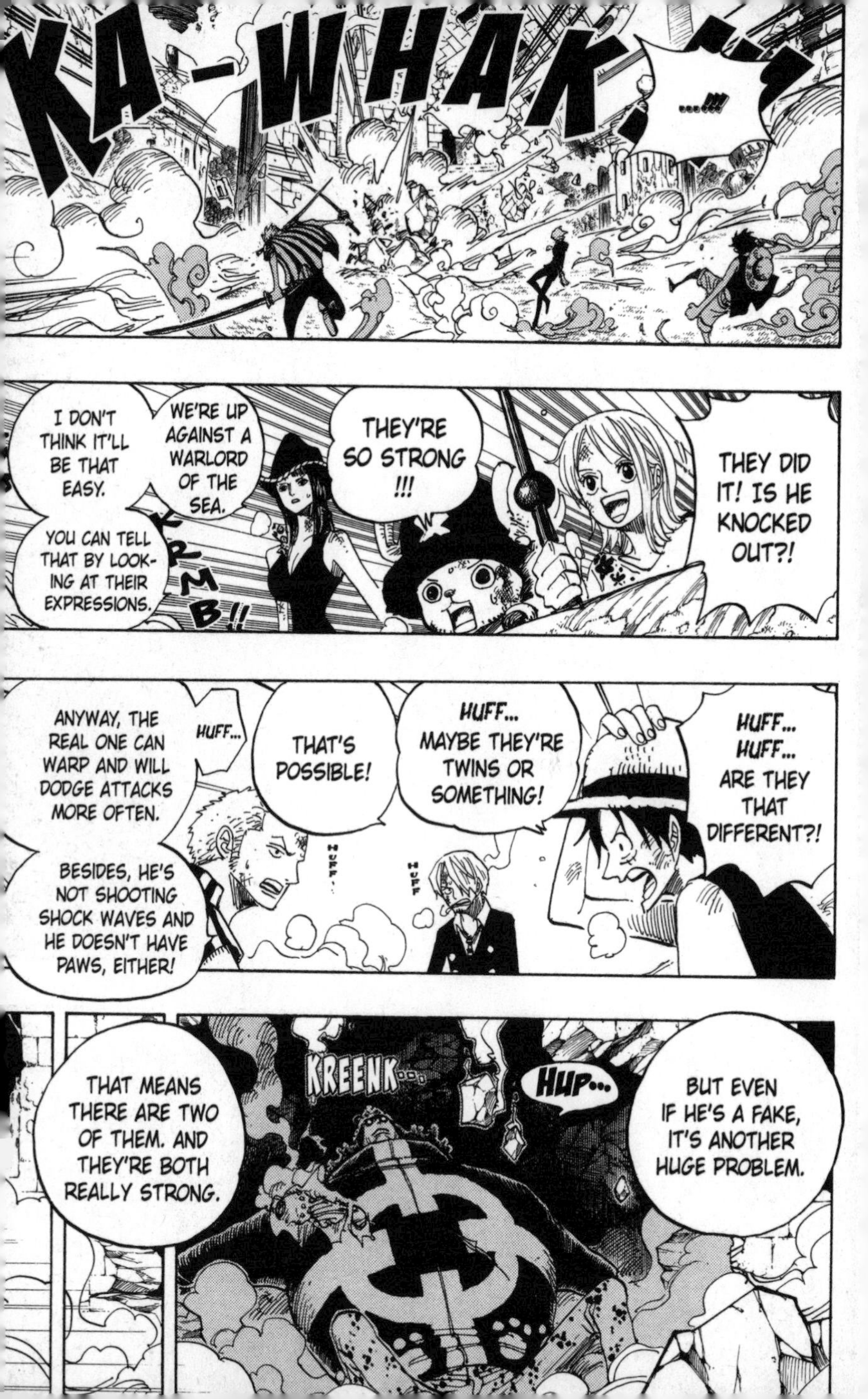
KA-WHAK
...!!!
THEY DID IT! IS HE KNOCKED OUT?!
THEY'RE SO STRONG !!!
WE'RE UP AGAINST A WARLORD OF THE SEA.
I DON'T THINK IT'LL BE THAT EASY.
YOU CAN TELL THAT BY LOOK-ING AT THEIR EXPRESSIONS.
KRMB!!
HUFF... HUFF... ARE THEY THAT DIFFERENT?!
HUFF... MAYBE THEY'RE TWINS OR SOMETHING!
THAT'S POSSIBLE!
HUFF
HUFF...
HUFF...
ANYWAY, THE REAL ONE CAN WARP AND WILL DODGE ATTACKS MORE OFTEN.
BESIDES, HE'S NOT SHOOTING SHOCK WAVES AND HE DOESN'T HAVE PAWS, EITHER!
BUT EVEN IF HE'S A FAKE, IT'S ANOTHER HUGE PROBLEM.
HUP...
KREENK...
THAT MEANS THERE ARE TWO OF THEM. AND THEY'RE BOTH REALLY STRONG.

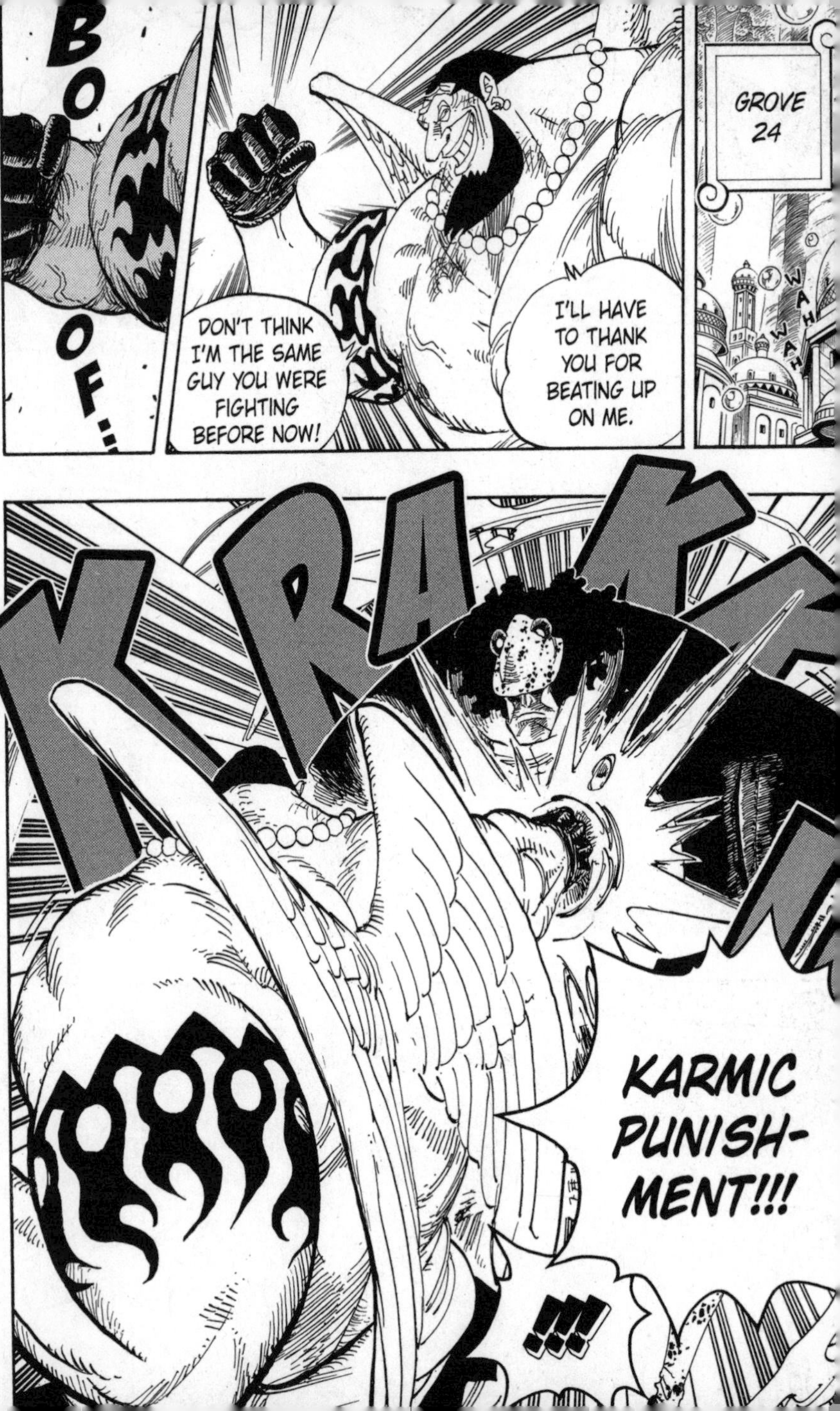

GROVE 24
WAH WAH
I'LL HAVE TO THANK YOU FOR BEATING UP ON ME.
DON'T THINK I'M THE SAME GUY YOU WERE FIGHTING BEFORE NOW!
BOOF...
KRAK
KARMIC PUNISH-MENT!!!
!!!

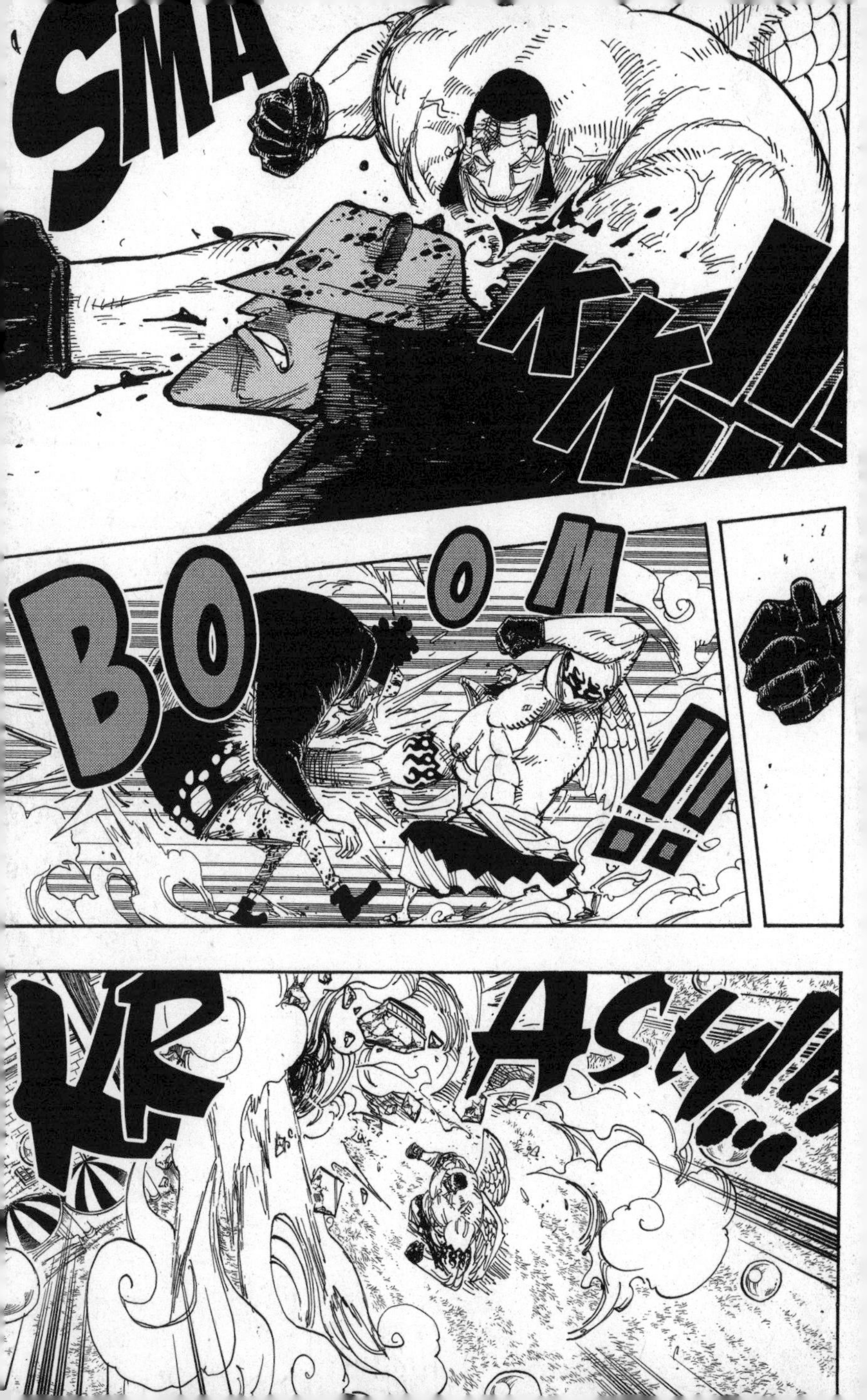
SMACK!!
BOOM!!
KRASH!!

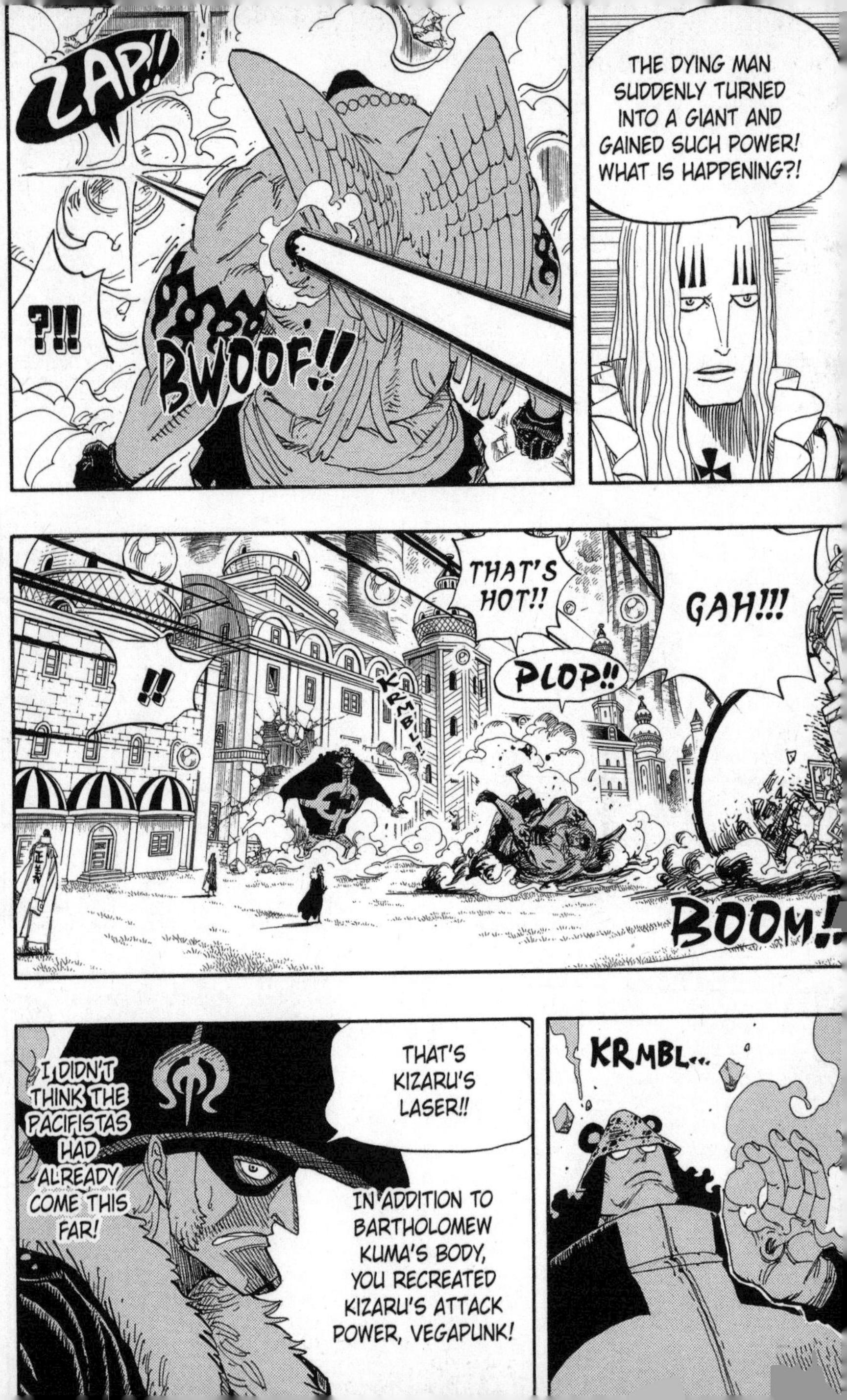
THE DYING MAN SUDDENLY TURNED INTO A GIANT AND GAINED SUCH POWER! WHAT IS HAPPENING?!
ZAP!!
BWOOF!!
?!!
GAH!!!
THAT'S HOT!!
PLOP!!
BOOM!!
KRMBL...
!!
KRMBL...
THAT'S KIZARU'S LASER!!
IN ADDITION TO BARTHOLOMEW KUMA'S BODY, YOU RECREATED KIZARU'S ATTACK POWER, VEGAPUNK!
I DIDN'T THINK THE PACIFISTAS HAD ALREADY COME THIS FAR!

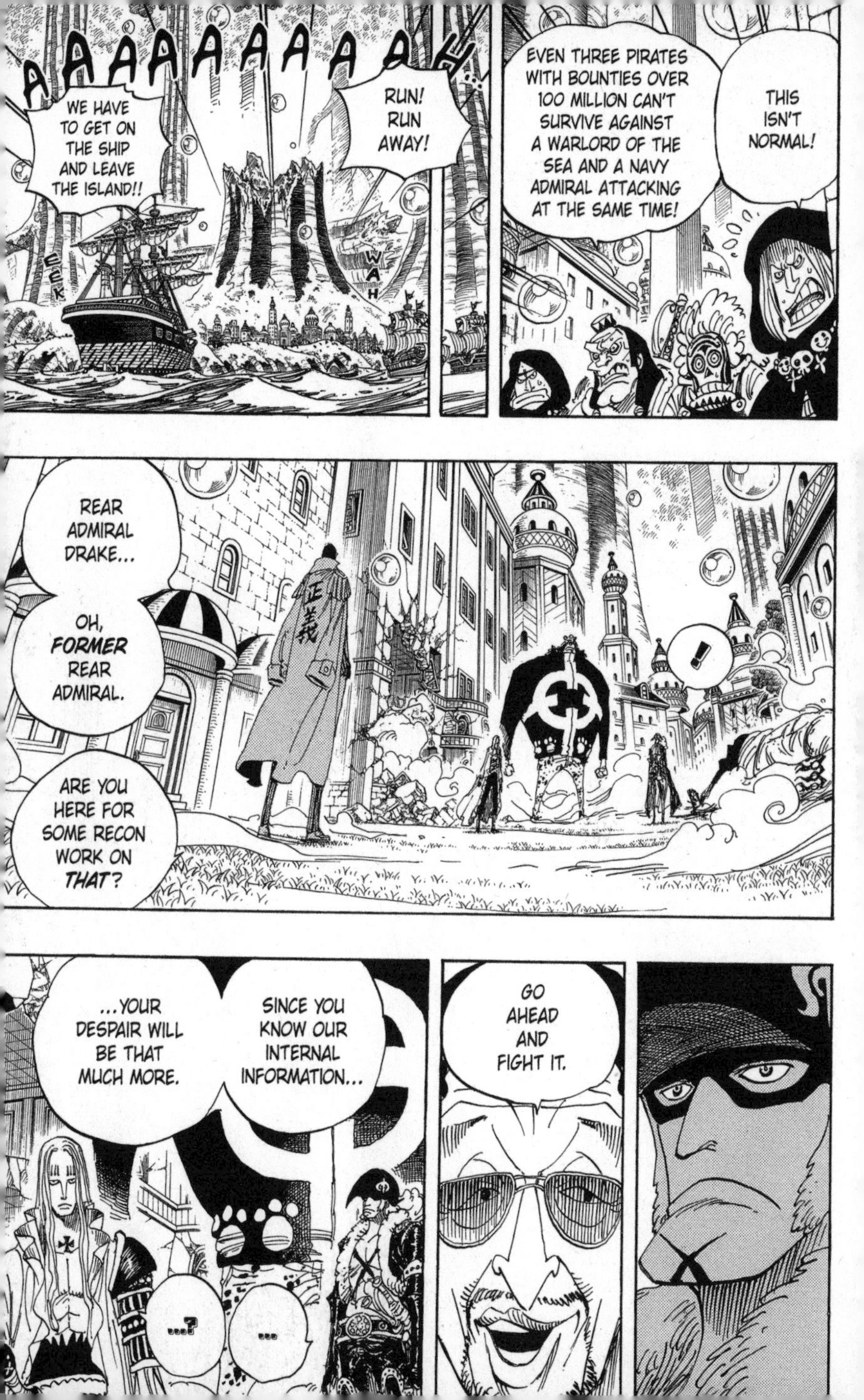
THIS ISN'T NORMAL!
EVEN THREE PIRATES WITH BOUNTIES OVER 100 MILLION CAN'T SURVIVE AGAINST A WARLORD OF THE SEA AND A NAVY ADMIRAL ATTACKING AT THE SAME TIME!
AAAAAAAAAH...
RUN! RUN AWAY!
WE HAVE TO GET ON THE SHIP AND LEAVE THE ISLAND!!
WAH
EEK
REAR ADMIRAL DRAKE...
OH, FORMER REAR ADMIRAL.
ARE YOU HERE FOR SOME RECON WORK ON THAT?
!
GO AHEAD AND FIGHT IT.
SINCE YOU KNOW OUR INTERNAL INFORMATION...
...YOUR DESPAIR WILL BE THAT MUCH MORE.
...
...?

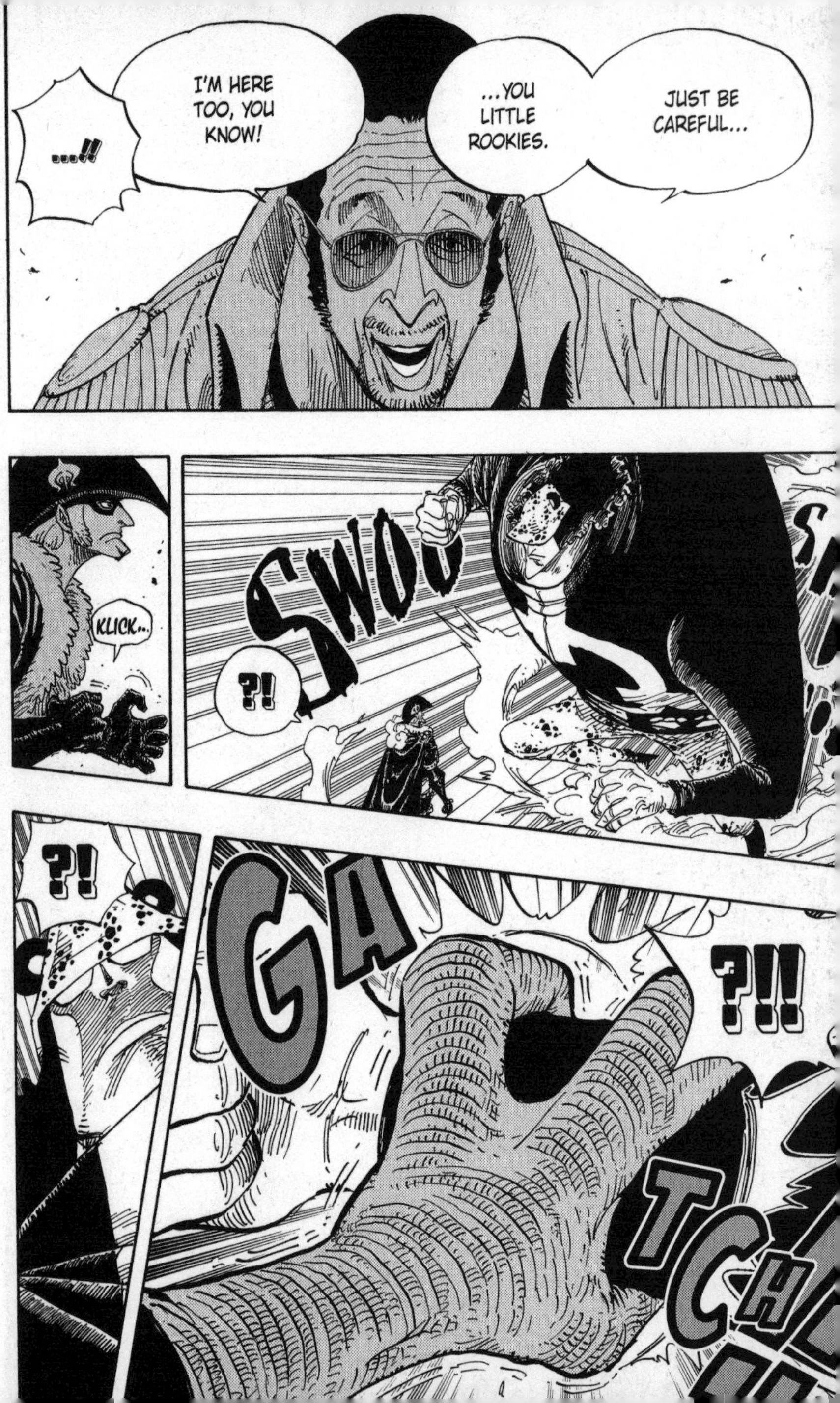
JUST BE CAREFUL...
...YOU LITTLE ROOKIES.
I'M HERE TOO, YOU KNOW!
...!!
SWOO
?!
KLICK...
TCH
?!!
GA
?!

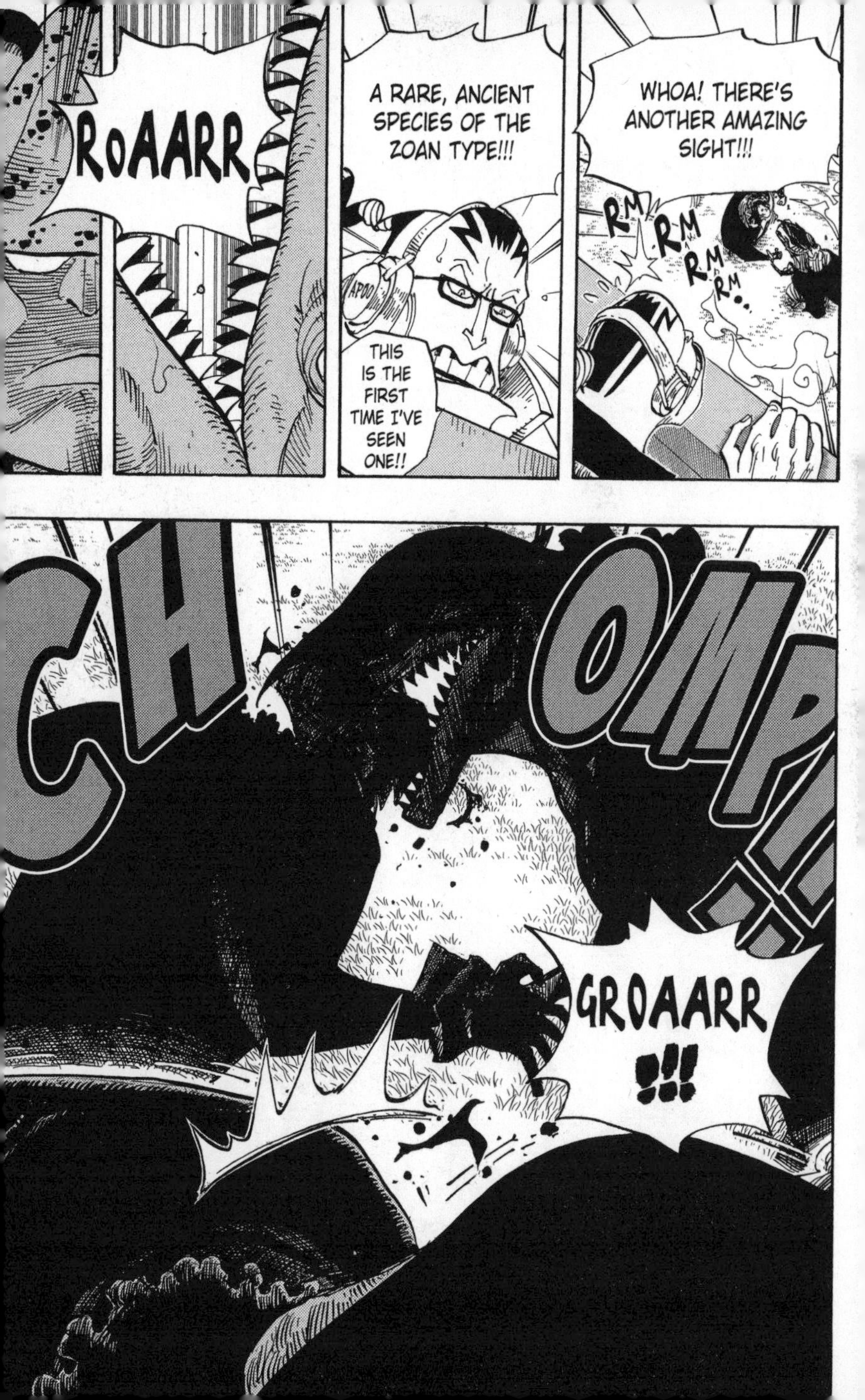
WHOA! THERE'S ANOTHER AMAZING SIGHT!!!
RM RM RM RM...
A RARE, ANCIENT SPECIES OF THE ZOAN TYPE!!!
APOO
THIS IS THE FIRST TIME I'VE SEEN ONE!!
ROAARR
CHOMP!!
GROAARR!!!

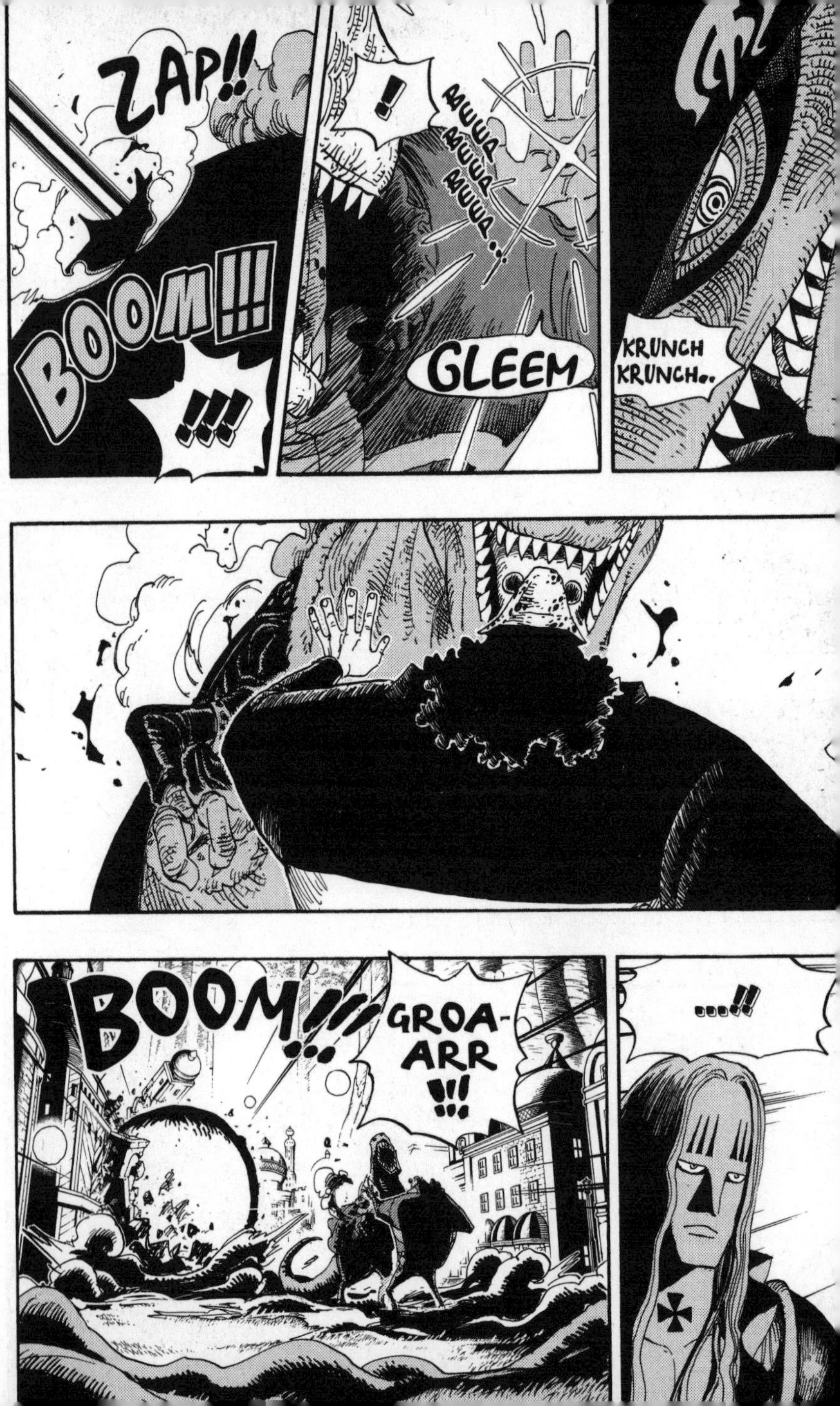
KRUNCH KRUNCH..
!
BWWA BWWA BWWA..
GLEEM
ZAP!!
BOOM!!!
!!!
...!!
GROA-ARR!!!
BOOM!!!...

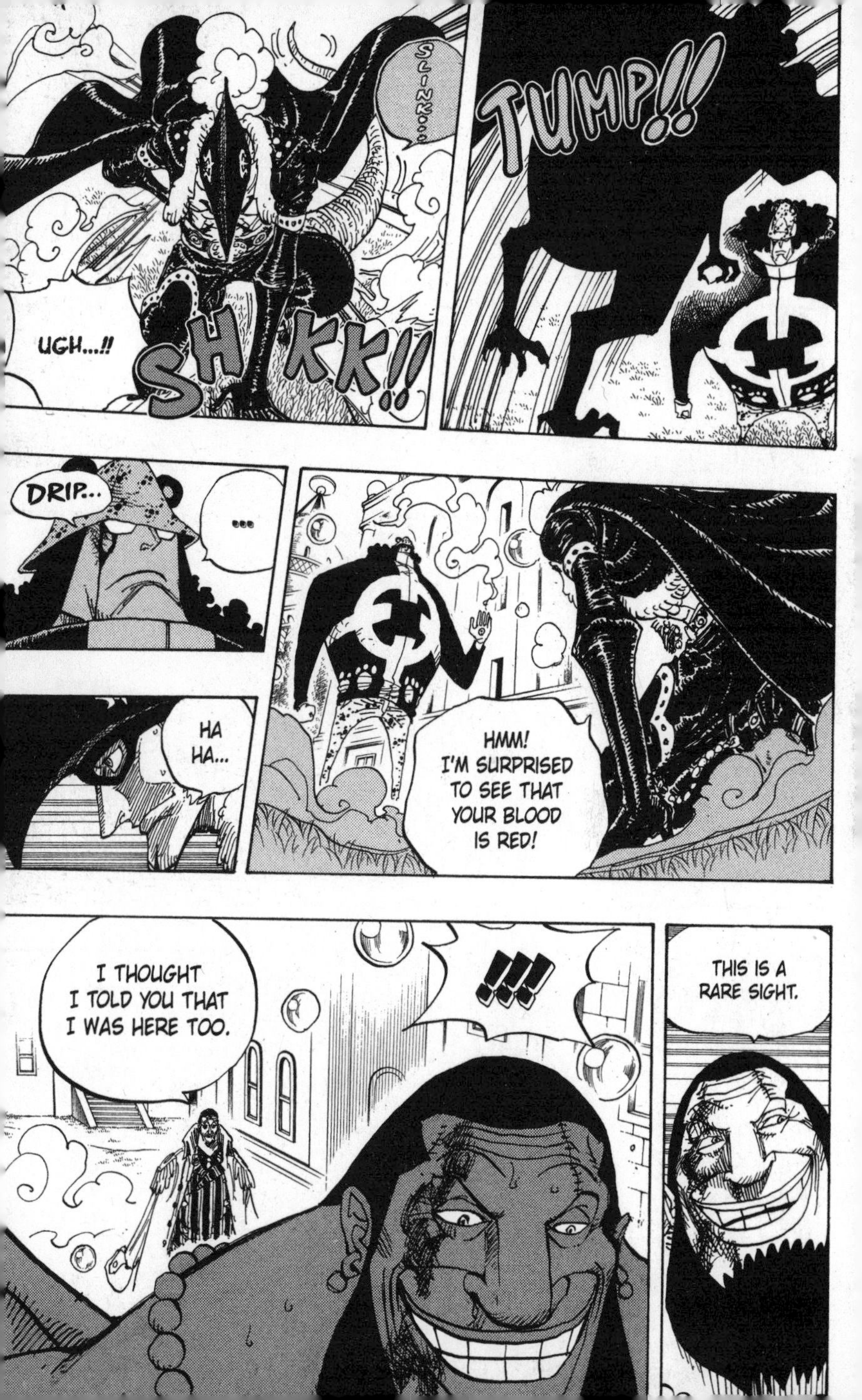
TUMP!!
SLINK...
UGH...!!
SHKK!!
HMM! I'M SURPRISED TO SEE THAT YOUR BLOOD IS RED!
DRIP...
...
HA HA...
THIS IS A RARE SIGHT.
!!!
I THOUGHT I TOLD YOU THAT I WAS HERE TOO.

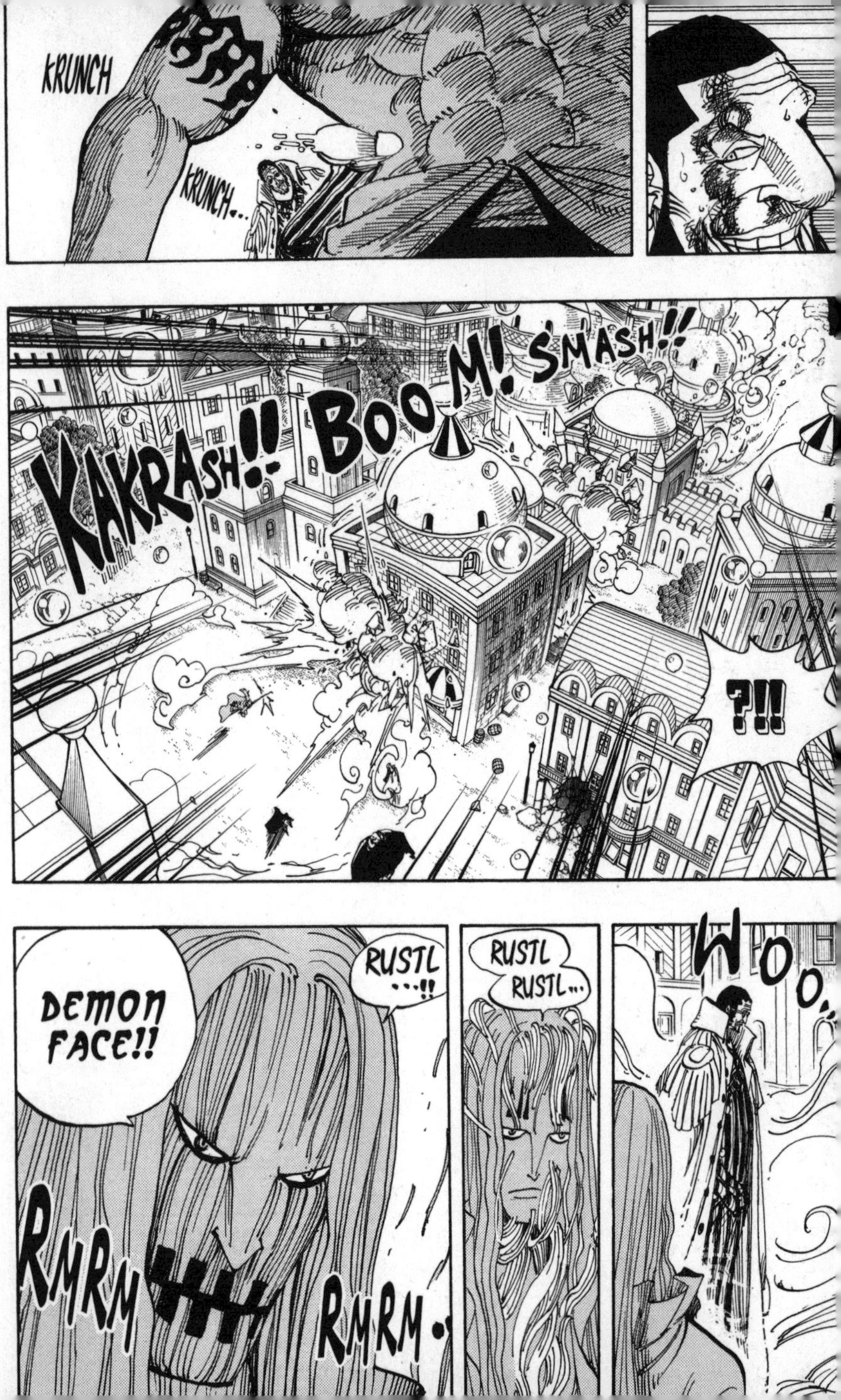

KRUNCH
KRUNCH...
KAKRASH!!
BOOM!
SMASH!!
?!!
WOO...
RUSTL
RUSTL...
RUSTL
...!!
DEMON FACE!!
RMRM
RMRM...

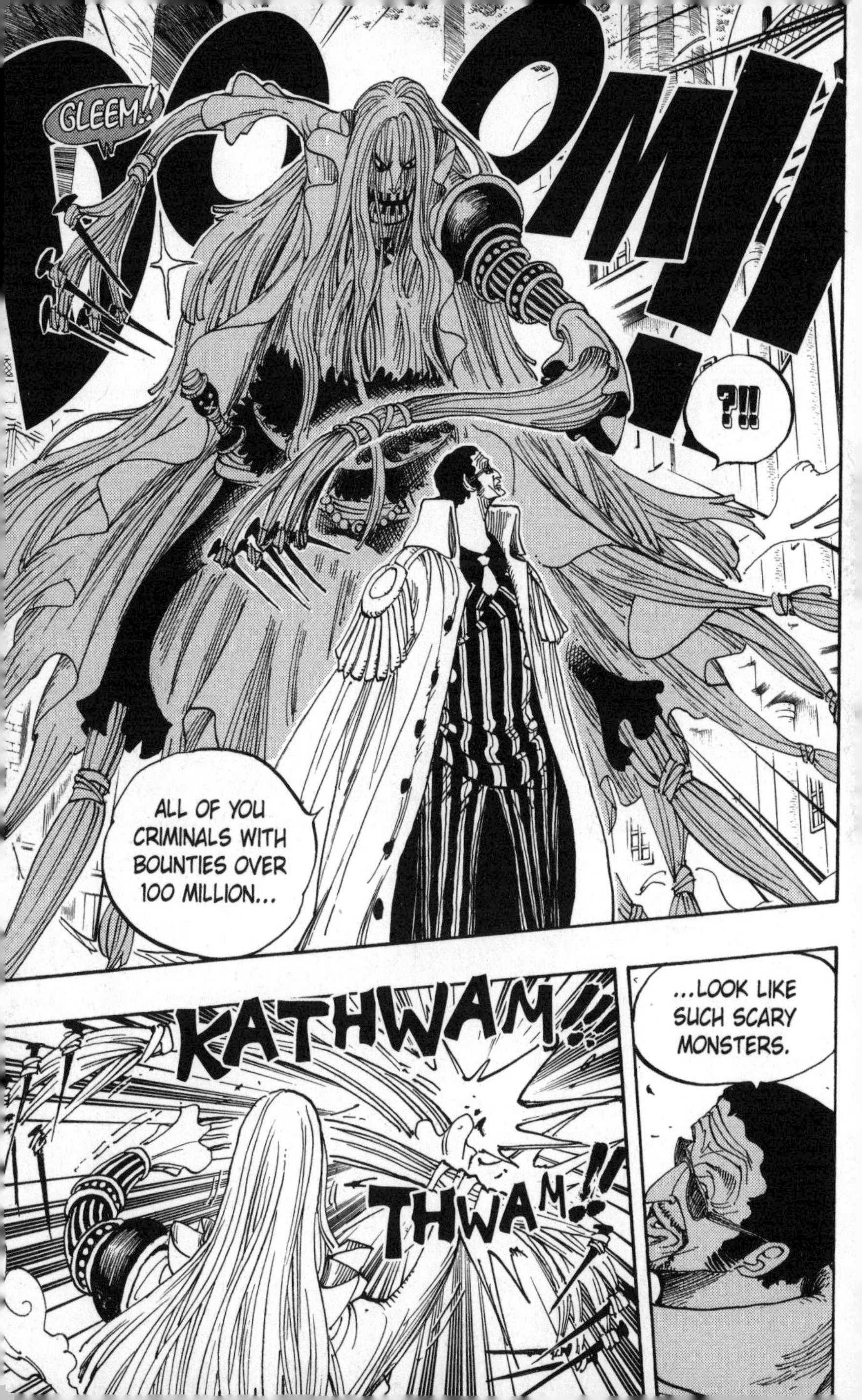
DOOM!!
?!!
GLEEM!!
ALL OF YOU CRIMINALS WITH BOUNTIES OVER 100 MILLION...
...LOOK LIKE SUCH SCARY MONSTERS.
KATHWAM!!
THWAM!!

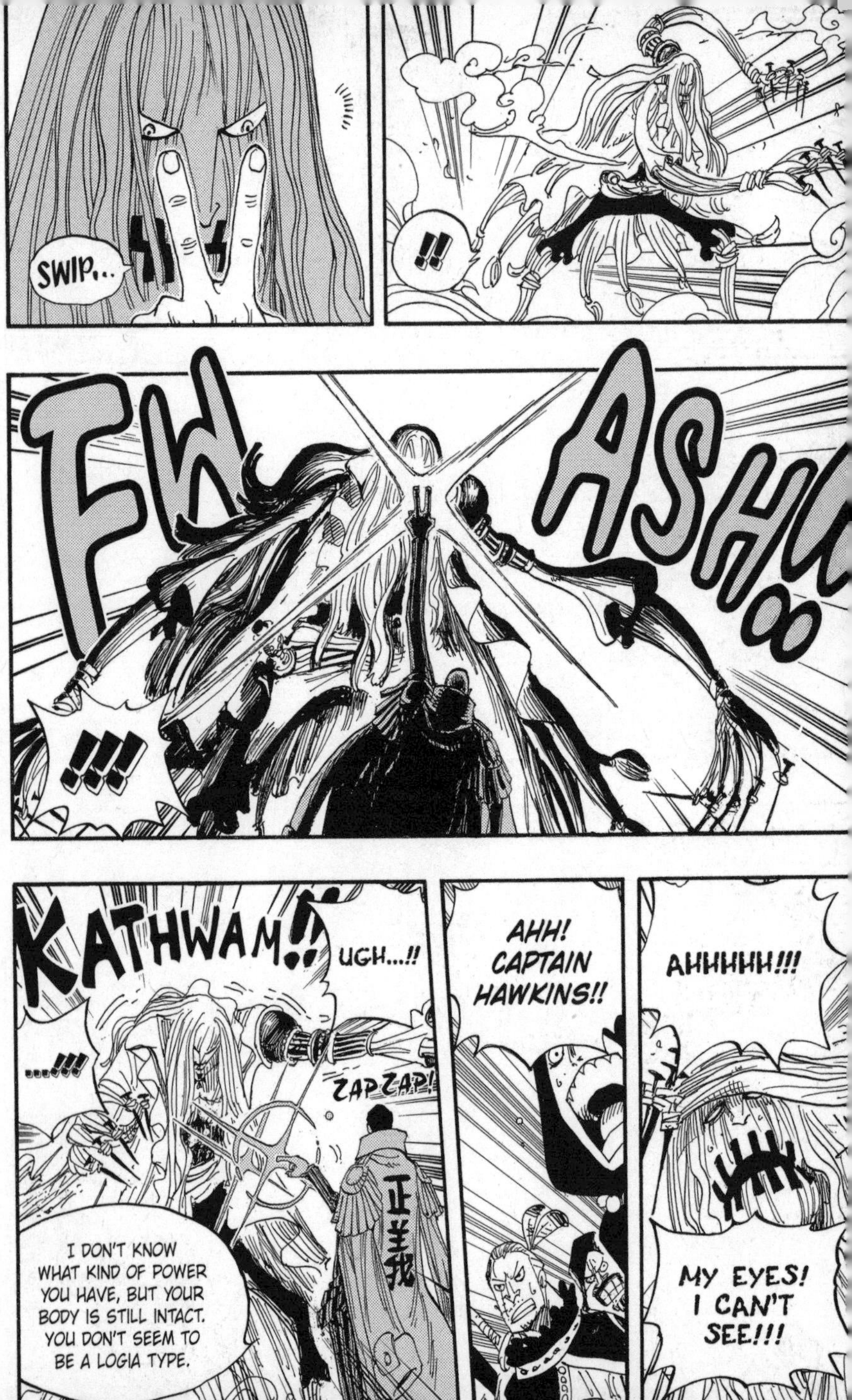
!!
SWIP...
FWASH..
!!!!
AHHHHH!!!
MY EYES! I CAN'T SEE!!!
AHH! CAPTAIN HAWKINS!!
UGH...!!
KATHWAM!!
ZAP ZAP!
...!!!
I DON'T KNOW WHAT KIND OF POWER YOU HAVE, BUT YOUR BODY IS STILL INTACT. YOU DON'T SEEM TO BE A LOGIA TYPE.

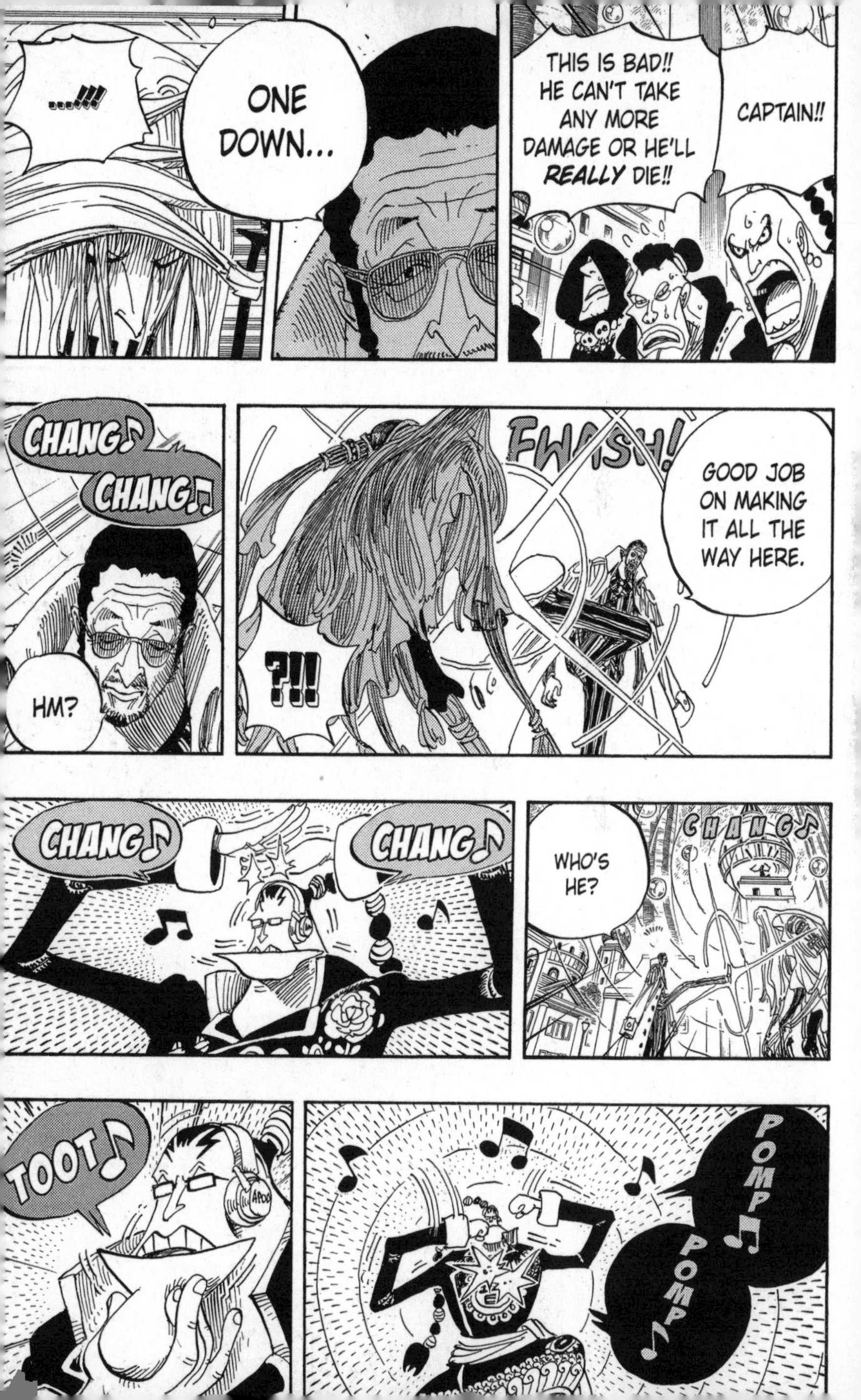
CAPTAIN!!
THIS IS BAD!! HE CAN'T TAKE ANY MORE DAMAGE OR HE'LL *REALLY* DIE!!
ONE DOWN...
...!!!
FWASH!
GOOD JOB ON MAKING IT ALL THE WAY HERE.
?!!
CHANG♪
CHANG♪
HM?
CHANG♪
WHO'S HE?
CHANG♪
CHANG♪
POMP♪
POMP♪
TOOT♪

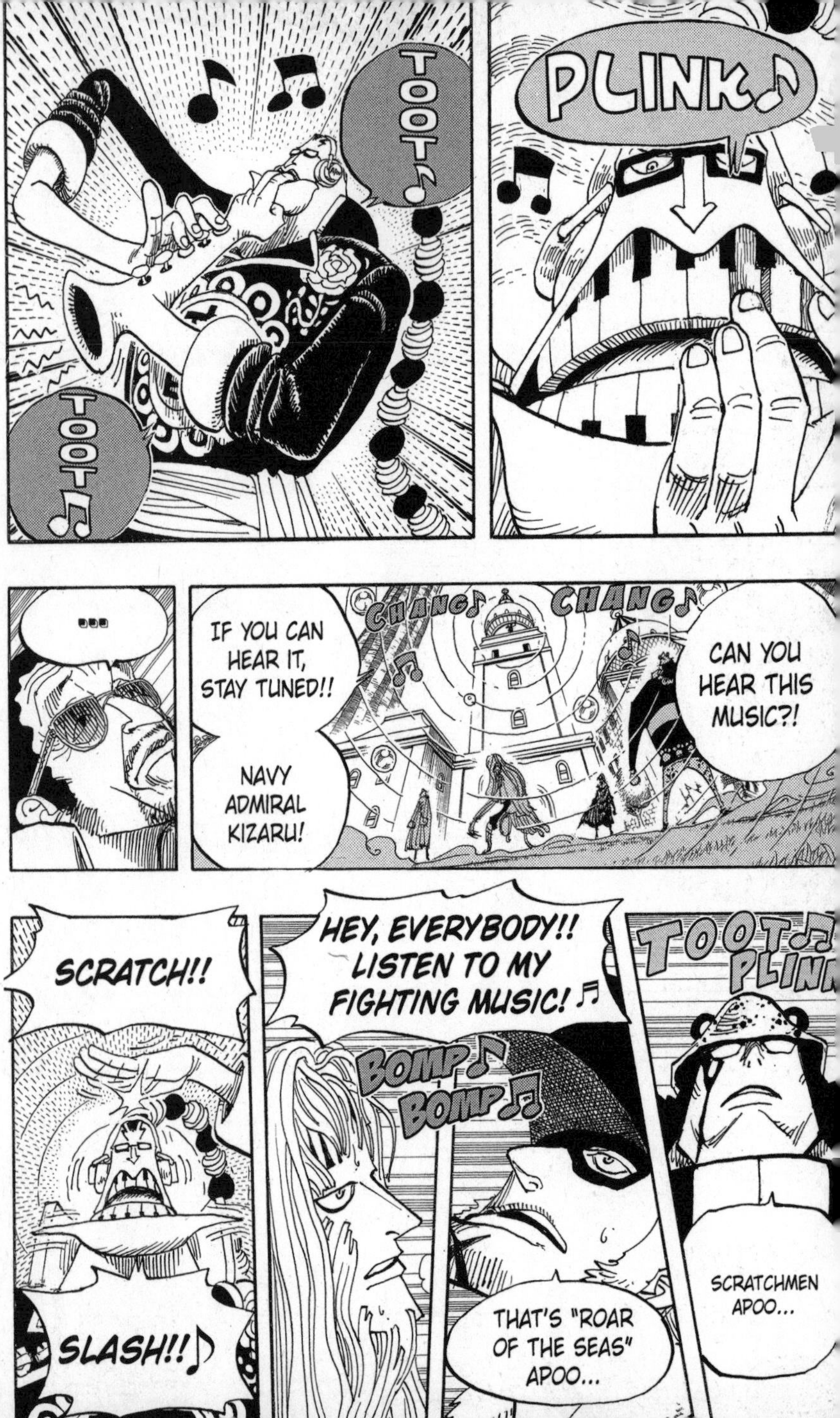
PLINK♪
TOOT♪
TOOT♪
CHANG♪ CHANG♪
CAN YOU HEAR THIS MUSIC?!
IF YOU CAN HEAR IT, STAY TUNED!!
NAVY ADMIRAL KIZARU!
...
TOOT♪
SCRATCHMEN APOO...
HEY, EVERYBODY!! LISTEN TO MY FIGHTING MUSIC!♪
BOMP♪ BOMP♪
THAT'S "ROAR OF THE SEAS" APOO...
SCRATCH!!
SLASH!!♪

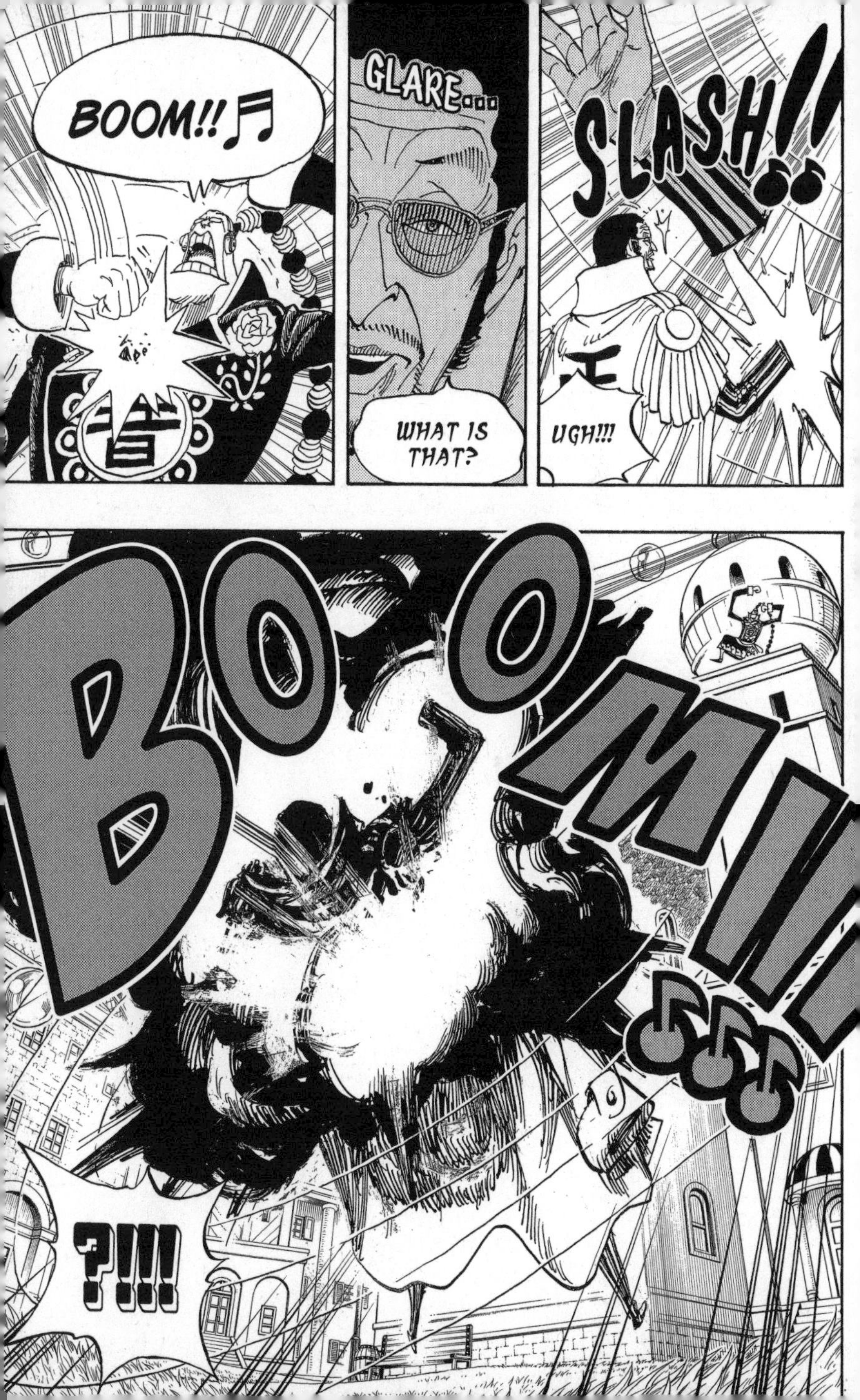
SLASH!!
UGH!!!
GLARE...
WHAT IS THAT?
BOOM!! ♫
BOOM!!
?!!!

SBS Question Corner

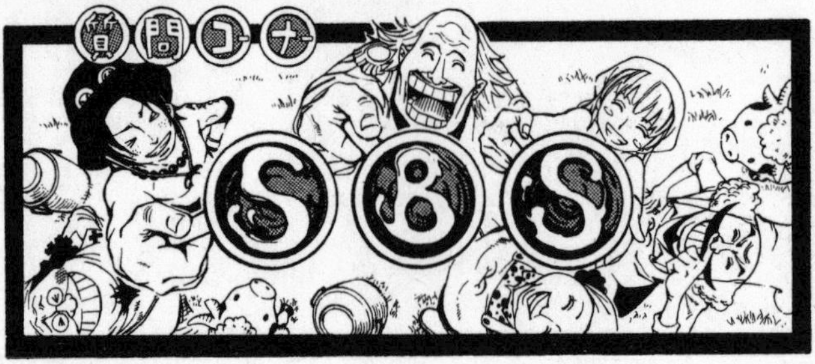
SBS

(Harry Milky, Tokyo)

HSK (Hello Silly Kids)
Thanks for waiting. I've been receiving many letters asking for voice actors' profiles for a long time now. I wonder which volume it was where I first said, "then let's do a voice actor Question Corner"... I'm known as a grown-up who always fulfills his promises, even if it takes a little extra time. So here I am, fulfilling a promise! What's up, guys?!

Well, first things first, let's start with the voice of our hero, Monkey D. Luffy! The prodigal voice actress Mayumi Tanaka is in the house!

Oda: Hello, Mayumi.

Tanaka: Yes, hello. What's the matter?

O: We're doing an SBS today.

T: Oh, that. The (S)low (B)reaks done (S)lowly.

O: You're sort of right, but the right answer is... Well, just try it out yourself. Here are the postcards you have to answer (Drops a stack).

T: Oh? They sent in this many questions?

O: Yup. My readers do this all the time. So, please, answer them!

Preview for the next Voice Actor Question Corner

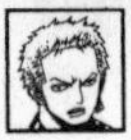
Zolo (Kazuya Nakai)

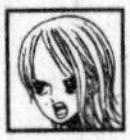
Nami (Akemi Okamura)

Chapter 510:
STRAW HAT PIRATES VS. WAR MACHINE

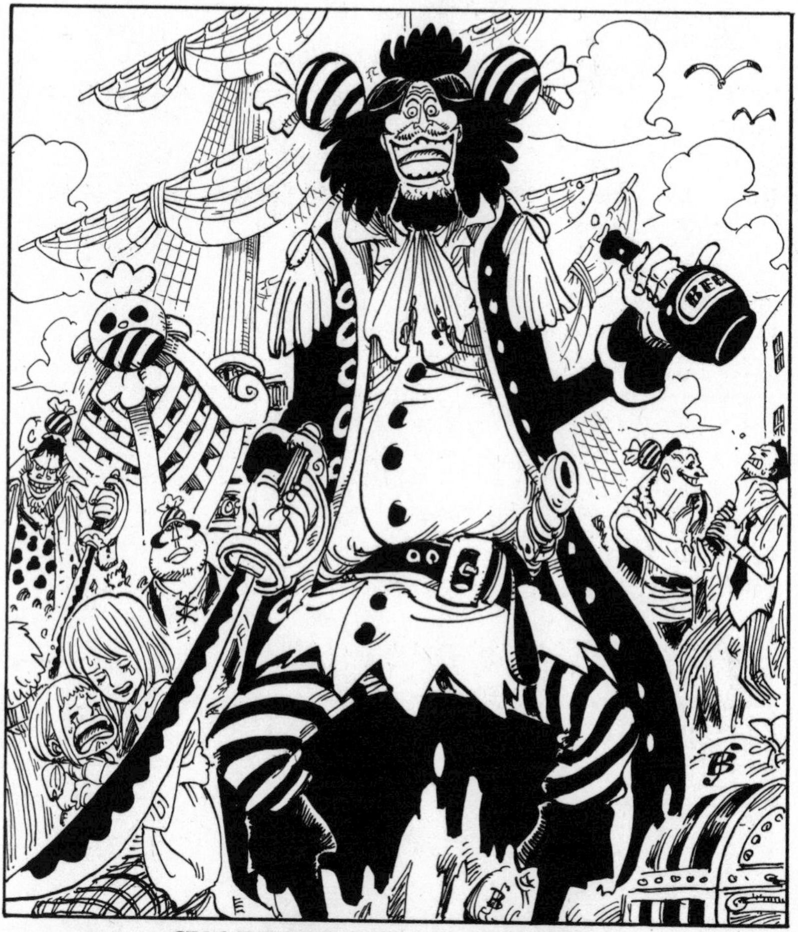

CP9'S INDEPENDENT REPORT, VOL. 18:
"CANDY PIRATES AT THE ST. POPLAR PORT!"

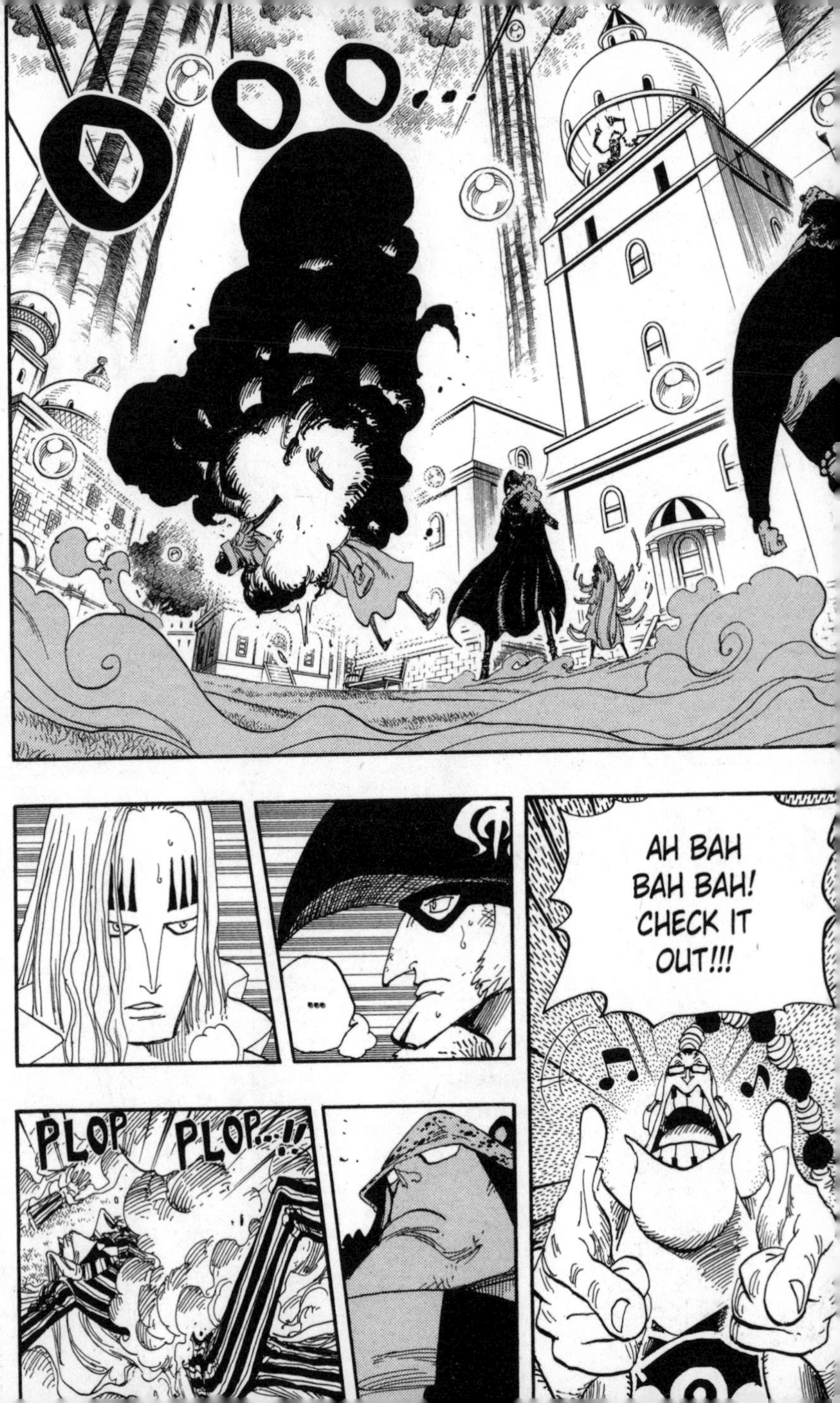
OOO...
AH BAH BAH BAH! CHECK IT OUT!!!
...
PLOP PLOP...!!

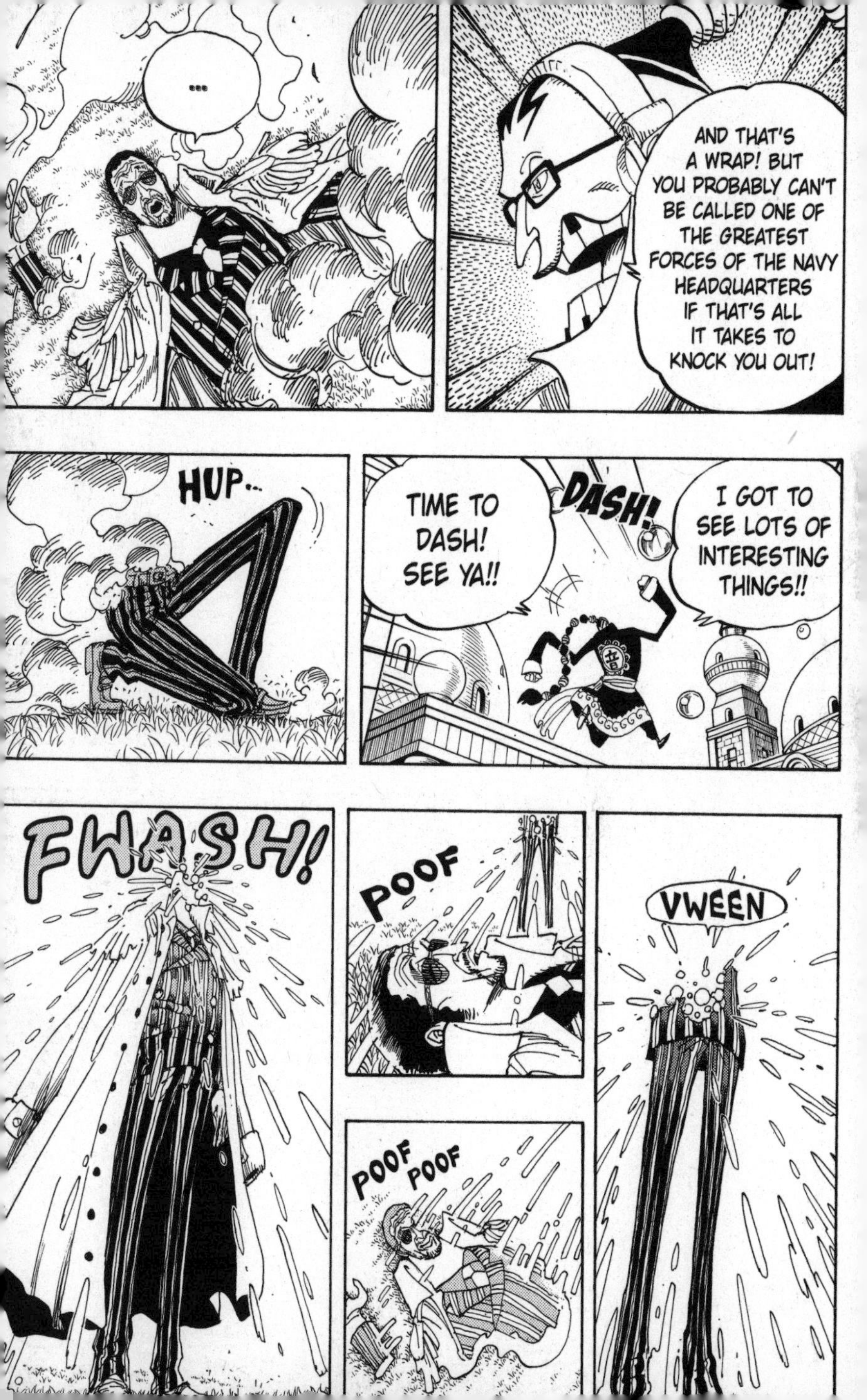
AND THAT'S A WRAP! BUT YOU PROBABLY CAN'T BE CALLED ONE OF THE GREATEST FORCES OF THE NAVY HEADQUARTERS IF THAT'S ALL IT TAKES TO KNOCK YOU OUT!
...
I GOT TO SEE LOTS OF INTERESTING THINGS!!
DASH!
TIME TO DASH! SEE YA!!
HUP...
VWEEN
POOF
POOF POOF
FWASH!

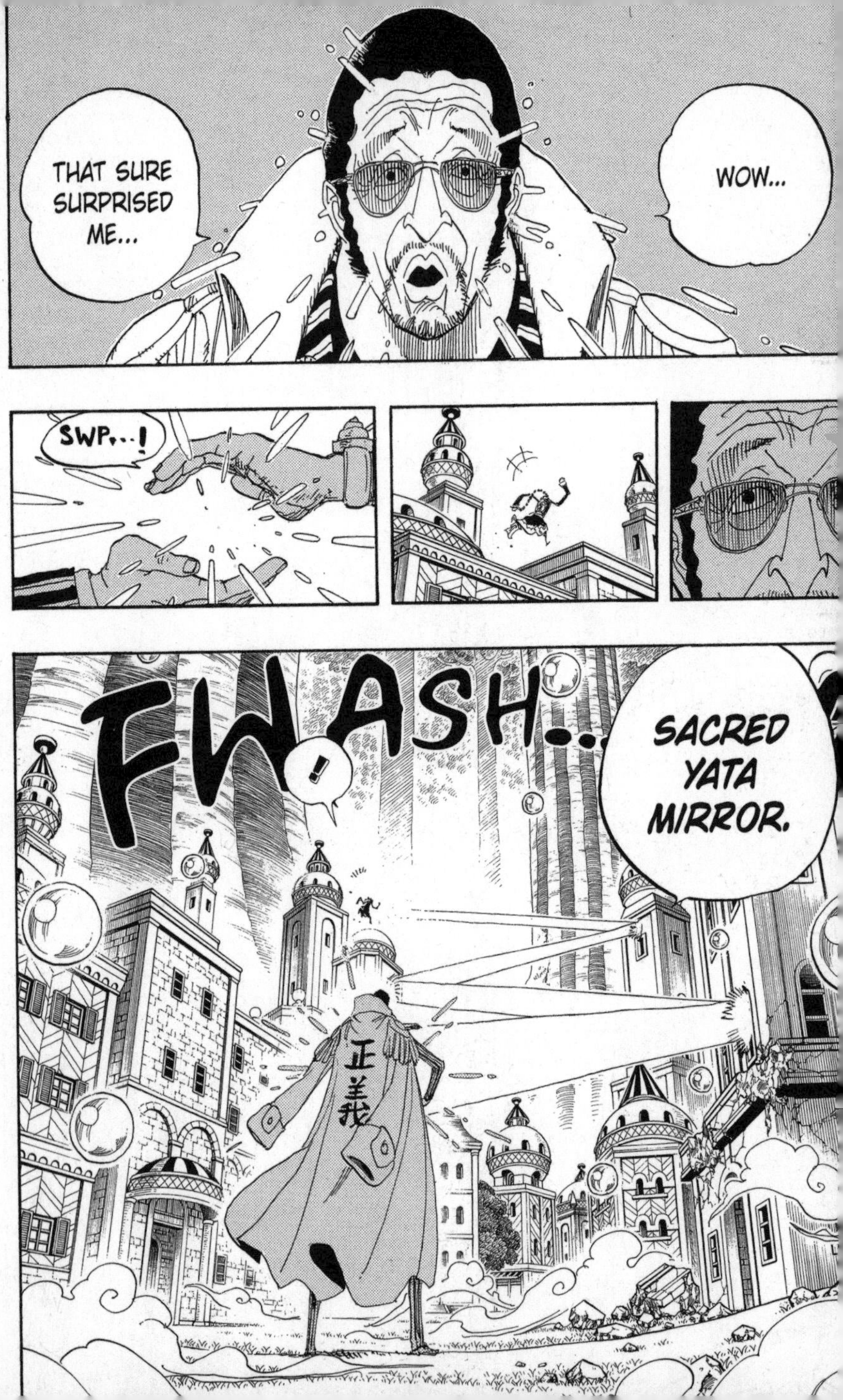
WOW...
THAT SURE SURPRISED ME...
SWP...!
SACRED YATA MIRROR.
FLASH...
!

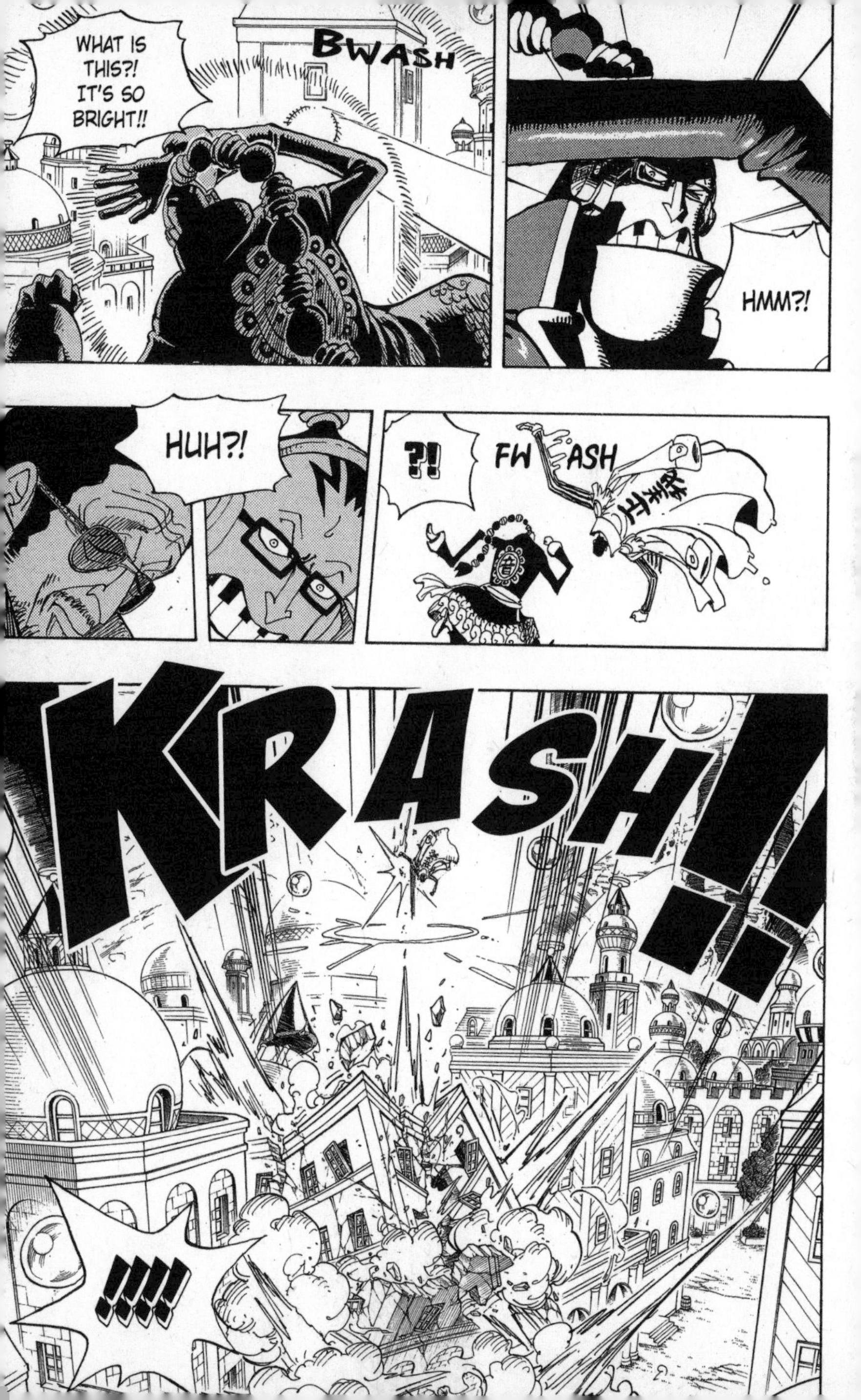
HMM?!
BWASH
WHAT IS THIS?! IT'S SO BRIGHT!!
FW ASH
?!
HUH?!
KRASH!!
!!!!

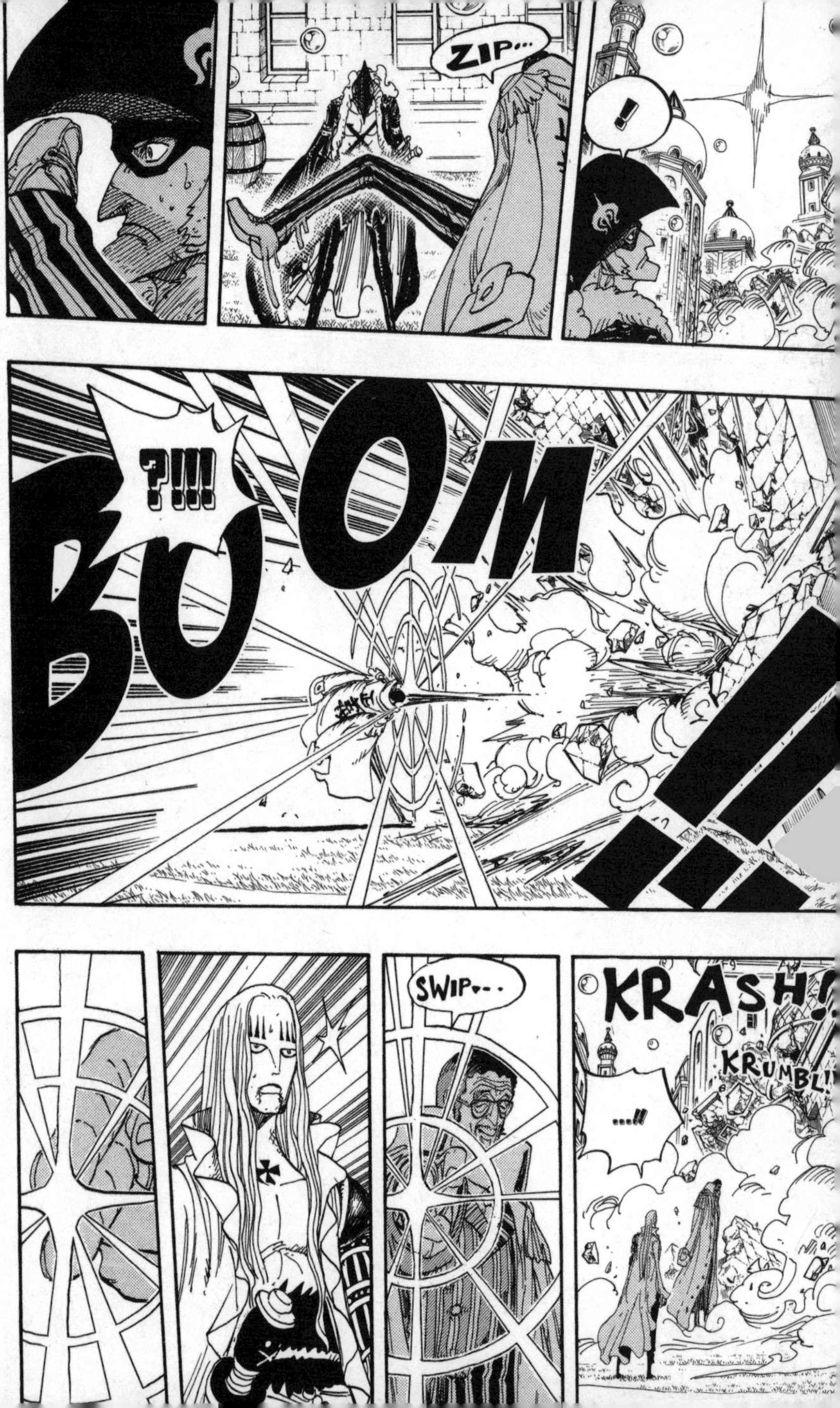
!
ZIP...
BOOM!!
?!!!
KRASH!
KRUMBL!
...!!
SWIP...

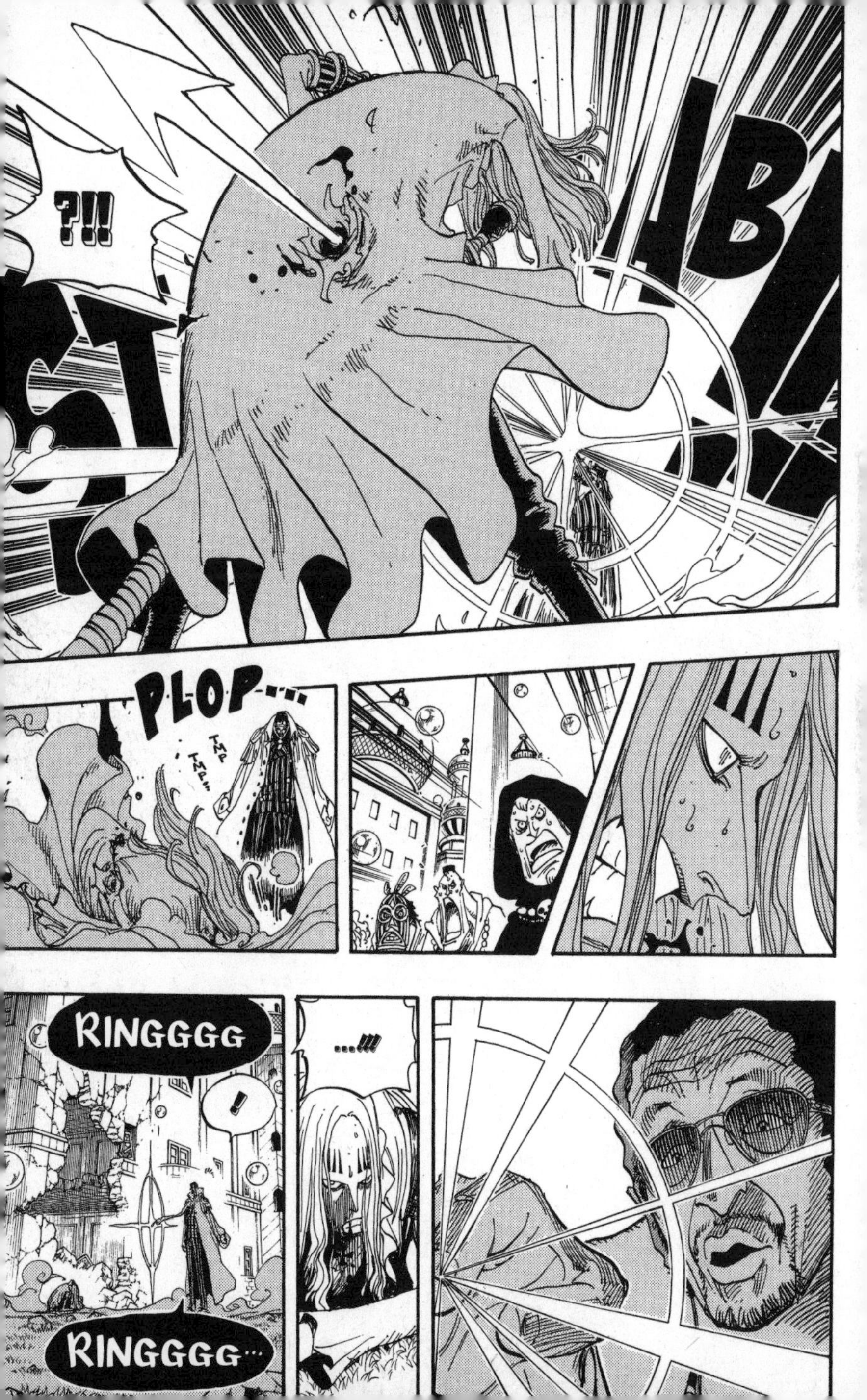
?!!
PLOP...!!
TMP TMP!!
RINGGGG
!
RINGGGG...
...!!!

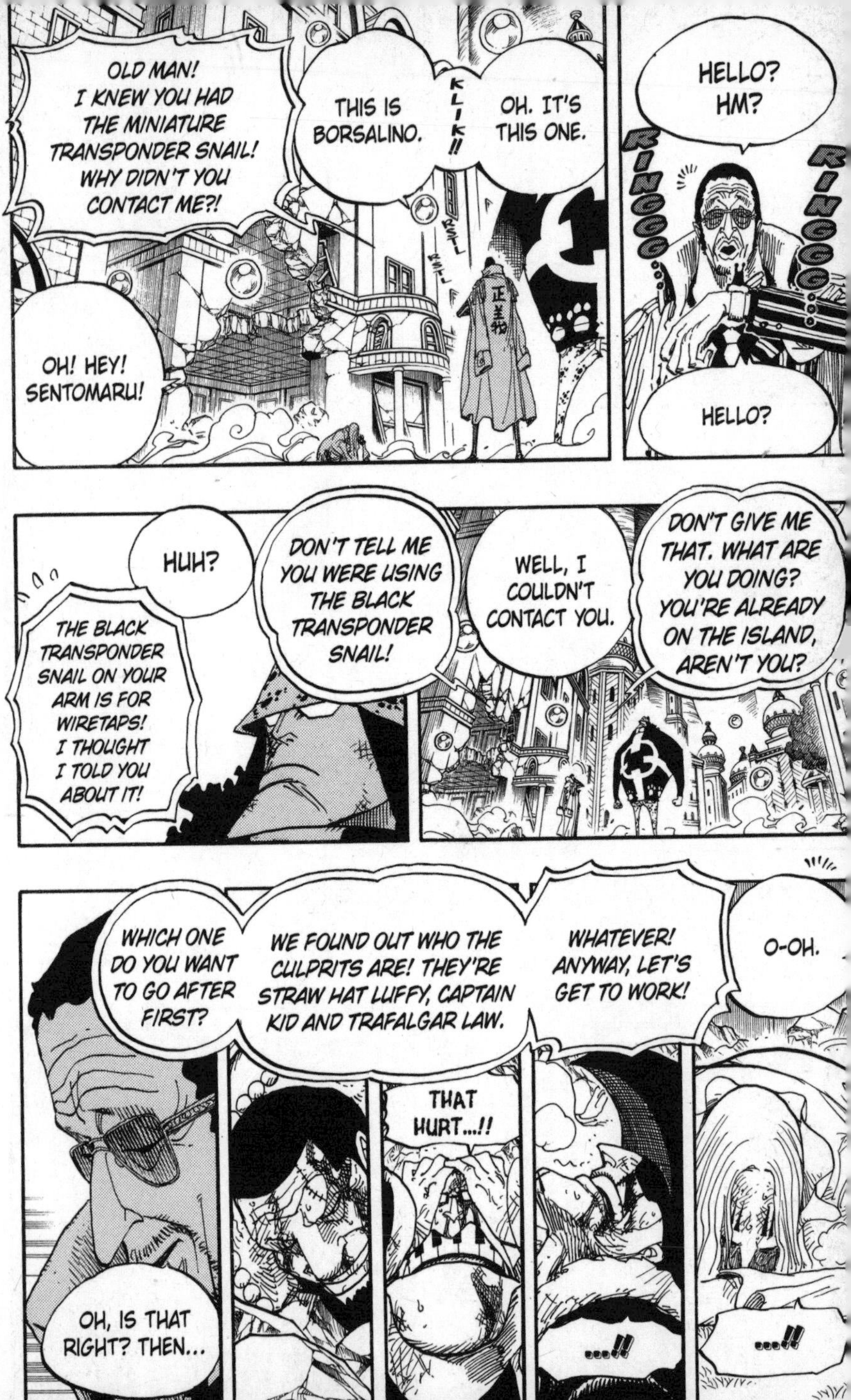
HELLO?
HM?
RINGGG
RINGGG
HELLO?
OH. IT'S THIS ONE.
KLIK!!
THIS IS BORSALINO.
RSTL
RSTL
OLD MAN! I KNEW YOU HAD THE MINIATURE TRANSPONDER SNAIL! WHY DIDN'T YOU CONTACT ME?!
OH! HEY! SENTOMARU!
DON'T GIVE ME THAT. WHAT ARE YOU DOING? YOU'RE ALREADY ON THE ISLAND, AREN'T YOU?
WELL, I COULDN'T CONTACT YOU.
DON'T TELL ME YOU WERE USING THE BLACK TRANSPONDER SNAIL!
HUH?
THE BLACK TRANSPONDER SNAIL ON YOUR ARM IS FOR WIRETAPS! I THOUGHT I TOLD YOU ABOUT IT!
O-OH.
WHATEVER! ANYWAY, LET'S GET TO WORK!
WE FOUND OUT WHO THE CULPRITS ARE! THEY'RE STRAW HAT LUFFY, CAPTAIN KID AND TRAFALGAR LAW.
WHICH ONE DO YOU WANT TO GO AFTER FIRST?
...!!
...!!
THAT HURT...!!
OH, IS THAT RIGHT? THEN...

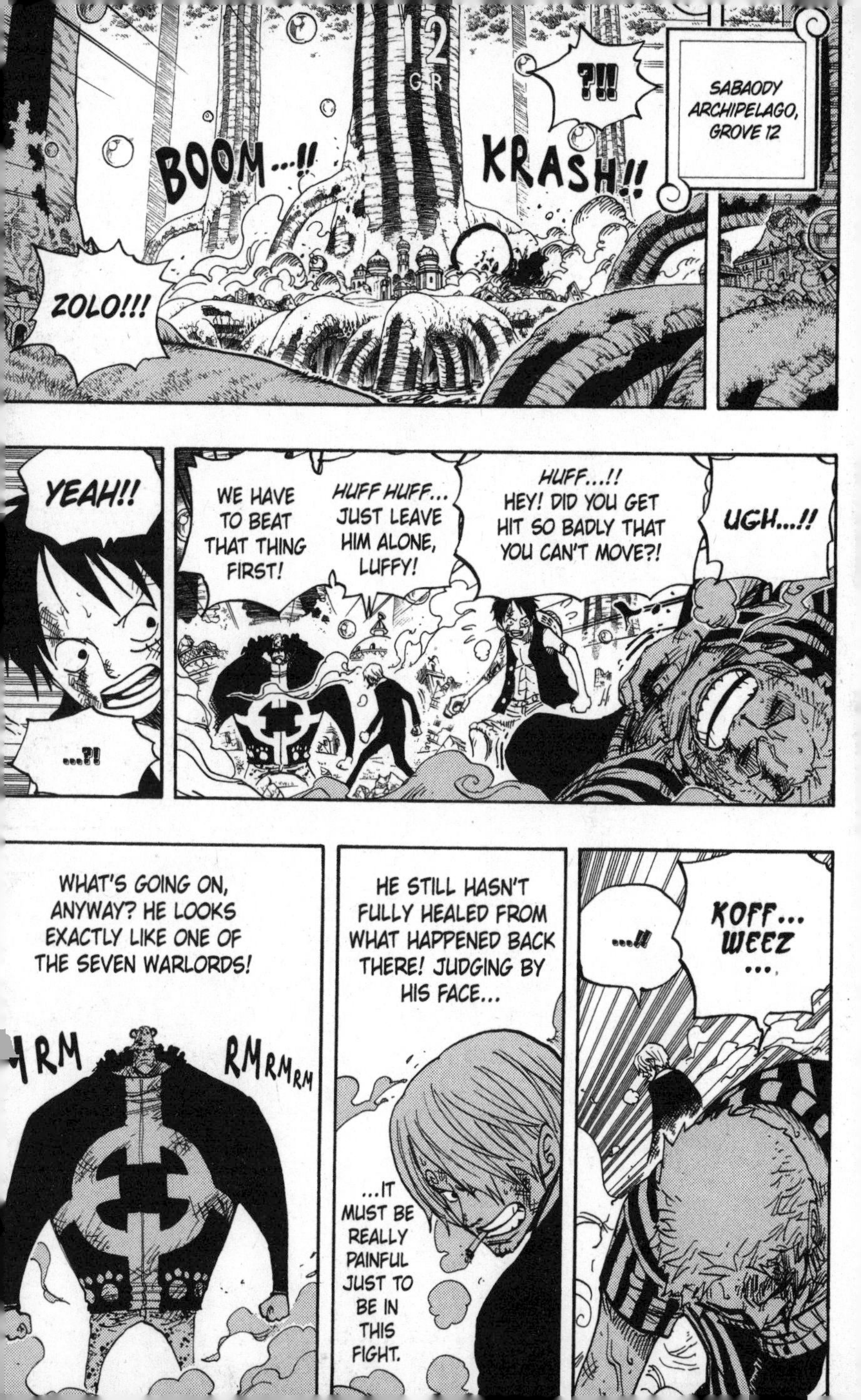
SABAODY ARCHIPELAGO, GROVE 12
?!!
KRASH!!
12 GR
BOOM...!!
ZOLO!!!
UGH...!!
HUFF...!! HEY! DID YOU GET HIT SO BADLY THAT YOU CAN'T MOVE?!
HUFF HUFF... JUST LEAVE HIM ALONE, LUFFY!
WE HAVE TO BEAT THAT THING FIRST!
YEAH!!
...?!
KOFF... WEEZ ...
...!!
HE STILL HASN'T FULLY HEALED FROM WHAT HAPPENED BACK THERE! JUDGING BY HIS FACE...
...IT MUST BE REALLY PAINFUL JUST TO BE IN THIS FIGHT.
WHAT'S GOING ON, ANYWAY? HE LOOKS EXACTLY LIKE ONE OF THE SEVEN WARLORDS!
RMRMRM
RM

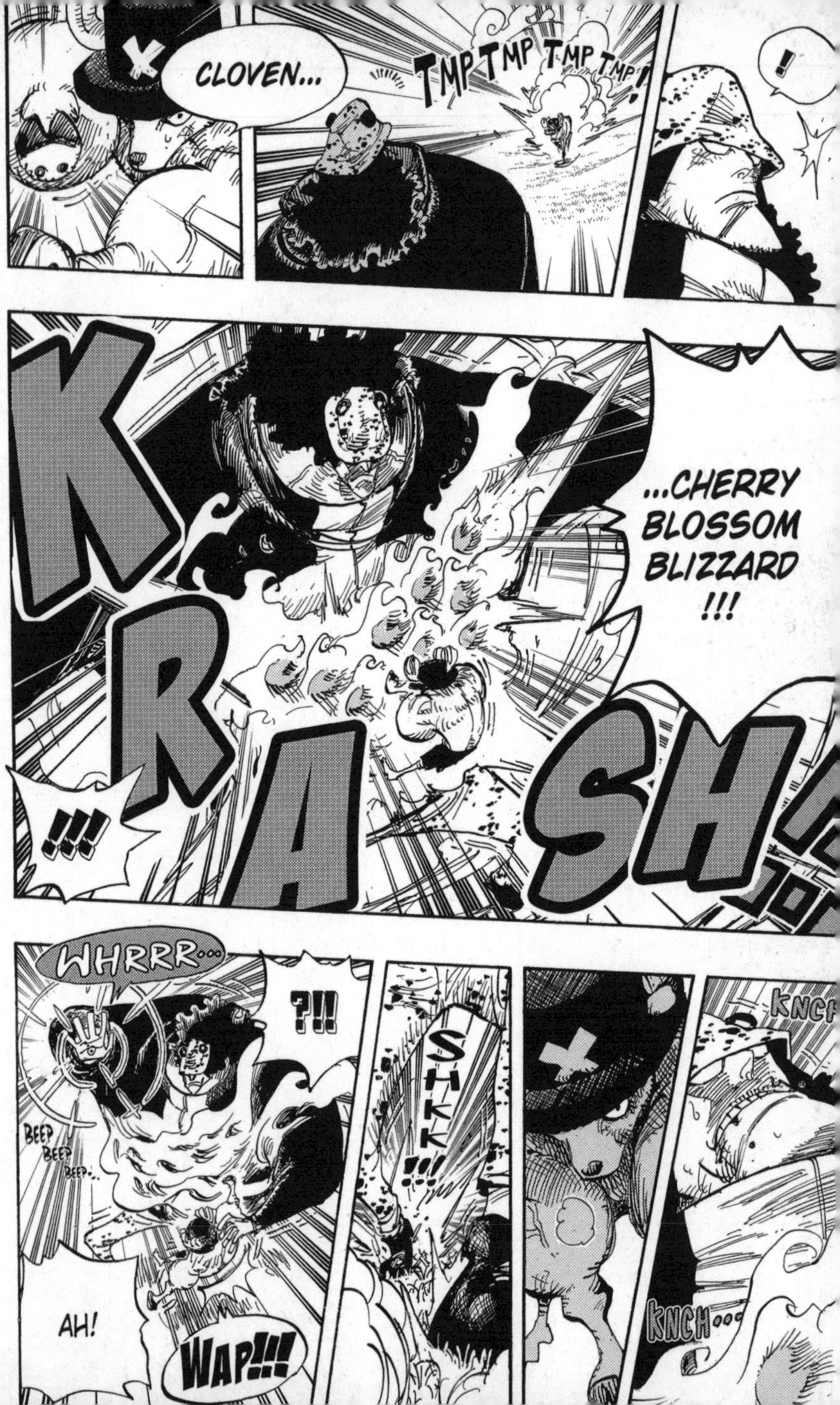
!
TMP TMP TMP TMP
CLOVEN...
...CHERRY BLOSSOM BLIZZARD !!!
KRASH
!!!
KNCH...
SHKK!!!
?!!
WHRRR...
BEEP BEEP BEEP...
AH!
WAP!!!

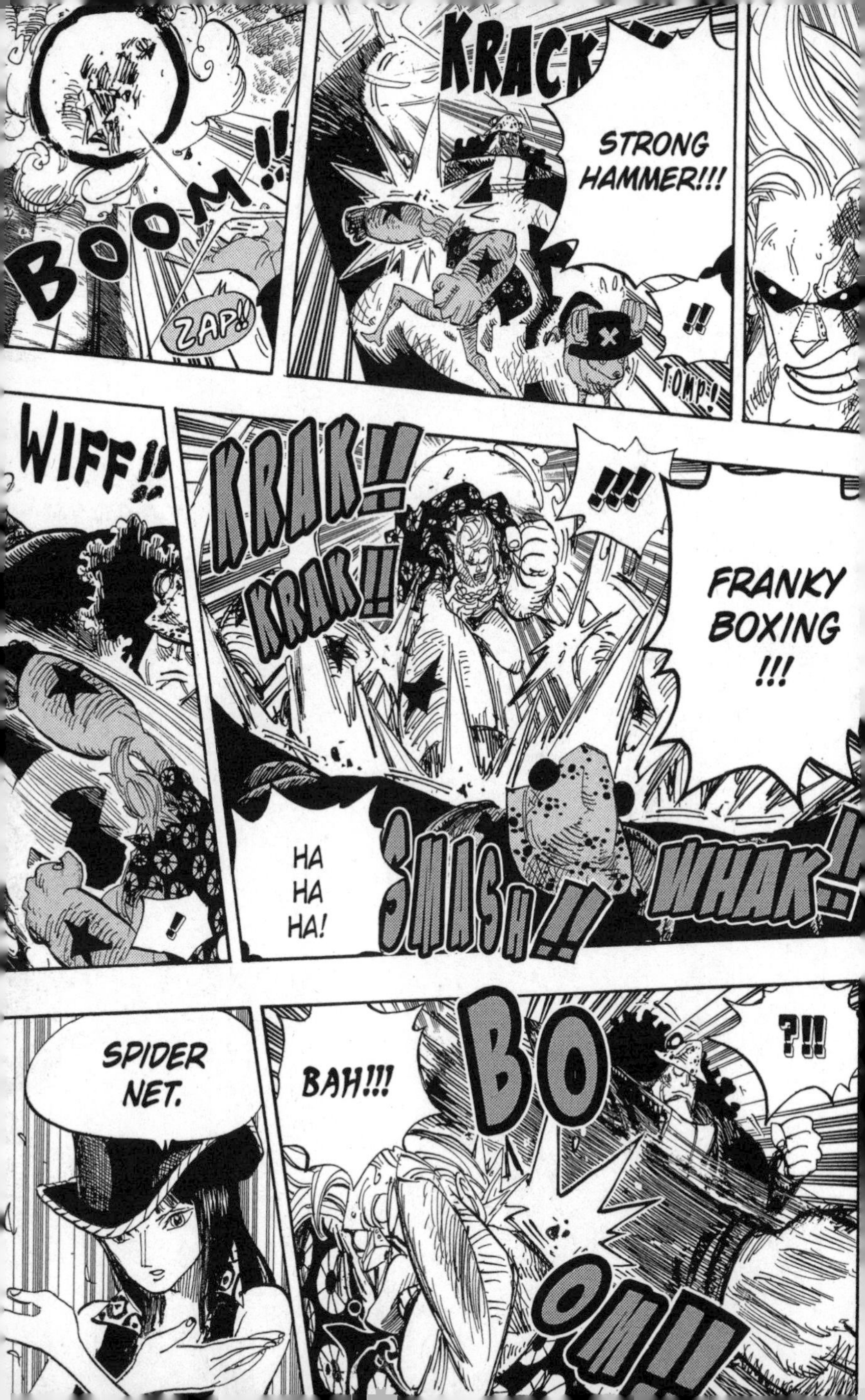
KRACK
STRONG HAMMER!!!
!!
TOMP!
BOOM!!
ZAP!!
!!!
FRANKY BOXING !!!
KRAK!!
KRAK!!
WHAK!!
SMASH!!
HA HA HA!
WIFF!!
!
?!!
BO
BAH!!!
OM!!
SPIDER NET.

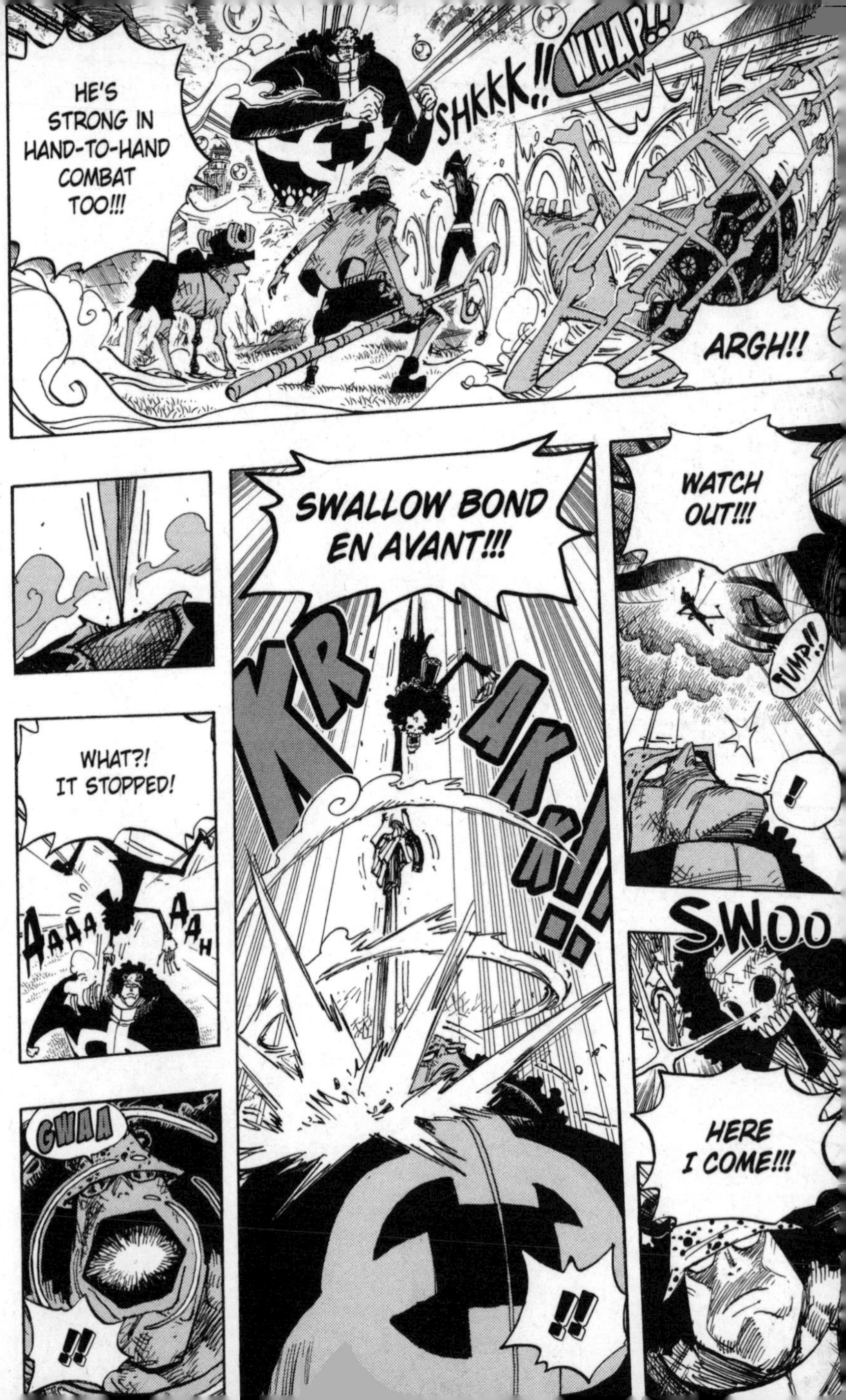
WHAP!!
SHKKK!!
HE'S STRONG IN HAND-TO-HAND COMBAT TOO!!!
ARGH!!
WATCH OUT!!!
TUMP!!
!
SWOO
HERE I COME!!!
SWALLOW BOND EN AVANT!!!
KRAKK!!
!!
WHAT?! IT STOPPED!
AAAAAAH
GWAA
!!

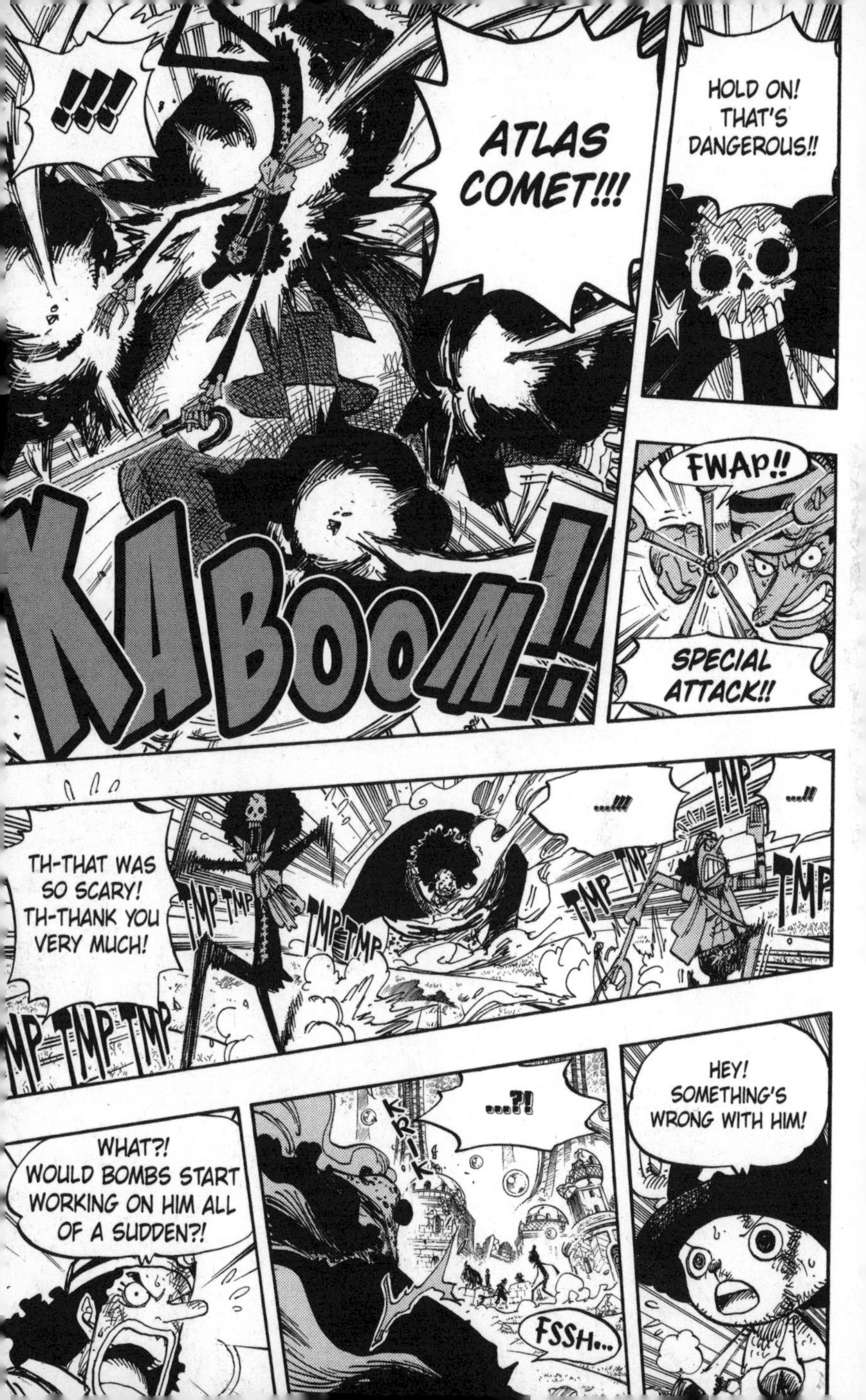
HOLD ON! THAT'S DANGEROUS!!
FWAP!!
SPECIAL ATTACK!!
!!!
ATLAS COMET!!!
KABOOM!!
...!!
TMP
...!!!
TMP TMP
TMP TMP
TH-THAT WAS SO SCARY! TH-THANK YOU VERY MUCH!
TMP TMP TMP
HEY! SOMETHING'S WRONG WITH HIM!
...?!
KRIK
FSSH...
WHAT?! WOULD BOMBS START WORKING ON HIM ALL OF A SUDDEN?!

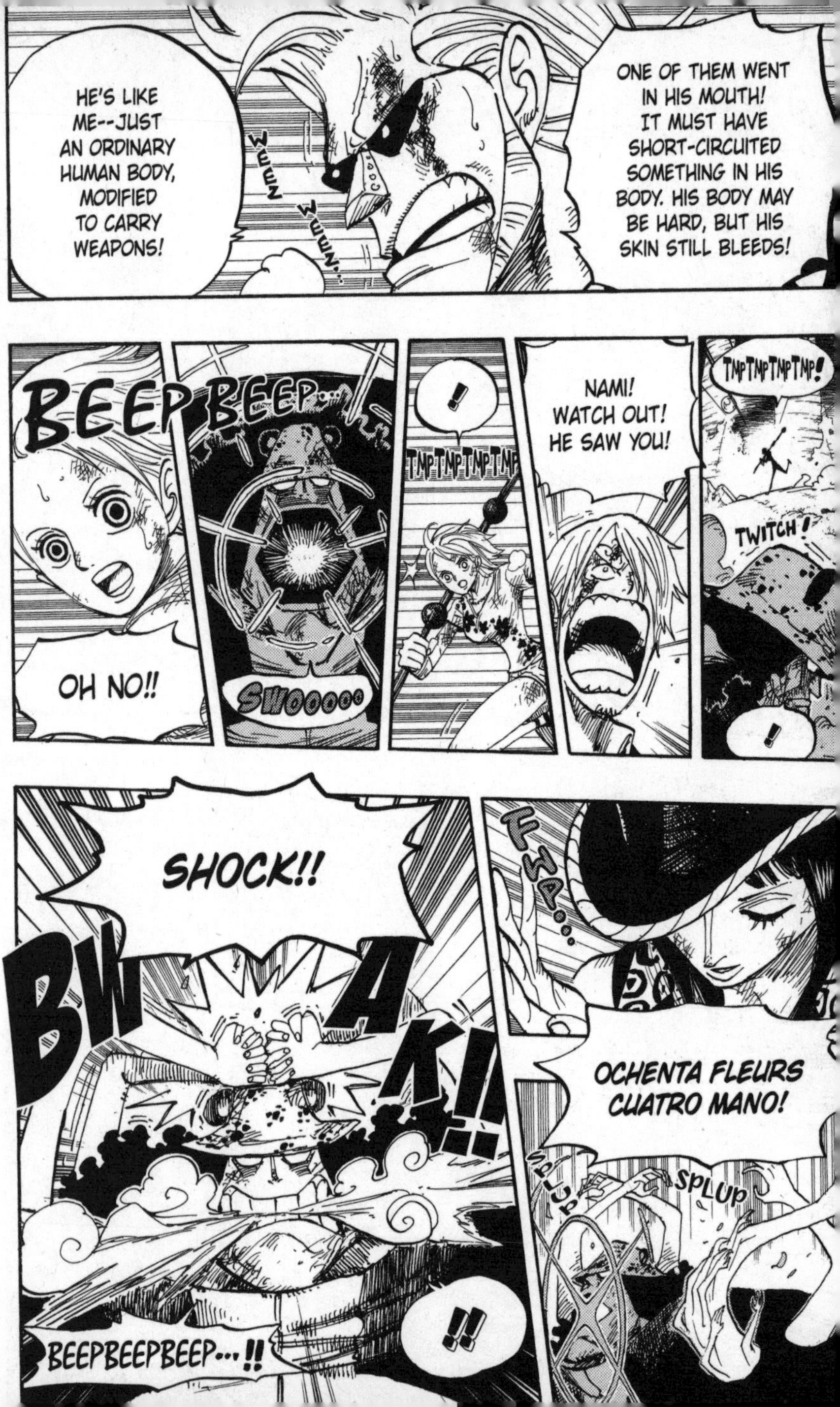
ONE OF THEM WENT IN HIS MOUTH! IT MUST HAVE SHORT-CIRCUITED SOMETHING IN HIS BODY. HIS BODY MAY BE HARD, BUT HIS SKIN STILL BLEEDS!
WEEEN
WEEEN...
HE'S LIKE ME--JUST AN ORDINARY HUMAN BODY, MODIFIED TO CARRY WEAPONS!
TMPTMPTMPTMP!
TWITCH!
!
NAMI! WATCH OUT! HE SAW YOU!
!
TMPTMPTMPTMP
BEEP BEEP...
SWOOOO
OH NO!!
FWP...
OCHENTA FLEURS CUATRO MANO!
SPLUP
SPLUP
SHOCK!!
BWAK!!
!!
BEEPBEEPBEEP...!!

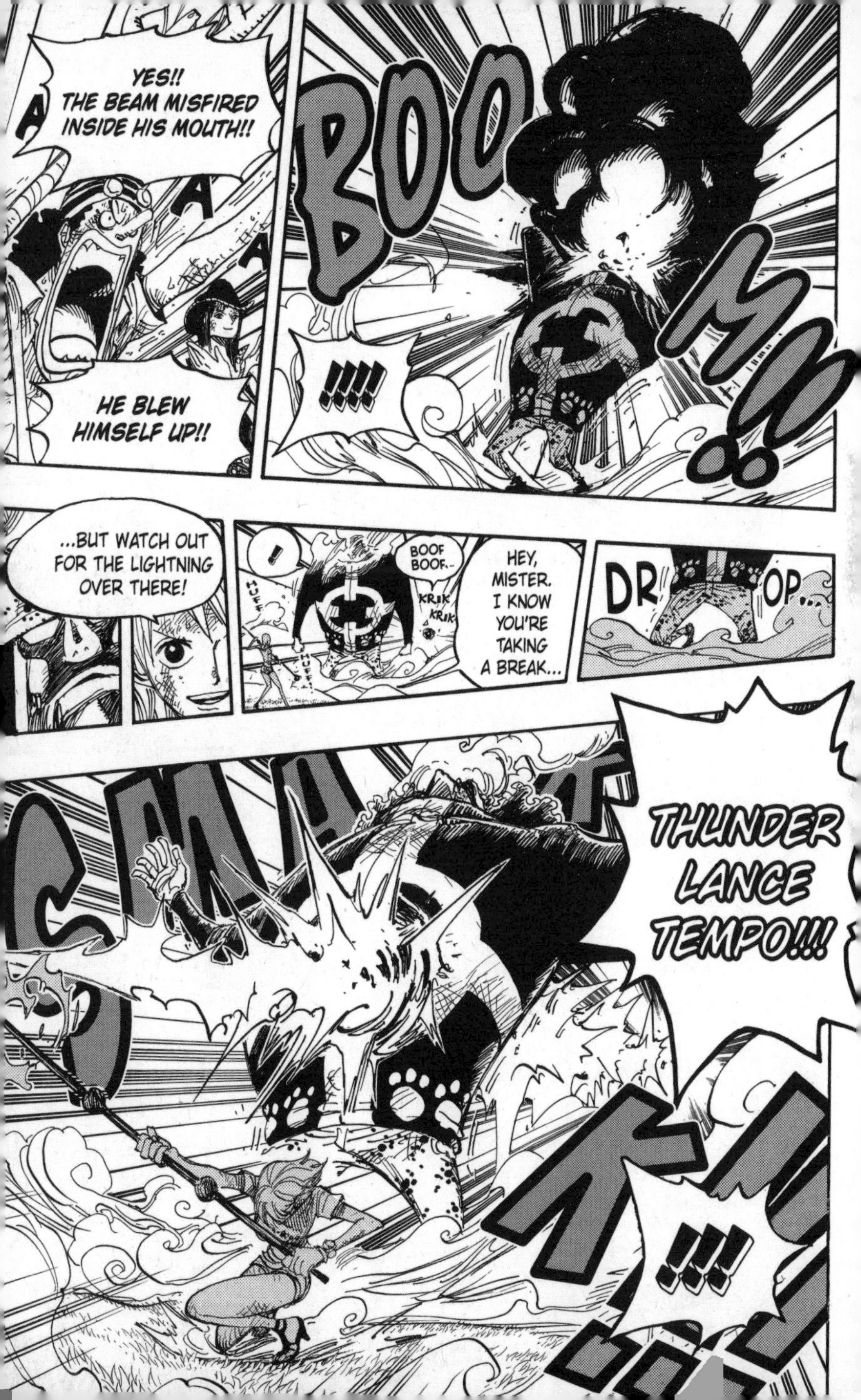
BOOOM!!
!!!!
YES!! THE BEAM MISFIRED INSIDE HIS MOUTH!!
AAA
HE BLEW HIMSELF UP!!
DR OP...
HEY, MISTER. I KNOW YOU'RE TAKING A BREAK...
BOOF BOOF...
!
KRIK KRIK
HUFF HUFF
...BUT WATCH OUT FOR THE LIGHTNING OVER THERE!
THUNDER LANCE TEMPO!!!
!!!

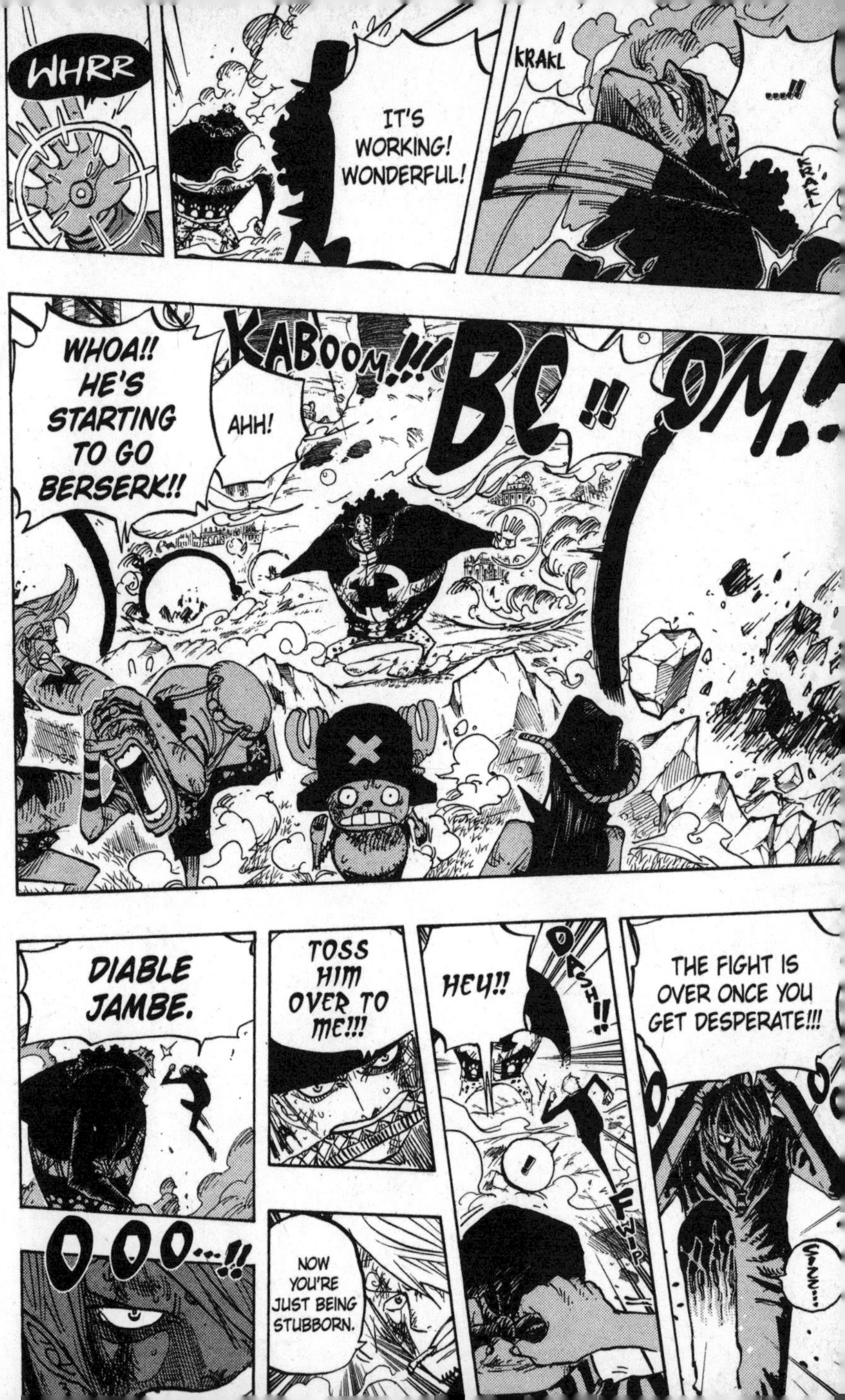
...!!
KRAKL
KRAKL
IT'S WORKING! WONDERFUL!
WHRR
BOOM!!
KABOOM!!!
AHH!
WHOA!! HE'S STARTING TO GO BERSERK!!
THE FIGHT IS OVER ONCE YOU GET DESPERATE!!!
HEY!!
DASH!!
!
FWIP
TOSS HIM OVER TO ME!!!
NOW YOU'RE JUST BEING STUBBORN.
DIABLE JAMBE.
O.O.O...!!

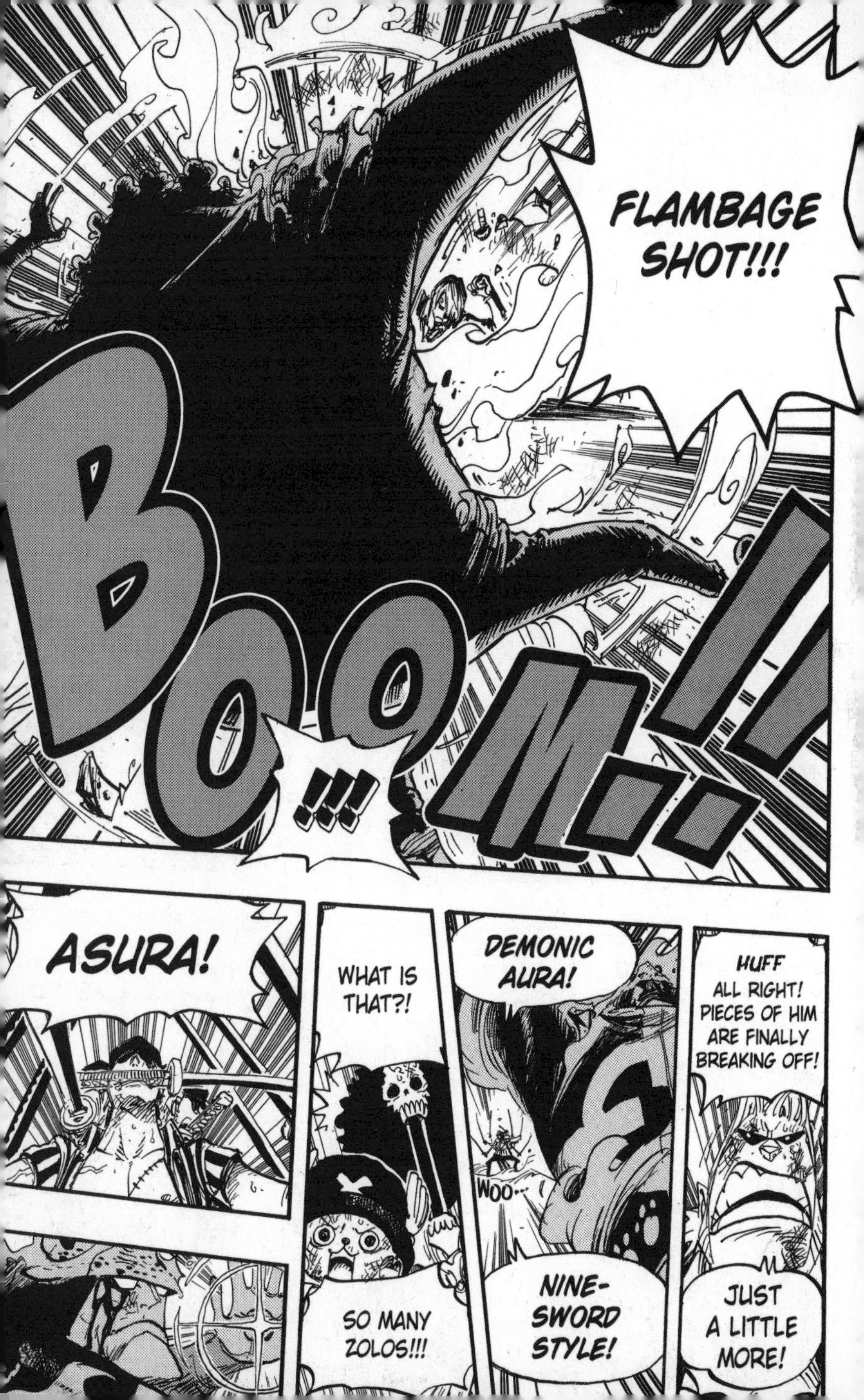
FLAMBAGE SHOT!!!
BOOO!!! M!!
HUFF
ALL RIGHT! PIECES OF HIM ARE FINALLY BREAKING OFF!
JUST A LITTLE MORE!
DEMONIC AURA!
WOO...
NINE-SWORD STYLE!
WHAT IS THAT?!
SO MANY ZOLOS!!!
ASURA!

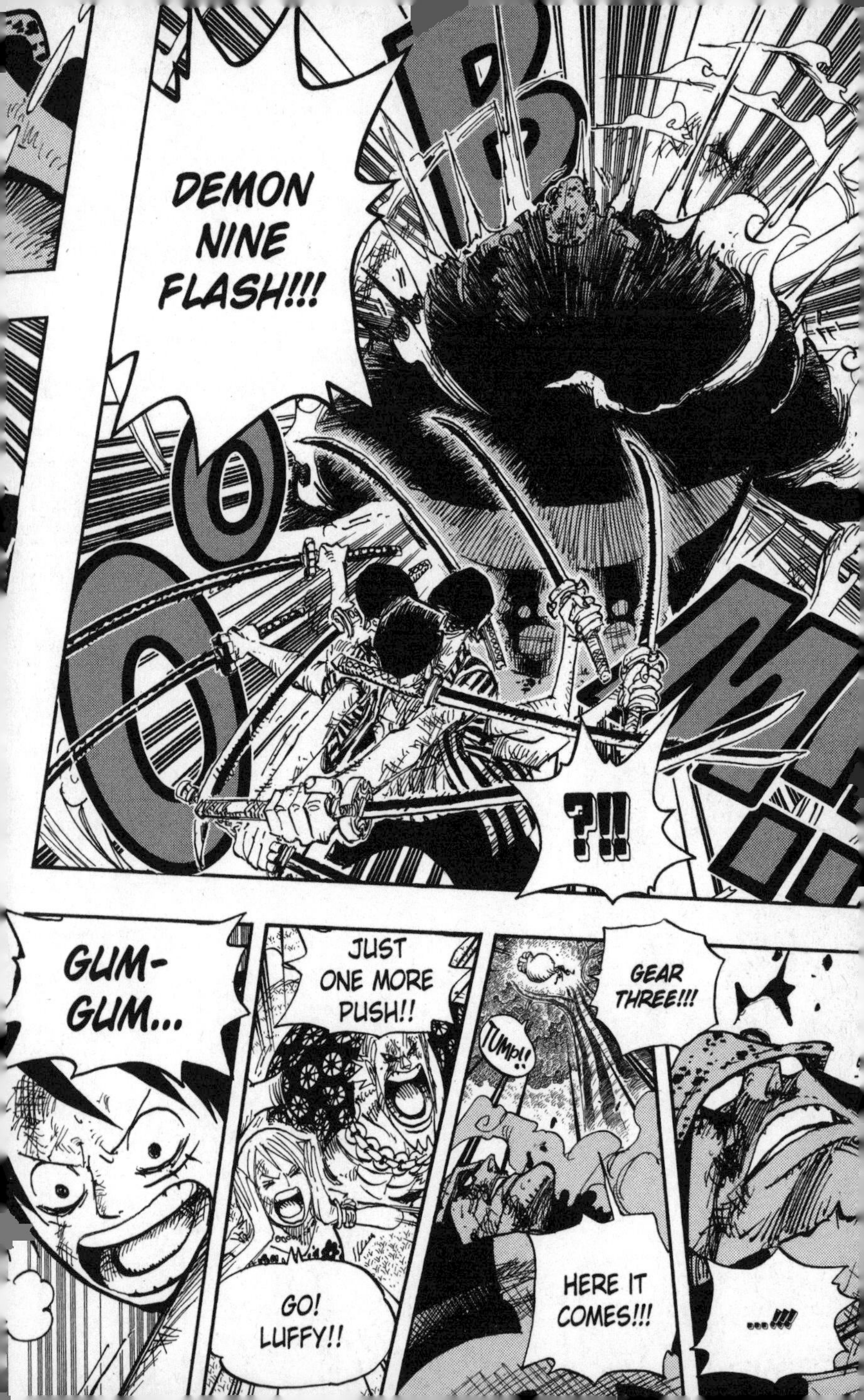
DEMON NINE FLASH!!!
?!!
...!!!
GEAR THREE!!!
TUMP!!
HERE IT COMES!!!
JUST ONE MORE PUSH!!
GO! LUFFY!!
GUM-GUM...

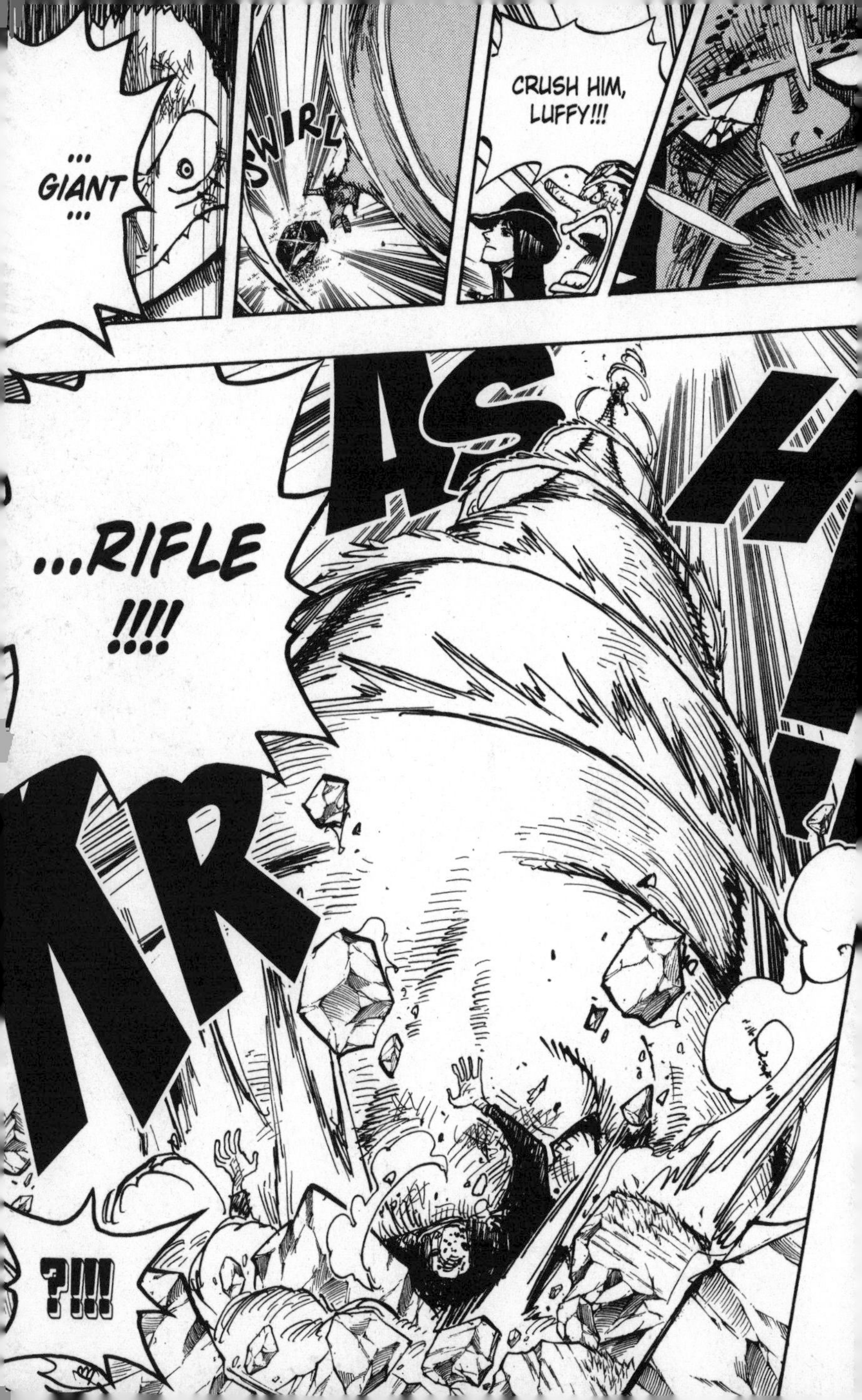
CRUSH HIM, LUFFY!!!
SWIRL
...GIANT...
...RIFLE !!!!
?!!!

SBS Question Corner

MAYUMI TANAKA, VOICE OF LUFFY!

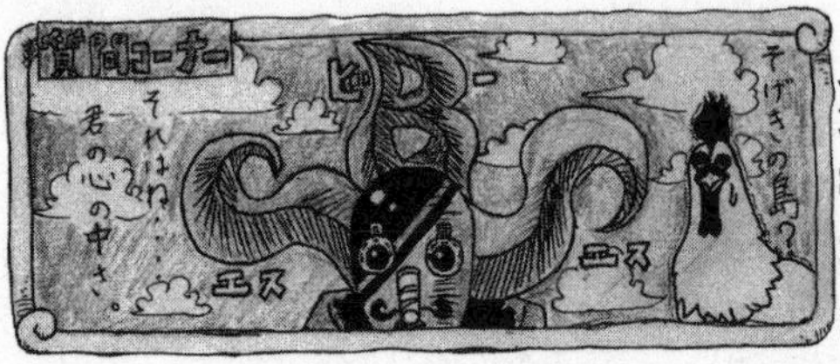
質問コーナー
そげきの鳥？
それはね……
君の心の中さ。
(Yasuhiro Yoshioka, Nagasaki)

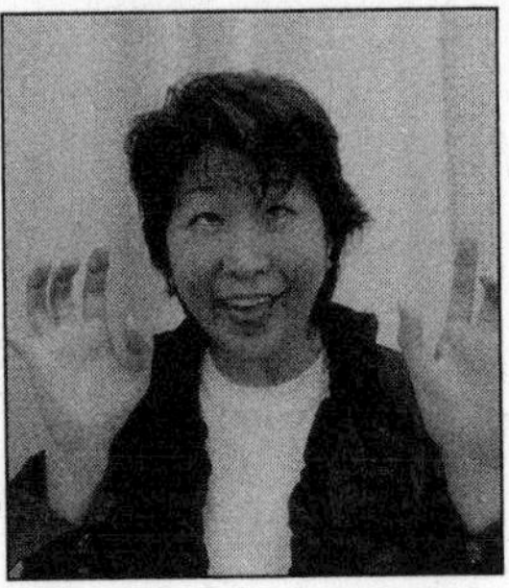

Reader: Hello. Unfortunately for Odacchi, I'm going to have Mayumi Tanaka start the Question Corner this time (smooch!). Please start, Mayumi Tanaka.✧

--Rubosu

Tanaka: Let's start the (S)low (B)reaks done (S)lowly!

Oda: I said that's not what it stands for! Oh, wait. Maybe it is...

Reader: Have you ever partied with the other Straw Hat Pirates voice actors?

--Kanna Kawahito

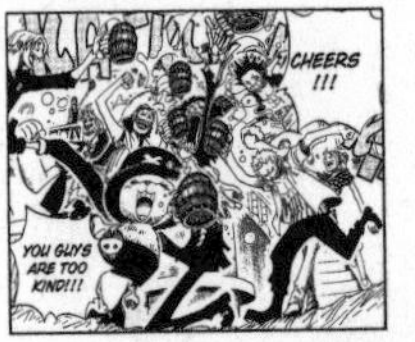
CHEERS !!!
YOU GUYS ARE TOO KIND!!!

T: I had a takoyaki party with the other One Piece actors in my training room at home. There was some children's bedding in that room, and the actor who does Usopp fell asleep in it. He's a big pain in the butt.

R: Don't mind me, just keep going.

--Usamickey

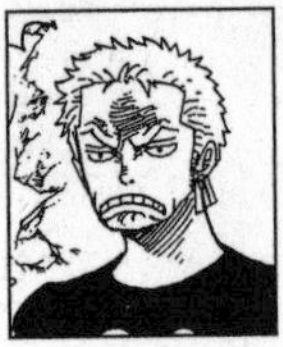

T: What? In Luffy's role? Usamickey, you want to play Luffy? Then I'll do Zolo.

R: Ms. Tanaka, I have a question. When you get telemarketers on the phone, do you talk to them in Luffy's voice? Please tell me.

--Windy

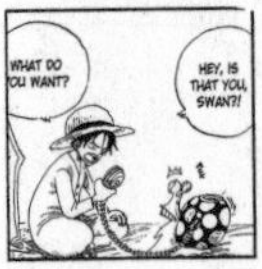
HEY, IS THAT YOU, SWAN?!
WHAT DO YOU WANT?

T: Once I was just talking normally and the telemarketer asked for my mother. I shouted back at him "I am the mom!" and he got freaked out. Serves him right!

R: I'm a huge fan! I've seen practically every single anime that you were featured in. By the way... "Take this! Negative Hollow!"

--Maron

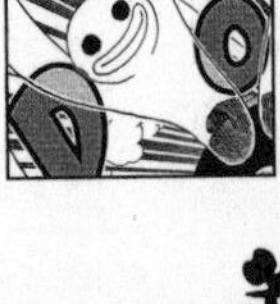

T: **I'M SO SORRY THAT A LITTLE OLD LADY LIKE ME IS DOING THE VOICE OF LUFFY...**

Chapter 511:
AXE-CARRYING SENTOMARU

**CP9'S INDEPENDENT REPORT, VOL. 19:
"MESSENGER OF JUSTICE"**

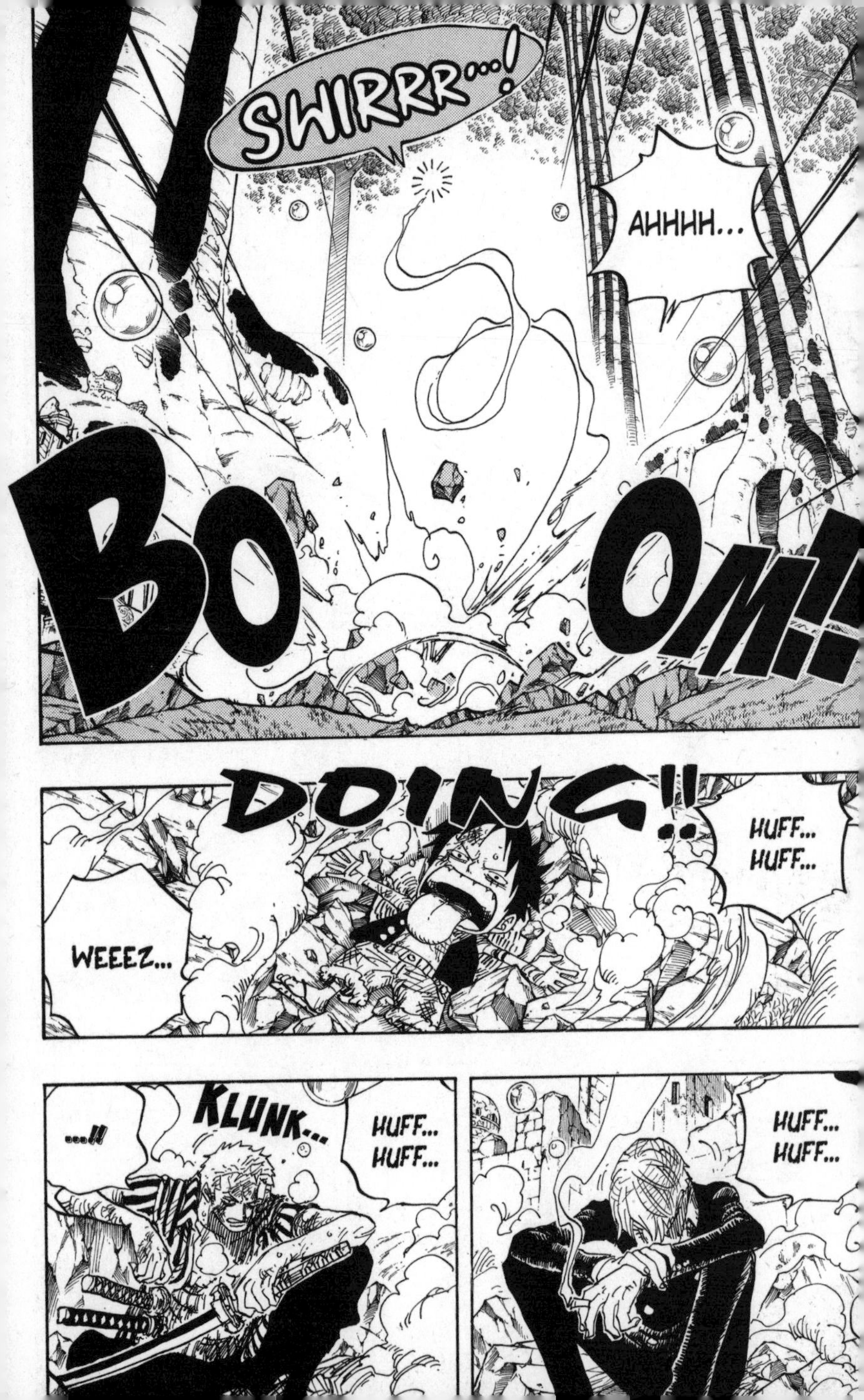
AHHHH...
SWIRRR...!
BOOM!!
DOING!!
HUFF... HUFF...
WEEEZ...
HUFF... HUFF...
HUFF... HUFF...
KLUNK...
...!!

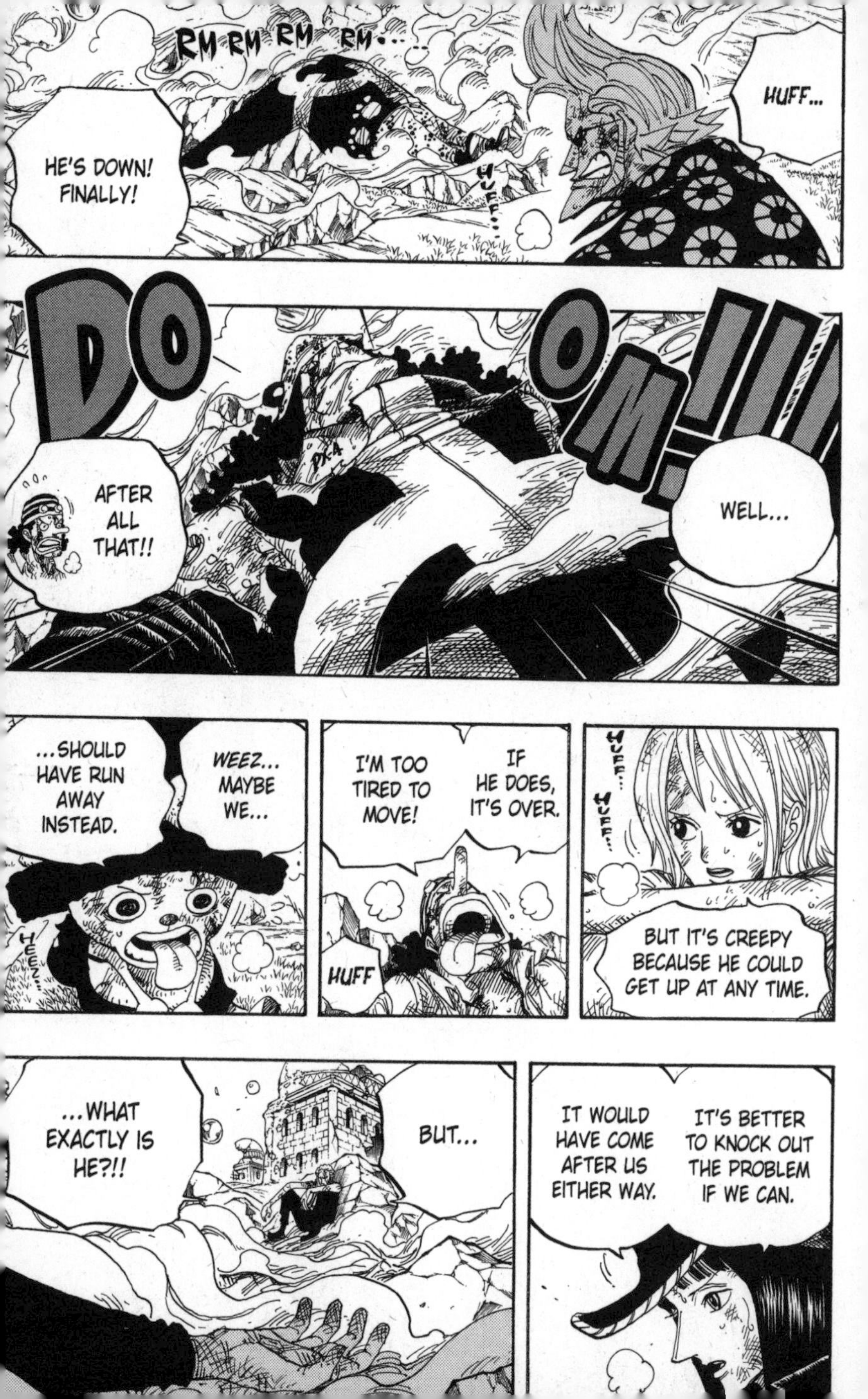
HUFF...
RM RM RM RM...
HUFF...
HE'S DOWN! FINALLY!
DOOM!!!
WELL...
AFTER ALL THAT!!
HUFF... HUFF...
BUT IT'S CREEPY BECAUSE HE COULD GET UP AT ANY TIME.
IF HE DOES, IT'S OVER.
I'M TOO TIRED TO MOVE!
HUFF
WEEZ... MAYBE WE...
...SHOULD HAVE RUN AWAY INSTEAD.
HEEZ...
IT'S BETTER TO KNOCK OUT THE PROBLEM IF WE CAN.
IT WOULD HAVE COME AFTER US EITHER WAY.
BUT...
...WHAT EXACTLY IS HE?!!

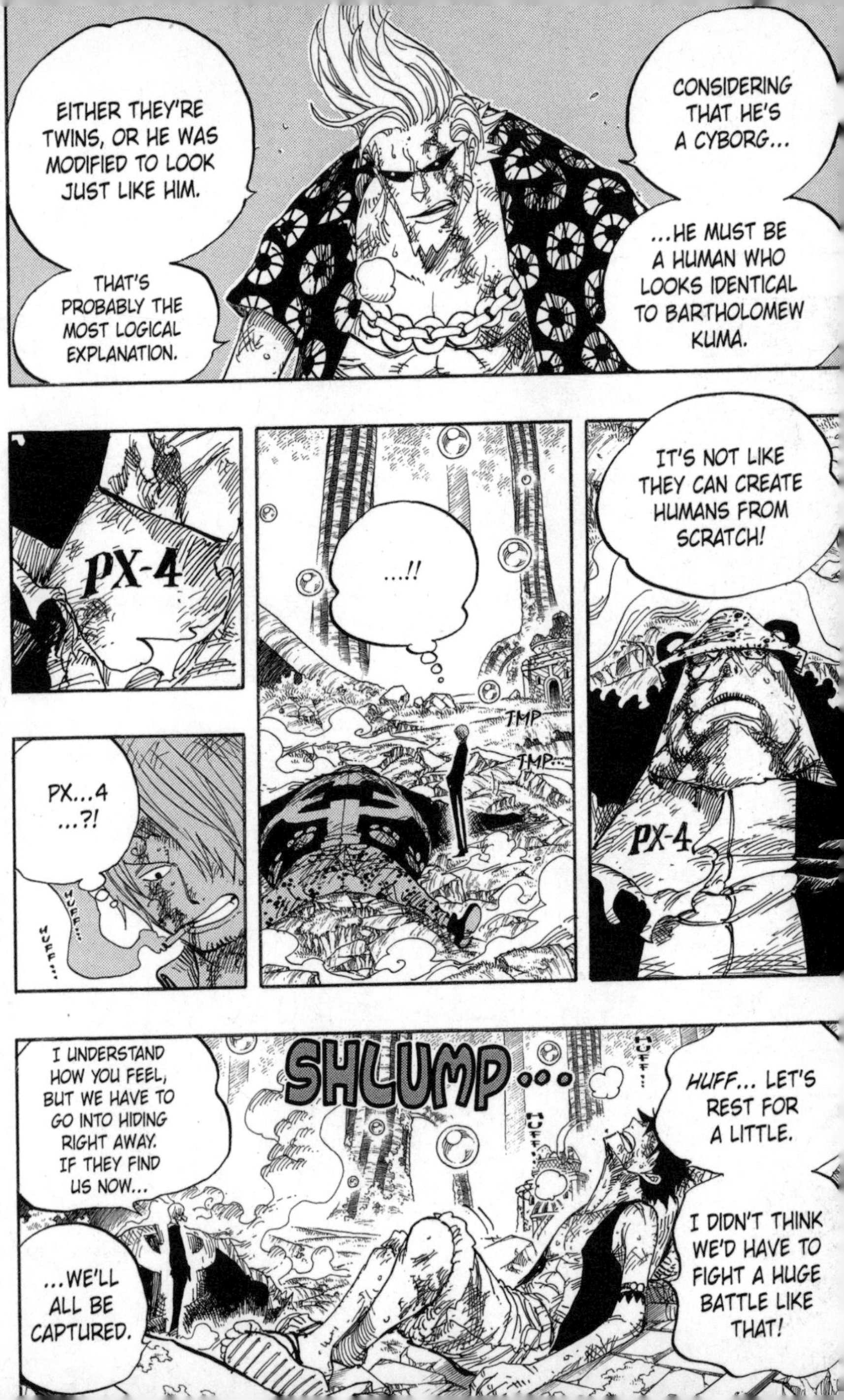
CONSIDERING THAT HE'S A CYBORG...
...HE MUST BE A HUMAN WHO LOOKS IDENTICAL TO BARTHOLOMEW KUMA.
EITHER THEY'RE TWINS, OR HE WAS MODIFIED TO LOOK JUST LIKE HIM.
THAT'S PROBABLY THE MOST LOGICAL EXPLANATION.
IT'S NOT LIKE THEY CAN CREATE HUMANS FROM SCRATCH!
PX-4
...!!
TMP
TMP...
PX-4
PX...4 ...?!
HUFF
HUFF...
HUFF
HUFF...
HUFF... LET'S REST FOR A LITTLE.
I DIDN'T THINK WE'D HAVE TO FIGHT A HUGE BATTLE LIKE THAT!
SHLUMP...
I UNDERSTAND HOW YOU FEEL, BUT WE HAVE TO GO INTO HIDING RIGHT AWAY. IF THEY FIND US NOW...
...WE'LL ALL BE CAPTURED.

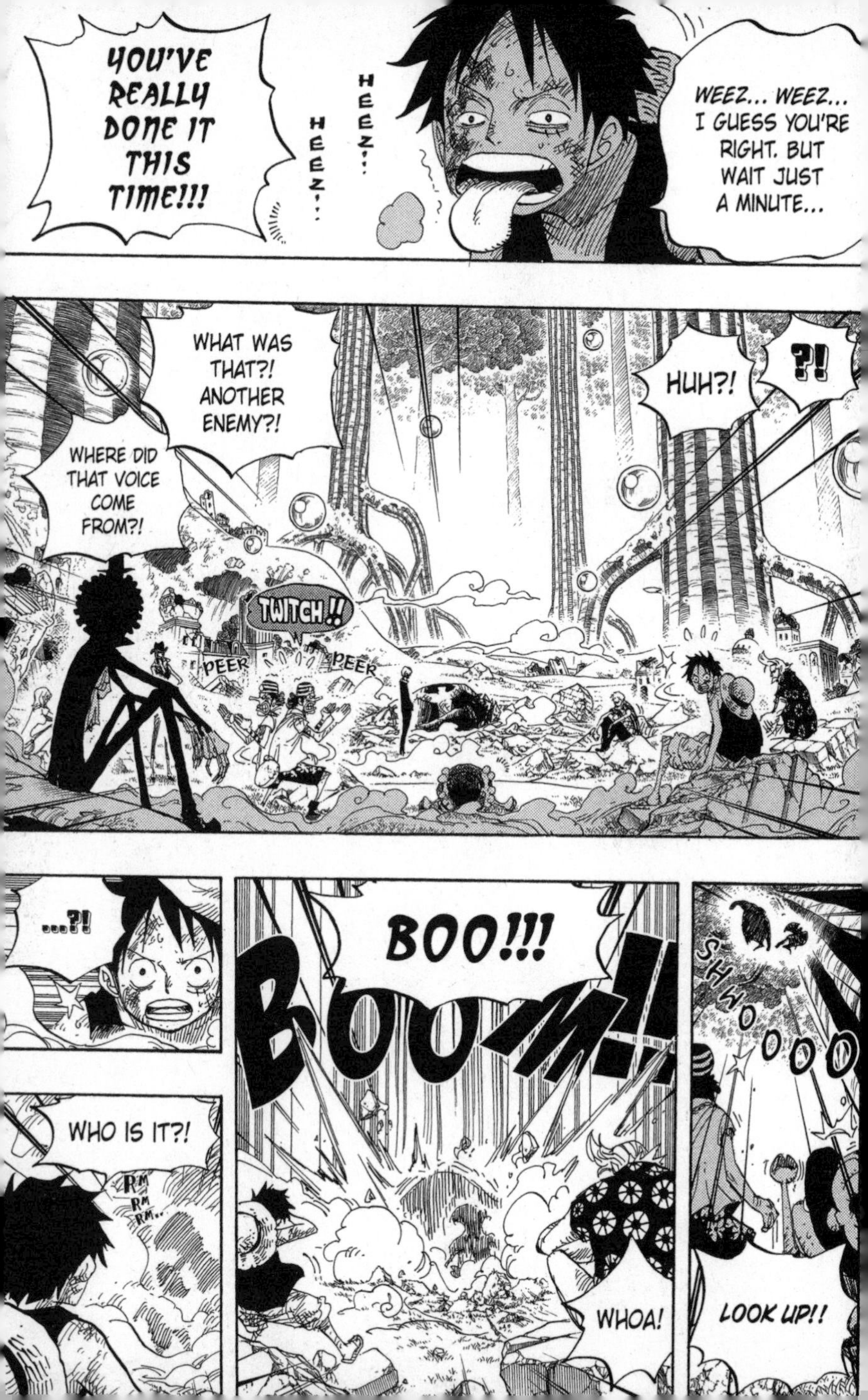
WEEZ... WEEZ... I GUESS YOU'RE RIGHT. BUT WAIT JUST A MINUTE...
HEEZ... HEEZ...
YOU'VE REALLY DONE IT THIS TIME!!!
?!
HUH?!
WHAT WAS THAT?! ANOTHER ENEMY?!
WHERE DID THAT VOICE COME FROM?!
TWITCH!!
PEER PEER
SHWOOOOO
LOOK UP!!
WHOA!
BOO!!!
BOOM!!
...?!
WHO IS IT?!
RM RM RM...

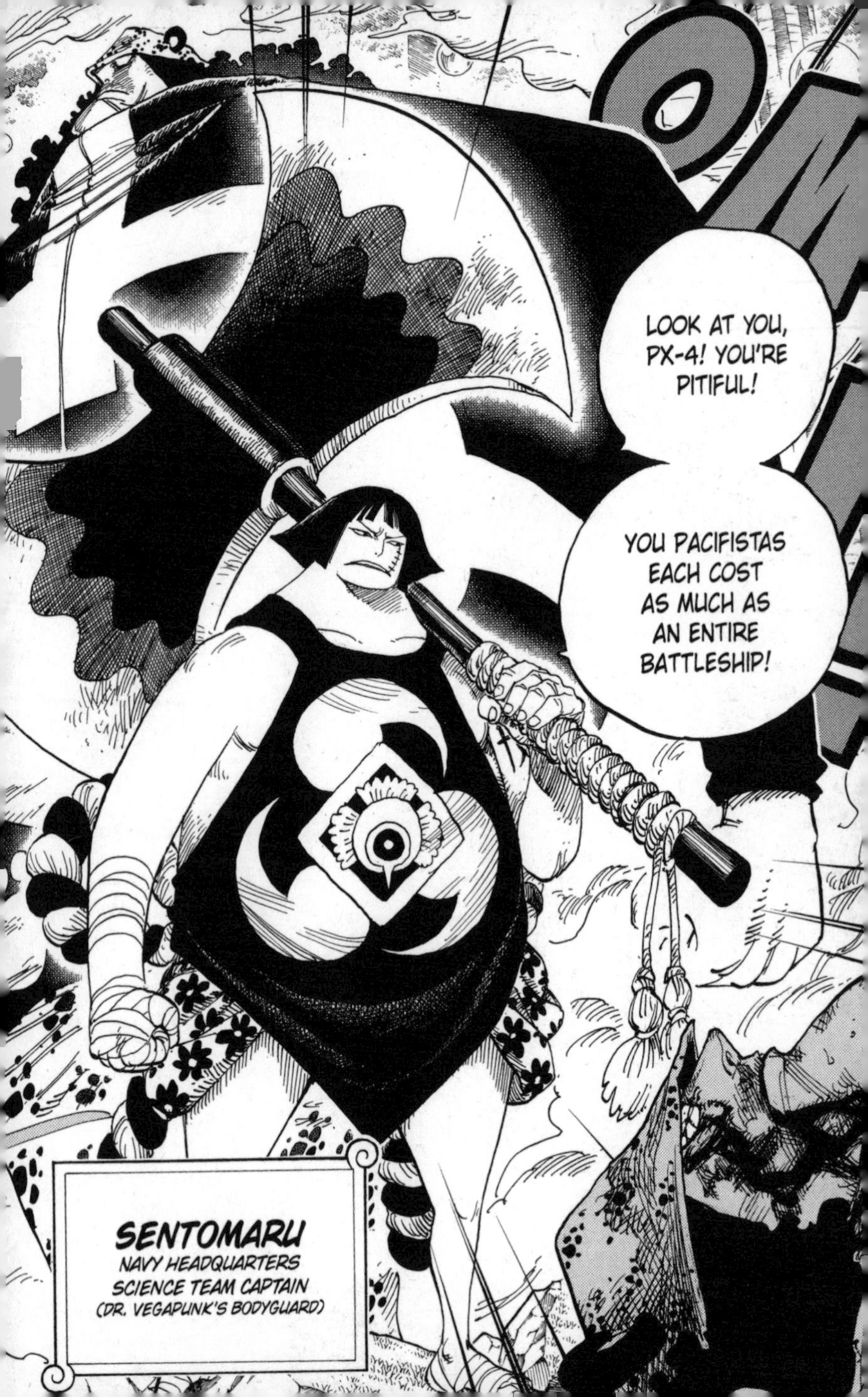
LOOK AT YOU, PX-4! YOU'RE PITIFUL!
YOU PACIFISTAS EACH COST AS MUCH AS AN ENTIRE BATTLESHIP!
SENTOMARU
NAVY HEADQUARTERS SCIENCE TEAM CAPTAIN (DR. VEGAPUNK'S BODYGUARD)

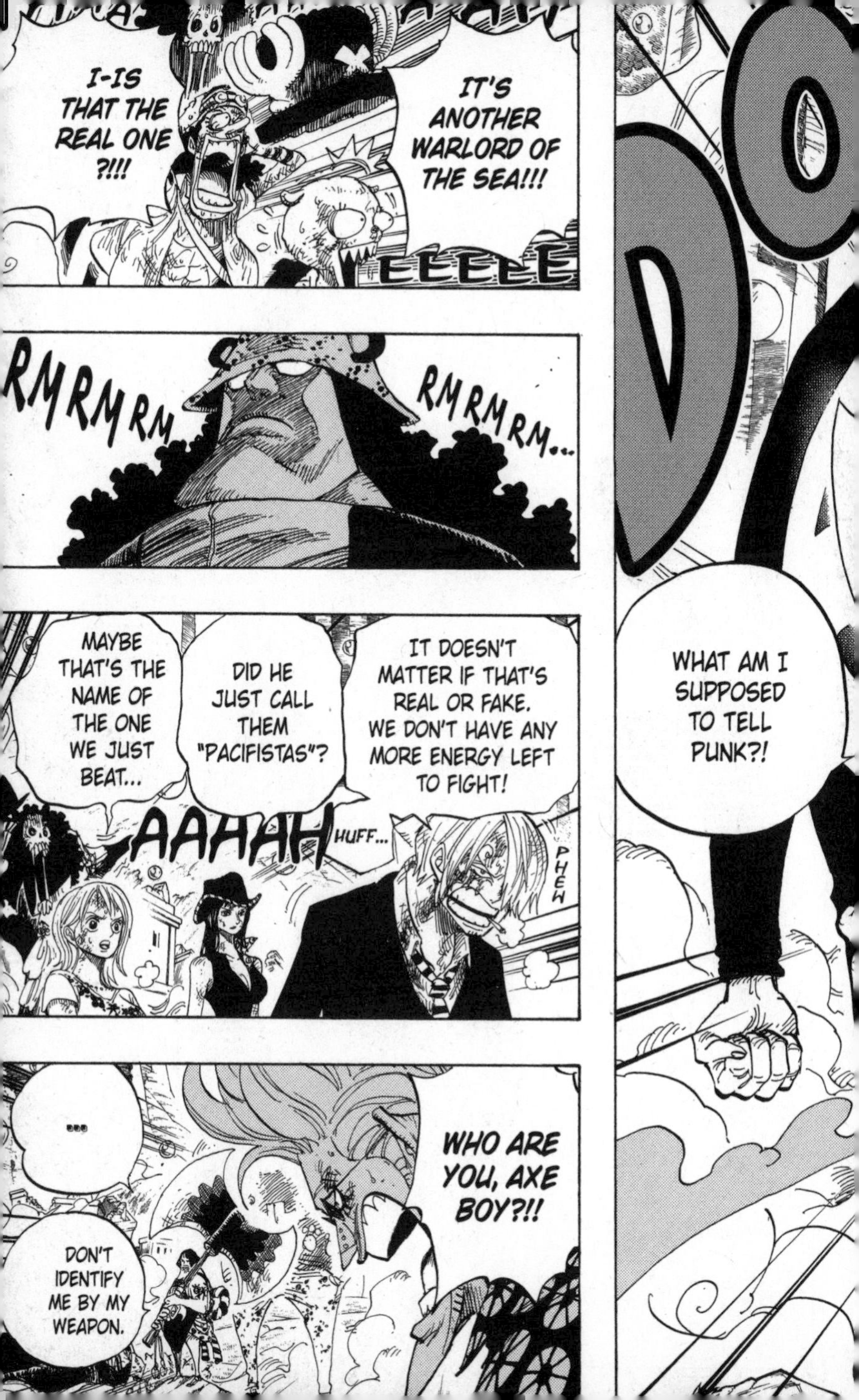
WHAT AM I SUPPOSED TO TELL PUNK?!
IT'S ANOTHER WARLORD OF THE SEA!!!
I-IS THAT THE REAL ONE ?!!!
EEEEEE
RMRMRM...
RMRMRM
IT DOESN'T MATTER IF THAT'S REAL OR FAKE. WE DON'T HAVE ANY MORE ENERGY LEFT TO FIGHT!
PHEW
HUFF...
DID HE JUST CALL THEM "PACIFISTAS"?
MAYBE THAT'S THE NAME OF THE ONE WE JUST BEAT...
AAAHH
WHO ARE YOU, AXE BOY?!!
...
DON'T IDENTIFY ME BY MY WEAPON.

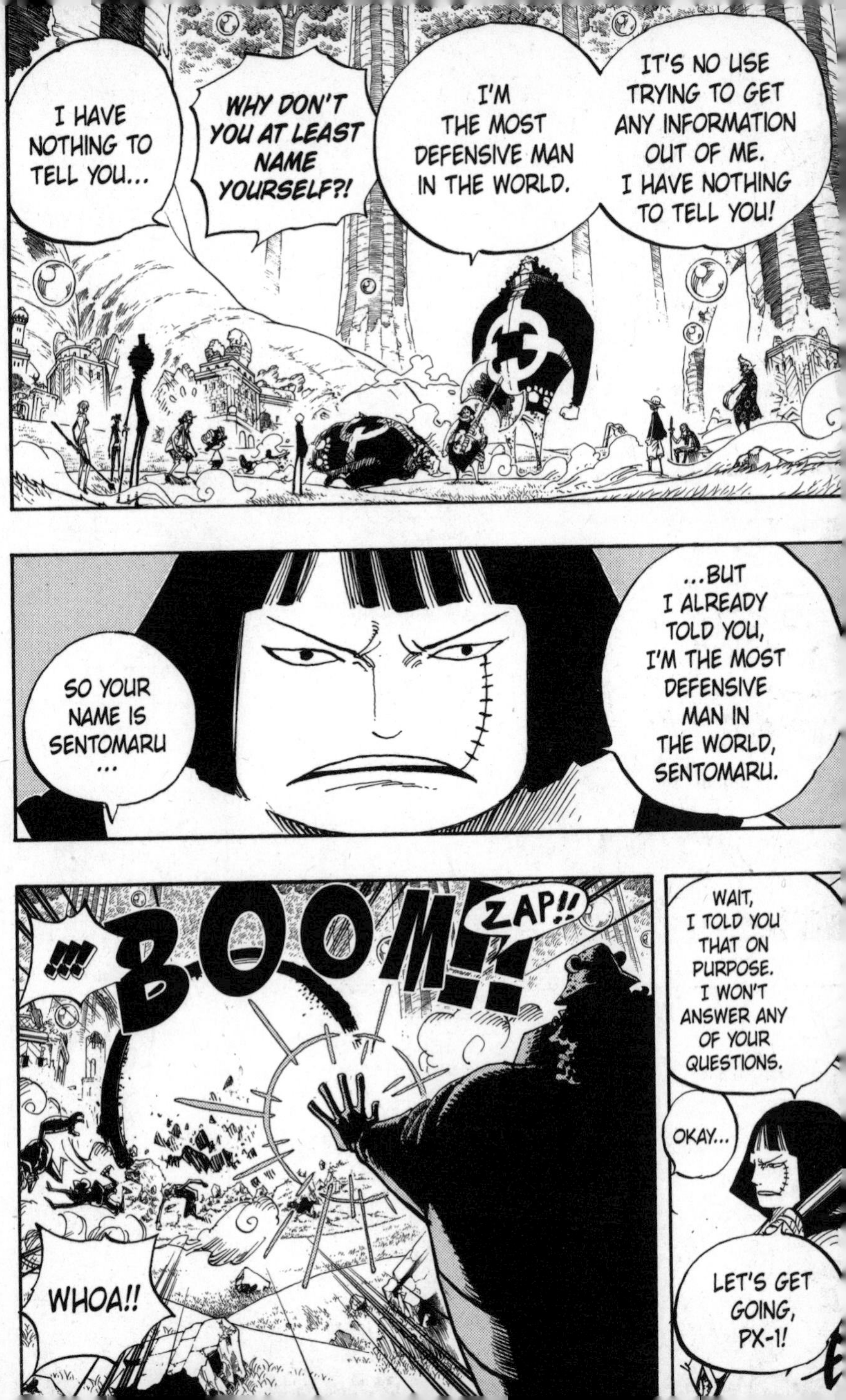
IT'S NO USE TRYING TO GET ANY INFORMATION OUT OF ME. I HAVE NOTHING TO TELL YOU!
I'M THE MOST DEFENSIVE MAN IN THE WORLD.
WHY DON'T YOU AT LEAST NAME YOURSELF?!
I HAVE NOTHING TO TELL YOU...
...BUT I ALREADY TOLD YOU, I'M THE MOST DEFENSIVE MAN IN THE WORLD, SENTOMARU.
SO YOUR NAME IS SENTOMARU...
WAIT, I TOLD YOU THAT ON PURPOSE. I WON'T ANSWER ANY OF YOUR QUESTIONS.
OKAY...
LET'S GET GOING, PX-1!
ZAP!!
BOOM!!
!!!
WHOA!!

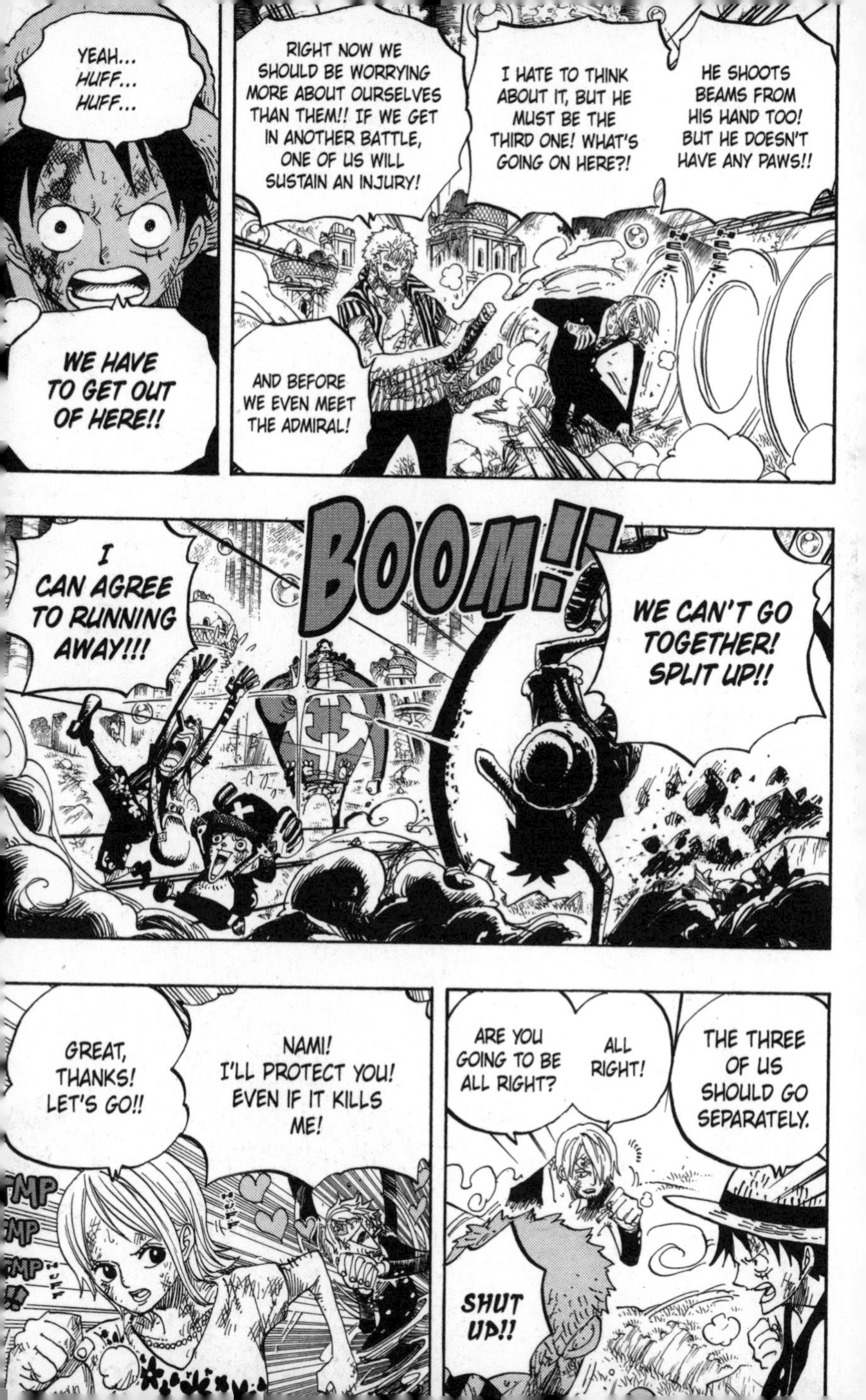
HE SHOOTS BEAMS FROM HIS HAND TOO! BUT HE DOESN'T HAVE ANY PAWS!!
I HATE TO THINK ABOUT IT, BUT HE MUST BE THE THIRD ONE! WHAT'S GOING ON HERE?!
RIGHT NOW WE SHOULD BE WORRYING MORE ABOUT OURSELVES THAN THEM!! IF WE GET IN ANOTHER BATTLE, ONE OF US WILL SUSTAIN AN INJURY!
AND BEFORE WE EVEN MEET THE ADMIRAL!
YEAH... HUFF... HUFF...
WE HAVE TO GET OUT OF HERE!!
BOOM!!
WE CAN'T GO TOGETHER! SPLIT UP!!
I CAN AGREE TO RUNNING AWAY!!!
THE THREE OF US SHOULD GO SEPARATELY.
ALL RIGHT!
ARE YOU GOING TO BE ALL RIGHT?
SHUT UP!!
NAMI! I'LL PROTECT YOU! EVEN IF IT KILLS ME!
GREAT, THANKS! LET'S GO!!

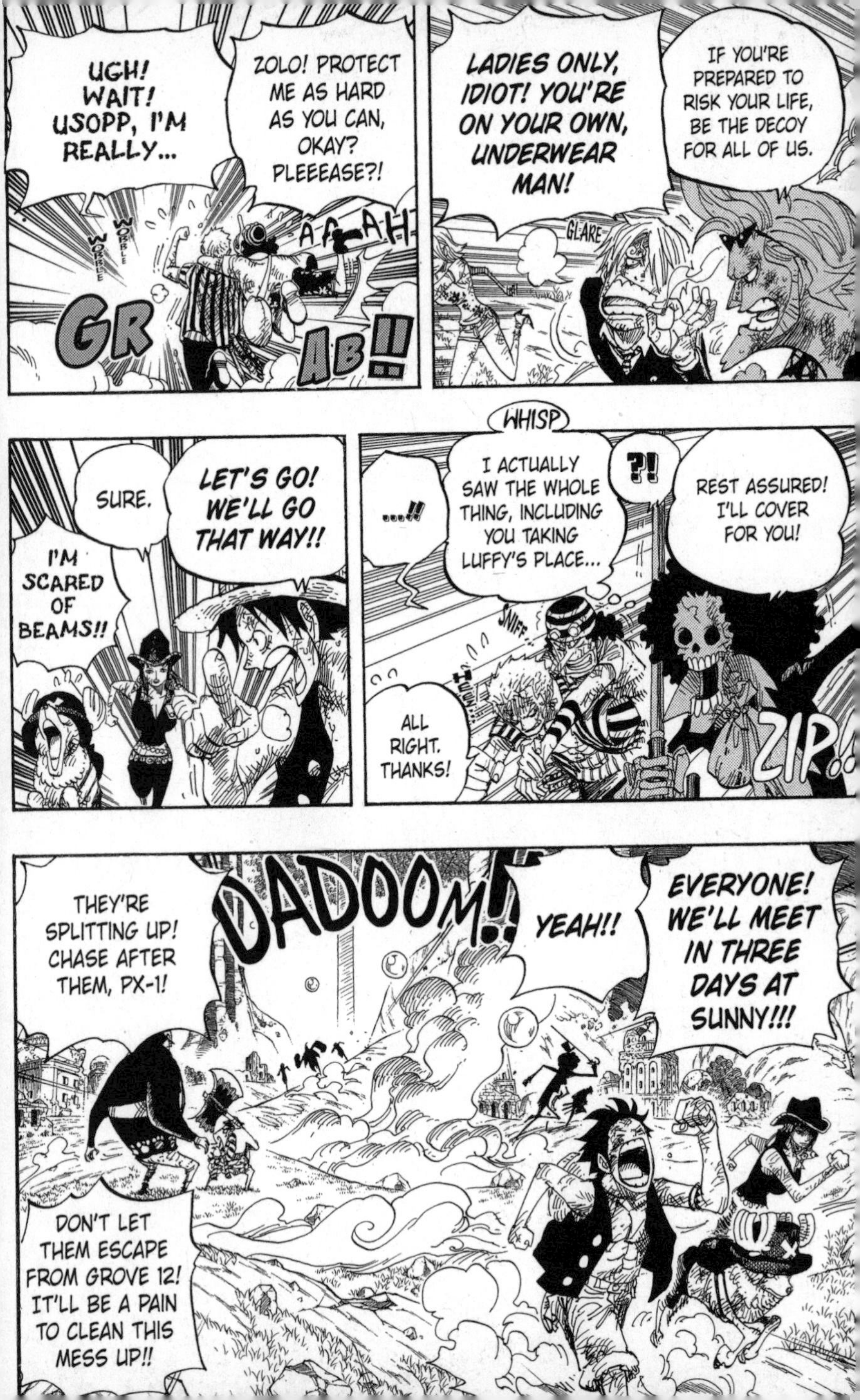
IF YOU'RE PREPARED TO RISK YOUR LIFE, BE THE DECOY FOR ALL OF US.
LADIES ONLY, IDIOT! YOU'RE ON YOUR OWN, UNDERWEAR MAN!
GLARE
ZOLO! PROTECT ME AS HARD AS YOU CAN, OKAY? PLEEEASE?!
UGH! WAIT! USOPP, I'M REALLY...
WOBBLE WOBBLE
GRAB!!
WHISP
REST ASSURED! I'LL COVER FOR YOU!
?!
I ACTUALLY SAW THE WHOLE THING, INCLUDING YOU TAKING LUFFY'S PLACE...
...!!
SNIFF...
ALL RIGHT. THANKS!
ZIP...
LET'S GO! WE'LL GO THAT WAY!!
SURE.
I'M SCARED OF BEAMS!!
EVERYONE! WE'LL MEET IN THREE DAYS AT SUNNY!!!
YEAH!!
DADOOM!!
THEY'RE SPLITTING UP! CHASE AFTER THEM, PX-1!
DON'T LET THEM ESCAPE FROM GROVE 12! IT'LL BE A PAIN TO CLEAN THIS MESS UP!!

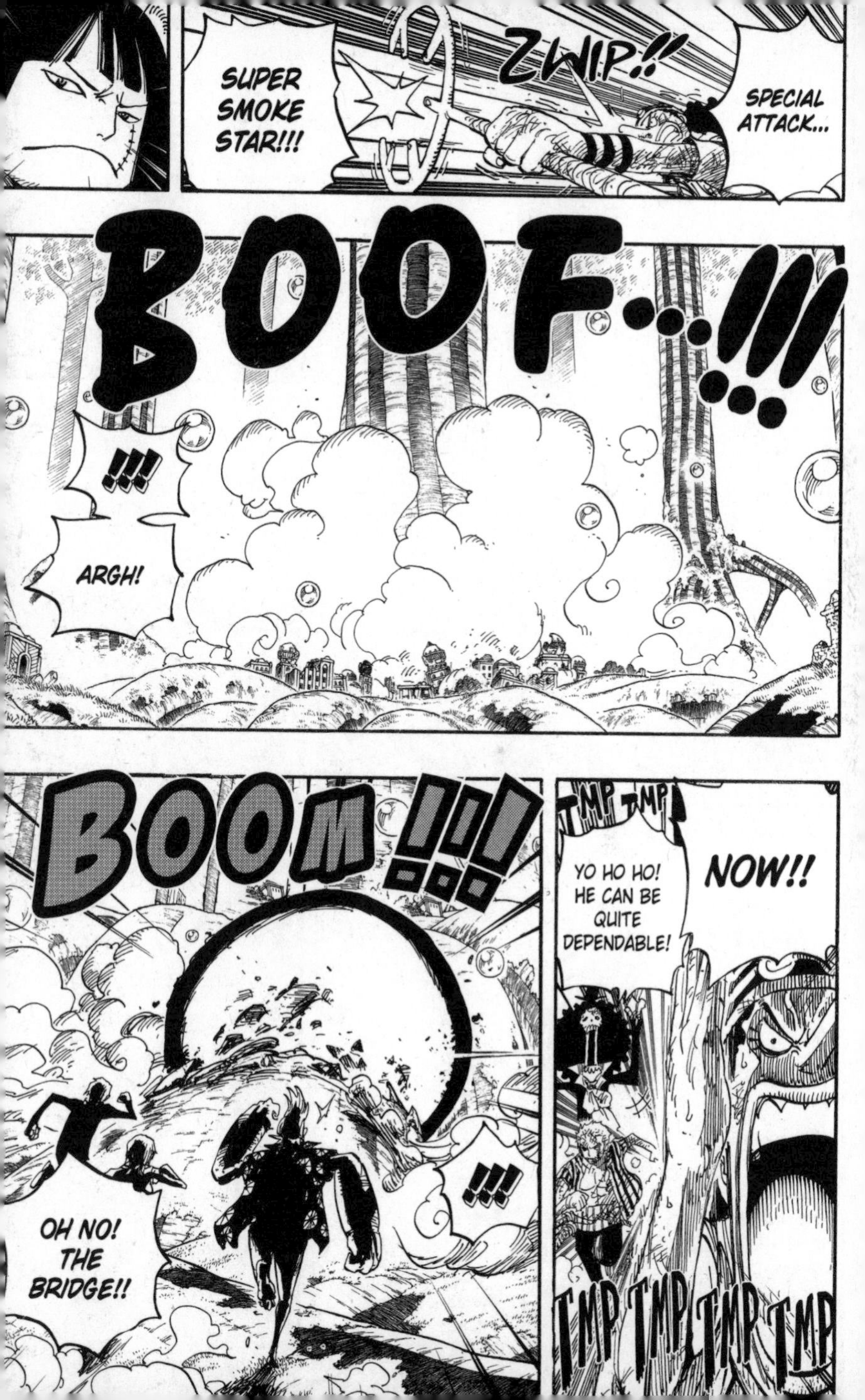
ZWIP!!
SPECIAL ATTACK...
SUPER SMOKE STAR!!!
BOOF...!!
!!!
ARGH!
TMP TMP
NOW!!
YO HO HO! HE CAN BE QUITE DEPENDABLE!
TMP TMP TMP TMP
BOOM!!!
!!!
OH NO! THE BRIDGE!!

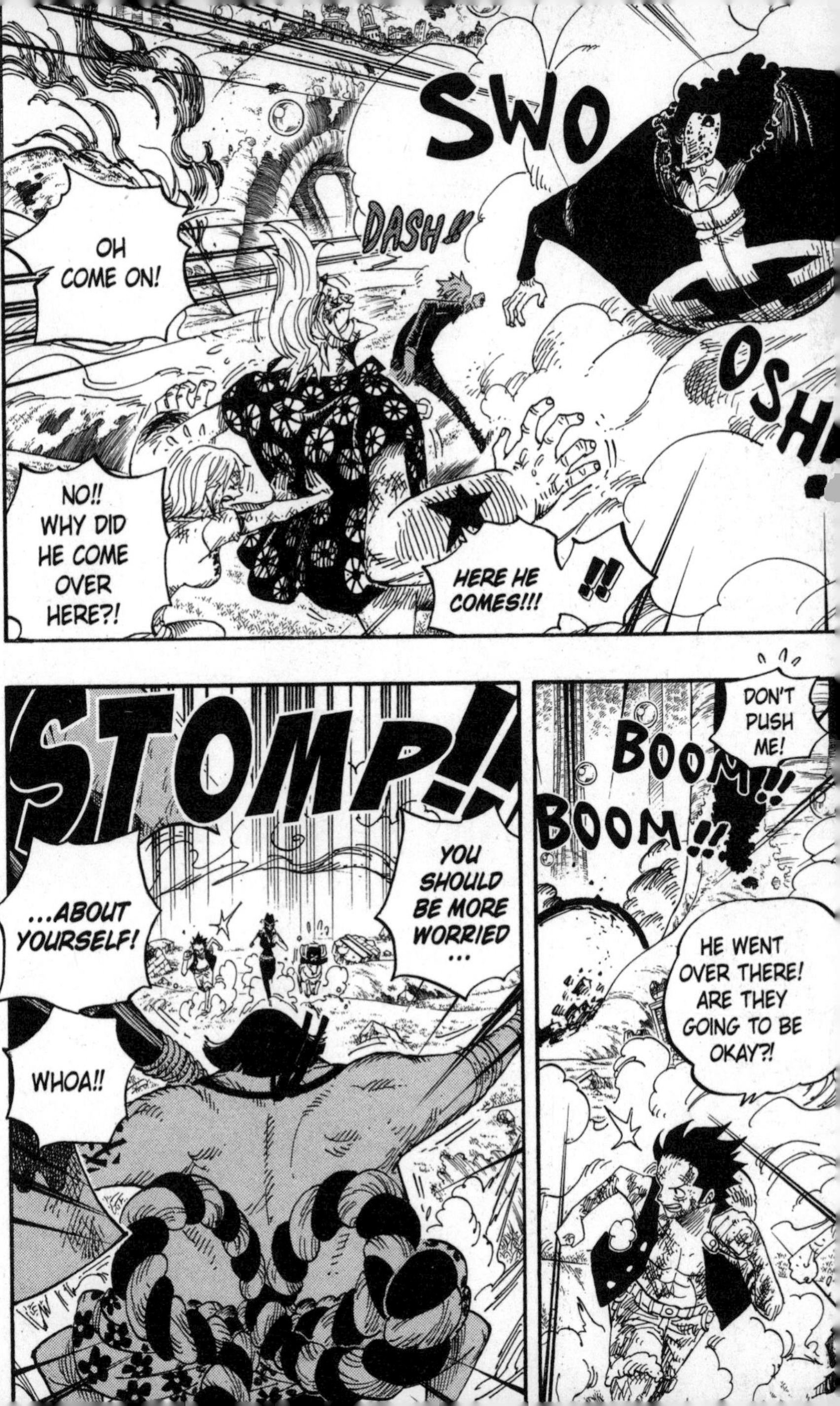
SWOOSH!
DASH!!
OH COME ON!
HERE HE COMES!!!
!!
NO!! WHY DID HE COME OVER HERE?!
DON'T PUSH ME!
BOOM!!
BOOM!!
HE WENT OVER THERE! ARE THEY GOING TO BE OKAY?!
STOMP!!
YOU SHOULD BE MORE WORRIED...
...ABOUT YOURSELF!
WHOA!!

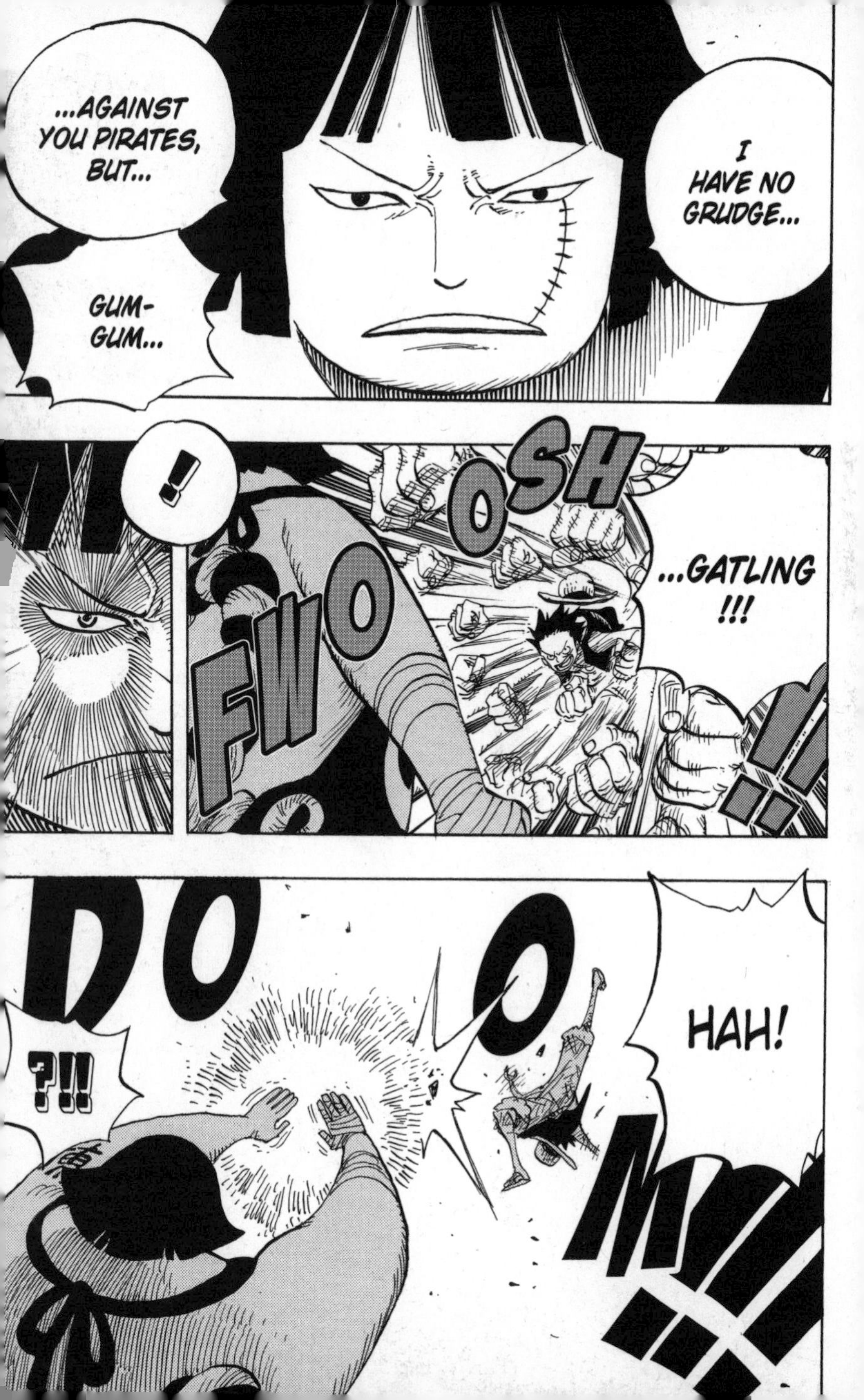
I HAVE NO GRUDGE...
...AGAINST YOU PIRATES, BUT...
GUM-GUM...
FWOOSH
...GATLING !!!
!
HAH!
DOOOM!!
?!!

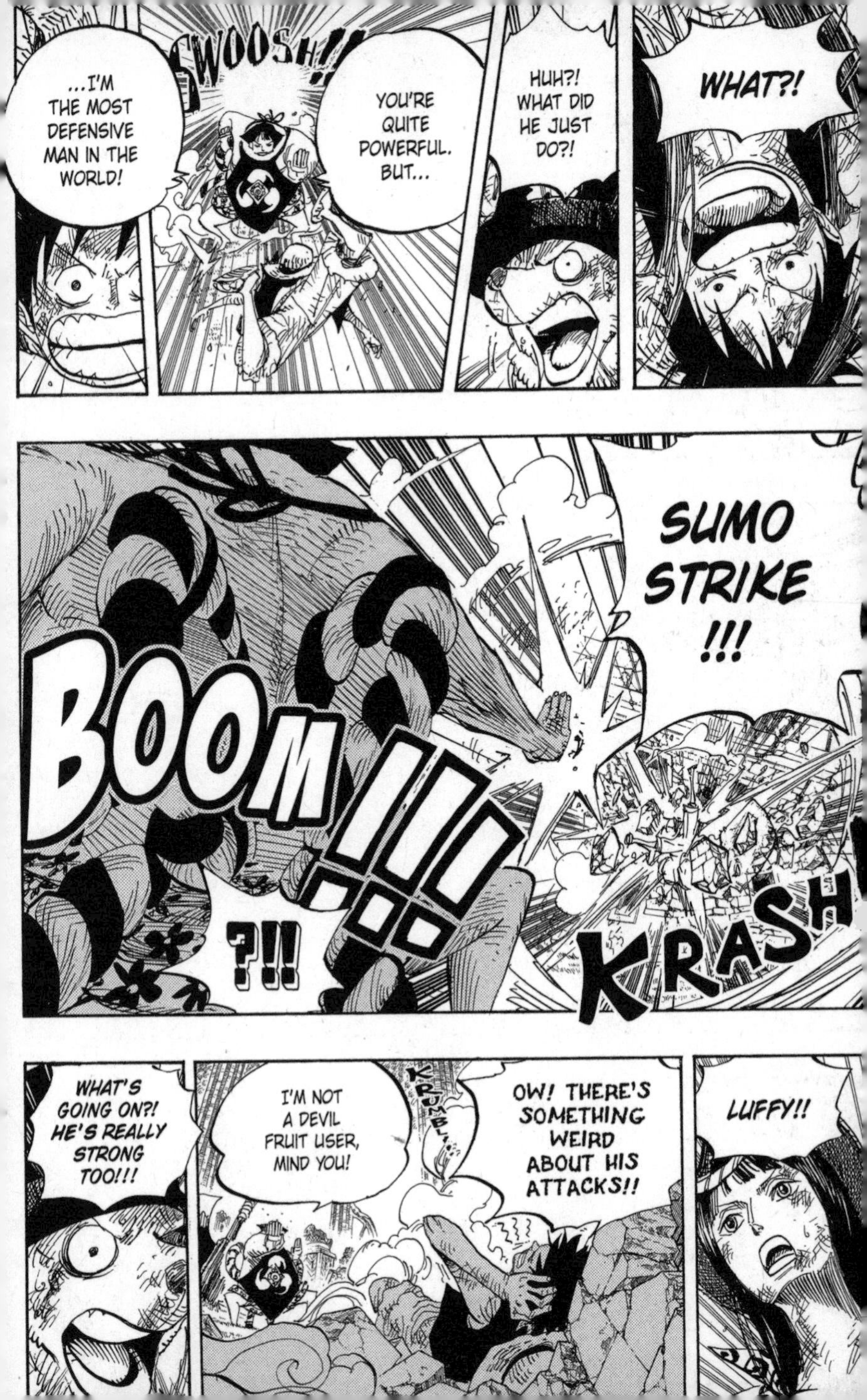
WHAT?!
HUH?! WHAT DID HE JUST DO?!
YOU'RE QUITE POWERFUL. BUT...
SWOOSH!!
...I'M THE MOST DEFENSIVE MAN IN THE WORLD!
SUMO STRIKE!!!
BOOM!!!
?!!
KRASH
LUFFY!!
OW! THERE'S SOMETHING WEIRD ABOUT HIS ATTACKS!!
KRUMBL...
I'M NOT A DEVIL FRUIT USER, MIND YOU!
WHAT'S GOING ON?! HE'S REALLY STRONG TOO!!!

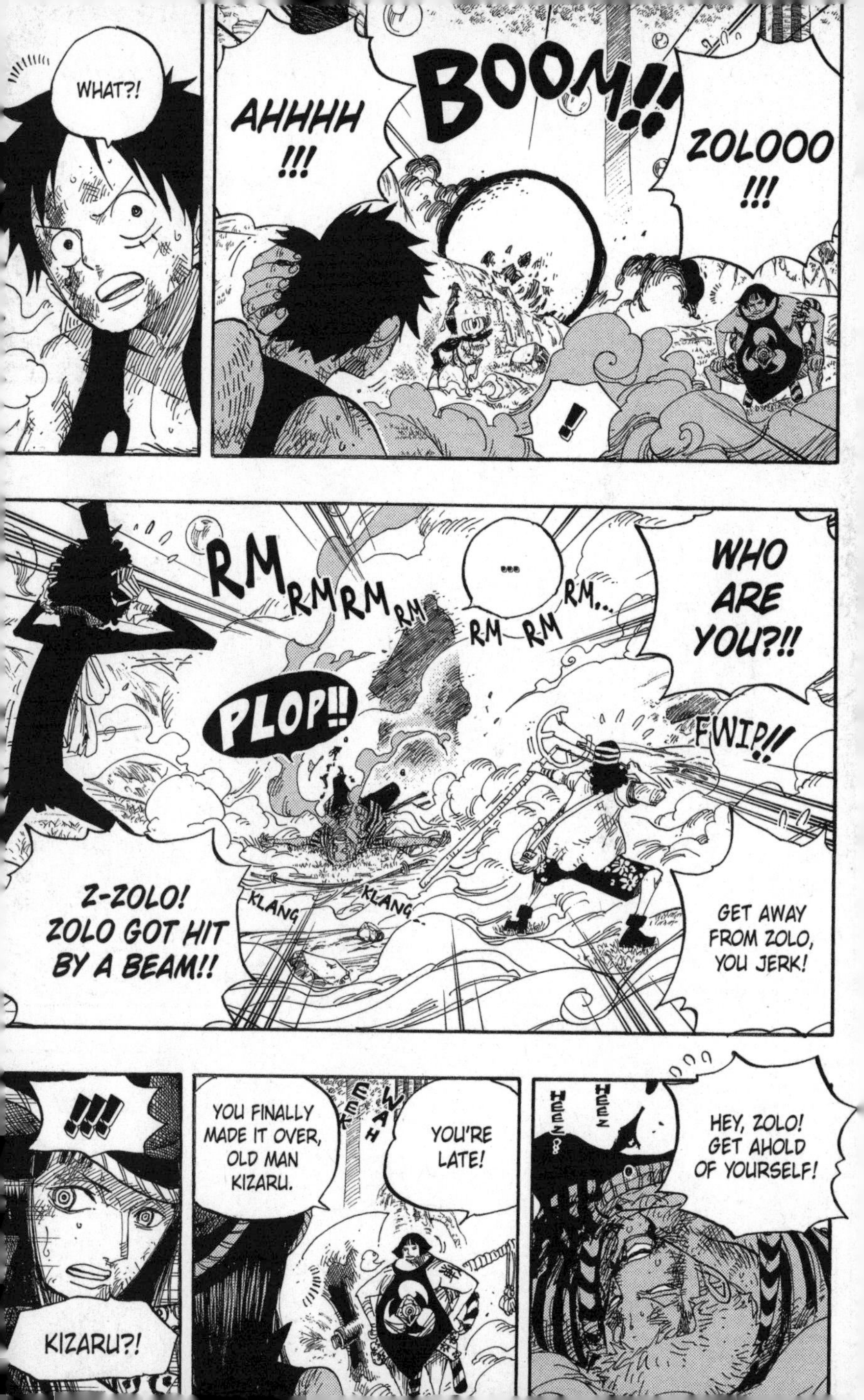
ZOLOOO !!!
BOOM!!
AHHHH !!!
!
WHAT?!
WHO ARE YOU?!!
...
RM RM RM RM RM RM RM...
FWIP!!
PLOP!!
GET AWAY FROM ZOLO, YOU JERK!
KLANG
KLANG
Z-ZOLO! ZOLO GOT HIT BY A BEAM!!
HEEZ
HEEZ
HEY, ZOLO! GET AHOLD OF YOURSELF!
KEE WAH
YOU'RE LATE!
YOU FINALLY MADE IT OVER, OLD MAN KIZARU.
!!!
KIZARU?!

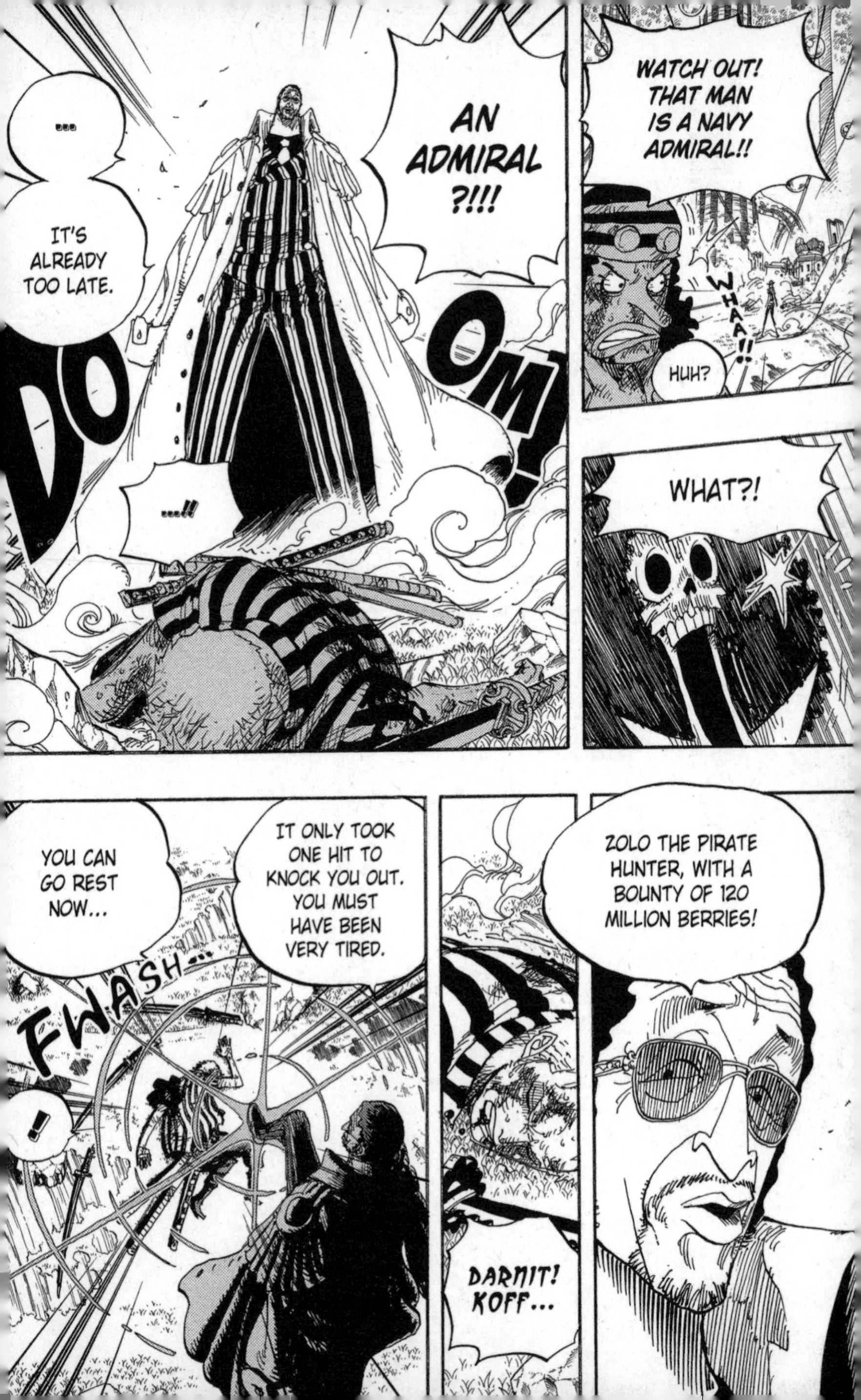
WATCH OUT! THAT MAN IS A NAVY ADMIRAL!!
WHAA!!
HUH?
WHAT?!
AN ADMIRAL ?!!!
...
IT'S ALREADY TOO LATE.
DOOM!
...!!
ZOLO THE PIRATE HUNTER, WITH A BOUNTY OF 120 MILLION BERRIES!
DARNIT! KOFF...
IT ONLY TOOK ONE HIT TO KNOCK YOU OUT. YOU MUST HAVE BEEN VERY TIRED.
YOU CAN GO REST NOW...
FWASH...
!

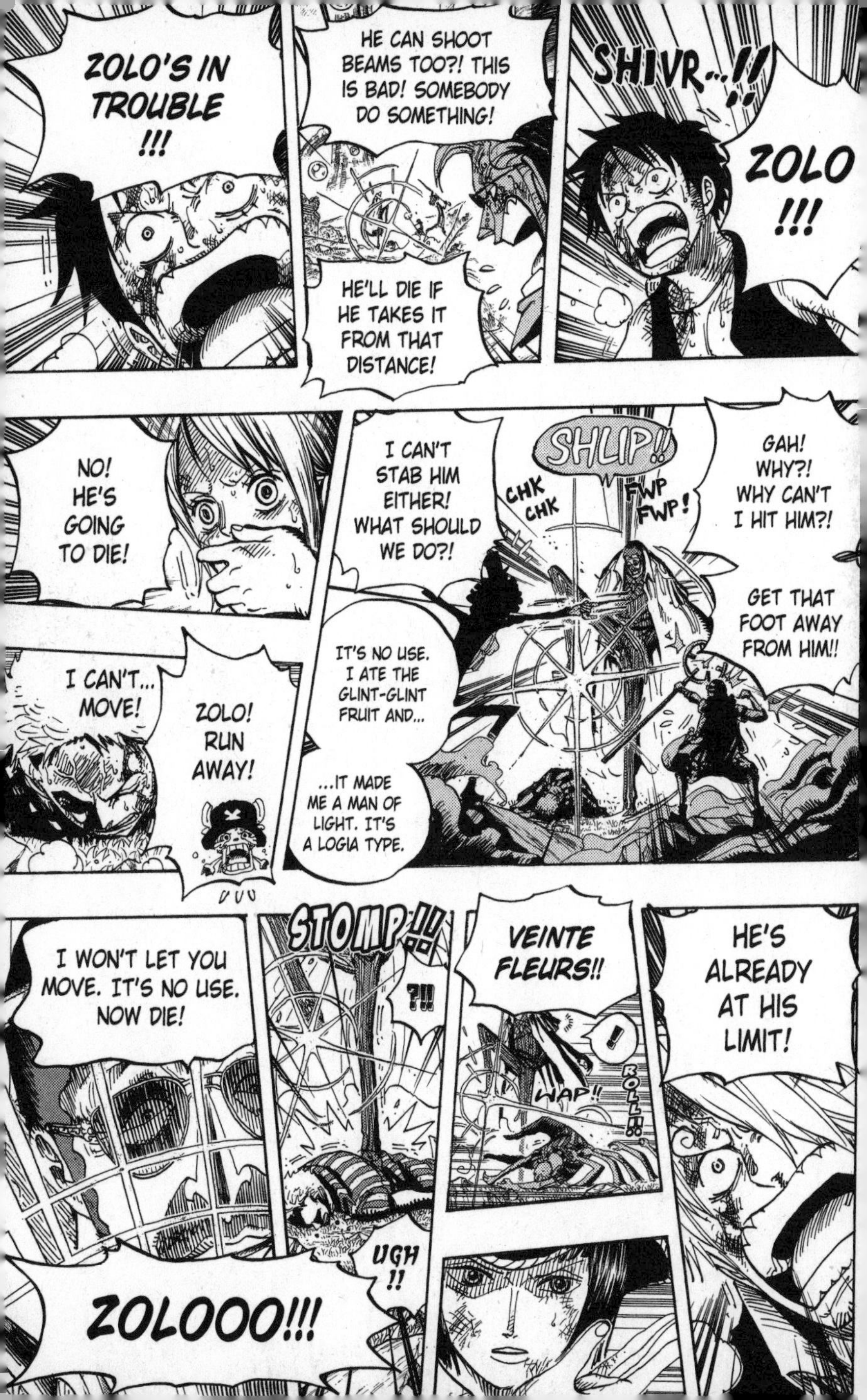
SHIVR...!!
ZOLO!!!
HE CAN SHOOT BEAMS TOO?! THIS IS BAD! SOMEBODY DO SOMETHING!
HE'LL DIE IF HE TAKES IT FROM THAT DISTANCE!
ZOLO'S IN TROUBLE!!!
GAH! WHY?! WHY CAN'T I HIT HIM?!
SHLIP!!
FWP FWP!
CHK CHK
I CAN'T STAB HIM EITHER! WHAT SHOULD WE DO?!
GET THAT FOOT AWAY FROM HIM!!
IT'S NO USE. I ATE THE GLINT-GLINT FRUIT AND...
...IT MADE ME A MAN OF LIGHT. IT'S A LOGIA TYPE.
NO! HE'S GOING TO DIE!
I CAN'T... MOVE!
ZOLO! RUN AWAY!
HE'S ALREADY AT HIS LIMIT!
VEINTE FLEURS!!
!
ROLL!!
WAP!!
STOMP!!
?!!
UGH!!
I WON'T LET YOU MOVE. IT'S NO USE. NOW DIE!
ZOLOOO!!!

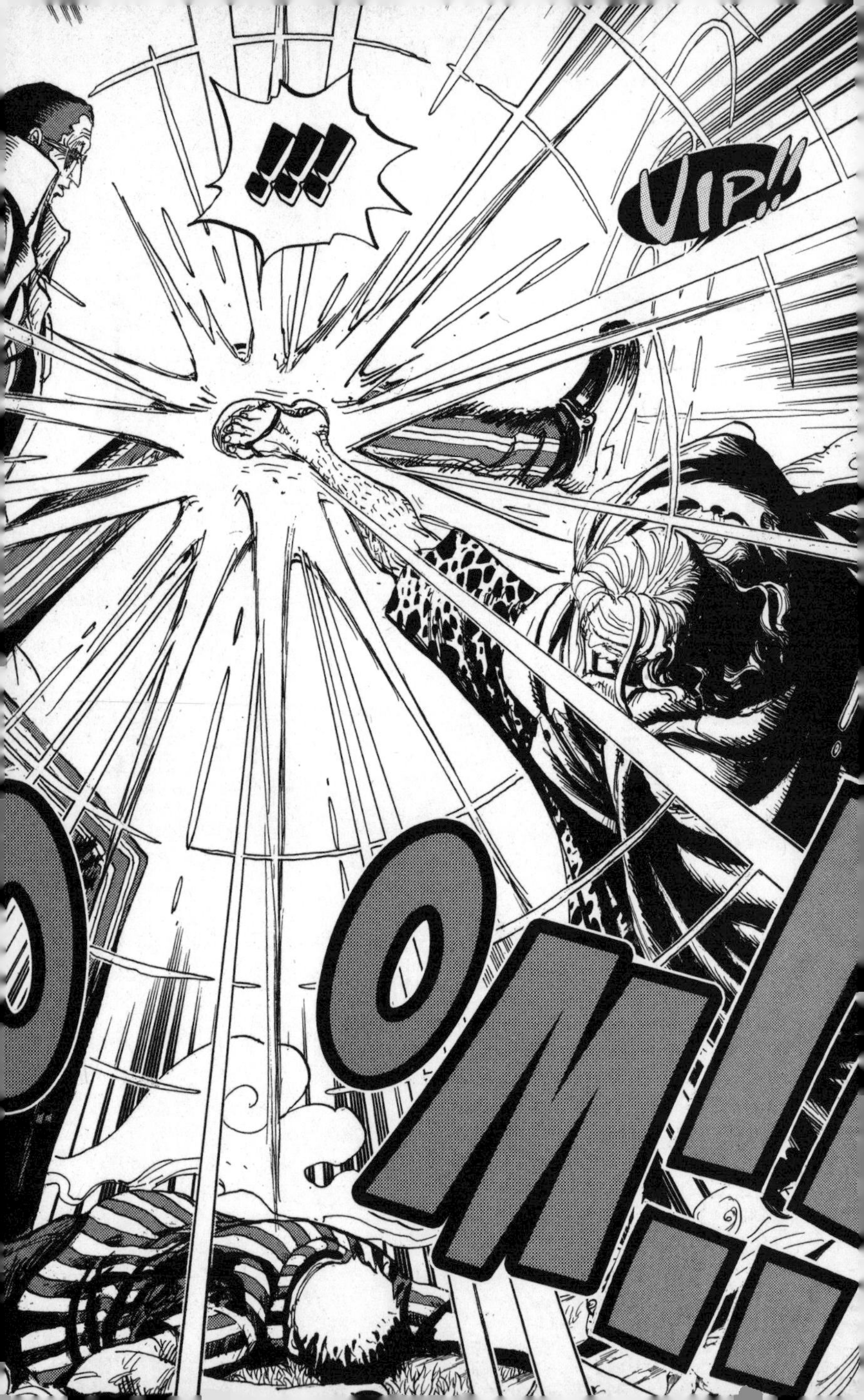
VIP!!
!!!

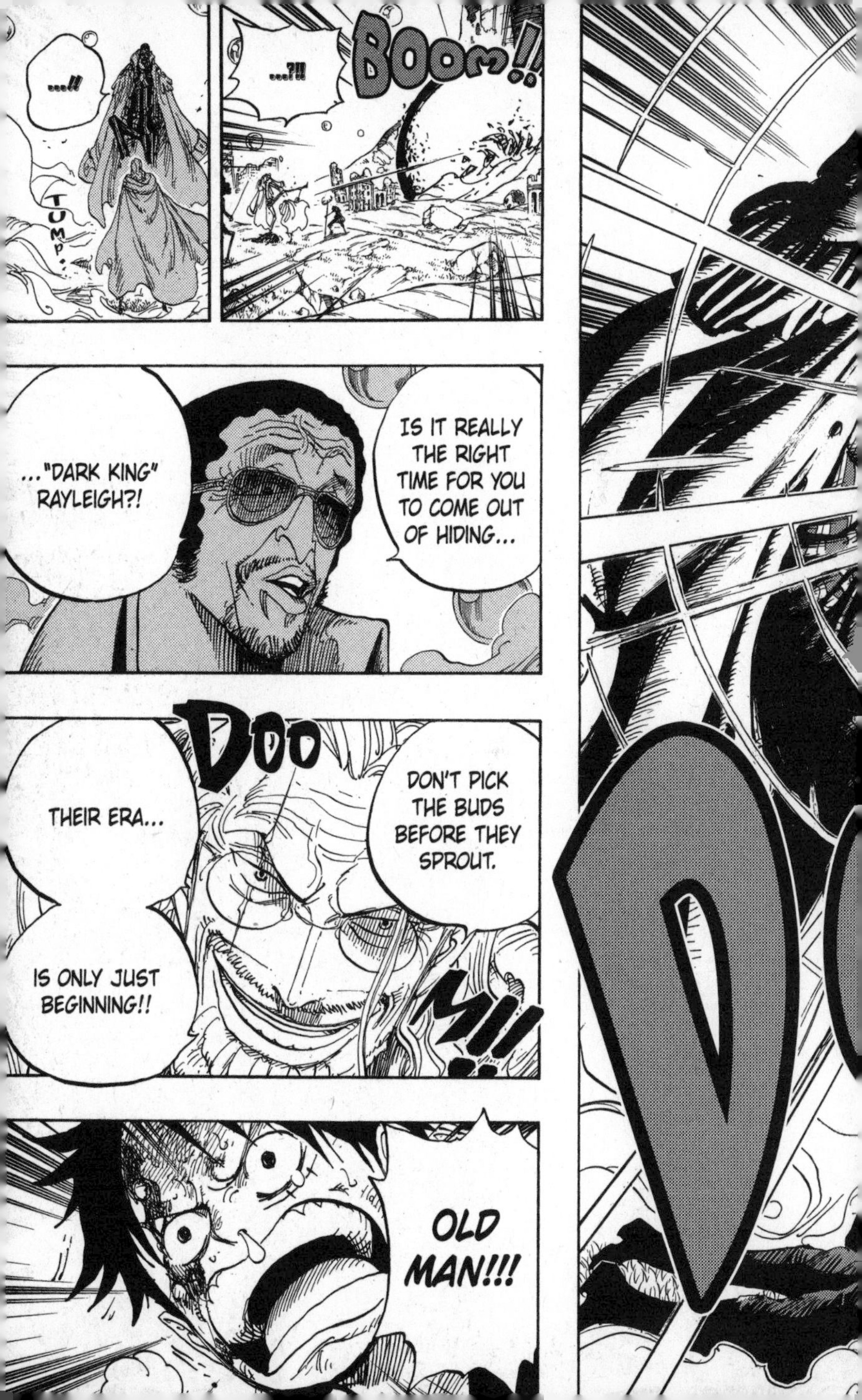
BOOM!!
...?!!
...!!
TUMP..
IS IT REALLY THE RIGHT TIME FOR YOU TO COME OUT OF HIDING...
..."DARK KING" RAYLEIGH?!
DOOMI!!
DON'T PICK THE BUDS BEFORE THEY SPROUT.
THEIR ERA...
IS ONLY JUST BEGINNING!!
OLD MAN!!!

CAPTAIN MAYUMI TANAKA'S QUESTION CORNER!!

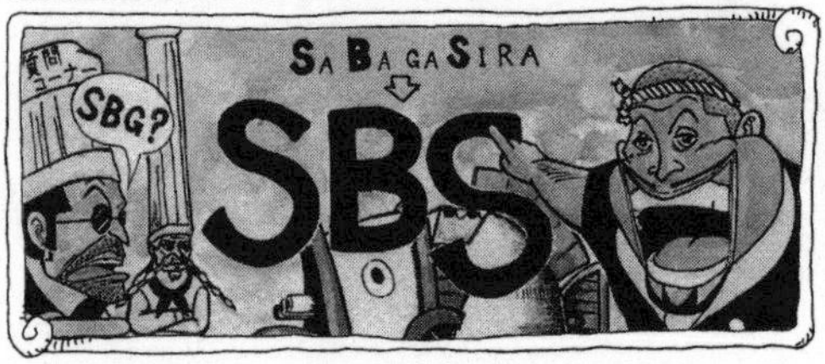
SBG?
SABAGASIRA
SBS

(Doromizu, Ibaraki)

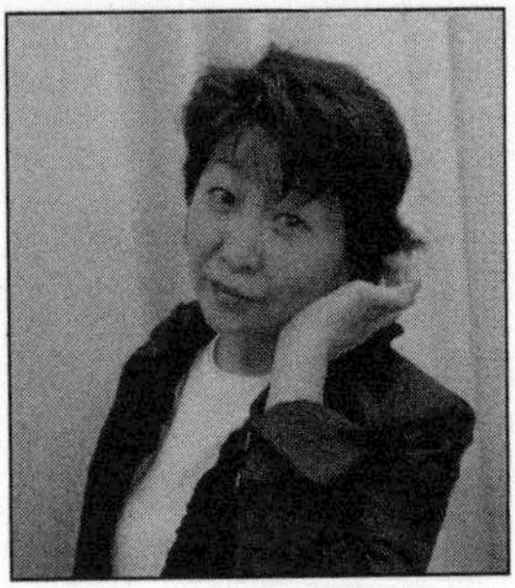

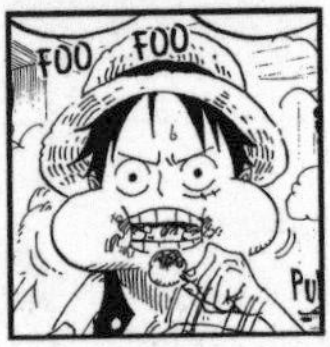
FOO FOO

R: I see Luffy talk while he's eating very often… Do you eat while you're voice acting? I've always wondered about that!

--Ayako

T: I always go for realism! I'm always eating the stuff that Odacchi drew!

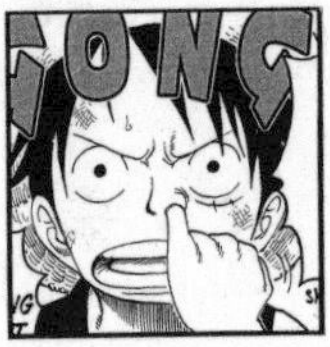

R: I enjoy watching the *One Piece* anime every week! When Luffy is talking while picking his nose, do you also imagine yourself picking your nose while saying it? Or do you actually pick your nose while you act?

--Hojirina III

T: I always go for realism! Always!

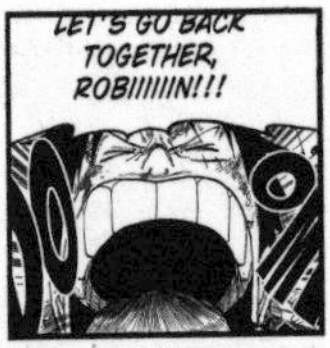
LET'S GO BACK TOGETHER, ROBIIIIIIN!!!

R: Luffy has a lot of lines that he shouts. Do those make you tired?!

--Calorie

T: I use up some strength every time I shout, and it makes me shorter. During the recording for the first episode of One Piece, I was 175 cm tall. But after ten years, I am now 147.5 cm.

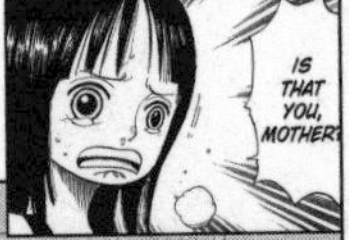
IS THAT YOU, MOTHER

R: Please be my mom!

--High Socks in the Winter Last Me Three Days

T: Sure. But I'll turn into your dad with a buzz cut sometimes. Are you sure you want that? (→)

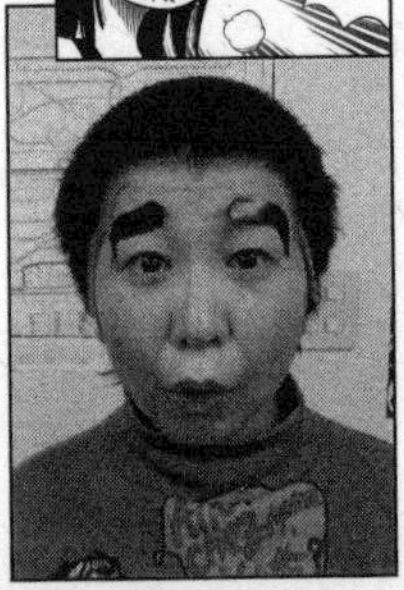

O: What in the world are you doing?! Whatever! Look forward to the next Voice Actor Question Corner!

Chapter 512:
ZOLO, GONE

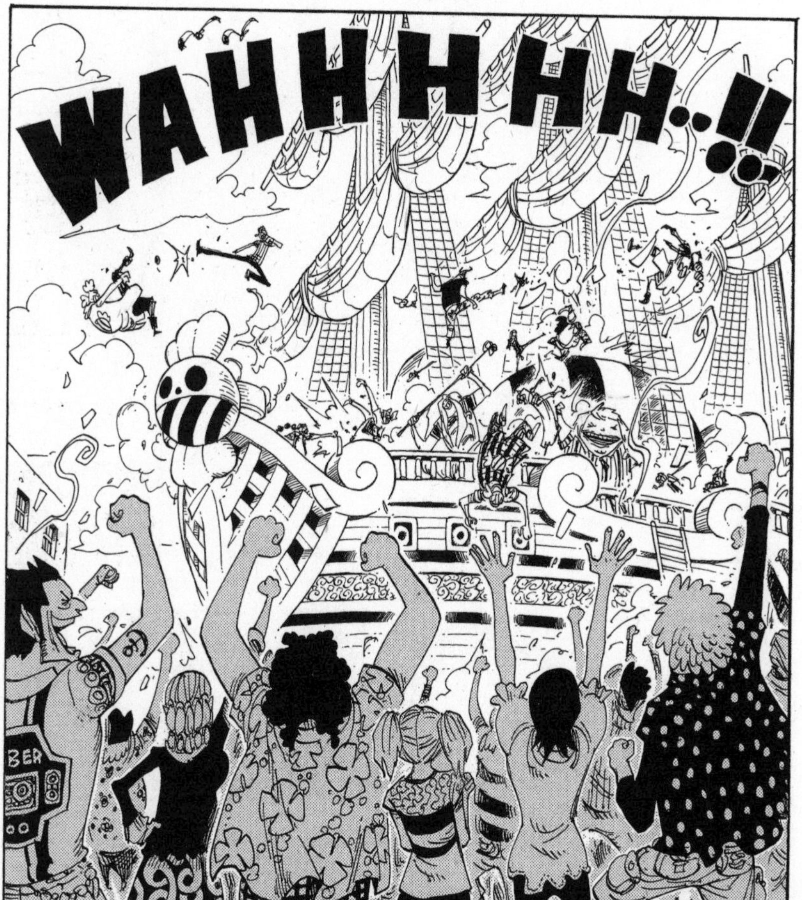
WAHHHHH..!!

CP9'S INDEPENDENT REPORT, VOL. 20:
"THE HEROES NEVER SEEN BEFORE"

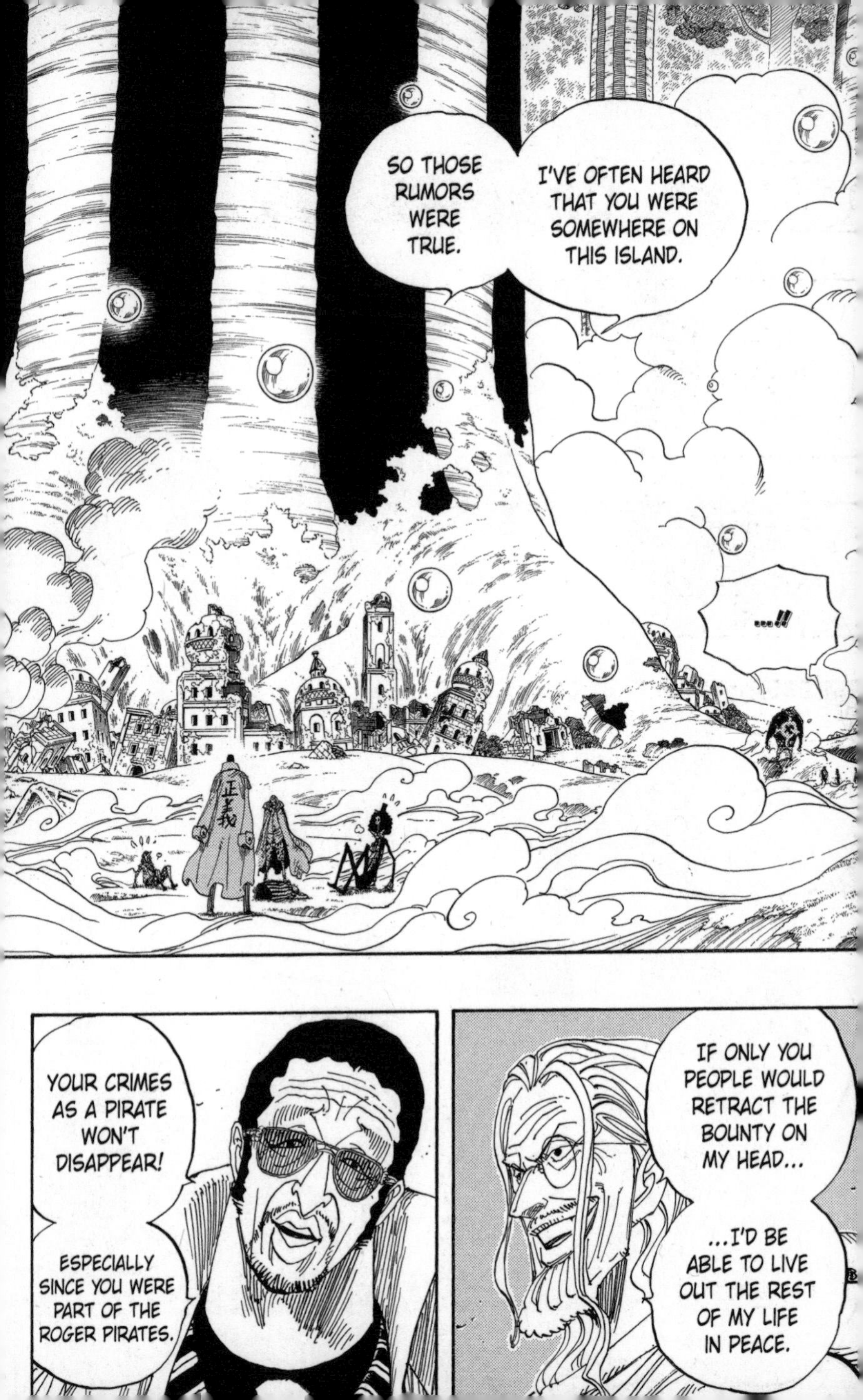
I'VE OFTEN HEARD THAT YOU WERE SOMEWHERE ON THIS ISLAND.
SO THOSE RUMORS WERE TRUE.
...!!
IF ONLY YOU PEOPLE WOULD RETRACT THE BOUNTY ON MY HEAD...
...I'D BE ABLE TO LIVE OUT THE REST OF MY LIFE IN PEACE.
YOUR CRIMES AS A PIRATE WON'T DISAPPEAR!
ESPECIALLY SINCE YOU WERE PART OF THE ROGER PIRATES.

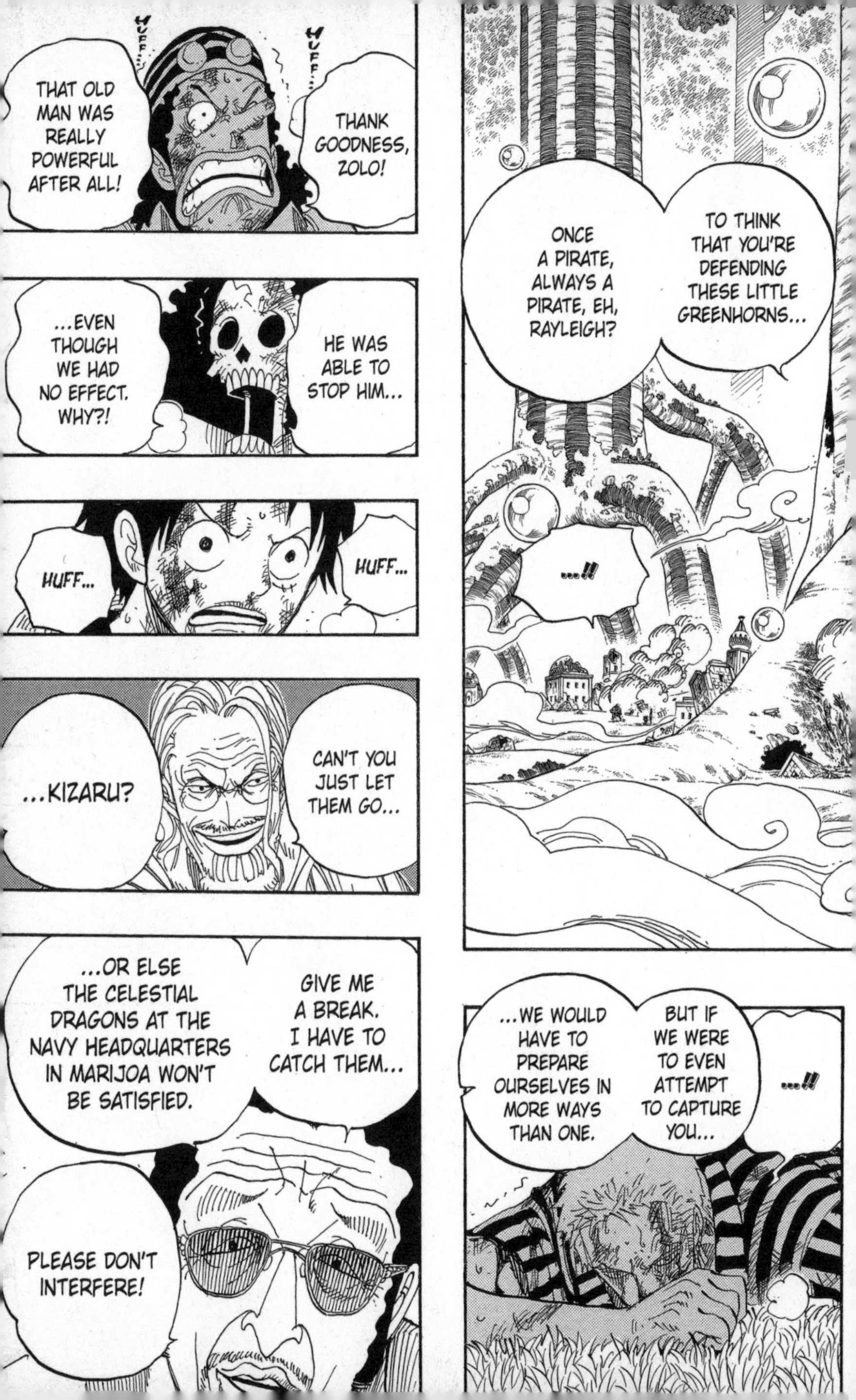
TO THINK THAT YOU'RE DEFENDING THESE LITTLE GREENHORNS...
ONCE A PIRATE, ALWAYS A PIRATE, EH, RAYLEIGH?
...!!
...!!
BUT IF WE WERE TO EVEN ATTEMPT TO CAPTURE YOU...
...WE WOULD HAVE TO PREPARE OURSELVES IN MORE WAYS THAN ONE.
HUFF...
HUFF...
THANK GOODNESS, ZOLO!
THAT OLD MAN WAS REALLY POWERFUL AFTER ALL!
HE WAS ABLE TO STOP HIM...
...EVEN THOUGH WE HAD NO EFFECT. WHY?!
HUFF...
HUFF...
CAN'T YOU JUST LET THEM GO...
...KIZARU?
GIVE ME A BREAK. I HAVE TO CATCH THEM...
...OR ELSE THE CELESTIAL DRAGONS AT THE NAVY HEADQUARTERS IN MARIJOA WON'T BE SATISFIED.
PLEASE DON'T INTERFERE!

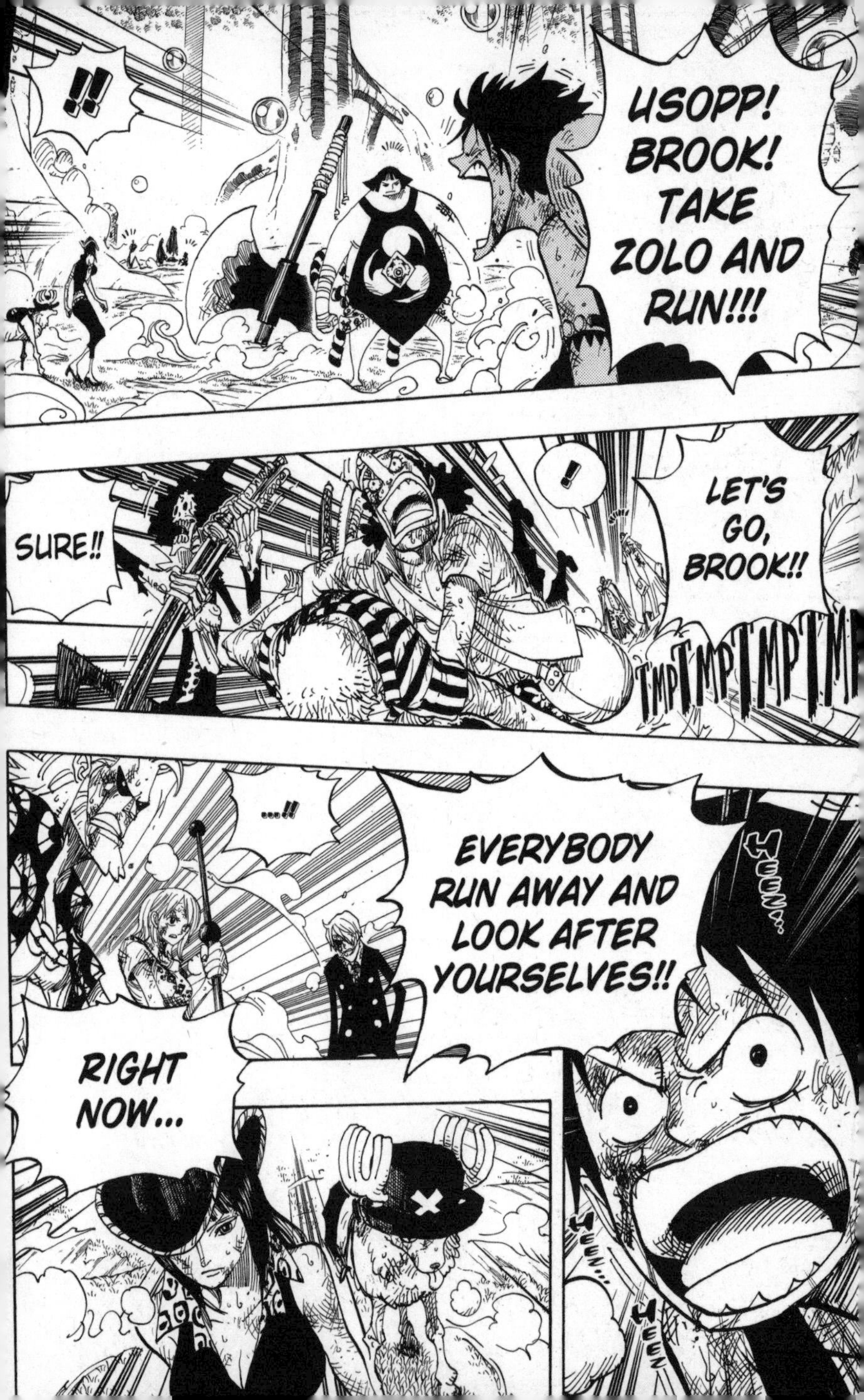
USOPP! BROOK! TAKE ZOLO AND RUN!!!
!!
LET'S GO, BROOK!!
!
TMP TMP TMP TMP
SURE!!
HEEN...
EVERYBODY RUN AWAY AND LOOK AFTER YOURSELVES!!
...!!
RIGHT NOW...
HEEN...
HEEN

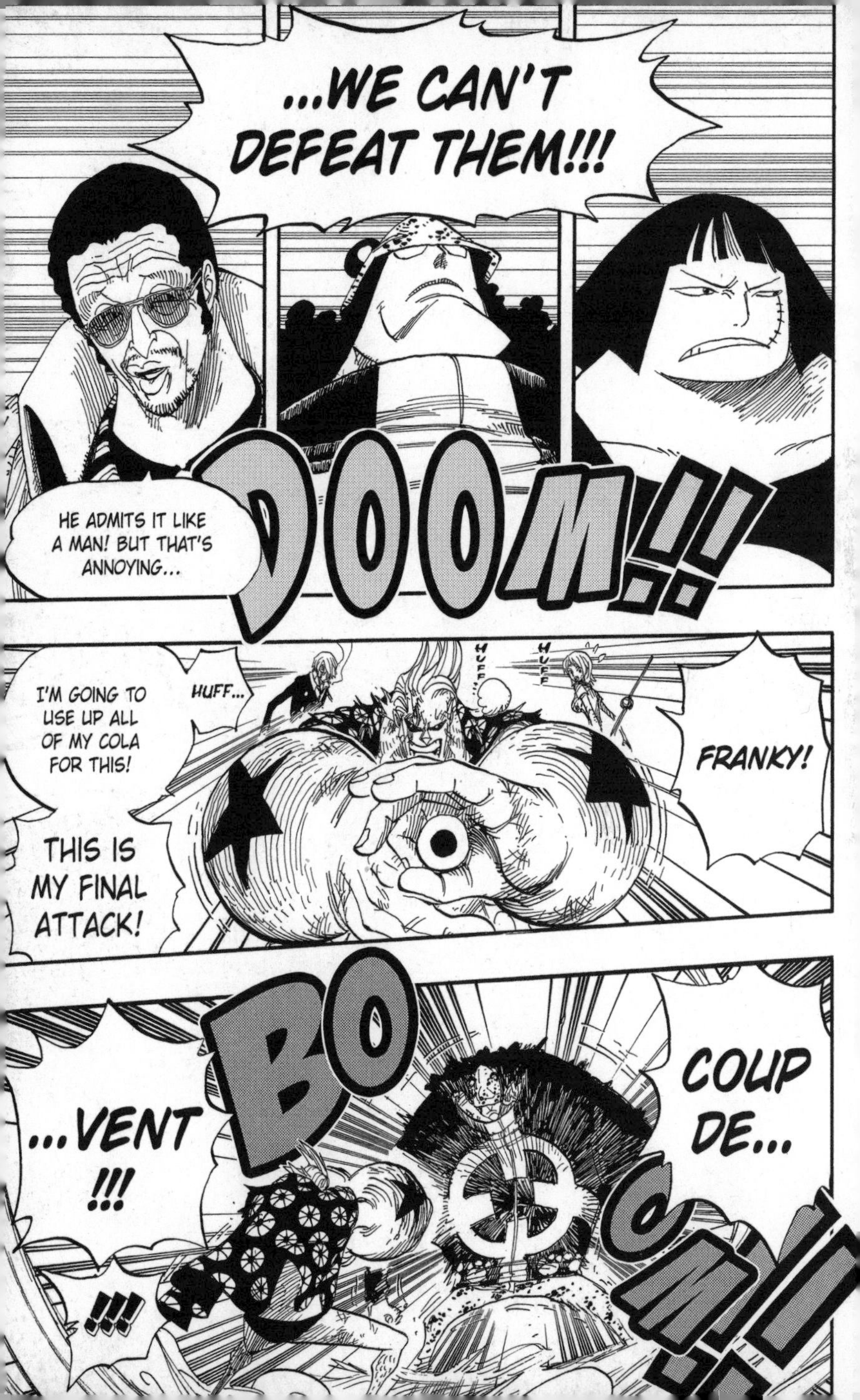
...WE CAN'T DEFEAT THEM!!!
DOOM!!
HE ADMITS IT LIKE A MAN! BUT THAT'S ANNOYING...
FRANKY!
HUFF
HUFF
HUFF...
I'M GOING TO USE UP ALL OF MY COLA FOR THIS!
THIS IS MY FINAL ATTACK!
COUP DE...
BOOOM!!
...VENT !!!
!!!

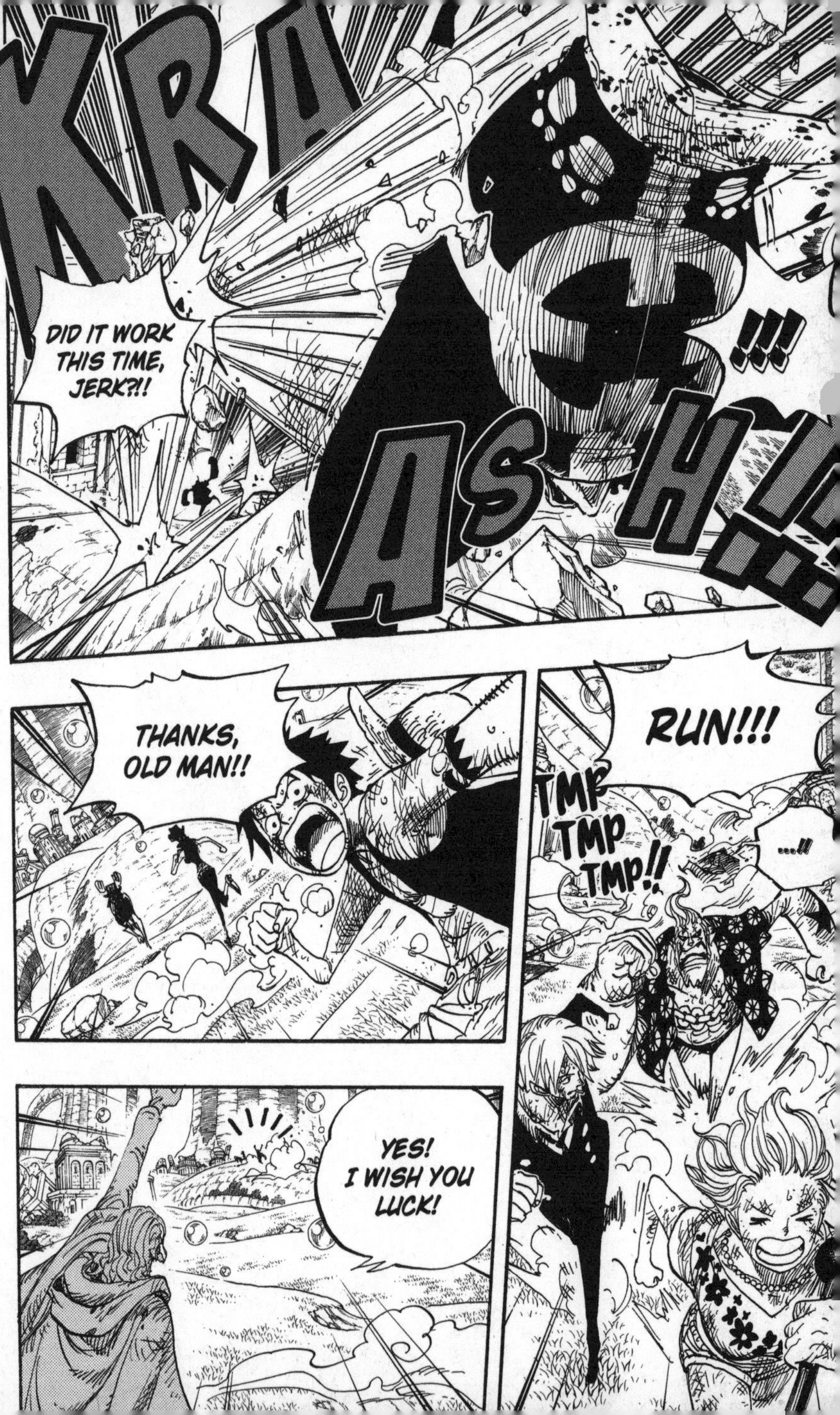
KRA
ASH!!!
DID IT WORK THIS TIME, JERK?!!
RUN!!!
TMP TMP TMP!!
...!!
THANKS, OLD MAN!!
YES! I WISH YOU LUCK!

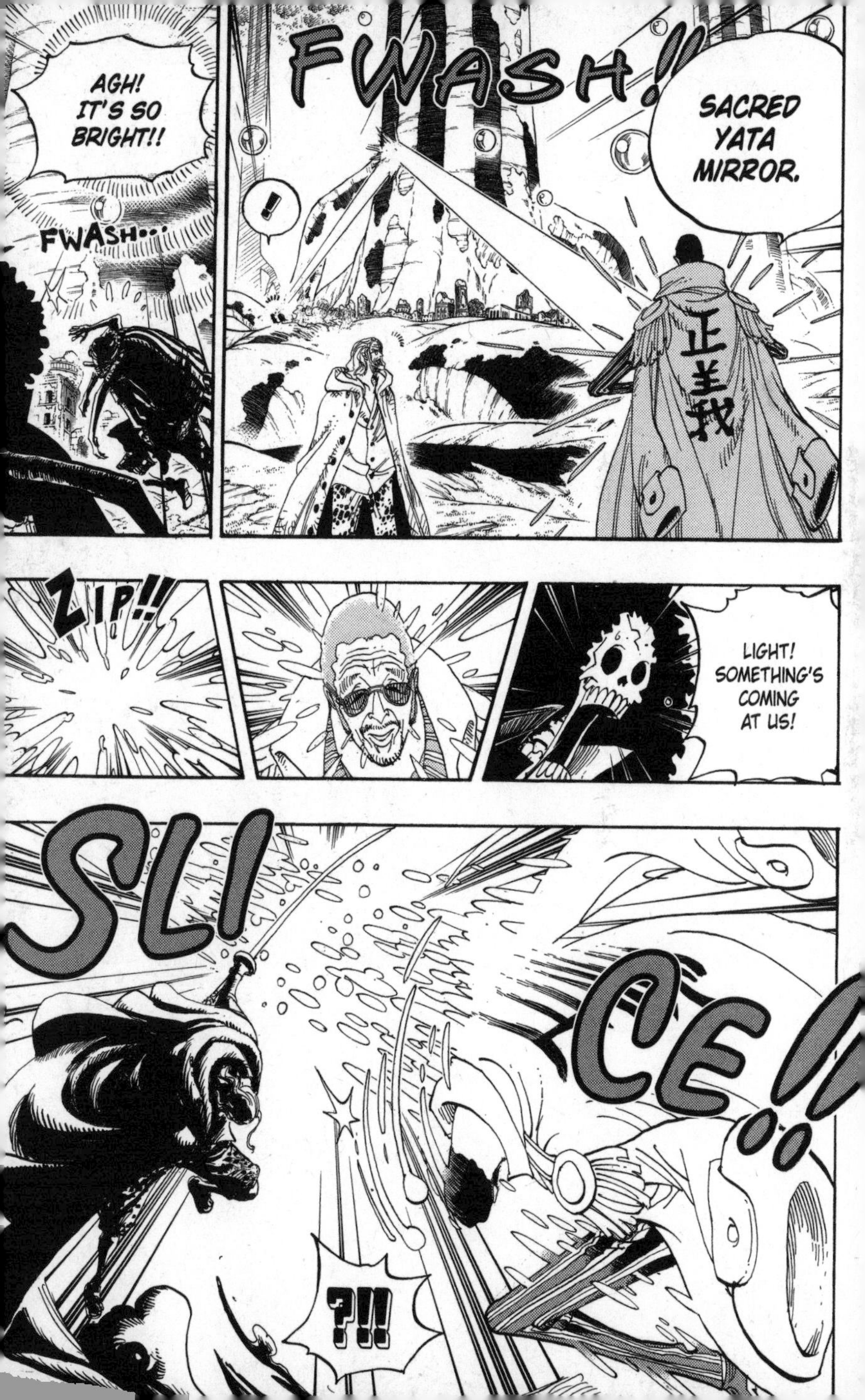
FWASH!!
SACRED YATA MIRROR.
!
AGH! IT'S SO BRIGHT!!
FWASH...
LIGHT! SOMETHING'S COMING AT US!
ZIP!!
SLICE!!
?!!

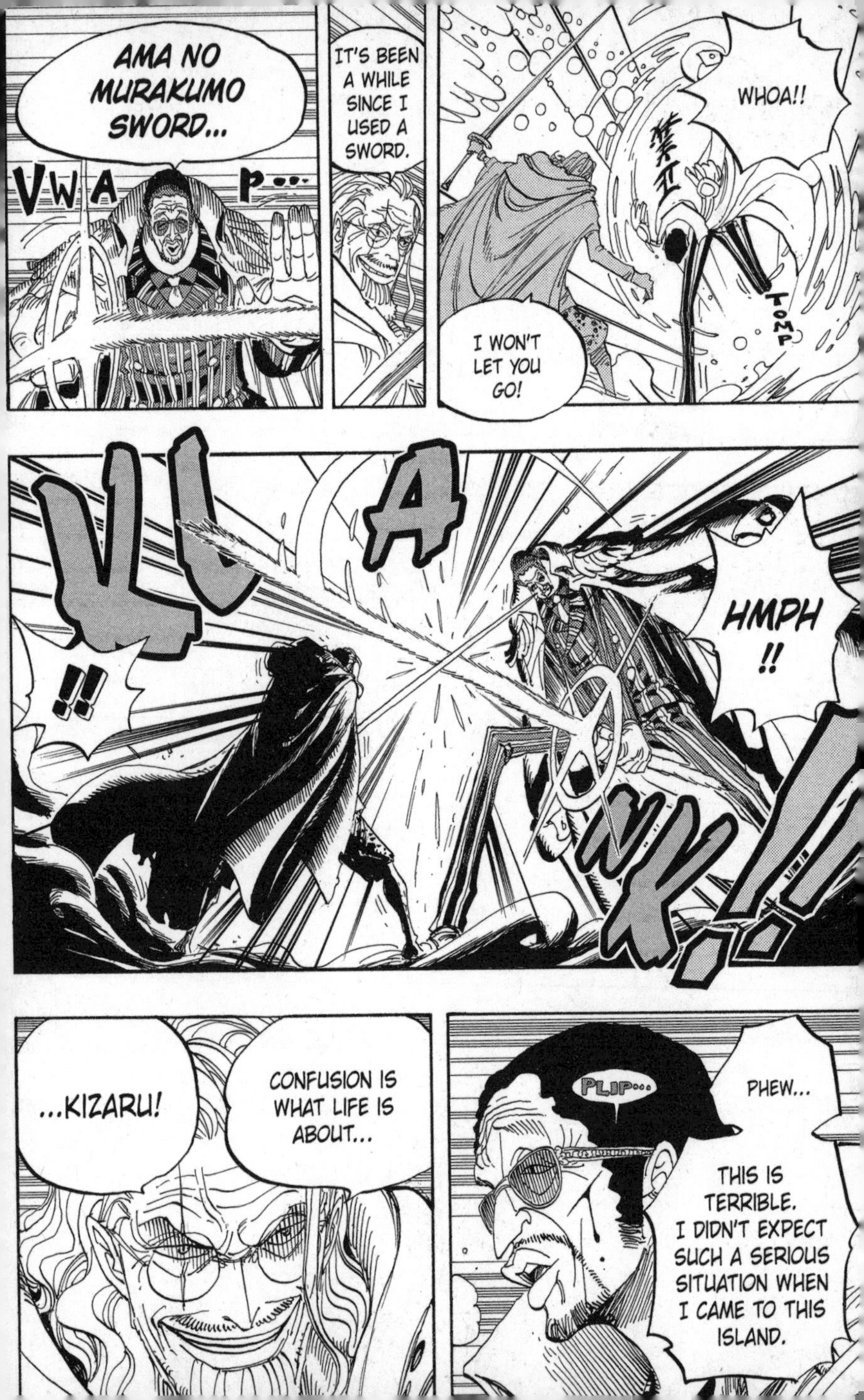
WHOA!!
TOMP
I WON'T LET YOU GO!
IT'S BEEN A WHILE SINCE I USED A SWORD.
AMA NO MURAKUMO SWORD...
VWAP...
HMPH!!
!!
PLIP...
PHEW...
THIS IS TERRIBLE. I DIDN'T EXPECT SUCH A SERIOUS SITUATION WHEN I CAME TO THIS ISLAND.
CONFUSION IS WHAT LIFE IS ABOUT...
...KIZARU!

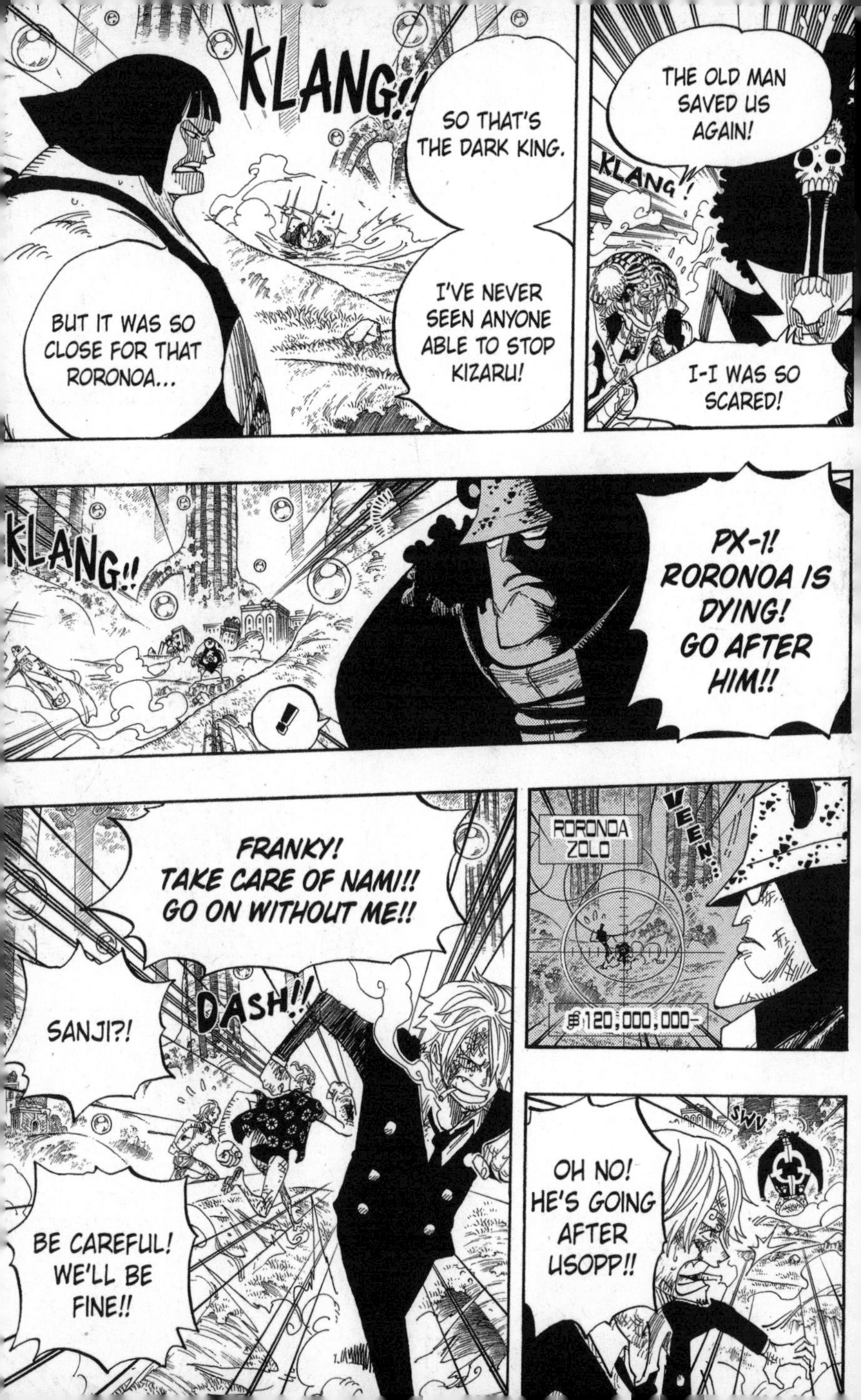
THE OLD MAN SAVED US AGAIN!
KLANG!
I-I WAS SO SCARED!
KLANG!!
SO THAT'S THE DARK KING.
I'VE NEVER SEEN ANYONE ABLE TO STOP KIZARU!
BUT IT WAS SO CLOSE FOR THAT RORONOA...
PX-1! RORONOA IS DYING! GO AFTER HIM!!
!
KLANG!!
VEEN...
RORONOA ZOLO
฿120,000,000-
SWV
OH NO! HE'S GOING AFTER USOPP!!
FRANKY! TAKE CARE OF NAMI!! GO ON WITHOUT ME!!
DASH!!
SANJI?!
BE CAREFUL! WE'LL BE FINE!!

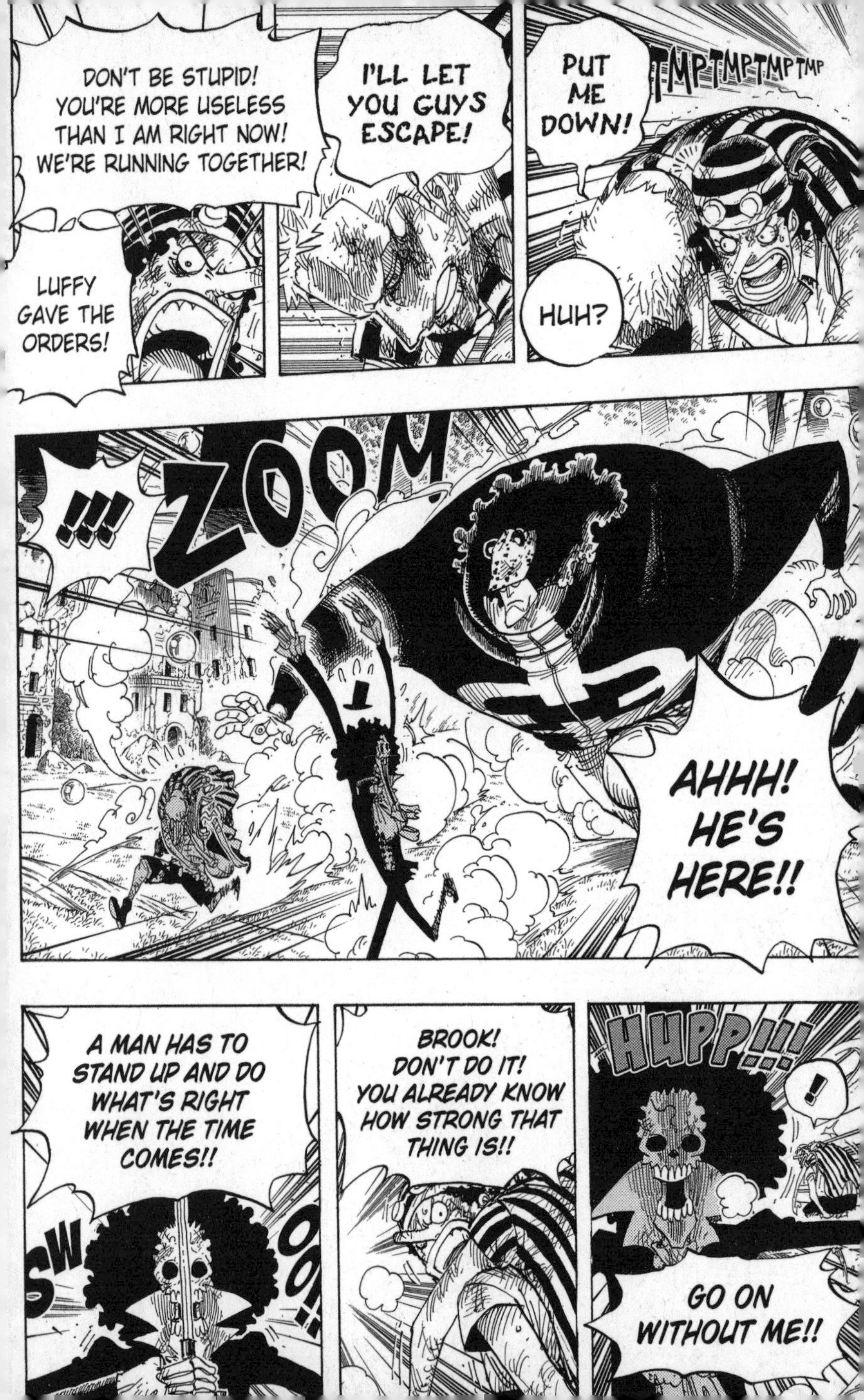
TMPTMPTMPTMP
PUT ME DOWN!
HUH?
I'LL LET YOU GUYS ESCAPE!
DON'T BE STUPID! YOU'RE MORE USELESS THAN I AM RIGHT NOW! WE'RE RUNNING TOGETHER!
LUFFY GAVE THE ORDERS!
ZOOM
AHHH! HE'S HERE!!
!!!
HUPP!!!
!
GO ON WITHOUT ME!!
BROOK! DON'T DO IT! YOU ALREADY KNOW HOW STRONG THAT THING IS!!
A MAN HAS TO STAND UP AND DO WHAT'S RIGHT WHEN THE TIME COMES!!
SW
OO!!

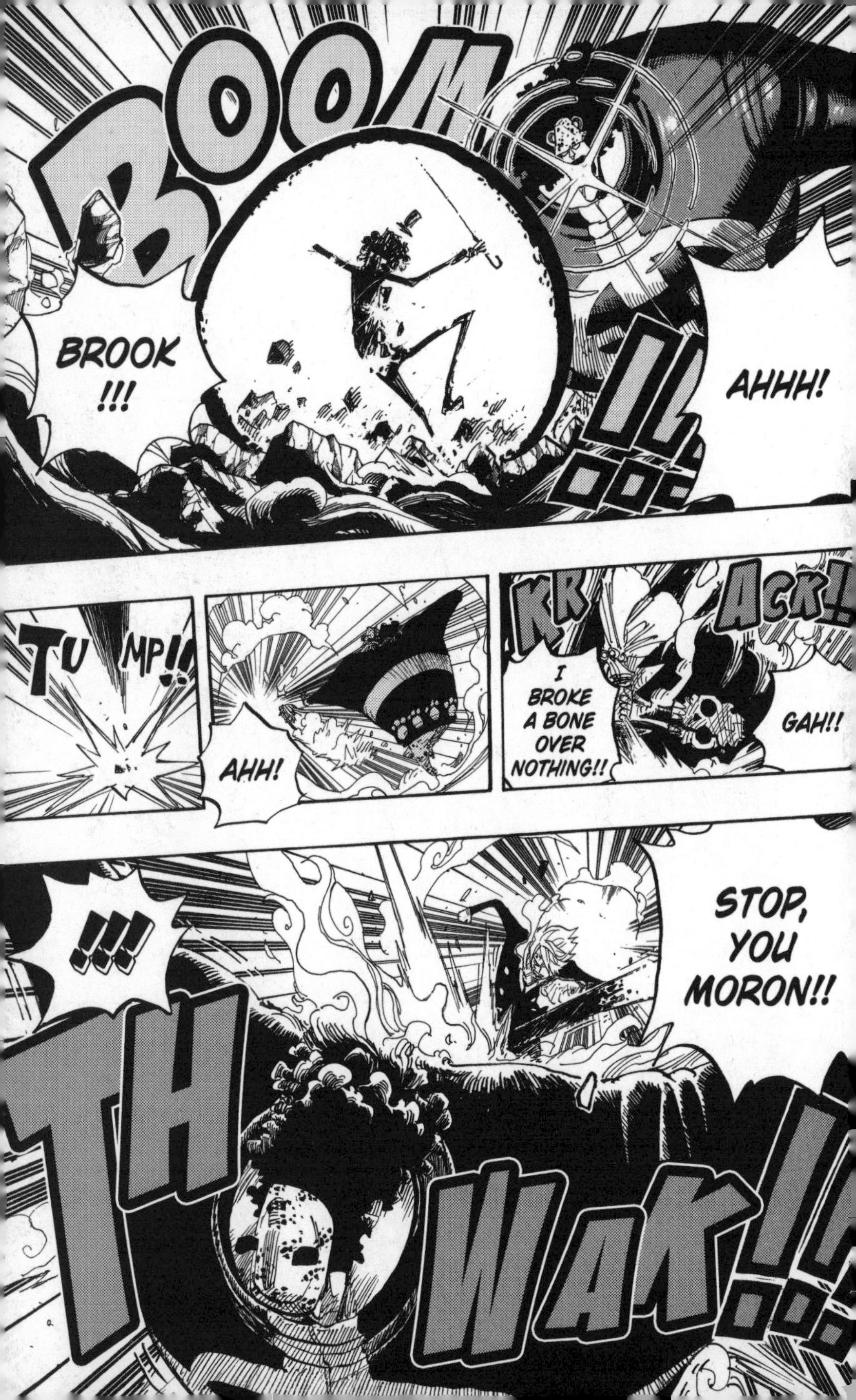
AHHH!
BOOM!!
BROOK !!!
KR ACK!!
GAH!!
I BROKE A BONE OVER NOTHING!!
AHH!
TU MP!!
STOP, YOU MORON!!
!!!
TH WAK!!

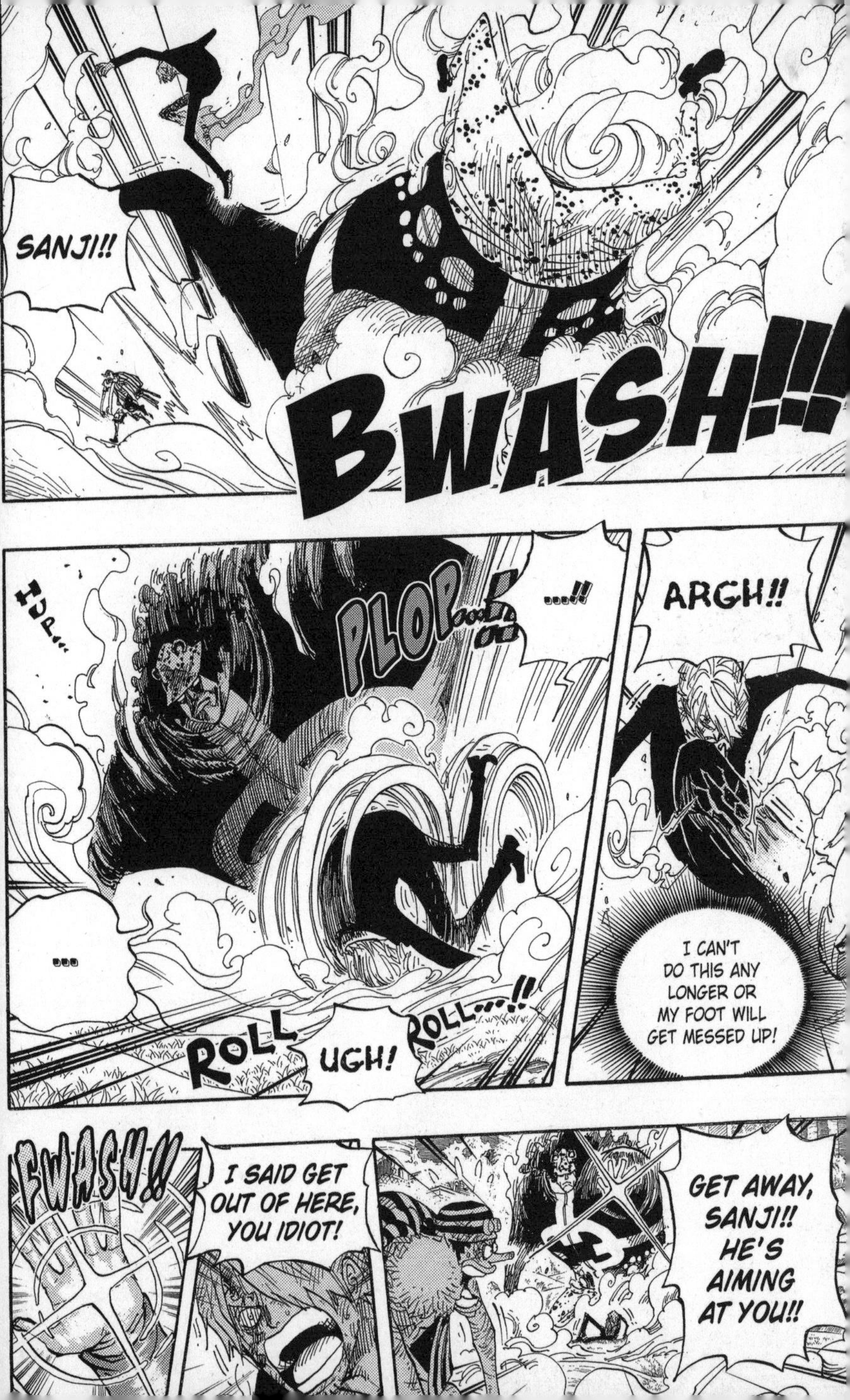
SANJI!!
BWASH!!!
ARGH!!
I CAN'T DO THIS ANY LONGER OR MY FOOT WILL GET MESSED UP!
...!!
PLOP...!
HUP...
...
ROLL...!!
UGH!
ROLL
GET AWAY, SANJI!! HE'S AIMING AT YOU!!
I SAID GET OUT OF HERE, YOU IDIOT!
FWASH!!

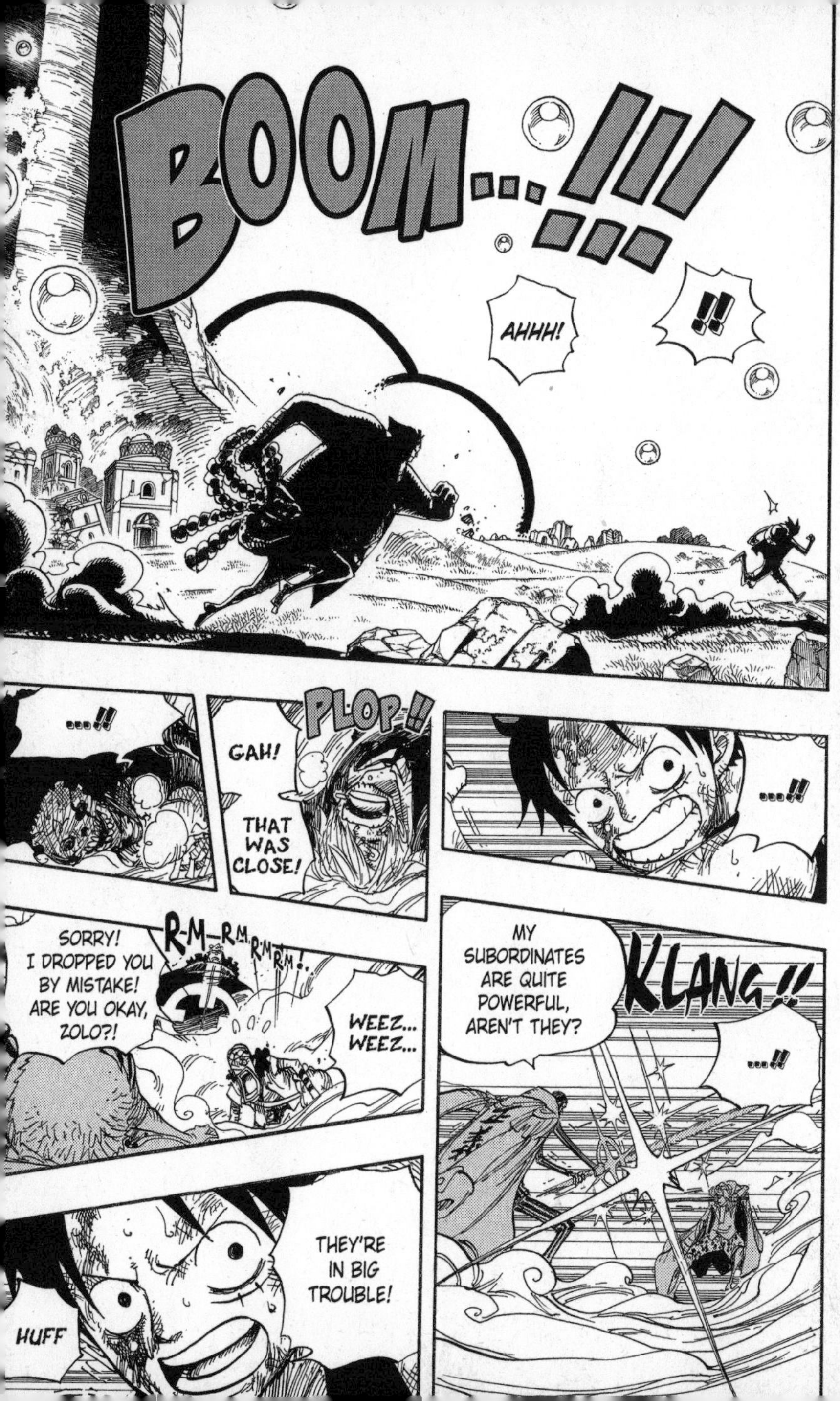
BOOM...!!!...
!!
AHHH!
...!!
PLOP!!
GAH!
THAT WAS CLOSE!
...!!
MY SUBORDINATES ARE QUITE POWERFUL, AREN'T THEY?
KLANG!!
...!!
R-M R-M R-M R-M!
SORRY! I DROPPED YOU BY MISTAKE! ARE YOU OKAY, ZOLO?!
WEEZ... WEEZ...
THEY'RE IN BIG TROUBLE!
HUFF

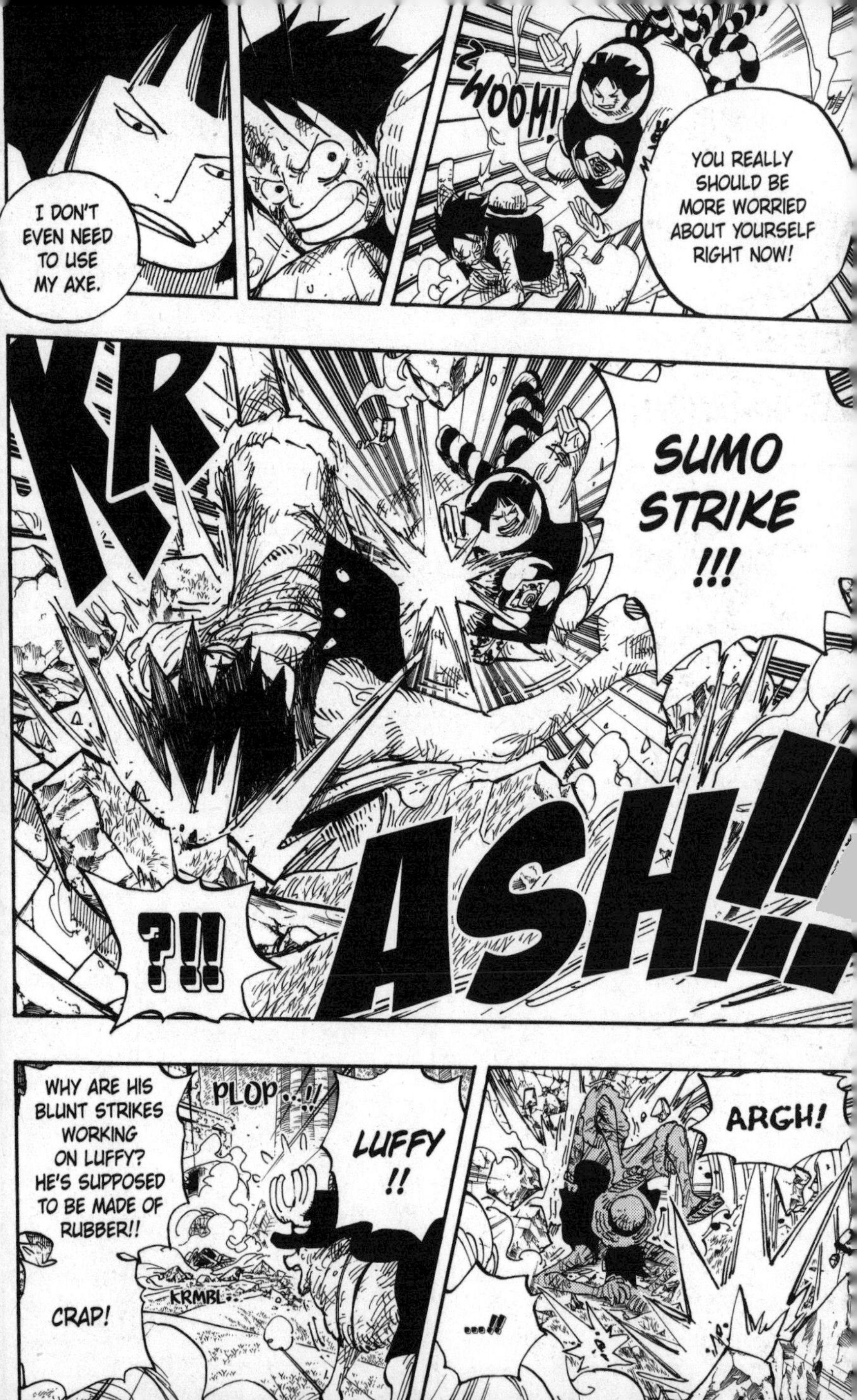
WHOOM!
YOU REALLY SHOULD BE MORE WORRIED ABOUT YOURSELF RIGHT NOW!
I DON'T EVEN NEED TO USE MY AXE.
SUMO STRIKE !!!
KR
ASH!!
?!!
ARGH!
...!!
LUFFY !!
PLOP..!!
WHY ARE HIS BLUNT STRIKES WORKING ON LUFFY? HE'S SUPPOSED TO BE MADE OF RUBBER!!
KRMBL..
CRAP!

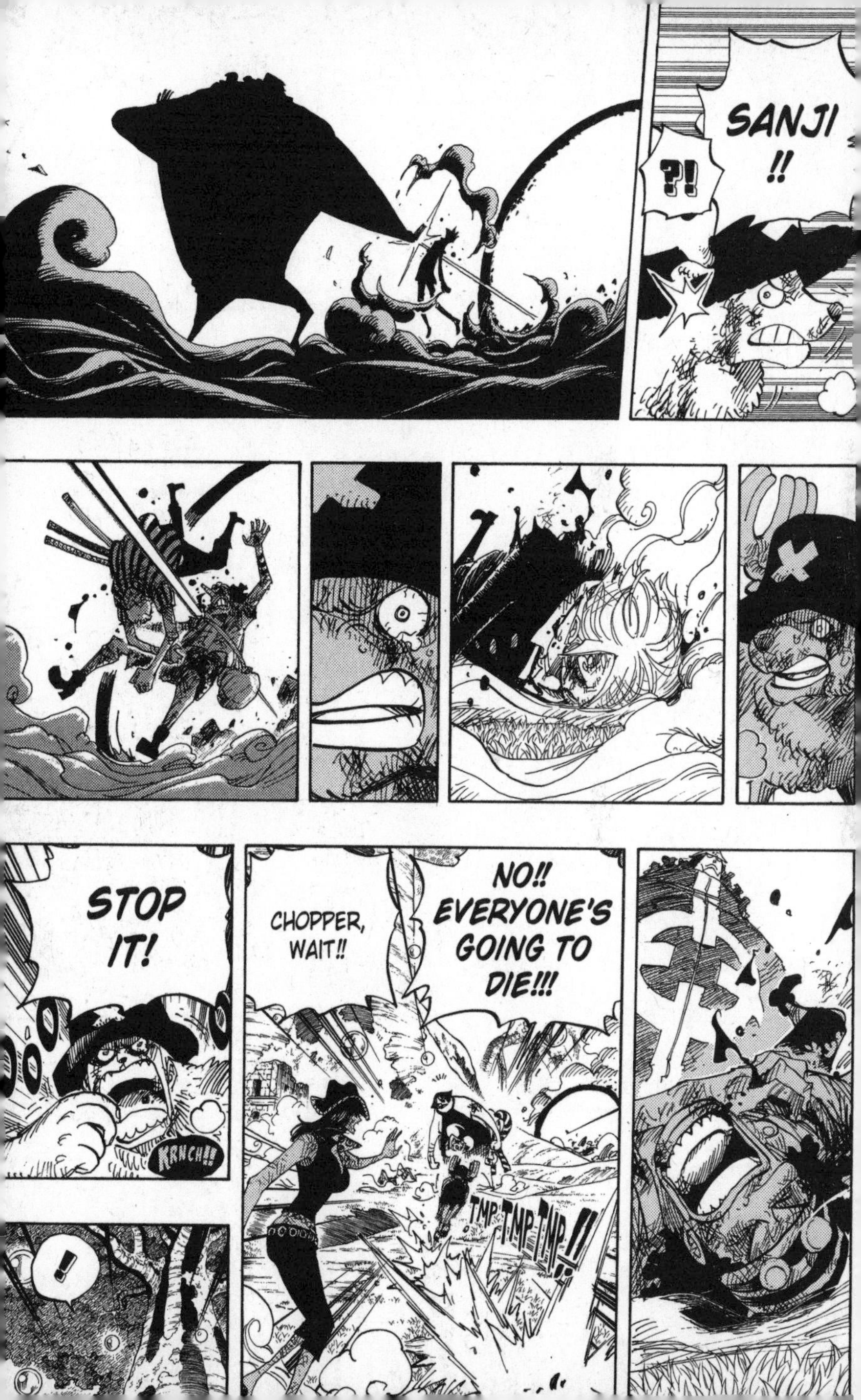
SANJI!!
?!
NO!! EVERYONE'S GOING TO DIE!!!
CHOPPER, WAIT!!
TMP TMP TMP!!
STOP IT!
KRNCH!!
!

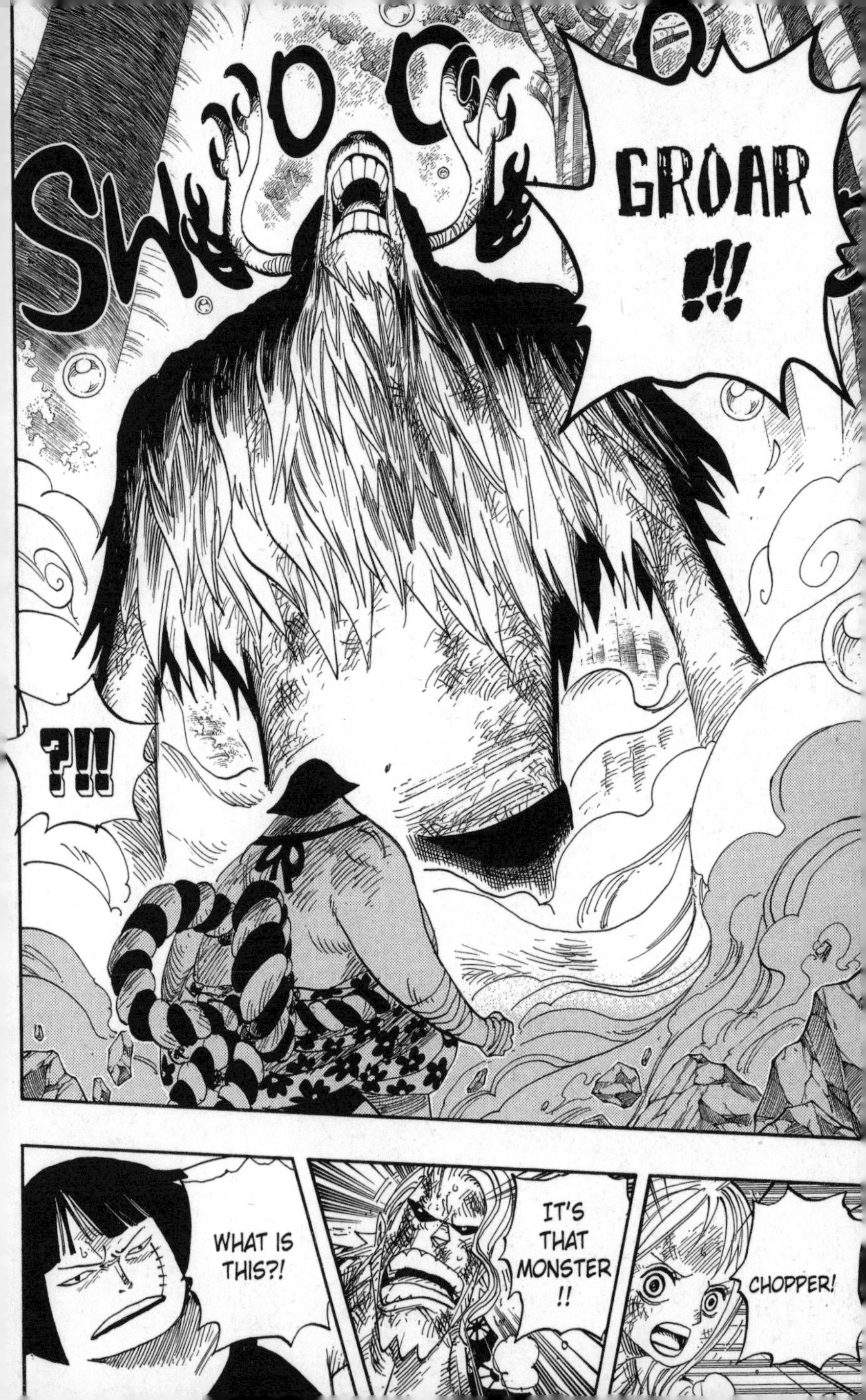
GROAR!!!
?!!
CHOPPER!
IT'S THAT MONSTER!!
WHAT IS THIS?!

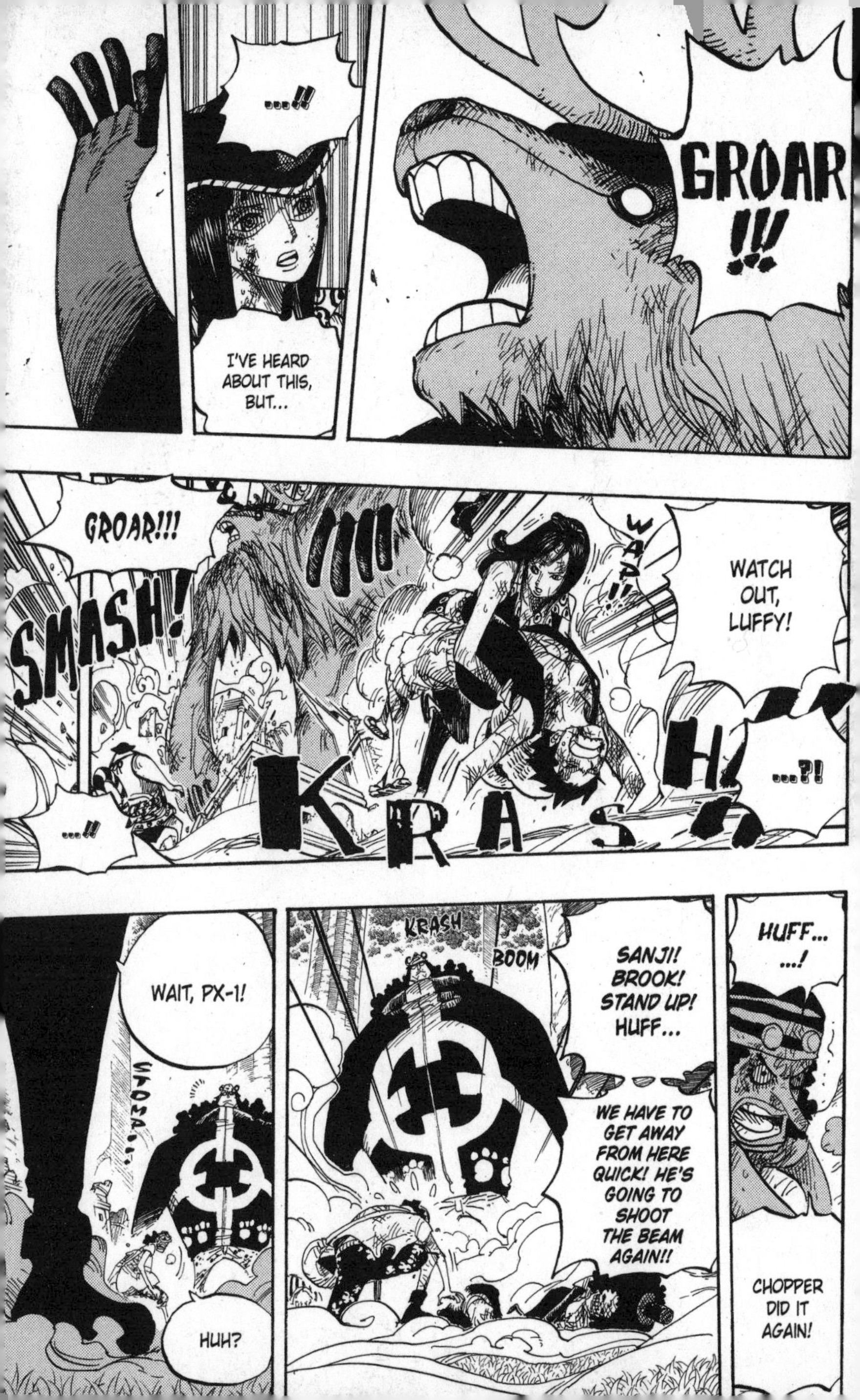
GROAR!!!
...!!
I'VE HEARD ABOUT THIS, BUT...
WATCH OUT, LUFFY!
WAP!!
...?!
KRASH
GROAR!!!
SMASH!
...!!
HUFF... ...!
CHOPPER DID IT AGAIN!
SANJI! BROOK! STAND UP! HUFF...
WE HAVE TO GET AWAY FROM HERE QUICK! HE'S GOING TO SHOOT THE BEAM AGAIN!!
BOOM
KRASH
WAIT, PX-1!
STOMP...
HUH?

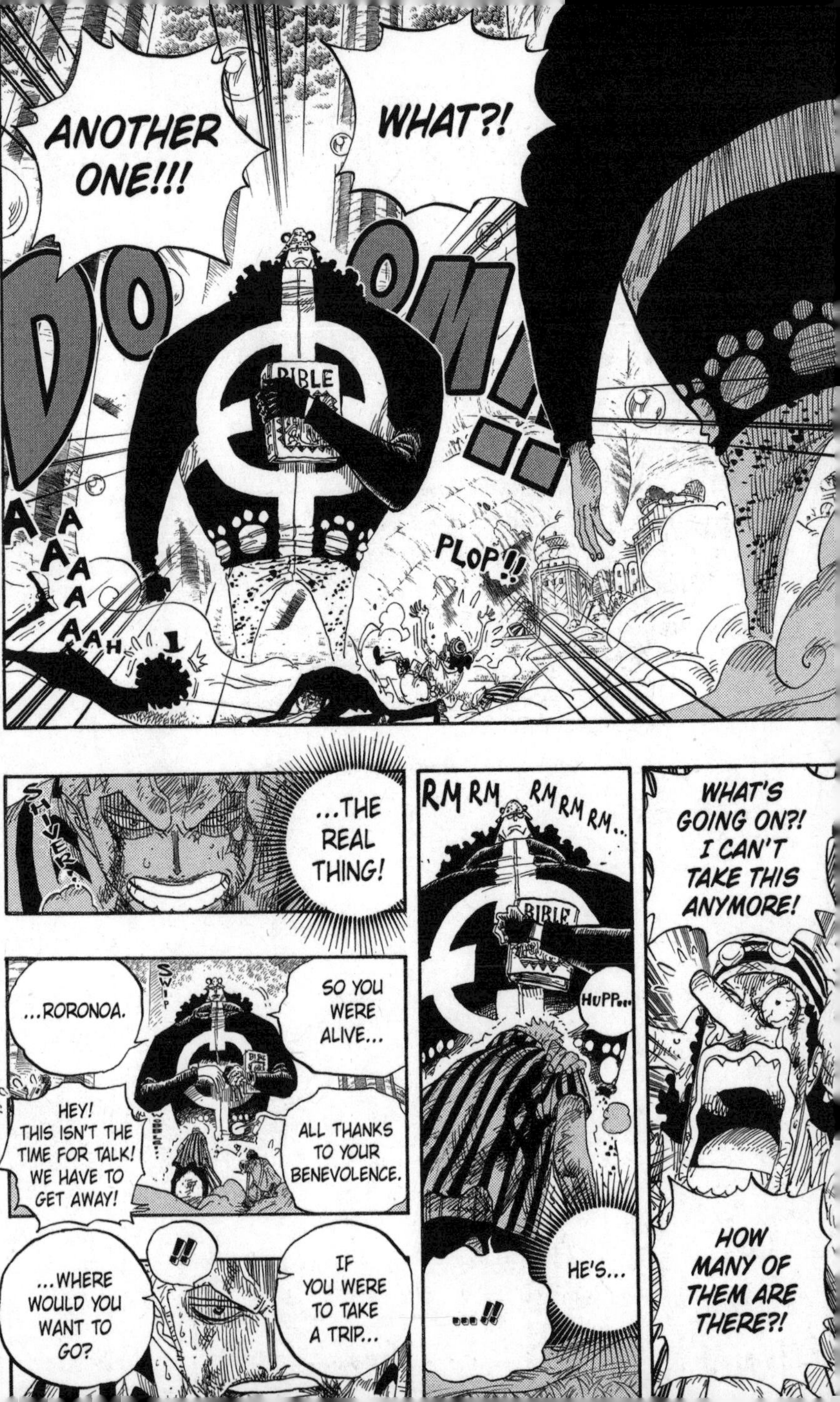
WHAT?!
ANOTHER ONE!!!
DOOM!!
PLOP!!
AAAAAAAH
WHAT'S GOING ON?! I CAN'T TAKE THIS ANYMORE!
HOW MANY OF THEM ARE THERE?!
RM RM RM RM RM...
BIBLE
HUPP...
HE'S...
...!!
SHIVER
...THE REAL THING!
SWIP
SO YOU WERE ALIVE...
...RORONOA.
ALL THANKS TO YOUR BENEVOLENCE.
HEY! THIS ISN'T THE TIME FOR TALK! WE HAVE TO GET AWAY!
IF YOU WERE TO TAKE A TRIP...
!!
...WHERE WOULD YOU WANT TO GO?

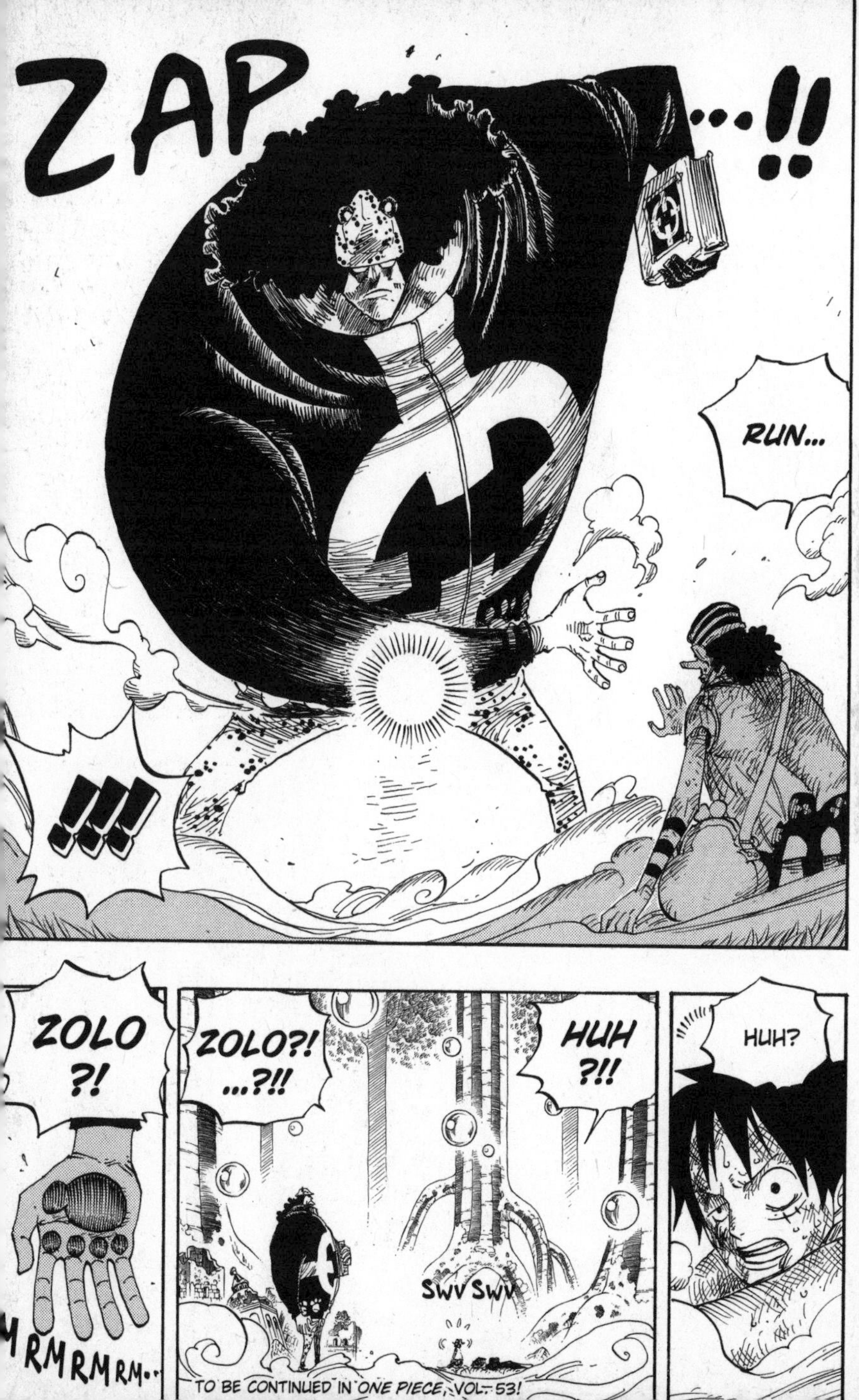
ZAP...!!
RUN...
!!!
HUH?
HUH ?!!
ZOLO?! ...?!!
SWV SWV
TO BE CONTINUED IN ONE PIECE, VOL. 53!
ZOLO ?!
MRMRMRM...

COMING NEXT VOLUME:

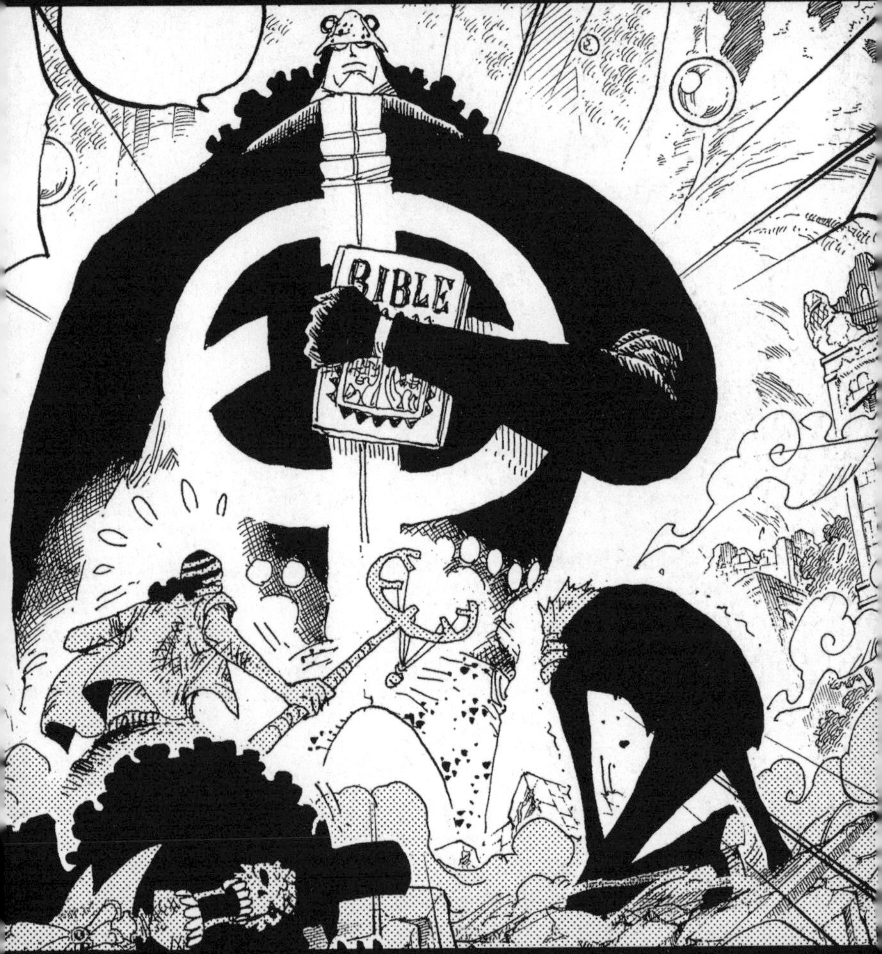
BIBLE

When the real Bartholomew Kuma shows up, the Straw Hats are powerless against this Warlord of the Sea's teleportation powers. Should they come in contact with his bare paw, they'll be sent flying to an unknown location. But if the crew gets scattered all around the world, will they ever be able to meet up again?!

ON SALE NOW!

BAKUMAN。

STORY BY TSUGUMI OHBA
ART BY TAKESHI OBATA

From the creators of *Death Note*

The mystery behind manga making REVEALED!

Average student Moritaka Mashiro enjoys drawing for fun. When his classmate and aspiring writer Akito Takagi discovers his talent, he begs to team up. But what exactly does it take to make it in the manga-publishing world?

Bakuman。 Vol. 1
ISBN: 978-1-4215-3513-5
$9.99 US / $12.99 CAN *

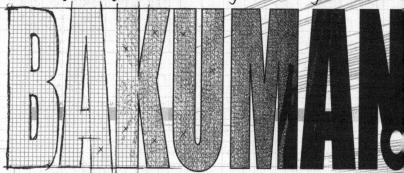

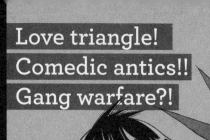

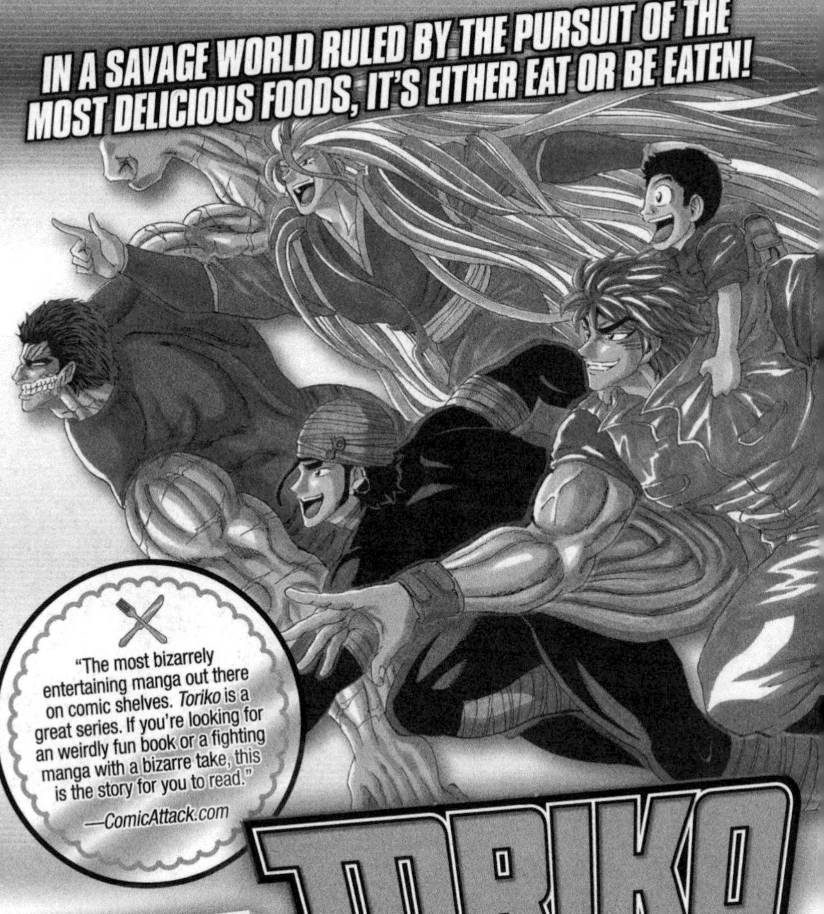
IN A SAVAGE WORLD RULED BY THE PURSUIT OF THE MOST DELICIOUS FOODS, IT'S EITHER EAT OR BE EATEN!
"The most bizarrely entertaining manga out there on comic shelves. Toriko is a great series. If you're looking for an weirdly fun book or a fighting manga with a bizarre take, this is the story for you to read."
—ComicAttack.com
TORIKO

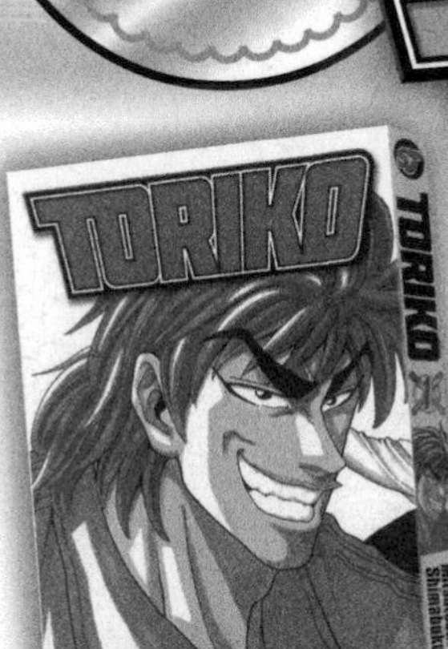
TORIKO
TORIKO
1
Mitsutoshi Shimabukuro
SHONEN JUMP MANGA
Story and Art by
Mitsutoshi Shimabukuro

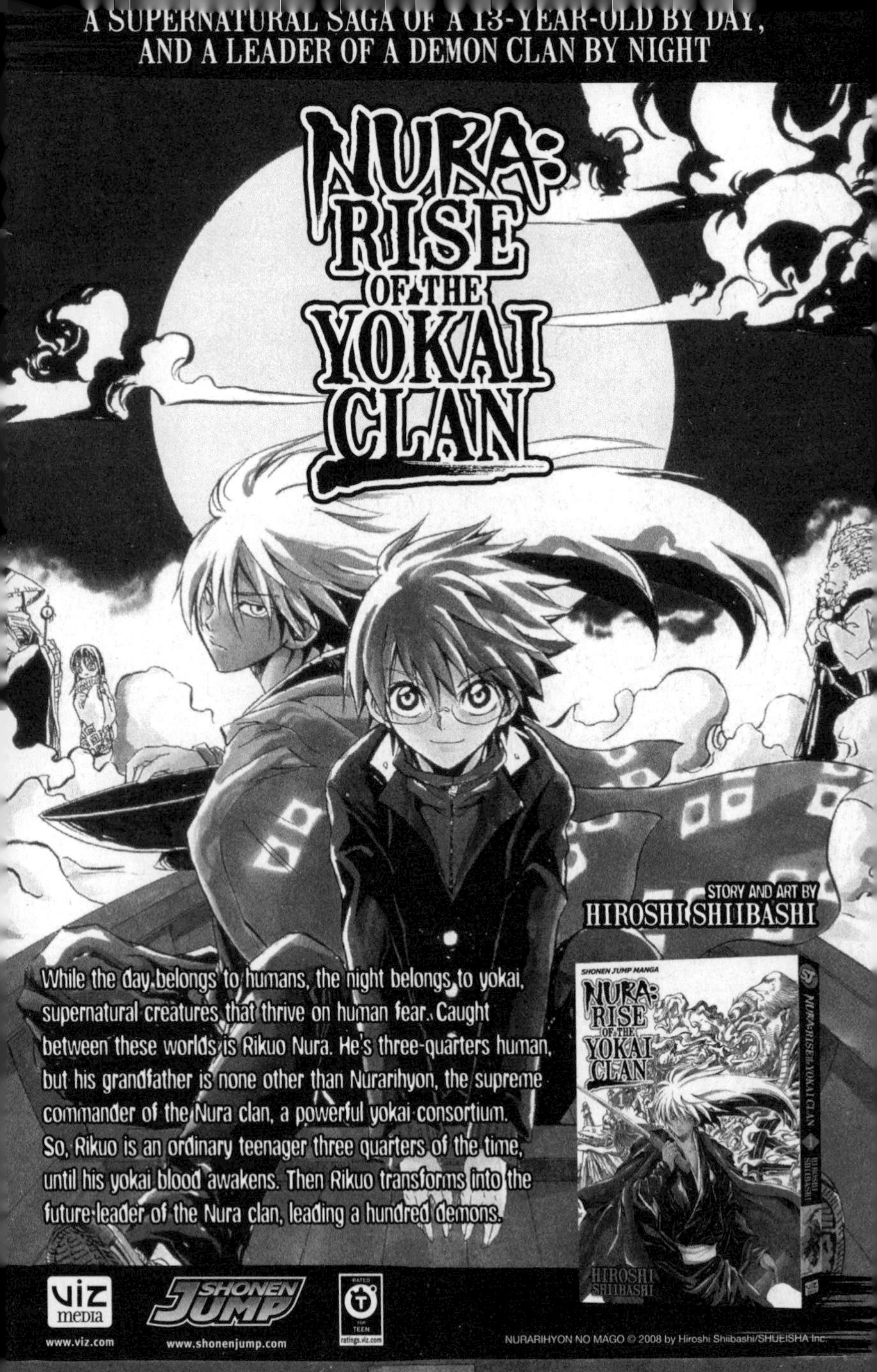
A SUPERNATURAL SAGA OF A 13-YEAR-OLD BY DAY, AND A LEADER OF A DEMON CLAN BY NIGHT
NURA: RISE OF THE YOKAI CLAN
STORY AND ART BY
HIROSHI SHIIBASHI
While the day belongs to humans, the night belongs to yokai, supernatural creatures that thrive on human fear. Caught between these worlds is Rikuo Nura. He's three-quarters human, but his grandfather is none other than Nurarihyon, the supreme commander of the Nura clan, a powerful yokai consortium. So, Rikuo is an ordinary teenager three quarters of the time, until his yokai blood awakens. Then Rikuo transforms into the future leader of the Nura clan, leading a hundred demons.
SHONEN JUMP MANGA
NURA: RISE OF THE YOKAI CLAN
HIROSHI SHIIBASHI
viz media
www.viz.com
SHONEN JUMP
www.shonenjump.com
RATED T FOR TEEN
ratings.viz.com
NURARIHYON NO MAGO © 2008 by Hiroshi Shiibashi/SHUEISHA Inc.

You're Reading in the Wrong Direction!!

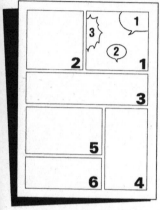

Whoops! Guess what? You're starting at the wrong end of the comic!

...It's true! In keeping with the original Japanese format, **One Piece** is meant to be read from right to left, starting in the upper-right corner.

Unlike English, which is read from left to right, Japanese is read from right to left, meaning that action, sound effects and word-balloon order are completely reversed...something which can make readers unfamiliar with Japanese feel pretty backwards themselves. For this reason, manga or Japanese comics published in the U.S. in English have sometimes been published "flopped"— that is, printed in exact reverse order, as though seen from the other side of a mirror.

By flopping pages, U.S. publishers can avoid confusing readers, but the compromise is not without its downside. For one thing, a character in a flopped manga series who once wore in the original Japanese version a T-shirt emblazoned with "M A Y" (as in "the merry month of") now wears one which reads "Y A M"! Additionally, many manga creators in Japan are themselves unhappy with the process, as some feel the mirror-imaging of their art skews their original intentions.

We are proud to bring you Eiichiro Oda's **One Piece** in the original unflopped format. For now, though, turn to the other side of the book and let the journey begin...!

—Editor